WRITINGS
OF
JOHN QUINCY ADAMS

THE MACMILLAN COMPANY
NEW YORK · BOSTON · CHICAGO · DALLAS
ATLANTA · SAN FRANCISCO

MACMILLAN & CO., LIMITED
LONDON · BOMBAY · CALCUTTA
MELBOURNE

THE MACMILLAN CO. OF CANADA, LTD.
TORONTO

WRITINGS

OF

JOHN QUINCY ADAMS

EDITED BY

WORTHINGTON CHAUNCEY FORD

VOL. VI

1816–1819

New York
THE MACMILLAN COMPANY
1916

All rights reserved

COPYRIGHT, 1916
BY MARY OGDEN ADAMS

Published March, 1916.

CONTENTS

1816

PAGE

April 6. To EDWARD PERKINS 1
    Slaves are property in the United States. Manner of returning a stowaway slave.

April 8. To JOHN ADAMS 2
    The Massachusetts election. Choice of Brooks a surprise. His claims to recognition and his supporters. A letter from Otis. Would have voted for Dexter.

April 9. To THE SECRETARY OF STATE 5
    Condition of Great Britain misrepresented. Abundance and taxation. Distress confined to landed interest. The national debt. Prospect of continued peace and France.

April 13. To EDWARD WYER 11
    Contents of his letters. Criticisms on the Ghent commissioners and charges of corruption against the administration.

April 14. To SAMUEL DEXTER 11
    Appreciates his approval. Their courses of conduct compared. Politics of the past reviewed. Project for disunion. The situation of Europe.

April 15. To THE SECRETARY OF STATE . . . 16
    Interview with Lord Castlereagh. Question of power to conclude on fisheries and disarmament upon the Lakes. Negotiation to be removed to Washington. The Cass-James correspondence. Restriction on passengers from Ireland.

CONTENTS

                                                          PAGE

April 30. To THE SECRETARY OF STATE . . . 19
    Instructions to negotiate on the fisheries sent to Bagot. Spain and Spanish affairs. Treatment of the patriots. Great Britain supporting demands of Onis. Orders on the fisheries.

May 6. To JOHN ADAMS 23
    Purchase of books. Bekker's *Monde Enchanté* and the *Defence of the American Constitutions*.

May 14. To GEORGE AND JAMES ABEL 24
    Trade with British East Indies.

May 14. To THOMAS ASPINWALL 25
    The negotiations with the Barbary powers. Information should be made public.

May 14. To LORD CASTLEREAGH 26
    Abolition of slave trade. Compensation for slaves under the Ghent treaty. Evidence for the charge and claim examined. British naval officers involved. Disposition of slaves condemned as prize of war.

May 15. To THE SECRETARY OF STATE 35
    Correspondence with Lord Castlereagh on slaves.

May 21. To GEORGE WILLIAM ERVING 36
    Peace should be kept with Spain. Signs of possibilities in Great Britain. Reported cession of Florida to Great Britain.

May 29. To JOHN ADAMS 37
    Discussion on the fisheries. Is preaching peace. War of 1812 characterized.

June 3. To EDWARD WYER 39
    His comments and criticisms. Conduct of the administration.

CONTENTS

	PAGE
June 6. To ABIGAIL ADAMS	40

Scott's *Antiquary*. Studies of his children. Marriages in the royal family. Meetings with some of the Dukes. Lord Holland's civilities. Difficult position of the American minister.

June 10. To GEORGE WILLIAM ERVING 45

Too much warlike humor in Congress. South America and Algiers. No distress in Great Britain. Arrest of Thorndike.

June 22. To THE SECRETARY OF STATE 48

Exmouth's expedition to Algiers, and its consequences.

July 12. To THE SECRETARY OF STATE 51

Salaries of ministers. Allowance to Castlereagh's mission. His own experience at St. Petersburg and London. Salaries to consuls.

July 30. To THE SECRETARY OF STATE 53

Passengers from Ireland. Trade with the British East Indies. Tonnage and other duties. Auction duties and a question of duties on iron. Machinery for the mint.

August 1. To JOHN ADAMS 58

Restoration of the Jesuits. The speech of Governor Brooks. Situation of the federalists. Separation of Maine from Massachusetts. Dislike of the United States in Europe. Decatur's toast. Deaths of Colonel Smith and Dexter.

August 7. To JOSEPH HALL 63

The Massachusetts election. Brooks' speech to the legislature. Conduct of the federalists. Separation of Maine. Trade conditions in the United States. Distress in Great Britain.

CONTENTS

August 16. To ABIGAIL ADAMS 68
    Social functions. The Princess Charlotte. Gossip on royal family fashionable.

August 19. To LORD CASTLEREAGH . . . 69
    Treatment of American prisoners at Dartmoor.

August 24. To ABIGAIL ADAMS 70
    Political parties in Great Britain. Resolutions of the city of London.

August 24. To THE SECRETARY OF STATE . . . 72
    Subjects on which British government will negotiate. Transport of ordnance stores to Canada. Exmouth and Algiers.

August 30. To ABIGAIL ADAMS 75
    An excuse for not writing. Attentions from the Lord Mayor. Entertainments given. Political aspect of the harvest. Cobbett's prophecy. Cheap wheat. Public feeling irritated.

September 17. To LORD CASTLEREAGH 80
    A treaty of commerce. Incompleteness of the convention of 1815. Trade with the West Indies. Countervailing restraints may become necessary. Duties upon American produce in Canada. Arrangement for making impressment unnecessary. Neutral and belligerent rights. Compensation for slaves.

September 18. To THE SECRETARY OF STATE . . . 87
    Little prospect of commercial negotiation. Neutral rights not neglected. Exmouth's expedition.

September 20. To ABIGAIL ADAMS 89
    Leslie has painted his portrait. Visit from Thacher and Bigelow. A cold summer and sun-spots. Their an-

cestors. Royal matrimony. Charges against the Princess of Wales and the ministry. Will remove to London.

September 27. To THE SECRETARY OF STATE . . . 94
Proposal for a treaty of commerce. Little prospect of success. Disposition to amuse the government. Possible change of ministry. The Regent's divorce.

September 28. To THE PRESIDENT 98
His letters delivered. Problems of British finance. The treaty of commerce. The ships at Venice. Purchase of the Nicobar Islands from Denmark. Rumors as to Naples mission.

October 5. To ABIGAIL ADAMS 101
American visitors and letters. Mrs. Tarbell on his neatness.

October 5. To THE SECRETARY OF STATE . . . 103
British commercial policy and counteracting legislation.

October 12. To THE SECRETARY OF STATE . . . 104
Passengers on vessels from Ireland. Case of the *Independence*. Conveyance of destitute American seamen. Matter of unoccupied tonnage. Emigration involved. Letters on it from America. Extra duties.

October 15. To ABIGAIL ADAMS 109
The quiet season at hand. Re-election of Lord Mayor Wood.

October 21. To P. VAN HUFFEL 109
Asks that his portrait be delivered to Mr. Connell.

October 29. To JOHN ADAMS 111
Speculations of the first philosophy. Is studying the heavens. Manilius and Franklin. Seal and mystical

CONTENTS

letter. Schooling of his sons. A Latin play. Thacher's departure. Otis in society. Peace of Europe.

November 4. To ABIGAIL ADAMS 116
    Story's eulogium of Dexter. An omission.

November 15. To GEORGE WILLIAM ERVING . . . 117
    Maps and magazines. Hunt's *Examiner*. Rise of Phillips. Case of the *William and Mary*.

November 16. To THE SECRETARY OF STATE . . . 119
    Return of destitute seamen. Distress meetings and riots.

November 19. To ABIGAIL ADAMS 120
    The dinner at Guild Hall. Aspland and his works.

November 26. To ABIGAIL ADAMS 121
    The reviews. Phillip's success. Meeting with Frend.

December 3. To JOHN ADAMS 123
    Cobbett the champion of parliamentary reform. The coming session.

December 11. To ABIGAIL ADAMS 125
    The distresses of the country. Napoleon at St. Helena.

December 19. To WILLIAM SHALER 126
    His negotiations with Algiers. A trick in the treaty. Movements of his friends.

December 24. To WILLIAM TEMPLE FRANKLIN . . 128
    Remembers Dr. Franklin. Welcomes the volume of his private correspondence.

December 25. To CHRISTOPHER HUGHES . . . 129
    Readings in international law. A list submitted.

CONTENTS

1817

January 3. To JOHN ADAMS 131
On returning to the United States. Hint of an appointment to the Department of State. No direct intimation received. Opinions and knowledge. Reading the Bible. Sends Franklin's *Correspondence*. The President's message and the political future.

January 13. To WILLIAM EUSTIS 137
As to the Secretaryship of State. The political changes in Massachusetts. Arrival of Everett. Contingent charges upon foreign missions.

January 17. To WILLIAM PLUMER 139
Approves his speech to the legislature. Decline of federalism. Madison and his successor. Dislike in Europe to America. Naval power jealousy. Causes for differences.

January 21. To THE SECRETARY OF STATE . . . 144
Parliament and a change of ministry. Excessive load of taxation. Policy of the opposition. Parliamentary reform and its champions. Produce of the revenue. A French loan in London.

January 25. To ABIGAIL ADAMS 150
Shipping and grain imports. Reading unitarian pamphlets.

January 28. To FRANCES FREELING 151
On respecting his official mail.

January 29. To THE SECRETARY OF STATE . . . 153
Prince Regent attacked on his return from opening Parliament. Meetings for demanding a reform of the Commons. Whigs are without a policy. Reformers not rioters. Distress apparent.

CONTENTS

January 30. To GEORGE WILLIAM ERVING . . . 155
    Diplomatic usage to accomplish nothing. The opening of Parliament. English periodicals.

February 12. To ABIGAIL ADAMS 157
    Effect of peace in the United States and Great Britain.

February 20. To THE SECRETARY OF STATE . . . 158
    Sacrifice of salaries by Regent and ministers. Rioters and reform meetings. The assault on the Regent. His gifts to the public. Rioters followers of Spence. The reformers. Suppression of outbreaks.

March 4. To THE SECRETARY OF STATE . . . 164
    Dealing with the Barbary powers. Their military power and trickery. Repressing seditious meetings. The ministry is stronger.

March 6. FROM JAMES MONROE 165
    Has appointed him to be Secretary of State.

March 20. To THE SECRETARY OF STATE . . . 167
    A treaty of commerce. Sees no ground for an agreement. The act of Congress not criticised.

March 31. To JOHN ADAMS 168
    A curious life of Napoleon. Treatment of the prisoner. Southey's inconsistency. His play of *Wat Tyler*. Cobbett driven away. Silencing the reformers.

March 31. To LORD CASTLEREAGH 172
    Case of W. B. Crosby. The treaty obligations. Lands not to be escheated to crown because of alienage.

April 10. To THE SECRETARY OF STATE . . . 174
    Spain deeply injured by the Portuguese invasion of Buenos Ayres. Question about Onis. Mediation of powers asked. Success of measures against sedition.

CONTENTS xiii

PAGE

April 17. To THE PRESIDENT 177
    Accepts the appointment of Secretary of State. Will embark in May.

April 25. To LORD CASTLEREAGH 177
    Has sent commercial propositions to Washington. The negotiation on the fisheries.

April 23—May 16. To ABIGAIL ADAMS 178
    Doubts his competency to fill office of Secretary, but has accepted. Is preparing for his departure. Passage engaged in the *Washington*. Public estimation of his appointment. As to possible want of harmony in views. Conception of his duty.

May 20. To WILLIAM EUSTIS 182
    Should return at his convenience. A chargé d'affaires and secretary. Application of George Joy.

May 31. To JOHN GRAHAM 184
    Has delivered his letter of recall. Exchange of friendly assurances. A present declined. Did not take leave of the Queen. Mr. Smith is chargé d'affaires.

August 21. To RICHARD RUSH 185
    Time of reaching Washington.

September 1. To JOSEPH ANDERSON 186
    Looks to a renewal of confidence and intimacy. Appointments in his department.

September 5. To FRANCES CALLEY GRAY . . . 187
    Question of indebtedness in past relations.

September 21. To ABIGAIL ADAMS 188
    Has had an interview with the President. Will take office on the morrow. Personal and family matters.

CONTENTS

                                                                         PAGE

September 24. To HYDE DE NEUVILLE 190
    An alleged Napoleonian confederation and its objects. Repressive powers of the government limited. Matter will receive consideration, and information is desired.

September 25. To THE PRESIDENT 191
    Answer sent to the French minister. Has expressed a wish for a publication of the documents.

September 26. To JOHN SPEAR SMITH . . . 193
    Regrets not having seen him at Baltimore. Prospect of becoming a legislator. Advice on conduct.

September 26. To WILLIAM CRANCH 194
    Recalls intimacy and friendship.

September 27. To THE PRESIDENT 195
    Conversation with the French minister. Knowledge of the plot asserted, but government had no proof. How papers could be published. Mr. Bagot's questions.

September 28. To ALEXANDER HILL EVERETT . . 200
    On his return to the diplomatic career. The position of chargé d'affaires in the Netherlands mission. Will not be backward in recommending him. Letters on England. Theory of checks and balances. His view of the British constitution not impartial. Opportunity for praise.

September 29. To THE PRESIDENT 204
    The alleged projects against other nations. A Mexican venture. Possible explanation. Captain Biddle for the northwest coast.

September 30. To THE PRESIDENT 207
    Reply to the French minister. Procrastinating policy of Spain. Assurances received.

CONTENTS

October 5. To JOHN ADAMS 208
    Is breaking into the office routine. The schooling of his sons. Political calm not lasting.

October 6. To ANDRÉ DE DASCHKOFF 209
    Reinstatement of Harris at St. Petersburg. Is received with great satisfaction.

October 8. To JOHN ADAMS SMITH 211
    President's town and reception. Subsiding of party spirit. Will not last long. Rush's appointment to London. His accounts.

October 8. To THE PRESIDENT 213
    Why the French minister raised a question on invading Spanish territory. Participation of Joseph Bonaparte.

October 9. To THE PRESIDENT 215
    Appointments to office. The clerkships in the Department of State. A letter from Morris Birkbeck.

October 11. To THOMAS JEFFERSON 217
    Returns a pamphlet by the Abbé de Pradt. Character of the writer. A report on weights and measures. Will recommend the adoption of the French metric system. Books wanted.

October 15. To ALEXANDER HILL EVERETT . . . 221
    Opportunities in the diplomatic service. His accounts should be settled. Need of punctuality in public accounts. His letters on England. Theory of balances once more. The elections.

October 29. To ALEXANDER HILL EVERETT . . . 226
    Reason for urging a settlement of his accounts. Will purchase Ebeling's library.

CONTENTS

	PAGE
November 2. To ABIGAIL ADAMS	227

Crowded with business. Rush and his desire to go to England in a war ship. Speculation to be aroused on rating of ships.

November 4. To GEORGE JOY 229

The consulate at Amsterdam. Consuls residing at a distance from their posts. The President's choice will probably fall on another. His conduct at Copenhagen. The insinuations against Erving. His writings in England.

November 6. To RICHARD RUSH 233

Instructions. Commissions under the treaty of Ghent. Arbitration by the Emperor of Russia. Discriminating duties. The commercial convention of 1815. Effect of war upon treaties. The fisheries and navigation of the Mississippi. Neutral and belligerent rights. Impressment of seamen. Precedents supplied by England. Power to treat. Forms of treaties and presents. Correspondence with the department Claims. Destitute seamen.

November 11. To DANIEL SHELDON 250

Delivery of sailors for trial. Murder and piracy to be tried wherever criminal is found.

November 14. To JOHN STUART SKINNER . . . 253

Charge of obtaining interested information from the Department of State. Asks for names.

November 16. To ALEXANDER HILL EVERETT . . 254

Appleton appointed secretary of legation in Belgium. Effect upon Everett's application. Everett named for chargé d'affaires. Vague insinuations to his disadvantage. Will be given an opportunity to reply. Should atone for his injustice to the President. Advice upon conduct.

CONTENTS xvii

PAGE

November 17. To JOHN ADAMS, JR. 258
Will not excuse rashness. His studies. Indulgence and its consequences.

November 23. To ALEXANDER HILL EVERETT . . 260
The elections and party spirit in Boston. His political articles. Claims of the federalists. Carey's *Olive Branch*. The question of the governorship. Brooks and Mason. Ebeling's library. Monroe's opinion upon it.

November 24. To JOHN ADAMS 265
Consequences of a public calling. Is not blind to the circumstances of his situation. What is under the election for representative in Boston. Revolt of a part of the federalists. J. T. Austin and the treaty of Ghent commission. Riley's accounts. Calhoun and Wirt.

November 30. To ALEXANDER HILL EVERETT . . 269
Advice offered, not a reproach. Has acted only from friendship.

December 15. To JAMES MADISON 271
His intercourse with Jeremy Bentham. Circular letter of Governor Nicholas. Copies of *Chrestomathia* sent. The journal of the constitutional convention of 1787.

December 21. To JOHN ADAMS 274
Plague of office seekers. Pertinacity of George Barrell. Sympathy for South America. Introduces Nathaniel Pope. Politics in Pennsylvania.

December 23. To JOSEPH HALL 277
Election of Mason is gratifying. The seers of brighter views.

December 26. To GEORGE WASHINGTON ADAMS . . 278
Employment of time in study. Subject for a dissertation. Advice.

CONTENTS

December 29. To ALEXANDER HILL EVERETT . 280
    Return of Mr. Eustis. Peace societies. An article on South America. Who is judge of conditions there. Identity of their cause with that of the united colonies of North America. Some differences noticed. Boston politics.

December 31. To CHARLES COLLINS 283
    Information on the occupation of Amelia Island. McGregor's authority. Republic of the Floridas and a provisional government.

1818

January —. SUPPRESSION OF PIRATICAL ESTABLISHMENTS 286
    Suggestions for a report by the House Committee on Foreign Affairs.

January 21. To PETER PAUL FRANCIS DE GRAND . . 289
    Has read his communication. Desires information on the plans of the L'Allemands. Aury and the Floridas. McGregor's intentions. Neutrality attacked.

January 27. To HYDE DE NEUVILLE 291
    Neutrality in South American contest. Occupation of Amelia Island. The case of the *Maby*.

February 2. MEMORANDUM ON THE BRITISH OFFER TO MEDIATE BETWEEN THE UNITED STATES AND SPAIN.... 294

March 1. To PETER PAUL FRANCIS DE GRAND . . 299
    Regrets the accident to him. Conditions on which money may be advanced to the L'Allemands. Distrusts half-confidences.

March 9. To RICHARD RUSH 300
    His conversation with Doctor Thornton. McGregor has sailed for England and should be watched.

CONTENTS

PAGE

March 25. REPORT ON SOUTH AMERICAN INDEPENDENCE 301

April 6. To ALEXANDER HILL EVERETT . . . 304
Ebeling's library given to Harvard University. Nothing done by Congress. Massachusetts politics.

April 20. To GEORGE WILLIAM ERVING . . . 306
Negotiations with Onis. Dispute over the Red River. Boundary asserted. British mediation. Interest in South American affairs. Cases of Meade and Robinson.

April 20. To PETER PAUL FRANCIS DE GRAND . . 310
The project against Texas.

April 27. To J. E. HALL 311
His election to the American Philosophical Society. A biographical sketch.

May 19. To ALBERT GALLATIN 312
South America and the negotiations with Spain. Onis and his claims. Amelia Island. A minister for La Plata. British mediation. Attitude of European powers towards the United States. European interposition in South America. Neutrality. Suggests a free communication of intentions.

May 20. To RICHARD RUSH 319
Compensation for slaves under the Ghent treaty. The voyage of the *Ontario*. Reserve of Europe on South America. What is known of their intentions. Neutrality and acknowledgment of independence. A memorial from Moscow. To invite confidence. Believes in South American independence.

May 21. To RICHARD RUSH 327
Return of extra duties levied on American commerce. An act of commercial retaliation. The approaching

termination of the commercial convention of 1815. A treaty suggested. Exception in favor of Nova Scotia.

May 22. To ALBERT GALLATIN 332
    Commercial convention of 1815. Points to be settled in a new arrangement. Indemnity for slaves under the Ghent treaty. Boundaries and fisheries.

May 24. To JONATHAN RUSSELL 336
    Form of correspondence.

May 25. To ABIGAIL ADAMS 337
    Collectorship at Plymouth. Wirt's *Patrick Henry*. Dearborn on Bunker's Hill. Decline of party spirit.

May 29. To RICHARD RUSH 339
    Economy in foreign expenditures. Commercial legislation. South American affairs. A European alliance.

May 30. To RICHARD RUSH 343
    President's departure from the city. Coöperation of the United States with Great Britain. Commercial matters.

June 1. To JOSEPH HOPKINSON 345
    Map of Louisiana.

June 18. To JOHN D. LEWIS 346
    Conduct of Harris as consul. Some explanation required from Lewis. Further affidavits wanted. Must be no personal violence between the parties. The affair between J. L. Harris and Lewis's brother.

June 22. To JONATHAN RUSSELL 351
    Commercial relations with Sweden.

June 22. To ALEXANDER HILL EVERETT . . . 352
    Soliciting office. Eustis explains his opinion of Everett.

CONTENTS

	PAGE
June 22. To CHRISTOPHER HUGHES	354

Impossible to answer private correspondents. A hint on his letters. Cannot relieve his disappointment. No permanency in Swedish mission. Jefferson's views on changes in office. What to write about.

June 26. CASE OF OBED WRIGHT 358

June 28. To GEORGE WASHINGTON CAMPBELL . . 359
  The Swedish treaty. May stop in Denmark and see Rosencrantz. Diplomatic relations with that country. Mr. Pederson's position. Consuls in the Danish West Indies. Claims not abandoned. The consulate at St. Petersburg. Consular fees. To watch European movements.

June 28. To GEORGE WASHINGTON CAMPBELL . . 366
  Commercial policy of the United States. Equality and reciprocity. Former approaches to Russia. Nothing to bargain for. Russian merchants. Church-money. The northwest coast of America. Russia and a navy. A settlement on Columbia River. Arbitration by Emperor of Russia. The Holy Alliance. Great Britain not a party. The European alliance and South America. Russia against the provinces. United States not informed and its position outlined. Its differences with Spain.

July 6. To WILLIAM PLUMER 380
  The convention journal. The President's declaration on internal improvements. The appointment to Russia. Inadequate compensation in missions.

July 8. To THE PRESIDENT 383
  Letters from commissioners to South America. Protest of the Spanish minister against Jackson's conduct.

July 20. To THE PRESIDENT 385
  Jackson fully justified.

CONTENTS

July 23. To Don Luis de Onis 386
    Reply to his protest on Jackson. Restraining the Indian. Spanish commander unable to perform his part. Respect for Spanish territory. Pursuing the Seminoles. Self defense urged. Spanish commanders unfriendly. Demands their punishment. Forts will be restored.

July 28. To Albert Gallatin and Richard Rush . 394
    Commercial treaty with Great Britain. West Indies and the navigation act. The colonial system maintained because of age. The free-port act. Return of tonnage duties. Boundaries. Settlement on the Columbia River. Difficulties in arbitration. The fisheries. Status of the treaty of 1783.

July 30. To Richard Rush 409
    The free-port act. Extra duties. Expensive commissions under the Ghent treaty. Consuls in opened ports. Jackson's acts in the Floridas.

August 3. To Francis Calley Gray 412
    Cannot disapprove his determination on Russian mission. The individual and public service. An American in Europe.

August 10. To Alexander Hill Everett . . . 415
    Has been appointed chargé d'affaires in the Netherlands mission. Commercial relations with the United States and duties. Negotiation not wanted. Colonial system out of date. Conspiracy against the United States. Claims against the Netherlands. Obligations independent of internal revolutions. Correspondence. Consuls.

August 12. To the President 429
    Rumor of cession of Florida to the United States. Aguirre's mission and troubles. The navigation act.

CONTENTS

August 13. To the President 431
    Aguirre's vessels and Onis' complaints.

August 15. To Richard Rush 433
    The British Order in council. How an acknowledgment of South American independence would be received.

August 20. To Richard Rush 434
    Parry and his manuscripts. Tigere and his preparation of paper. Castlereagh and the executions by Jackson. Fishing vessels interfered with.

August 23. To the President 438
    Barlow's allowance. The President and execution of criminals. Is about to leave the city. Rush's interview with Aguirre.

August 24. To the President 441
    Relations with South American agents. Time of recognition. Complaints by the British government.

August 24. To Don Luis de Onis 444
    No violation of law in vessels at New York. Discussion of Jackson's conduct unseasonable. Forts to be restored. Is gratified by prospect of treaty.

August 27. To Don Manuel H. De Aguirre . . 446
    The United States neutral in contest between Spain and South America. Advantages of a friendly intercourse extended to his country. Right to buy ships and arms. Has been informed of his powers.

August 27. To Thomas Sumter 452
    His disclosure of the proposed European mediation. Consul Ray's position. Seamen from the *Penguin*. Consuls in the Cape de Verde islands.

CONTENTS

October 31. To Don Luis de Onis 455
    Rights of the United States to the Mississippi beyond controversy. The captured forts restored. Cession will quiet dispute. Claims cannot be admitted. A boundary stated. Renunciation of certain claims. Flag covering property. No necessity for new laws. Is authorized to conclude a treaty.

November 2. To John Adams 462
    Death of his mother.

November 2. To Albert Gallatin and Richard Rush 464
    Impressment of seamen. What the British government offered. Permanent peace between the two countries incompatible with impressment. Duration of the treaty. Authorizing a call for a list of the crew. Suppression of the slave trade. Suggested system not applicable to the United States.

November 16. To Peter Paul Francis De Grand . 472
    His plan for a government currency.

November 28. To George William Erving . . 474
    Demands of Spain on Jackson's acts. A part already complied with. How the occasion for occupying the forts arose. Origin of the Seminole war. British invasion of Spanish territory. Conduct of Colonel Nicholls. The negro fort. Alexander Arbuthnot. Jackson crosses the border. Fort St. Marks. The Governor of Pensacola. Pensacola and Barrancas occupied. No censure will be passed on Jackson. Demand for the punishment of Spanish officers. Spain must cede or protect her possessions. Pizarro's statements examined. Arbuthnot and Hambly. The case of Ambrister. McGregor and Woodbine. Characteristics of Indian warfare. British instigation. Summary.

November 30. To Don Luis de Onis . . . 503
    The western boundary withdrawn. Jackson's defence.

CONTENTS

Failure of Spain to fulfil her treaty obligations. Conditions cannot be mistaken. Arbuthnot's real purposes. No indemnities for damage. Is ready to proceed in making a treaty.

November 30. To ALBERT GALLATIN 511
    Justification of Jackson's acts in Florida. Responsibility of Spain. Trusts the example will be efficacious.

December 31. To DAVID C. DE FORREST . . . 514
    On the recognition of Buenos Ayres. Cannot issue an exequatur to him. Is the independence of Buenos Ayres complete? Equality and reciprocity should be the rule in commerce.

1819

January 1. To RICHARD RUSH 520
    Treatment of deputies from the South American revolutionary governments. Equality not possible. A temporary state of things. Mediation by the allies. Attitude of the United States. A consul general to be received and recognition may be given.

January 20. To JOHN HOLMES 526
    Retention of Amelia Island.

January 29. To DON LUIS DE ONIS 526
    His proposition on boundary not acceptable. Will not continue discussion if powers are incompetent to conclude.

February 14. To JOHN ADAMS 528
    Whimsical choice of weapons with which to attack him. The South American situation and Jackson. As a party question. How the enemies of Jackson became his enemies. Letters of Algernon Sydney.

CONTENTS

	PAGE
February 19. To Don Luis de Onis	533

Sends copy of treaty which must be accepted without alteration.

February 19. Certificate on Captain Barron . . 534

March 17. To Hyde de Neuville 535
   Questions on certain grants of land in Florida made by Spain, but rendered void by the treaty.

March 20. To Don Luis de Onis 537
   His disavowal of grants will be made known in Madrid. The captain general at the Havana should be notified. The archives of the ceded territory.

March 31. To Hyde de Neuville . . . 539
   Would prefer a general commercial treaty to an arrangement covering only certain points. His leave of absence and services.

April 14. To the President 540
   Scott's difference with Jackson. The position of the President.

April 15. To Hyde de Neuville 543
   Unlawful armaments in the ports of the United States. Privateers with blank commissions as pirates. A treaty could be negotiated.

May 2. To Richard Rush 545
   His private correspondence. Scattering of the diplomats. Difficulties endured by foreign ministers. Bagot commended. Regard for De Neuville. Efficacy of the good offices of France. The British government and Arbuthnot and Ambrister. Humanity limited to black slaves.

May 24. To Ward Nicholas Boylston . . . 551
   Prizes for elocution and their conditions. The pro-

fessorship and its requirements. Clerical profession not well suited to it.

May 31. To HENRY CHANNING 554
    Recommendations for appointment to office.

June 24. To FREEMAN TYLER 555
    Cannot serve as a director in the Planters' Bank. Banks and suspension of specie payments.

October 23. To HYDE DE NEUVILLE 557
    Spain to send a confidential person on the treaty. Asks him to remain in America during the winter. Preservation of peace the object.

December 16. To WILLIAM LOWNDES . . . 559
    Spain bound in honor to ratify the treaty. United States has right to compel the performance of a solemn engagement.

December 21. To WILLIAM LOWNDES . . . 562
    Treaty held up by Spain for fear of recognition of South America. France and Russia and the occupation of Florida. Spanish troops in Cuba.

December 25. To THE PRESIDENT 565
    First calls on members of Congress. Practice when he was a Senator. Indebtedness to that body. The rule followed by himself and Mrs. Adams. An avoidance of invidious distinctions.

December 29. To THE VICE PRESIDENT . . . 569
    The etiquette of first visits and his position in the matter.

WRITINGS
OF
JOHN QUINCY ADAMS

WRITINGS OF JOHN QUINCY ADAMS

TO EDWARD PERKINS [1]

LONDON, 6th April, 1816.

SIR:

The circumstances mentioned in your letter of the 3rd instant are of a nature which make it proper for me to observe, that the advice which at Captain Fales's request I shall very cheerfully give, must be considered merely as that of an individual having no authority to interfere officially in the case.

By the laws of North Carolina and at Georgetown (whether in South Carolina or in the District of Columbia) slaves are property, and by the constitution of the United States slaves, escaping from their masters into a state where slavery does not exist, are to be restored them on demand. Captain Fales is therefore in the situation of a person having *found* on board his ship the property of another man, which he is of course bound to restore. I conceive it to be consequently his duty to take the man back to the United States, to deliver him, if he arrives at Boston, to the marshal of the district, who, upon a warrant from a magistrate founded upon Captain Fales's affidavit of the manner in which the man was found on board the vessel and of his own statement that he is the slave of Mr. Collins, will be authorized to take him into custody until he can be sent back to his master. Captain Fales should also give notice to Mr. Collins of the facts. He has, I presume, a fair claim upon Mr. Collins

[1] United States Vice Consul at Bristol, England.

for payment of reasonable charges for the subsistence of the man while in his involuntary custody, as well as for those of sending him back; and I should recommend that in giving Mr. Collins the means of recovering his slave, Captain Fales ought to call upon his sense of justice and humanity most earnestly for a promise that he will exercise no personal rigor towards the slave by way of punishing him for this elopement. I am, etc.

TO JOHN ADAMS

EALING, 8 April, 1816.

MY DEAR SIR:

Your indifference as to the result of the elections to the Presidency of the United States and to the office of governor of your own Commonwealth of Massachusetts, which I find avowed in your favor of 7th of February, is the best of all possible political symptoms. It proves first, that you consider all the candidates as more likely to fill the respective stations, if suited to them, with credit to themselves and usefulness to the country. Secondly, that you consider no important principle of administration, external and internal, to be involved in the issue. Thirdly, that the violence of party spirit continues to subside among us, and that there are no conflicting interests to immediate operation threatening our national union, or the unutterable horrors of civil war.

Of this there has been a deep impression upon my mind of great and imminent danger; and although I cannot share in your total indifference between the candidates mentioned by you, I not only concur in the belief that no material public injury will result from the success of either of them, but that compared with the interest which two years ago I should have felt in the prospect of these events, that of the present moment is not to be named.

The selection of the federal candidate for governor of Massachusetts has much surprised me. In November you gave me a list of nine names then talked of, but that of Brooks [1] was not among them. Assuredly the General would have my vote in preference to most of them, for I never heard of him as a Hartford Conventionist; but he has been so little known in public life at all, and has gone along in such an easy even tenor, that I should not have dreamt of him as the candidate of those who plotted that notable conspiracy. It is the worst thing I ever knew of him. I have seen the electioneering address in his favor, and find that not only his own honorable services in the revolutionary war are very properly alleged in support of his pretensions, but also that he is said to have had two sons in the public service during the late war, and that one of them fell in the glorious battle upon Lake Erie. These are to *my mind* strong titles to public gratitude and would be powerful motives to influence my vote. But what can they be to those who grudged even a vote of thanks for the victory on Lake Erie, and all others achieved by their own countrymen? To those who in the struggle of life and death hailed the enemy as the bulwark of our holy religion? To those who not only avowed their approbation of the infamous principle of the press gang, but who while *thousands* of their own brethren natives of their own state were groaning under the bondage of British

---

[1] John Brooks (1752–1825). "Mr. Erving, who has arrived in Paris, writes me, that in Boston the Trinitarians are increasing and the Federalists diminishing, *and putting water into their wine*. Their liquor will require much more diluting yet. I have nothing to say against General Brooks, much against those whose candidate he is. By the returns that we have seen his majority will be meagre enough, and too consumptive to be long lived." *To Abigail Adams*, May 20, 1816. Ms.

impressment, instituted a mock legislative inquiry, and reported in the face of mankind that they could ascertain only *eleven* citizens of Massachusetts who had been subjected to it? Now can those aiders and abettors of the man-stealer hold it up as a claim of merit in General Brooks, that he had a son who died in a cause so reprobated by their abhorrence?[1] But I should be still more embarrassed to account for this, had I not been informed that my old friend Otis writes to his correspondents in this country, that the issue of the war has been to give our people a consciousness of their own strength and confidence in themselves; and he has even given warning that if Great Britain should again provoke us into a war, she will find us far more united against her than we were in the last. Burke says that Charles Townshend always hit the House of Commons between wind and water. Otis has spent his life in hitting the opinions of the people of Massachusetts between wind and water. After his exploits at the Hartford Convention and his παραπρεσβεία to Washington, when he was so seasonably accompanied from Baltimore to that city by the messenger bearing the treaty of Ghent,[2] it was certainly very gratifying to me to be told that he was writing to his friends in England that the *next* war between the United States and Great Britain would exhibit us more united than the last. Not that I placed much reliance upon it as a promise; but it was the evidence to me where the wind and water line now is, and has been since the peace. As the election is at this moment decided, there can be no harm in the avowal that my vote should have been for Dexter; one reason for which would have been precisely because he has *not* been so skilful in aiming at the wind and water line as

[1] John Brooks, Jr. (1783–1813). He was killed at the battle on Lake Erie.
[2] Morison, *Harrison Gray Otis*, II. 160.

my friend Otis, and because he did not wait till the next war to take the side of his country in a quarrel with Britain.

. . . .

TO THE SECRETARY OF STATE

No. 39.   [JAMES MONROE]

LONDON, 9 April, 1816.

SIR:

From the representations of the present condition of this country, contained in all the newspapers that you will receive and repeated day after day, and week after week, in the parliamentary debates, it is to be apprehended that erroneous impressions of the reality may be made unless these highly colored pictures should be received with suitable allowances. It might perhaps be stated that there never was a period in the history of this island, when there was less of real suffering among the people than at this moment. There certainly never was a period, when the public tranquillity was more profound. The great and immediate cause of complaint is excessive plenty, the consequence of which, in point of fact, is that the whole people are fed. The nature of their want will give a striking idea of their real state. They want a year of scarcity. It is nevertheless true that this overflowing abundance, combining with the load of taxation with which they are oppressed, bears with peculiar hardship upon one particular class of the people, a very important part of the community—the small farmer. Nothing can be more simple than that the calculation of this load of taxation has been doubled upon them by the depreciation of their stock to one-half the value at which it could be sold during the war. Hence the inability of many of them to pay their rents and their tithes. Hence the reduction in the wages of laborers, which increases the numbers to be supported or assisted by the poor rates. Hence a falling off in the income of the landlords, some of whom are compelled to retrench their expenses, and others to intrench upon their capitals. Hence a diminution of consumption in the articles of commerce and luxury, and hence finally an augmented number of distresses for rent and executions for the payment of taxes. To what extent this may be carried hereafter I will not undertake to say; but if it should amount to anything that can deserve the name of national distress, it will be discovered by symptoms far, very far differing from any that have been hitherto discernible. It is clear that neither [this] nor any other government can levy taxes upon the poor absolutely poor. Taxation must in its nature be levied upon superfluity. But there is a state of society just above that of poverty, and from which the government may, and this government does, commence the extraction of part of its superfluity; and as that part was a large proportion of the whole when the stock and income of this class of people was double what it is at present, now that these have been reduced one-half in value, the part extracted absorbs the whole superfluity, and encroaching upon the stock itself, ruins the man and casts him upon the parish for subsistence. Cases of this kind have undoubtedly become numerous and every individual case is of great hardship. But on the other hand, it should be considered that the property of the fund-holders has risen in value in proportion as that of the land-holders has fallen. The three, and four, and five per cents have nominally risen but little. The prices at the stock exchange are nearly as they were. But the forty millions a year, which the bank paid out two years ago to the stockholders as interest upon their funded property, was worth not more than twenty-five millions of gold or silver. It is now equivalent to specie. Here is then fifteen millions in value added to the circulating superfluity of the nation, and the fundholders are enabled to enlarge their scale of expenditure as much as the landed proprietors are obliged to retrench theirs. This appears to be the circumstance which will falsify the predictions of those who have foretold a great falling off in the revenue as a consequence inevitable from the distress of the landed interest. The fact has hitherto proved directly the reverse. All the taxes upon consumption and expenditure yielded more in 1815 than they ever had in any preceding year. The returns upon the 5th of this month for the first quarter of the present year indicate no symptoms of deficiency. The excise, the assessed taxes, the stamps, are all as productive as they ever have been, and hence it is demonstrated that the consumption of luxuries as well as of necessaries, the transfers of property, and the commerce of internal circulation, are as great and as active as ever; while the other fact, that the exchange and consequently the balance of trade of all the world is in favor of Great Britain, amply refutes the clamors of commercial distress in which the merchants are indulging themselves, rather for the sake of keeping in tune with the farmers, than from any real participation in their sufferings.

The distress therefore about which so much is said both in and out of Parliament is not the distress of the nation, but it may with propriety be termed the distress of the landed for the benefit of the funded interest. That its tendency must be, should it long continue, to destroy the harmony between those two important parts of the community, is very obvious, and the consequences may be serious, if the attention of the nation should be allowed to fix itself for a length of time upon its internal state, so that the debt and the taxes may have their full undisturbed operation. It is the opinion of many distinguished political economists here, that the debt, however large, is no burthen upon the nation, because they consider the nation both as debtor and creditor. The nation, say they, owes to itself. A more correct view of the subject seems to be that the result of the debt is to make one-half the nation debtors to the other, and the government is the mere agent of the creditor for the collection of the payment. The burden of taxation has evidently become insupportable to the debtor part, and the rejection of the proposal to continue the property tax at a reduced rate is the first unequivocal indication of that fact. But the relief from immediate pressure has been obtained only by postponing the attempt to obtain any permanent relief. The sinking fund now pays off but twelve millions of the debt yearly by the loss of the property tax, and the war tax on malt. The government is compelled to add by loans or by issuing Exchequer bills fifteen millions to the debt. But as there is reason to expect that the remaining revenue will yield three millions more this year than it did the last, the sum of debt will probably be at the end of the year about the same that it was at the beginning. Much is said by the ministers in Parliament to represent the actual state of things as an intermediate stage between war and peace, and they hold out the prospect of being able to reduce their expenditures six or five millions lower the next year than this. That however is a very precarious promise. Upon the principles on which they found their naval and military establishments for the present year, it is more likely they will find the want of increased expenses for the next, than that they will think themselves enabled to make further retrenchments. There is therefore little reason to expect for years to come any alleviation of the national debt; but there is nothing in the present condition of the nation that demonstrates inability to bear it. The distress which is represented as pressing upon the nation is in point of fact limited to a small, though important, portion of the people. It is even unbalanced by a corresponding augmentation of the wealth of another part of the community; and however afflictive the operation of this process may be upon individuals, and however it may be justly taken for the symptoms of a deep and most dangerous disease in the state, it would be an utterly erroneous conclusion to infer from it that it has any effect to impair the present strength or resources of the nation.

The general aspect of affairs in Europe seems to promise a durable tranquillity. No solid confidence can, however, be placed in it so long as France shall remain in her present forced and unnatural condition. By the treaties this is to continue at least three, and contingently five years. If the people of France should for that length of time submit to this new and extraordinary form of government, it may be foretold with the most undoubting confidence, that the necessity for keeping up the same guaranty to maintain the authority of the Bourbons will, at the end of the five years, rather be greater than less than it was when the arrangement was made. Even if the present king, the least obnoxious to the French people of the whole family, should live through the period of this royal servitude, he will certainly need the foreign armies to protect his authority; so that it will be impossible for him to dispense with them. To his *legitimate* successors they will be still more necessary than to him. But even should the course of nature change in their favor, and should they feel their hold upon the affections of the nations to be so strong that they can venture to dismiss their allied guardians, it may be doubted whether England, Austria, Prussia or Russia, will be equally convinced of the expediency, either of withdrawing their troops or of restoring the fortresses which place France so completely under their control. From the duress under which France is now held there appear to be only two possible issues. One by the dissolution of the European alliance against her, of which hitherto there is not the slightest prospect; and the other by the impatience and desperation of the people of France breaking out in abortive insurrections, which would inevitably lead to further dismemberment and to the final partition of the country. The elements of civil society in France are dissolved. Her military power is annihilated. The conflict of political opinions and of individual interest is inveterate, irreconcilable. There is no real government. No genuine tie of allegiance from the subject to the sovereign, or of protection from the sovereign to the subject. Religion itself, after losing all its salutary control, has yet just influence enough left to be the cause of deadly dissension. It is scarcely possible that France should escape the fate of Poland. The manner in which this event is to be consummated and the distribution of the spoils will form perhaps for some years the great subject of negotiation and discussion among the European allies. I am, etc.[1]

[1] "Mr. Fry [of Glennie, Son and Company] entertained me with melancholy prophecies of great and numerous approaching failures in America. He says there will be enormous, overwhelming losses upon all the late commercial speculations from America to every part of Europe and to India; and indeed that he shall be afraid to hear from 'The States.' He says also that the repeal of the discriminating duties, according to the commercial convention, though it appears upon paper to be fair, will operate entirely against America; that the American vessels cannot stand a competition for freight with the Scotch; that the Scotch can navigate their vessels at half the expense, and feed their sailors at half the cost. I asked him how the speculations upon British manufactures to America now answered. He said, he

TO EDWARD WYER

LONDON, 13th April, 1816.

SIR:

. . . .

I ought perhaps in candor to inform you that shortly after I had the pleasure of meeting you at Gothenburg, several letters written by you accidentally fell into my hands open. They contained animadversions upon the persons then commissioned on the part of the United States for the negotiation of the peace which I thought unsuitable, and which the event has happily proved to have been ill-founded. I was not individually named in those remarks, but neither was I excepted from them. You had delivered to me at Gothenburg several letters of recommendation from worthy and most respectable friends of mine in America, and you had expressed to me sentiments of regard which I thought inconsistent with the general censure passed upon all the commissioners in your letters written at the same time, and should however have overlooked everything that merely concerned myself. But there was in two or three of the letters a charge of the foulest *corruption* upon the present administration of the United States, a charge which I hope you are now convinced was rash and utterly groundless, a charge which I then thought and still think unbecoming in the letters of a person bearing a commission under that very administration. If you have copies of those letters you can recur to them, and if not, you will doubtless recollect

---

did not know. They did not meddle with the dry goods line. Young Glennie said they had declined executing many orders that they had received to purchase goods, knowing that if they should send them, they would sell to a loss." April 8, 1816. *Ms. Diary.*

the substance of them. If you have any explanation to give concerning them I shall be happy to receive it, and to find it such as to justify the confidence of those gentlemen who so strongly recommended you to mine.[1] Meanwhile I remain, etc.

TO SAMUEL DEXTER

LONDON, 14th April, 1816.

DEAR SIR:

Some months since Captain Stuart upon his arrival in this country with Colonel Aspinwall delivered to me your favor of 14 October, which I received with much pleasure. I have found in Captain Stuart an agreeable and intelligent acquaintance. He has lately left England with some others of our countrymen upon a tour to France.

Nothing could be more gratifying to me than your obliging suffrage to the usefulness of my services since my present residence in Europe; but in the sincerity of my heart I assure you that they are not to be compared to the services which during the same time you have rendered to our common country. My path of duty has been clear. Whatever success has attended it must be attributed, first, to a wiser disposer of human affairs than any of us, secondly, to the glorious energy of our countrymen upon the ocean and upon the land—an energy which neither our foreign enemy, nor those wise men of the east who built their system of politics upon contempt for the American character had

---

[1] In replying Wyer stated that his "severity on the commissioners was occasioned by the very unhandsome conduct I had received from Mr. Russell; and from the *vile behavior* of Mr. Barker, captain of the cartel *Chauncey*." He denied intending to make any charge of corruption against the administration. Wyer was United States consul at Riga.

taken into their account. Thirdly, to the wisdom, moderation, and pure patriotism of the President, Congress and government of the United States who commenced and prosecuted the war, and authorized the conclusion of the peace upon principles founded in the honor, independence and real welfare of the Union. Fourthly, to the able and honorable colleagues with whom I have been associated. With all these aids, and with a line of conduct so plainly marked out as the only one that could with propriety be pursued, whatever anxious moments have weighed upon me during the career through which I have passed, there has certainly been no extraordinary effort either of intellect or of virtue required of me in any of the situations wherein I have been placed. I have not been called upon to rise at the dictate of my own conscience above the very atmosphere of party politics; to act in opposition to all or most of those with whom I had acted before; to bear the sufferings of the most inveterate of political enemies, " the foes who once were friends"; to lose the affection, and even the esteem of those whom I had most highly regarded and respected; to be branded as an apostate from my principles for the very stubbornness of my adherence to them; to have my inflexible devotion to my duty construed into a base and sordid dereliction of it: to encounter the glance

"of hard unkindness' altered eye,"

and the more mortifying candor of those whose compassion was willing to acquit my honesty at the expense of my understanding, and scored to the account of folly whatever they deducted from the charge of vice. Of all this I had some, and not a little, experience for two years before I left the United States, and of all this I think you have had no small share during the last three years. It is precisely the period of my whole public life to which I look back with the greatest satisfaction, and in which to my own mind my services were, though less successful, yet more meritorious than anything that I have done in Europe. I am aware that of the measures of that time your opinion was and continues to be unfavorable. Whether they were the best measures might then, and may still, be very fairly questioned. Nor shall I deny that the policy and wisdom of the declaration of war when it was made, might at the time and may yet be far from unquestionable, and that different views of the common interest may lead upon the fairest grounds to opposite conclusions on this question. It was not the constitutional opposition, it was the spirit of faction and the project of discussion in the New England leaders that I held in abhorrence. It is this which you have so boldly, and in the end so successfully resisted, and by resisting it with the weight of your character and the power of your eloquence have rendered service to the Union and even to New England, which the whole lives of the whole Hartford Convention will never equal. I yet hope that at the moment I am writing a majority of the people of Massachusetts have testified their sense of this most important service by placing you at the head of their government. But should it be otherwise, should the bulwark and the press gang combination still be strong enough to carry a candidate whom I should be sorry to rank among them, and whom I believe they took up more for your sake than for his own, more to keep you out than to get him in, you will enjoy a reward superior to anything that parties or people can bestow, the imperishable reward of a self-approving mind. The plan for separating New England from the rest of the North American Union has, I suppose, been again for the present moment laid aside. But it has been so long formed, so repeatedly sunk into the shade at seasons of national prosperity, and reappeared with increasing maturity at times of general difficulty and danger; it has taken such deep root in the speculative opinions of some semi-Solons, and opened such a field for the petty ambition of some demi-semi-Cæsars, that I take it for granted it is not dead, but will be watered into bloom again by the first shower of public calamity that may occur. I am apprehensive that this pernicious system will survive all its founders, and that there is a school of younger politicians arising, deeply infected with its doctrines. As disunion is the only fatal mischief which in the natural course of events can for many ages befall our country, I hope that a school not less ardent and zealous, and far more wise and learned, will be reared at the same time to repel and explode its errors. In the physical world it is said that the poisonous plant and its medicinal antidote are usually found growing in the neighborhood of each other. May the same guardian care of providence be extended to our political world!

The prospects of Europe are not more propitious to the freedom and happiness of its inhabitants than they have been for the last thirty years. Europe has escaped from servitude to France, but it yet remains for France to escape from servitude to Europe. In shaking off the fetters of a French military despotism, Europe is passively submitting to be reshackled with the manacles of feudal and papal tyranny. She has burst asunder the adamantine chains of Bonaparte, to be pinioned by the rags and tatters of monkery and popery. She has cast up the code of Napoleon, and returned to her own vomit of Jesuits, inquisitions, and legitimacy or Divine Right. With this state of things it is impossible that Europe should be long contented. Europe is not even now contented. Very little however of the voice of discontent can be heard. The cry is drowned in the louder noise of the soldiers' drums. The further dismemberment and the final partition of France will probably for some time furnish occupation for the rest of Europe, but according to every probability, the rights of individuals and of nations will be trampled upon as they have been.

May our country display forever the reverse of the picture! Such is the prayer of, Dear Sir, your very faithful, etc.

TO THE SECRETARY OF STATE

No. 40.   [JAMES MONROE]

LONDON, 15 April, 1816.

SIR:

At the request of Lord Castlereagh I called upon him last Tuesday,[1] when he informed me that the British government were prepared to make a proposal for an arrangement of the question relating to the fisheries, and to meet that of the government of the United States relative to naval armaments on the North American lakes, so far as to avoid everything like a contention between the two parties which should have the strongest force there. He asked me if I considered my powers adequate, and if I had instructions which would authorize me now to conclude an agreement upon these points. I told him that I did not consider my power as extending to the first, and should not feel myself warranted in concluding an article upon the second without further instructions. I had transmitted to you copies of all the papers which had passed between Lord Bathurst and me concerning the fisheries, and I was in daily and hourly

[1] April 9. See Adams, *Memoirs*, under that date.

expectation of receiving instructions upon the note from Lord Bathurst proposing a negotiation upon that subject; but possibly they might contain only observations upon the proposal and no new power. He said as the fishing season was now approaching, perhaps it would be most expedient to make the proposal directly to the government of the United States at Washington, and to send a power and instructions for that purpose to Mr. Bagot, so that the instructions to the British naval officers on the American station might be given accordingly. With regard to the force upon the lakes, he said, excepting the vessels which might be necessary to convey troops occasionally from station to station, the British government did not wish to have any ships in commission or in active service, and all the armed vessels now existing there might be laid up, as it was called here, in ordinary. I said that understanding it as now agreed that no new additional force should be commenced upon the lakes on either side for the present, and all the effects of a positive engagement as existing from this time, there would be ample time for the concerting of an express article which might be satisfactory to both governments, and in many respects it might be most convenient that this should be concluded at Washington. I therefore readily assented to his suggestion, and wished that a power and instructions should be sent out to Mr. Bagot upon both the points, which I trust will immediately be done.[1] I then observed that while speaking of the means of preserving the peace between the bordering possessions of the two countries, I would again ask his attention to the correspondence between the Governor of the Michigan Territory and Colonel James, copies of which I had lately transmitted to him, and inquired if anything had been done upon the

[1] See *Letters and Despatches of Lord Castlereagh*, XI. 278, 285, 316, 346, 355.

note which I had addressed to him on this subject.[1] He had probably not read either my note or the correspondence, and if he had, he retained no recollection of their contents. I recapitulated to him all the facts: the manner in which the Indian had been killed; the letters from Colonel James to Governor Cass; the coroner's inquest; the reward offered by the Canadian magistrates of five hundred *dollars*, and the proclamation of Governor Cass in defense of the jurisdiction of the territory; and I reminded him of the imminent danger there had been that acts of violence and of hostility between the two jurisdictions would have ensued from these transactions. He said that a strong instruction should be sent out to the colonial government, and the persons complained of should be called upon to show if they had any explanation to give for their proceedings.

I asked him if the discrimination between the ships of the two countries in relation to the carrying of passengers had been removed. He said that without admitting the right, orders to that effect had been sent to Ireland. I understood him that it had been left to the Irish government to determine, whether the restriction upon British ships should be increased, or that upon American vessels diminished. I told him that this must be at the option of the government. But I apprehended if they should make the restriction of one passenger to five tons universal, it would be almost equivalent to a total prohibition of commerce between the United States and Ireland. The decision upon this matter has been much procrastinated, and I should have pressed for it with more importunity; but that it is yet uncertain here whether the convention has been carried into effect in the United States. This government has been loudly called upon to suspend the operation upon that

[1] McLaughlin, *Lewis Cass*, 103.

account, and I expected Lord Castlereagh would have spoken to me of it. But he did not, and the act of Parliament for carrying the convention into effect here has passed. Since this interview with Lord Castlereagh I have received from him a note respecting the slaves carried away from the United States after the ratification of the peace. A copy of it is enclosed; to reply to it at present would be to no purpose. I shall wait for your further instructions.

I am, etc.[1]

TO THE SECRETARY OF STATE

No. 43.   [JAMES MONROE]

LONDON, 30 April, 1816.

SIR:

I called again yesterday upon Lord Castlereagh, and showed him your letter to me of 27 February, directing me to consider it as an authority and instruction to negotiate a convention respecting the fisheries. After perusing which he asked me, if a new power had been sent to me. I told him there had not. But I was authorized to show him that letter, which you had undoubtedly considered as containing

---

[1] "I am glad that my father's portrait and yours have at length been obtained from Mr. Stewart, and regret very much that the engraving of my father's was not made from Stewart's picture, instead of Mr. Morse's. The design of Mr. Delaplaine's collection is very good, but the execution is far from corresponding with it. Some of the portraits are badly painted, and others ill-engraved. There came a man here some months ago with the whole collection. I took as many of them as were not absolute caricatures; but that was scarcely one-half. I likewise took Perry's victory on Lake Erie, but Mr. Alston tells me it is good for nothing." *To Abigail Adams*, April 18, 1816. Ms.

a power sufficient for the purpose. He said that conformably to the agreement at our interview on the 9th instant he had already sent out authority and instruction to Mr. Bagot for this negotiation, which it would be more convenient to have conducted at Washington, because he was authorized also to give instructions to the British commanders on the coast according to the result of the discussions. I replied that it would be personally more satisfactory to me, and I presumed more convenient to my own government, to have the arrangement made at Washington. As however this authority had been transmitted to me it was my duty to lay it before him, and to act upon it, if this government should be so disposed. He said he thought it would only make the subject more complicated, without bringing it nearer to any result. I readily acquiesced in this opinion. Lord Castlereagh has not communicated to me the nature of the proposition which Mr. Bagot is authorized to make, but I have no reason to believe that my reply to Lord Bathurst's note has produced any alteration whatever in the views of the British government on this subject. I trust you have long before this received copies of that reply, dated 22 January, and transmitted to you with my dispatch No. 28. No answer has been given to it, but Lord Castlereagh told me immediately after reading it that they should adhere to their doctrine with regard to the abrogation of the treaty.[1]

. . . .

My letters of 22 and 31 January, and 8 February, have given you a very full account of the execution of your instructions of 10 December, and of the views of this government in relation to Spain and Spanish affairs. The debates

---

[1] See Adams, *Memoirs*, April 30, 1817.

in Parliament have occasionally furnished since then further elucidations of the British policy. At the very commencement of the session of Parliament, Mr. Brougham made a motion in the House of Commons for an address to the Prince Regent, requesting him to interpose in behalf of the Spanish patriots who are suffering under prosecutions by the government of Ferdinand VII. On that occasion, after a very long speech of Mr. Brougham and an animated debate, Lord Castlereagh closed the whole by a speech equally long, the main object of which was to inculpate the Spanish patriots, and to defend the proceedings of Ferdinand's government against them; but in which he at the same time said, that this government had interposed and were yet interposing in behalf of the patriots. If he had mentioned this at the time when Mr. Brougham gave notice of his motion, the whole debate would have been suspended, and it appears that the motive for letting the debate take its course must have been to have the opportunity of displaying in the face of Europe a formal defense of Ferdinand's government. The interference in behalf of the patriots was thus an ostensible compliance with the strong public sentiment of the country, while the Spanish government easily understood that against these representations it might assert all its spirit of independence without much offending the remonstrants. It does not appear that there has been any relaxation of rigor in the treatment of the patriots, but the Madrid *Gazette* has given the utmost publicity in Spain to Lord Castlereagh's defense of Ferdinand. Since then, in other debates, notice has been taken of the commerce between this country and South America, and of the British subjects taken at Carthagena by Morillo. Lord Castlereagh said this government were taking all the measures in their power to increase the commerce with South America, and that the Spanish government were disposed to treat the British subjects taken at Carthagena with *indulgence*. From all this, and especially from a comparison between Lord Castlereagh's speech on Mr. Brougham's motion, and what he was nearly at the same time saying to me concerning Spain under an injunction of confidence, the present British policy towards that country may be accurately ascertained.

That the Spanish government relies upon the support of that of Great Britain in making the demands set forth in Mr. Onis' letters cannot be doubted. Great Britain, you will recollect, did at the Ghent negotiation very decidedly manifest her disposition upon this subject. And the conclusion of the peace had probably produced no change in that respect. You will particularly notice what Lord Castlereagh said to me on the 25th of January, and in the discussion of every question of difference between the United States and Spain we must always take it for granted that the British feeling and policy will be against us. But that Mr. Onis' demands have been instigated by this government I am not warranted to assert. There was, I believe, some communication between Spain and this country before Mr. Onis' instructions were sent out, upon which he addressed those letters to you. Yet I do not think it was the wish or intention of this cabinet that the question should be brought to an immediate issue of war. The Spanish Ambassador here has evidently been concerned at the prospects of extremities which have been presented by the reports of the correspondence which have lately circulated here. He lately told me that Onis had written of the rupture as of unfounded calumnies—that Onis was *satisfied*—that he had indeed asked personally for leave of absence on account of his private affairs, but that it would not be granted. From the whole tenor of his conversation I should rather infer, if any counsel from the country has lately been given to Spain, it has been rather of a cooling than of an inflammatory character.

I ought to mention, that some intimation has been conveyed to me of new orders having been recently issued to the British naval officers at Newfoundland and on the North American coast, of special vigilance in the prevention of contraband, which has probably relation to the fisheries. I am, etc.

TO JOHN ADAMS

EALING, 6 May, 1816.

DEAR SIR:

I keep a constant search on foot for the books which in any of your letters you have expressed the desire of procuring, but the excessive prices at which all books are held deter me sometimes from taking those that I find, and I am not always successful in finding those for which I am on the lookout. The translation of the New Testament by Beausobre and L'Enfant is in two quarto volumes, and there is an additional volume of commentary. They ask for the whole 2½ guineas, which I have not paid, having the expectation of meeting with another copy upon better terms. I have not yet discovered Balthasar Bekker's *Monde Enchanté*. But I have met with one odd volume of an English translation of it under the title of the *World bewitched*. If the work had been complete, I would have taken it and sent it to you; though on the blank leaf of the volume that I met with there was a manuscript anonymous caution against the *impieties* contained in it, with the remark that they had been often refuted. Bekker was a clergyman, and was not perhaps aware that in writing down the devil he was laboring to demolish his own employment.

It is impossible to find any separate first volumes of the *Defence of the American Constitutions;* but complete sets of the work are to be had of many of the booksellers—little if anything under the original cost of the second edition. Stockdale has been some time dead.[1] His widow still keeps a shop, but his establishment opposite Burlington House is broken up. I have found two copies of my *Silesian Letters*, one of which I shall send you, and keep the other as a curiosity for my children. Copies of it are easily to be had, but at a price beyond what I am willing to pay for them. To collect an hundred of them would cost as much as to print a new edition at Boston or Philadelphia.

I have no letter from you later than of 7 February, and no accounts of my dear mother's health later than of the 19th of the same month. We are all well and anxiously waiting to hear again from Boston and Quincy.

Ever affectionately.

TO GEORGE AND JAMES ABEL

13 Craven Street, 14 May, 1816.

GENTLEMEN:

Immediately after receiving your favors of the 20th ultimo with its enclosures, I addressed a note upon the subject of it to Lord Castlereagh, and I have the satisfaction of stating to you by information from His Lordship, that a bill has been submitted to Parliament, to allow vessels of the United States to clear out from any port of this king-

[1] John Stockdale died June 21, 1814. He had issued two editions of the *Defence* in 1794, with different titles.

dom for any of the principal settlements of the British dominions in the East Indies: viz., Calcutta, Madras, Bombay, and the Prince of Wales's Island, with any articles which may legally be exported from the United Kingdom to the said settlements. I am, etc.[1]

TO THOMAS ASPINWALL

Private.   LONDON, 14 May, 1816.
SIR:

The enclosed letters are returned according to your desire. I think it would be expedient to publish that from Mr. Shaler and that from Commodore Shaw, with the exception of the last two lines. A reason for omitting them is, that the present state of affairs being a suspension of hostilities, it is not necessary to give the public any conjectural anticipation of a declaration of war by the Dey, or of its consequences. If, as you suppose, the effect of the publication would be to raise the price of insurance, that may be a farther motive for making it. The letters are written to you for the express purpose of giving public notice of the actual state of things to all persons interested in our trade in the Mediterranean. The underwriters are as much interested, and have as much right to the information as those who have insurance to be made. What the effect may be upon either of those parties of the facts is their concern and not ours. As public officers our province is to give them all alike the information affecting their interests in our possession. An extract also of Mr. McCall's [2] letter, which I have marked between crotchets with a pencil,

[1] See Adams, *Memoirs*, April 29, 1816.
[2] Richard McCall, United States Consul at Barcelona.

or a paragraph to the same purport, may be published with the other two letters. In giving the information to the public there is no possible event which can hereafter attach blame to you for it. But if the truce should be broken by the Dey, and misfortune should happen to any of our countrymen trading or navigating in the Mediterranean, we should regret that we had not given them all information which we possessed and which might have guarded them against it.

. . . . . .

I am, etc.

TO LORD CASTLEREAGH

The undersigned Envoy Extraordinary and Minister Plenipotentiary from the United States of America has had the honor of receiving Lord Castlereagh's note of the 27th ultimo, together with the enclosed copies of the act of Parliament for the abolition of the slave trade, and of the Order of Council of 16 March, 1808, consequent upon it. All which he will take the earliest opportunity of communicating to the government of the United States.

Unwilling to protract any discussion upon this subject beyond the bounds of absolute necessity, the undersigned will not anticipate the reflections which the perusal of those documents may suggest to the American government. He will confine himself to those observations, which he feels it to be his duty to make in reply, to the remarks of his Lordship upon the testimony which the undersigned had the honor of transmitting to him with this last note upon this subject.

In the pursuit of this inquiry it is very material constantly to bear in mind its real nature and origin. The American plenipotentiaries appointed to negotiate the treaty of peace were instructed to endeavor to obtain the restoration of the slaves taken from citizens of the United States by British officers during the war, or payment of their value to their owners. As a proper consideration in support of this claim to indemnify, it was alleged in a dispatch from the American Secretary of State to be known that a traffic had been carried on in the West Indies of slaves taken from the United States by those who professed to be their deliverers. Although no indemnity was obtained for the sufferers by the treaty of peace, the American government has been repeatedly and urgently called upon for evidence that the existence of this traffic was known. And what evidence could be more conclusive than the avowal of the practice to various persons made by several individuals whose names are given, and belong to the very class of persons to whom it had been imputed?

Under this view of the question the undersigned has the honor of requesting that Lord Castlereagh would take the trouble of a further perusal of the depositions of John Hamilton Browne, of Freeman Tyler, and of Michael Taney, copies of which the undersigned has transmitted to his Lordship. He takes the liberty of making the reference, because his Lordship will find that in those depositions the names of persons stated to have made the declarations to the purpose are given, and that they are not mere expressions of opinion, but unequivocal avowals of the traffic. In the deposition of Browne it is stated that Captains Nourse, Armistead, Wainwright and Ramsey, and Colonel Browne, an aid of General Ross, told the deponent that negroes and tobacco were considered as the private emolument of the officers; that likely negroes were worth from 900 to 1,000 dollars each in the West Indies; that this was the object of the officers in taking them, and that the British government was to know nothing of it. The deposition of Tyler states the fact of two negroes forcibly taken from him and carried away by Major Jones, and leaves that officer to account for the manner in which they were disposed of. The deposition of Michael Taney presents the facts of seventy-one slaves taken and carried away by a party of armed men, under the command of Captain Joseph Nourse, commander of his Majesty's ship *Severn*, after the same Captain Nourse had pledged his honor as a gentleman and a British officer, that if the deponent remained at home in his farming occupation, none of his family or anything he had should be molested either by himself or any of his Majesty's fleet; and after the deponent confiding in the efficacy of this solemn promise had abandoned the precaution with which he had previously removed his slaves and property out of the reach of the British force, and exposed them to the fate which then awaited them. The names, ages and sexes of these twenty-one slaves are given in this deposition, which attests also a declaration by two of the men under Captain Nourse's command, precisely conformable to that of Captain Nourse himself in Browne's deposition—that negroes and slaves were taken as private plunder.

It is proposed in Lord Castlereagh's note to inform the American government of the ultimate disposal of such slaves as can be proved to have placed themselves under the protection of officers serving against the United States, and it is intimated that many precautions were adopted with respect to these negroes in particular. From the above depositions, and from the whole mass of evidence communicated by the undersigned to His Majesty's government, it appears that during the war both persuasion and force were used by the British officers as means for taking and carrying away slaves from the United States. The negroes were invited by a proclamation from the naval commander in chief. They were urged by individual officers to place themselves under the protection of the British army and navy, and when allurement failed, the officers did not hesitate to carry them away by force. It becomes a question under these circumstances, whether the same or a different treatment was experienced by the negroes who voluntarily resorted to British protection, and by those who were carried away against their will. The undersigned does not precisely understand whether Lord Castlereagh intends to make a distinction between the two different modes of capture, and to admit that those taken by warlike operations were condemned as prize of war, while the voluntary fugitives were received, protected, and provided for, as freemen. This must be known to his Majesty's government, but the undersigned must consider Lord Castlereagh's proposal as an offer to account for the disposal and condition of *all* the slaves taken by British officers from the United States during the war, whether carried away as prize, or received into protection as deserters.

The deposition of Patrick Williams was certainly not as Lord Castlereagh supposes, the only foundation of the original allegation in the dispatch from the American Secretary of State. It was the only evidence in the form of an affidavit which had then been transmitted to the American government attesting the practice. The American government had instituted an inquiry upon the subject. Their knowledge of it had come to them by the means of public notoriety. They had made no research for evidence to particular facts. This deposition had not been taken by their desire or by their order. Lord Castlereagh attaches great importance to a judicial investigation of the special case mentioned in that deposition, inculpating the captain of the *Moselle* and Mr. Wood. But let it be supposed that the statement concerning those individuals was unfounded, the result could only be their acquittal from the charge of felony, upon which his Lordship proposes that they should be tried. Its effect could only be to discredit one witness to one fact. It would no more disprove the traffic alleged nor its notoriety, than the acquittal of one individual upon a trial for smuggling would disprove the assertion that smuggling is practised and notorious. Let it further be supposed that the depositions of Hall and Ironmonger should upon inquiry be proved incorrect, founded upon misapprehension, or even wilfully false. Whether explicit avowals of so many British officers to many witnesses of unimpeached veracity remained uncontradicted and unexplained, will not the allegation in the dispatch of the American Secretary of State be completely justified? While British officers in various parts of the southern states were taking and carrying away the slaves of American citizens, and were frankly avowing to their owners that their object in taking them was plunder, to sell the slaves in the West Indies, can it be imagined that this acknowledged traffic would not be notorious among the sufferers who lost their slaves? Notorious throughout the United States? If Browne's deposition be true, if the British Captains, Nourse, Wainwright, Ramsey, Colonel Browne, and others, held such discourse with him as he attests, they were either speaking truth, or practising deception upon him. If they spoke true, the traffic alleged is proved; if they deceived him, the charge against the British navy is at their own door. It is for them to wipe away the stain shed by themselves upon their country and upon its naval and military service.

It is also remarkable that with these avowals, the persons attested to have made them are stated to have added that of this traffic the British government were to know nothing. In connection with which the undersigned begs leave to invite attention of Lord Castlereagh to the facts which have already come to light in relation to the slaves taken from Rawleigh W. Downman. In that case it appears by the testimony upon oath of four witnesses, besides the allegations of Mr. Downman himself, that eleven slaves were taken by a vessel under the special privileges of a flag of truce, and sent in the face of day on board the British squadron in the Chesapeake. There is also evidence that they were transported to and landed at Bermuda, from whence one of the slaves escaped and returned to his master. And yet it appears by the report of Captain Barrie and of Admiral Cockburn, then commander of that British squadron, that neither of them had any knowledge of these transactions whatever. Giving the most entire confidence to the reports of these two officers which Lord Castlereagh has communicated to the undersigned, and extending the same credit to the deposition upon oath of four American citizens, the facts established by them are, that eleven slaves were taken by a British squadron from the American coast and transported to Bermuda, entirely without the knowledge of the commander of the squadron. Is it a strained inference from all this that multitudes of other slaves were in like manner taken and transported to the West Indies, unknown to the Commanders of the squadrons by which they were conveyed? Or that the only possible object of such clandestine transactions was to make sale of the slaves? Or that it could not be more difficult to effect a secret sale of them when once landed in a West India island, than to conceal from the commander of the squadron their capture, transportation and landing?

But without recurring to the supposition of secret sales, the decree of the Vice-Admiralty Court of Jamaica on the case of the *Wilhelmina* still appears to the undersigned to exhibit the proof of a sale of captured slaves, accomplished in the forms of a judicial process which might be applied to all other similar cases of capture. He is aware that the decree does not in terms authorize a sale of the slaves; but it appears that two persons, Auffroy and O'Hara, had been admitted as *claimants* of the vessel, cargo and slaves, all of which had by a prior decree of the court been delivered over to those claimants upon a bail bond given by them under a penalty of 3091 pounds currency, and that when the whole property was condemned as prize, the subsequent decree of the court was, not that the slaves or other property should be given up by the claimants, not that the slaves should be delivered over to the collector of the customs, but that the claimants should forthwith bring into the registry the 3091 pounds, the whole penalty of the stipulation bond which was thereupon to be cancelled. The undersigned certainly understood that by this course of proceedings the vessel, cargo and slaves, were left to remain in the possession of the claimants. If they were not, how could the whole penalty of the stipulation bond be exacted? If they were, the transaction was in substance a sale of the vessel, cargo, and slaves, to the claimants. If the undersigned has mistaken the purport of the decree, it will appear on the return to the inquiries which Lord Castlereagh informs him have been directed to be made in the island of Jamaica, how these slaves were disposed of after the bail bond which made the claimants responsible for them was cancelled. But if they were left in the possession and at the disposal of the claimants, the case not only proves a substantial sale of slaves captured as prize of war, but furnishes a precedent of a mode of transfer by which sales, not ostensible but real, could be effected in all other cases of capture, without being fettered by the act of Parliament for the abolition of the slave trade, or by the Order in Council for giving it effect.

The undersigned deems it his further duty to remark, that neither of these two documents does in terms limit the disposal of *all* negroes captured at sea and condemned to the king as prize of war to their enlistment in the army or navy, or to their being bound to apprenticeships for a term of years. The act and the Order both confine the authority to make this disposal of negro prisoners of war to *natives of Africa*, and consequently neither of these provisions could apply to the slaves taken from the United States, none or scarcely any of which were natives of Africa. The act provides that all slaves taken as prize of war shall *for the purposes only* of seizure, prosecution, and condemnation, be adjudged as slaves and property; that they shall be condemned as prize of war, *for the purpose only* of divesting and barring the proper right and property of their owners; and that they shall nevertheless in no case be liable to be sold or disposed of as slaves, by the king, or by any person claiming under him, or by force of the sentence of condemnation. But the provision of the act relative to the disposal after condemnation of slaves other than natives of Africa is merely negative—that they shall *not* be sold or treated as slaves by the king. How they shall be treated the act does not prescribe. The crown itself is not authorized compulsorily to enlist them, or to bind them to apprenticeships, the proviso containing that authority being limited to natives of

Africa. The Order in Council follows exactly the expressions of the act. It authorizes the collectors of the customs to receive, protect, and provide, for other negroes condemned as prize of war; but neither the act nor the Order in Council directs or authorizes the manner in which they shall be protected or provided for, and by expressly prescribing that they shall *not* be sold or treated by the king as slaves, without including them in the exception of the proviso, the act obviously exempts them from the liability to compulsory enlistment or apprenticeship to which the natives of Africa are subjected. It may be added that if the slaves condemned to the king in the case of the *Wilhelmina* had been received, protected, and provided for by the collector of customs according to the regulations of this act of Parliament and this Order in Council, there would be no necessity at this time for referring to the island of Jamaica to ascertain how they had been disposed of, the sentence of the Court of Vice-Admiralty which condemns them to the king being dated on the 31st of August, 1813, and the Order in Council expressly requiring the collector of the customs authorized to receive, protect, and provide for such condemned negroes, to transmit an annual report of all his proceedings under this authority, with accurate accounts specifying the numbers, names, sexes, and ages, of the negroes by him received and disposed of, to his Majesty's principal Secretary of State for the Colonial Department. If no such return has been made, and if it should prove that the ultimate disposal of those slaves was altogether different from that prescribed by the act of Parliament and the Order in Council for natives of Africa, his Majesty's government can have no difficulty in ascertaining in how many other cases of capture of slaves the forms of the Vice-Admiralty Court observed in the case of the *Wilhelmina* were applied during the war.

The undersigned prays Lord Castlereagh to accept the assurance of his high consideration.

Craven Street, 14 May, 1816.

TO THE SECRETARY OF STATE

No. 44.   [JAMES MONROE]

LONDON, 15 May, 1816.

SIR:

. . . .

On the 4th instant I received from him the note dated 27 April, a copy of which is herewith enclosed, together with copies of the act of Parliament for the abolition of the slave trade, and of the Order in Council of 16 March, 1808. My reply to his Lordship's note was sent to him yesterday. I also transmit a copy of it. The earnestness with which the subject continues to be pressed indicates an object not exclusively confined to the vindication of the character of the British nation. There appears great confidence that the depositions which testify to open sales of the slaves will be totally disproved, and you will observe Lord Castlereagh's disposition to confine the investigation to the special facts stated in those depositions. The stronghold of this confidence is that such sales would be felony, and this of itself tends to discredit the testimony of Patrick Williams and of Hall. I have made no remark on the character of the emancipation bestowed by the act of Parliament, but if its bounties, its enlistments, and its apprenticeships, have been applied to the slaves from the United States to whom freedom was promised, it is no wonder that such freedom should have been taken for another face of slavery.

I am, etc.[1]

TO GEORGE WILLIAM ERVING

EALING, 21 May, 1816.

MY DEAR SIR:

On the 28th of March I enclosed under cover to Mr. Hottinguer letters for you from the Duke of Sorentino, with a few lines of most pacific exhortation of my own. I hope you received the whole upon your arrival in Paris. A few days since I had the pleasure of receiving your favor of the 5th instant from Havre, and thank you cordially for the information contained in it. I have no copy of the cipher which you mention, and if I had could say nothing more than what I have said, keep the peace with Spain. You know that six frigates have been sent out with troops to the Bahama Islands, *to keep down the negroes.* You know that Colonel Nicholls brought over here certain pretended Creek Indians, one of whom has received a Major's commission in the British service.[2] You know that Lord Exmouth [3] has made peace for Sardinia and Naples with Algiers, and ransomed their prisoners at 500 and 1000 dollars a man. You know that the Dey has returned Decatur's treaty as a dead letter, and that we have another peace to make there. You

---

[1] On May 12 Adams had a conversation with Lord Castlereagh and Lord Melville, first lord of the admiralty, on Exmouth's expedition to the Barbary States. It is fully given in the *Memoirs*, under that date, and a copy was sent to the Secretary of State as dispatch No. 45, May 18.

[2] The prophet Francis was made a brigadier general in the royal service.

[3] Edward Pellew, Viscount Exmouth (1757–1833).

know that this country continues armed cap-a-pie by sea and by land, that the bank has carte blanche to coin paper for two years longer, and yet that the guinea scarcely fetches a pound note and a base shilling. Beware of breakers and keep the peace with Spain. I have the most positive assurance that there has been no cession nor talk of cession of Florida to Great Britain. Don't believe the stories they tell you about distress in this country and Ireland. There never was so little distress and never so little discontent—a riot here and there since bread has grown dear again notwithstanding. . . .

I remain, etc.

TO JOHN ADAMS

EALING, 29 May, 1816.

MY DEAR SIR:

It was only three days since that Mr. Prescott called out here and left your kind favor of 2 and 11 September last, enclosing one from Mr. Richard Sears, of Chatham, concerning the subject of the fisheries. I happened at the time when Mr. Prescott came to be in London, and have not yet had the pleasure of seeing him.

The question relating to the fisheries has been largely discussed between me and the British government, but hitherto without any other result than a proposal from them to negotiate an amicable arrangement of the matter at issue between the two countries, and an acceptance of that proposal on the part of the United States. Authority and instructions were sent to me to negotiate a convention to this effect, but it arrived too late to be acted upon. A power to negotiate on the same point had already been sent to Mr. Bagot, and the business will be done at Washington. How the pretensions of the parties can be reconciled I cannot anticipate. I have done the utmost in my power to maintain our rights, and hope they will be more effectually maintained in abler hands.

Whatever may be the natural and necessary propensities of mankind to war, my special duty at present is to preach peace. And from the bottom of my soul I do preach it, as well to those to whom, as to those from whom I am sent. I am deeply convinced that peace is the state best adapted to the interest and the happiness of both nations. All things considered, my countrymen appear to me inclined to be rather more proud than they have reason of the war from which they have so recently emerged. They look too intently to their triumphs, and turn their eyes too lightly away from their disasters. It was a war from which, if the account of disgrace and glory were fairly balanced, we should have something, but not much to boast of. May we do better the next time! and that we may do better, let us not be hasty to enter again upon the contest. At the same time it is not "ignoble ease and peaceful sloth" that I would counsel. An efficient revenue and a growing navy, these are the pillars of my peace.

We are all well. I have but one excuse for writing short letters, but that is now always the same. I hope to write to my mother next week. Meantime I am as ever, etc.

TO EDWARD WYER

LONDON, June 3, 1816.

SIR:

Your favor of 23 April O. S. has come to hand, and I hasten to assure you that I have no resentful recollection of the letters mentioned in my last. It was on the contrary in candor and in kindness to you that I mentioned my having seen them. The charge of corruption against the administration of the government of the United States was in general terms, and as far as I recollect in vague and figurative language. It was repeated nearly in the same words in two or three of the letters which were addressed to friends apparently confidential. The sentiment respecting the commissioners was, that if the government had honestly intended to make peace, they would have appointed *other men*. There was nothing said particularly of me that I could think improper, and as the event has vindicated the sincerity of the government and the competency of the commissioners for the attainment of peace, there was certainly little or nothing in your remarks for me to forgive.

As you have no copies of the letters, and my own remembrance of them is obscured by the lapse of nearly two years, it would be useless to discuss their contents any further. You are now convinced that the conduct of the administration of the United States has been just and honorable, and you will be sensible that while holding a commission as a mark of their confidence, some confidence in return was due from you to them, that this confidence ought not to have been shaken either by a misunderstanding between you and one of the commissioners, or by the misconduct of the captain of the *Chauncey;* that you may derive from the whole transaction a rule useful to yourself for the regulation of your sentiments and the government of your conduct in future is the sincere wish of your very humble and obedient servant.

TO ABIGAIL ADAMS

EALING, 6 June, 1816.

MY BELOVED MOTHER:

. . . .

I sent you lately by Mr. William C[ranch] Bond the last number of the *Edinburgh Review*. Mr. and Mrs. Perkins are now about returning to Boston, and have taken charge of the *Antiquary*, a new novel by Walter Scott, which I hope will afford you and my father some amusement. Its predecessors, *Waverley* and *Guy Mannering*, are already so well known in America that I presume you are acquainted with them. Whether Scott has withheld his name from the public from shame, considering it a degradation to sink from a poet into a novelist; or from the pride of rising a second time from nameless obscurity into eminence, I am not informed; but the celebrity of these three novels, which ought perhaps rather to be called romances, is not inferior to that of his most admired poems.

Your friendly admonitions to forbear overplying the tender constitutions of our children with study, come most opportunely to them at the eve of a new vacation of six weeks, which the too ready indulgence of their masters and parents will widen into two months. Your own authority, that we must be content to take children for children, would have had the greatest weight with me. But that of Dr. Priestley which you quote is in my scales lighter than his own dephlogisticated air. I have no faith either in his religion, his politics, or his morals. "Unstable as water" is the motto of them all.

If I could inspire the souls of my three boys with the sublime Platonic idea of aiming at ideal excellence; if I could persuade them to soar for their standard of emulation to the lofty *possible*, instead of crawling upon the ground with the dirt-clogged *real*, there might be danger that in cheering an ambition already over-eager I might expose their health to suffer from the excess of their application. But my own time is too short for the discharge of my official duties. I have not one hour of leisure in the twenty-four to devote to them. I must and do leave them to their teachers and masters. They are all, thanks to God, boys of good tempers and good dispositions. But the great and constant effort of them all, including George, is to escape from study, and to this effort I have given up all opposition as vain. I comfort myself with the reflection that they are like other children, and prepare my mind for seeing them, if their lives are spared, get along in the world like other men. I certainly can *imagine* something more flattering than all this. Quintilian's description of the boy that will make a valuable man is very different from that commonplace personage that Dr. Priestley's wisdom is for humoring into value. But I am aware that no labor will ever turn a pebble into a diamond. If the pursuit of knowledge at or very soon after George's age is not a passion which will seek its own gratification, I know how useless it is to impose it upon youth as a task.

It is probable that at the very moment while you were writing the letter of 2 May to my wife, in which you anticipated the nuptials of the Princess Charlotte,[1] we were listening to her responses in the marriage ceremony. The service

[1] To Prince Leopold of Saxe-Coburg.

was extremely well read by the Archbishop of Canterbury, and the Princess answered as if she was resolutely determined to "love, honor, and obey." I never had heard a lady so distinctly and audibly pronounce the answers as she did.

This marriage we are told is to be followed in a very few days by another between the Duke of Gloucester and the Princess Mary. They were both children when you were in this country, but since the commencement of this year they have both turned the corner of forty. The Princess Sophia of Gloucester, the Duke's sister, though three years older and quite a handsome woman, still lives in single blessedness.

The Duke of Cumberland has, to make assurance doubly sure, been twice married to the same lady. She is a sister of the late Queen of Prussia, and we had seen her at Berlin, as the young and beautiful widow of the king's brother, Prince Louis of Prussia. While we were there, she was married to a Prince of Solms. The Duke of Cumberland is her third husband. But although the marriage had the official sanction of the Prince Regent, which by the laws of this country was necessary to make it legitimate, it has not obtained the approbation of the Queen, at whose court the Duchess has not made her appearance. The reasons of the Queen's objections have not been made public.[1]

The Duke of Kent has a country seat at Castlebar Hill, within two miles of this house. I have of late frequently met him and the Duke of Sussex at public meetings and dinners of charitable and scientific associations, at which one of them usually presides. The Duke of Kent intends very shortly to leave this country, to reside three or four years at Bruxelles. His object in this determination is said to be, to reduce his establishment, and apply part of his

[1] Adams, *Memoirs*, April 1, 1817.

income to the discharge of his debts. We had known the Duke of Sussex at Berlin, and found upon meeting him here that he still retained the recollection of our acquaintance. From some misunderstanding between him and the Prince Regent, he does not appear at the levees, although he does at the Queen's Drawing Rooms. He sides in politics with the opposition, as do the Dukes of Kent and Gloucester, though not to the same extent. There was lately some coolness between the Regent and the Duke of Gloucester, who, as well as the Duke of Sussex and the Duke and Duchess of Cumberland, was *not* present at the marriage of the Princess Charlotte. There was, I believe, some question of the rank and precedence to be assigned to Prince Leopold, whether it should be immediately before, or after, the Duke of Gloucester. It was however ultimately determined in the Duke's favor, and Prince Leopold follows instead of preceding him. This has produced a reconciliation, and perhaps led to the Duke's marriage with the Princess Mary. He bears a very respectable character, and is much esteemed by all classes of people.

Among the persons whom I had formerly known upon the continent, and whom I have again met here, is Lord Holland.[1] His summer residence is on the way between this place and London. I have been the more indebted to him for his civilities, as they had been rather avoided by me, than sought, and as I had little reason to expect them. I owe him a reparation without exactly knowing how to make it, and I feel the more forcibly the obligation, because I believe him to be one of the most respectable noblemen of this land, and one of the best men living. He is now as to politics in the opposition; but in my estimation his conduct

[1] Henry Richard, third Baron Holland (1773–1840), who married Elizabeth Vassall.

in Parliament has done and does honor to himself and his country. He is also distinguished by his love of literature and the cultivation of science. The library at Holland House is one of the finest that I have seen in this country.[1]

An American minister is an object of more willing and friendly notice to the city and opposition parties, than to the court and the cabinet. But in the politics of the country I, of course, take no part and manifest no opinions. Among the ministerialists I find occasionally old acquaintances of Berlin who are yet willing to know me; and from the ministers I have received every personal attention that I could pretend to, and more than can be desired by one who, for reasons well known to you, cannot stand with them upon the equal footing of reciprocal hospitality. An American mission abroad is a perpetual lesson of humility, not to say of humiliation. It fixes a man in the condition of a parasite, and then tells him to maintain his self-respect and the consideration of his country. Among the advantages of our residence at this distance from town, I reckon that of being relieved from many invitations which we could not avoid there, and which we never could return. I know very well the benefit to a public minister of associating with the people of rank and consequence in the country where he is accredited; but I *feel* that he ought rather to shun than to seek such society, when he can appear in it only as a retainer, receiving unrequited favors, and not as an equal, sharing and dispensing by turns the interchange of social good offices. If I cannot join in the chorus of the convivial song "and let *him* spread the table tomorrow," I would fain not be listening to it at the table of another.

We are all well. George is to perform a part in Terence's Andria at the school next week, after which he and his brother

[1] Adams, *Memoirs*, June 2, 1816.

will write. All send love and duty to my father and to you.

TO GEORGE WILLIAM ERVING

EALING, 10 June, 1816.

DEAR SIR:
Your favors of 28th ultimo and 2nd instant came to hand only the day before yesterday. I accept your amendment to turn away the esquires as well as the excellencies from our tête-a-tête withinside our letters. But for the superscriptions going by post, the simple name might excite a suspicion of Jacobinism which might tempt the legitimate to inspect their contents.

I thought you had stouter nerves than to admit the conjuring up of devils of any color by my croaking spells. If you think that in my two last letters my discretion got the better of my valor, I can only say that much of my alarm came from home. There seemed to me too much of the warlike humor in the debates of Congress—propositions even to take up the cause of the South Americans; predictions of wars with this country to the end of time, as cool and as causeless, as if they were talking of the expense of building a light house, or of adding five cents to the salary of the Secretary of State, which you see they have had the magnanimity to refuse. I say nothing of the foreign missions, only to congratulate you upon the failure of the discriminating plan. But a quarrel with Spain for any cause can scarcely fail of breeding a quarrel with Great Britain—for the cause of the South Americans it would be infallible.

You know the purport of Lord Exmouth's treaties at Algiers, and you will soon hear of his second visit there, to protest against the application in any case to Great Britain of the eighteenth article of our last Algerine treaty. Pacific as I am, I hope we shall never again, after beating Algiers, truckle to her in substance, and then swagger as if we had obtained a triumph. A real and a glorious triumph awaits us there, if we will but undertake to win it. But we must have fighting as gallant and skilful as heretofore, and no trifling negotiations, no gratuitous restitutions, no consular presents, no bullying articles against tribute, and tacit ticklings of the pirates' palm. This war, if we have it, will be quite as much as we can manage well, and will not necessarily, nor even probably, lead us into any other. Its tendency would on the contrary be to cement our peace with the rest of the world, by increasing at once our moral strength in the respect of mankind, and our physical power of defense in the naval bulwark. War! say I, with Algiers, and peace with the universe beside.

You will continue to hear much talk about the distresses of this country, and to see highly colored pictures of petty riots among workmen to raise their wages, or to reduce the price of bread. Notwithstanding which I remain fixed in the opinion that never in our time was there so little prevailing distress, and never so little discontent throughout the island as at this time. You have seen the most confident and formidable predictions that there would be a falling off of thirty or forty per cent in the revenue; and if a hundredth part of the clamor about distress had been founded, that effect would have been inevitable. The revenue in all its branches is increasing instead of diminishing, and although fifteen or sixteen millions of annual taxes have been abolished, the stocks are constantly rising. The whole amount of loans for the present year will not equal the sum discharged by the sinking fund, the exchanges with all the world are largely in favor of this country, and yet the Bank makes paper money *ad libitum*. The government will this year face an expenditure of thirty millions, besides the interest of the debt. Parliament have been trifling with economy, retrenchment, agricultural distresses, tithes, poor laws, and all the standing themes of declamation; but trifling is all they have done. If there was more than usual distress, Parliament could not get rid of the subject by speeches and abstract resolutions. If there was real distress among the classes above pauperism, the assessed taxes upon luxuries and the excise upon luxurious consumption would and must fall off. If there was extraordinary distress among the poor, how could there be a complaint of excessive plenty? I will not say what the state of things may come to, but I rely upon it that if real distress ever comes, it will be in a very different shape from that in which it has yet appeared.

I had lately a letter from Mr. McCall, consul at Barcelona, who wishes much for your arrival in Spain. He complains much of the arrest of Mr. Andrew Thorndike and of irregular proceedings against him. He adds that we are much out of favor with the Spaniards.

I shall hope to hear from you at Madrid and remain, etc.

TO THE SECRETARY OF STATE

No. 47.   [JAMES MONROE]

LONDON, 22 June, 1816.

SIR:

. . . . . .

From the communication of Lord Castlereagh to me, the account of which was given in my last two dispatches, and from the general purport of Lord Castlereagh's observations, I am convinced that Lord Exmouth has on this occasion misunderstood the real object and intentions of his instructions. His government was perfectly satisfied with the result of his first negotiation at Algiers. They had manifested their indignation at the practice of Barbary warfare in making Christian slaves. They had charged their noble Admiral to read a moral lecture to the Dey, and having paid this tribute to the public feeling of Christendom, they were quite content to encourage the Dey to abolish the practice of making Christian slaves in future, by stipulating the payment of a heavy ransom for those he had already made. But the Bey of Tunis and, as Lord Castlereagh a few days since told me, the Bashaw of Tripoli were found so tractable under Lord Exmouth's admonitions that they issued declarations renouncing for the future the practice of reducing Christian captives to slavery, and Lord Exmouth seems to have been tempted by the success of his exhortations to those two minor potentates to renew with more vigor, or at least with more menace of energy, the experiment of obtaining a similar declaration from the Dey of Algiers. If I have not grossly mistaken the views of his government, they will be so far from thanking him for his renewed zeal to carry this part of his instructions into execution that they would most willingly have dispensed even with the declarations from Tunis and Tripoli. Lord Castlereagh told me that the only thing they expected Lord Exmouth to have done upon his return to Algiers was, to make that little protest against the application to Great Britain of the 18th article of the late Algerine treaty with the United States. But Lord Exmouth's demonstration of hostility, followed by his subsequent retreat, have not only placed this government in an awkward and mortifying position, but by the public advices from that quarter of a later date than Mr. Shaler's letter, have produced further unpleasant and even tragical consequences. At Oran it is said that several British vessels were immediately seized and their crews, with the British consul, sent prisoners to Algiers. From later accounts however it appears that they were afterwards released and restored. But at Bona there has been a massacre of two hundred Christians and upwards on the 27th of May, and among them was included by the reports now circulated the British consul. There have also been rumors that the Bey of Tunis had been deposed by his own son, in consequence of the declaration which Lord Exmouth had obtained from him, and that a squadron had issued from Tunis, by which new depredations were committed on the coast of Italy.

Some notice of these extraordinary transactions has been taken in the House of Commons where Mr. Brougham moved for the production of Lord Exmouth's treaties.[1] Lord Castlereagh declined producing them, and Mr. Brougham ultimately withdrew his motion. But in the debate the spirit of indignation against the Barbary states, was manifested by the friends and supporters of the minis-

[1] June 18, 1816.

ters as strongly as by their opponents. Lord Castlereagh alone withstood the general current, and sufficiently indicated that it is not the intention of the British government to extinguish these piracies on the African coast. On the contrary I am persuaded that a new negotiation will take place, in which Lord Exmouth's proceedings, if not disavowed, will be explained away on the ground of misconception; new sacrifices will be made to pacify the Dey of Algiers, and the commerce of all the secondary maritime states and the Christian shores of the Mediterranean will continue to be harassed and ransomed by the depredations of the Barbarians as heretofore, and probably worse. The next British negotiator at Algiers will understand his instructions and the real object of his government. In the late occurrences they appear to have been better understood by the Dey than by Lord Exmouth himself. For although his Lordship was ordered to give very grave and charitable counsel to the Dey, and was also explicitly authorized to use force, if necessary, yet it was certainly not expected either that the advice should be followed, or that the force should be used.

. . . . .

I am, etc.

TO THE SECRETARY OF STATE

No. 49.   [JAMES MONROE]

LONDON, 12 July, 1816.

SIR:

I had on the 5th instant the honor of receiving your favor of the 14th of May, and had previously received your report upon the projected augmentation of the salaries of the ministers of the United States at foreign courts, and on the proposal for the allowance of a compensation in the form of salary to the consuls, with copies of the letters from Mr. Crawford and Mr. Clay to you on those subjects.

With regard to the first question I am not aware that I can add any further information to that contained in those documents, unless it be the result of my own experience. The salaries allowed by the British and French governments to their ambassadors and ministers are correctly stated in the list annexed to your report, but the allowances to them for contingent expenses are usually an additional expense equal in amount to the salary. They are also entitled after a few years of service to pensions for life, proportioned to the length of time they have been in service, and equal upon the average from one-third to one-half the annual salary, and they are permitted to receive presents from the governments to which they are accredited, which in these treaty making times form no inconsiderable part of their emoluments. The account of expenses of Lord Castlereagh's three special missions to the continent was laid before Parliament at the late session. They embraced a term short of eighteen months, their amount was forty-three thousand pounds. There was no allowance for salary, but he received at the same time the salary of £6,000 a year as Secretary of State for Foreign Affairs, and the presents made him on the conclusion of treaties amounted to a much larger sum. The Russian and Austrian governments pay their ministers abroad much upon the same scale as France and England. The Russian ambassador at this court has a salary of sixty thousand dollars and a house to live in rent free.

During the five years and a half of my establishment at St. Petersburg my expenses fell little short of but did not exceed the salary and outfits allowed me. But I certainly could not disguise to myself, nor do I feel it necessary to conceal from you, that it was impossible to proportion my establishment to that standard without a great sacrifice of that consideration which attends the character of a foreign minister, much of which sacrifice doubtless fell upon myself far less to my regret than that part of it which was unavoidably shared by my country. It is not probable that any other minister of the United States in Russia will ever find it practicable to reduce his expenditures within the same compass. I have not found it possible here. I may state with perfect confidence that no minister of the United States at this court has ever found it profitable to limit his expenses within the public allowance of salary and outfit. And while it is notorious that a salary fixed twenty-five years ago was then inadequate to the necessities of the station, it is equally notorious that every expense of a domestic establishment in this country has doubled in that interval. The salary therefore at present is not only inadequate, but to a degree that no man can confine his expenses to it without positive degradation in the eyes of the people of this nation and of his own countrymen; for it will neither enable him to return the hospitalities of those with whom he is associated by his station, nor to show the attention of common civility to the numerous Americans who come recommended to them from the most respectable characters, and from all quarters of the Union. Such are the inevitable effects of this situation upon the estimation of a country whose representative is thus exhibited to the public view, that I am convinced there must be a change of the system. The permanent missions abroad must be exclusively given to men of large fortune, willing to expend it liberally, or there must be a considerable increase of the salaries.

I am not of opinion that an allowance of a salary to consuls would be either necessary or expedient. But a consul general in England, France, and perhaps each of the maritime countries of Europe where there is no diplomatic mission, might be useful, and would require a salary or some equivalent mode of compensation. I have already more than once suggested the indispensable necessity of a salary to the consul at the port of London, or of bestowing the office upon a merchant who would hold it in connection with a commercial establishment.

. . . .

I am, etc.

TO THE SECRETARY OF STATE

No. 52.   [JAMES MONROE]

LONDON, July 30, 1816.

SIR:

Since I had the honor of writing you I have received a packet from your Department containing a file of the *National Intelligencer* from the 1st to the 13th of June.

I have heretofore enclosed to you a printed copy of the

first act of Parliament passed at the late session, for carrying into effect the Commercial Conventions of 3 July, 1815. I now transmit copies of two other acts supplementary to it, and of my correspondence with this government relating to several objects connected with and depending on it.[1]

1. Conveyance of passengers from Ireland to the United States.

By an act of Parliament passed the 24th of June, 1803, it was provided that foreign vessels taking passengers from the ports of the United Kingdom should be permitted to take only one person for every five tons. From December last I have been receiving frequent letters from Ireland complaining of this regulation as affecting the shipping of the two countries, and operating as a discrimination in favor of British and to the disadvantage of American vessels in the ports of Ireland. I have already enclosed to you copies of my first note to Lord Castlereagh upon this subject, of his answer, and of my reply. And I have reported the substance of several conversations with him and with Mr. Robinson, the Vice-President of the Board of Trade in relation to it. It was at first contended that the discrimination did not come within the purview of the treaty, and Lord Castlereagh insisted that the policy of the act was not the discrimination of shipping, but to check emigration. After some time, however, he promised that the shipping of the two countries should be placed on the same footing, and the result is the act of 1 July, 1816, by which the restrictions of the prior law laid upon foreign vessels are now extended to British vessels. I send you a printed copy of both the acts.

2. Clearance of American vessels direct from British European ports to British ports in India. After the passage

---

[1] For a conversation with Lord Castlereagh on the questions between the United States and Great Britain, see Adams, *Memoirs*, July 18, 1816.

of the first act of Parliament carrying the convention into effect, clearances were refused to American vessels here bound to British ports in India. Messrs. G. and J. Abel and Co., after failing in applications for that purpose to the India House and to the Board of Control, addressed a letter to me, with copies of the answers which they had received from those offices. I made immediate application to Lord Castlereagh and furnished him with copies of those papers. After some time he informed me that a bill would be introduced into Parliament to allow those clearances. In the interval there had been some discussion between Mr. Robinson and me, whether this direct trade in American vessels from Great Britain to the British ports in India was implied in the commercial convention or not. He observed that even any indirect trade from the United States to British India was not expressly stipulated in the convention, and urged that it could not be supposed that Great Britain intended to permit American vessels to go from her own ports in immediate competition with her own subjects. I admitted that the indirect trade from the United States was contained in the convention, not by express words but only by necessary implication. Mr. Robinson did not contest that it had been so fully understood at the conclusion of the convention, and I observed that it was explicitly recognized in the notes of the British plenipotentiaries during the negotiation. And the general indirect trade being thus conceded, I insisted that no exception from it of the European British ports was to be presumed; but that if such an exception had been intended, it must have been expressed. I also insisted that this exception, if persevered in, could have ultimately no effect to give the British navigation exclusive privilege. It would only put American vessels to the trouble, perhaps with some trifle of additional expense, to clear out for intermediate ports. The act of Parliament has removed all question in this respect. There had been also a refusal to clear an American vessel for Batavia, although that colony had been receded by treaty to the Dutch. Upon my application to Mr. Robinson an order was dispatched to the collector at Liverpool to allow their clearance.

3. Tonnage duties, Ramsgate harbor dues, etc.

There were various charges of this nature levied upon American vessels beyond those to which British vessels were subjected. Upon a representation of it to me by Captain Aspinwall, I immediately addressed a note to Lord Castlereagh. I was informed that these duties being granted to chartered companies could not be repealed, but that the amount of them should be refunded by the officers of the customs, as was practised in the case of Portuguese vessels. Copies of my note to Lord Castlereagh on this subject, of his answer, and of the order from the Lords of the Treasury for the repayment of the extra duties, are among the present enclosures.

After the close of the session of Parliament I received a letter from an American house at Liverpool, complaining that a duty of five per cent upon the sale at auction of merchandise imported in American vessels was exacted, to which goods imported in British vessels were not liable when sold in the same manner. I spoke of it to Lord Castlereagh, who assured me that orders should immediately be given to cease requiring this duty. He said something at the same time of a distinction made in the new tariff of duties in the United States between *rolled* and hammered iron—the same manufacture being effected in this country by the process of rolling which in Sweden is done by hammering. This difference of duty he thought operated to the disadvantage of the British iron and as a preference to the Swedish, and he expressed the hope and professed the disposition that the fullest operation might be given on both sides to the equalizing principle of the convention.

With the act of Parliament empowering the secretaries of state to authorize the exportation of machinery for the use of the mint of the United States, I enclose copies of my note to Lord Castlereagh asking for such a permission and of his answer. Never having seen a copy of the bill while it was before Parliament, I had not the opportunity of suggesting a correction of the mistake in the preamble, which states that the machinery is wanted to erect and establish a mint in the United States. It will, however, of course have no effect upon the execution of the law. The power conferred upon the executive government you will perceive is more extensive than was requested, and may be used to obtain licenses for the conveyance of artificers, if they should be wanted, as well as of machinery. I have received two letters from Messrs. Belles and Harold of Birmingham, mentioning orders to them from Mr. Patterson, the Director of the Mint, for six pair of rollers to be sent to Philadelphia, and that they would be about this time ready for exportation from Liverpool.

I have the honor, etc.

TO JOHN ADAMS

EALING, 1 August, 1816.

MY DEAR SIR:

The multiplicity of business, and of things that consume more time than business, have in spite of all my efforts broken down to such a degree the regularity of my private correspondence that I am now to acknowledge the receipt of your favors of 20 and 28 March, of 10 and 20 May, and of 16 and 25 June, every one of which contains matter upon which, if I had the time and the talents, I could write you a volume in return.

You are alarmed at the restoration of the Jesuits; but whether it is that I was fascinated by my good old friend, the Father General at St. Petersburg, or that I have a firmer reliance upon the impossibility of reviving exanimated impostures, I have not been able to work myself up into anything like fear of evil consequences at this event. I had a diplomatic colleague in Russia, a man of excellent heart, of amiable temper, of amusing and sportive wit, a profound classical and mathematical scholar, an honest moralist and a conscientious Roman Catholic Christian, who used to maintain to me with the most diverting seriousness and from the deepest conviction of his soul that Father Malebranche was the only metaphysician, and that Locke was the veriest pestilence of modern times. Locke was the father of the Encyclopaedists; Locke was the founder of the French Revolution and of all its horrors. I understand that there is a learned Theban laying it down to the people of France in the *Moniteur*, that all the miseries of mankind in the present age are imputable to the pretended reformation of Luther; and at Madrid a professor of mathematics has commenced a course of lectures by announcing to his pupils that he shall omit all the higher branches of the science, because it has been proved by experience that they lead to Atheism. But if Julian, the genius, the conqueror, the philosopher, the master of the world, did but kick against the pricks when he undertook to restore the magnificent mythology of the Greeks, is it conceivable that the driveling dotards of this age can bring back the monkeries and mummeries of the twelfth century? Oh! No! Europe is tyrannized not by priests but by soldiers. It is overshadowed by a military despotism. Let the bayonets be taken away, and there will be no danger of the Jesuits.

A friend of mine has sent me a large parcel of Boston newspapers, mostly of the last days of June. By them and by other accounts I learn that Governor Brooks' speech has not given satisfaction to those who patronized his election. It is, however, such as I should have expected from the man before he was their candidate. His total silence upon the merits of his predecessor [1] is eloquence of the best kind. I always entertained a very respectful opinion of the character of General Brooks; but when I found him selected as the candidate of the Junto men, I could not avoid the suspicion that he had condescended, or would condescend, to some compromise of principle which could not fail to sink him in my estimation. He has steered clear of this rock in his speech. But he has a year of painful probation to go through, and with a prospect almost certain of being deserted by his supporters if he maintains his own independence. Since the peace it has evidently been the great struggle of the faction still calling themselves federalists, not as during the war to grasp or destroy the national government, but merely to maintain their own ascendency in the

[1] Caleb Strong.

states where they had obtained it. They have, however, failed even of that in Vermont, New Hampshire, and New York. In Massachusetts, Connecticut, and Maryland, their majorities have dwindled almost into nothing. Should no national misfortune befall us I anticipate their complete overthrow in another year. It is hinted to me that the separation of the District of Maine will prolong their dominion perhaps a year or two more in the remnant of old Massachusetts; but as the new state will immediately be redeemed from their misgovernment, it will weaken them in the national councils and scatter their ranks nearly as much as if they were reduced to a minority in the whole Commonwealth.

If I were merely a man of Massachusetts I should deeply lament this dismemberment of my native state. But the longer I live the stronger I find my national feelings grow upon me, and the less of my affections are compassed by partial localities. My system of politics more and more inclines to strengthen the union and its government. It is directly the reverse of that professed by Mr. John Randolph, of relying principally upon the state governments. The effort of every one of the state governments would be to sway the whole union for its own local advantage. The doctrine is therefore politic enough for a citizen of the most powerful state in the union, but it is good for nothing for the weaker states, and pernicious for the whole. But it is the contemplation of our external relations that makes me specially anxious to strengthen our national government. The conduct and issue of the late war has undoubtedly raised our national character in the consideration of the world; but we ought also to be aware that it has multiplied and embittered our enemies. This nation is far more inveterate against us than it ever was before. All the restored governments of

Europe are deeply hostile to us. The Royalists everywhere detest and despise us as Republicans. All the victims and final vanquishers of the French Revolution abhor us as aiders and abettors of the French during their career of triumph. Wherever British influence extends it is busy to blacken us in every possible manner. In Spain the popular feeling is almost as keen against us as in England. Emperors, kings, princes, priests, all the privileged orders, all the establishments, all the votaries of legitimacy, eye us with the most rancorous hatred. Among the crowned heads the only friend we had was the Emperor Alexander, and his friendship has, I am afraid, been more than cooled. How long it will be possible for us to preserve peace with all Europe it is impossible to foresee. Of this I am sure, that we cannot be too well or too quickly prepared for a new conflict to support our rights and our interests. The tranquillity of Europe is precarious, it is liable to many sudden changes and great convulsions; but there is none in probable prospect which would give us more security than we now enjoy against the bursting of another storm upon ourselves. I can never join with my voice in the toast which I see in the papers attributed to one of our gallant naval commanders.[1] I cannot ask of heaven success, even for my country, in a cause where she should be in the wrong. *Fiat justitia, pareat cœlum.* My toast would be, may our country be always successful, but whether successful or otherwise always right. I disclaim as unsound all patriotism incompatible with the principles of eternal justice. But the truth is that the American union, while united, *may* be certain of success in every rightful cause, and may if it pleases never have any

---

[1] Stephen Decatur, who gave the toast at Norfolk, Va., April, 1816: "Our country! In her intercourse with foreign nations, may she always be in the right; but our country, right or wrong."

but a rightful cause to maintain. They are at this moment the strongest nation upon the globe for every purpose of justice. May they be just to secure the favor of heaven, and wise to make a proper application of their strength. May they be armed in thunder for the defense of right, and self-shackled in eternal impotence for the support of wrong.

We have been much affected by the intelligence of the decease of Colonel Smith,[1] following in such quick succession upon that of his two brothers. It has severely distressed his son, in whom I have an industrious, attentive and faithful assistant. He had been in some measure prepared for the event by the accounts he had previously received. The news of Mr. Dexter's [2] death came upon us sudden and unexpected. We first heard of it on the 5th of June. I had written him a long letter on the 14th of April, in answer to one that I had received from him by Captain Stuart. It must have arrived in America after his departure and I hope will not fall into improper hands.

I shall write as soon as possible to my dear mother. We are all in good health, only as I have been troubled with six weeks of holidays, my three boys are now beginning to complain of a relapse into the school headache. They write by this opportunity for themselves.

I remain, etc.

[1] William Stephens Smith, brother-in-law of John Quincy Adams, died at Lebanon, New York, June 10, 1816.
[2] Samuel Dexter died at Athens, New York, May 3, 1816.

TO JOSEPH HALL

EALING, near London, 7 August, 1816.

DEAR SIR:

Your obliging favor of the 13th of June has come safely to hand, but I have not been so fortunate as to receive the preceding letter of 24 December to which it refers. This is a circumstance which I greatly regret, as the loss of any one of your letters is a privation of much valuable information and of the soundest views of our political affairs.

I was not surprised at the issue of the late election in Massachusetts, though I had been much at the selection of the federal candidate. As the federal majority in 1814 had been of more than ten thousand votes, and in 1815 had only fallen to seven thousand, I had little or no expectation that in the space of one year more it would fall off in a proportion so much accelerated as to change it into a minority for the time. The late Mr. Bayard was of opinion that the result of the peace would be to strengthen and increase the federal party throughout the Union. My own anticipation was that it would have a contrary effect, but with a slow, gradual and uniform operation. The recovery from an inflammatory disease is seldom so rapid as the progress of the disease itself, nor is the most sudden generally the most effectual convalescence. The improvement of the public spirit has been quite equal to my expectations; and to find the Massachusetts federalists reduced to the necessity of holding up General Brooks for their candidate was quite as satisfactory a demonstration to me of the tendencies of the popular sentiment, as the triumph of the Republican party in Vermont, New Hampshire, and New York.

I have read with much satisfaction the new Governor's

speech to the legislature, and have observed with still more pleasure the temper with which it has been received by both parties. The republicans have approved and applauded it without reserve. The federalists, applauding it apparently with equal warmth, seem only to vent their chagrin at the thought that *their* Governor has pleased and conciliated their adversaries. Governor Brooks has neither insulted nor calumniated the government of the nation. His immediate predecessor [*a line missing*] last three or four years seem to have considered that practice as by far the most important of their official duties. A snarling Governor, a snarling Senate, a snarling House of Representatives, such is the picture of Massachusetts under Strong's last administrations. Pious eulogies upon the bulwark of our Holy Religion; black letter law in favor [*blank*] in the face of mankind that they could find no more than eleven natives of Massachusetts impressed into the British Navy; sanctified resolutions that a moral and religious people ought not to rejoice at the victories of their country; processions and illuminations to celebrate the triumphs of the public enemy; the territory of the state abandoned to the invader, and Hartford Conventions to dissolve the Union—these, with periodical insult and calumny upon the government of the Union, these are the beams of glory with which Strong's second administration of Massachusetts will go down to posterity. Sound, sound was the sense of Governor Brooks when he turned a deaf ear to the [demand] which urged him to pledge his unsullied fame to the approbation of this mass of [*blank*].

It is a strong proof at once of the desperate condition to which the junto federalists find themselves reduced, and of the narrow scale upon which all their politics are graduated that they have reconciled themselves to the dismemberment of the Commonwealth by the separation of the province of Maine, merely because it may secure to them a year or two longer the dominion of the remnant of the state, though with a prospect equally apparent of introducing into the Senate of the Union two new members to counteract the influence of their own. I regret the separation of Maine, because it will sink my native state from the first down to the second or third rate among the members of the Union, and because I should have hoped that the weight which her strength and population must always have given her, would in future times be directed to the true honor and general interest of the country, although they had been so miserably misapplied for some years past. But as the objects of administration to which the state governments are generally confined may best be superintended by authorities compassed within small local divisions, as there was necessarily much inconvenience to the inhabitants of Maine by reason of their distance from the seat of government, and by their separation from its territory and the intervention of New Hampshire, and as our legislature had already become so enormously unwieldly, and was growing more so from year to year, I have made up my mind to be contented with the measure; and if the states of New York, Pennsylvania and Virginia would be partitioned in the same manner, I should be perfectly satisfied with this operation of our political arithmetic which multiplies by dividing, and adds to the whole body whatever it subtracts from each individual member.

The accounts that we receive from all the commercial cities of the United States are in some respects unpleasant. Trade is said to be by no means in a flourishing state. Excessive importations of goods that can neither be disposed of nor paid for: floods of discredited paper and a total exhaustion of gold and silver: provisions and all the necessaries of life at immoderate prices, and foreign goods unsaleable at prime cost; the public credit extremely low, and showing no symptom of recovery—these appearances give serious concern to the friends of our country, and afford some consolation to the people of this nation who are beginning to suffer severe distress themselves. Among them it is a great and as yet unsettled question to what cause their distress is to be imputed. The friends of the government and loyal subjects ascribe it to the transition from the state of war to that of peace, and to two or three successive seasons of extraordinary plenty. The Jacobins charge it upon the extravagant expenditures of the government, the insupportable load of taxation, and the wars against the French Revolution. The complete final success of those wars and the splendid victories of their armies in the late years have given the loyal party an irresistible ascendency over all their opponents, and there was probably never a period in the history of the island when there was such general submission to the government, so little disaffection throughout the country, and such a universal feeling of national pride and exultation as that which immediately succeeded the battle which they call the battle of Waterloo. The pressure upon the farmers had indeed begun to be felt some time before, but it was for several months after lost in the general shouts of triumph. It was, however, in the autumn of the last year that the complaints of agricultural distress began to be heard. The produce of the land sunk in value so that the farmers were unable to pay their rents. The country banks called in their paper and many of them failed. The manufacturers were compelled to dismiss their workmen. The paupers multiplied until many parishes became unable to maintain them. Yet these effects were all so limited and partial when Parliament met in February, that the Regent's speech congratulated them upon the flourishing state of commerce and the revenue, and took no notice of any distress as existing anywhere. The proposal on the part of the Ministers to continue the property tax, though reduced from ten to five per cent, produced a struggle against it, and many petitions from all parts of the kingdom. It was lost by a small majority in the House of Commons. Parliament sat five months, in which there was much speech making about distress and economy, but nothing more was done to relieve the distress, and an expenditure of thirty millions for the present year was sanctioned to illustrate the economy. In the meantime the complaints have been increasing and growing louder, at last they have resorted to a public subscription to relieve the sufferers. The most alarming symptom of the disease has but just shown itself, that is, a diminution of the revenue. The quarter which ended on the 5th of July was the first in which this deficiency appeared. If that should continue and increase as the present prospect threatens, the government will find it difficult to fulfil its engagements with the public creditors. Some slight appearances of discontent have lately been manifested in various parts of the country, and here and there hunger has produced an occasional popular riot which has been immediately suppressed by the soldiers. But hitherto the popularity of the government has suffered little. A foreign war might again divert the attention of the people from their own situation, and again make it supportable to them; but unless that, or some extraordinary turn of affairs should happen, I think it impossible that two years more should pass away without bringing the conflict between the land and the funds, the debtor and creditor of this nation to a crisis, which will dissolve the spell of her overgrown power, and reduce her to her fair proportions in the scale of Empire.

Mrs. Adams joins me in the desire to be kindly remembered to Mrs. Hall, and in the best wishes to yourself with which I am, Dear Sir, etc.

TO ABIGAIL ADAMS

EALING, 16 August, 1816.

MY DEAR MOTHER:

The receipt of all your letters to that of 30 June has been acknowledged. To answer them, I must have time to think—a privilege which I so seldom enjoy that I cannot even anticipate when I may be indulged with it. Mr. Tuckerman [1] brought your last letter. I saw him and his lady once; but they were only three or four days in London, and are gone upon a tour into the country. Mr. Tuckerman says his health has been restored by the voyage.

The Queen's evening party on the Prince Regent's birthday closed the fashionable assemblies for the season. We have avoided them as constantly as we could without impropriety. Yet they have for the last six months consumed a large portion of my time, and broken in upon the regularity of my life. You ask the character of the Princess Charlotte. But I have seen her only twice, and with little opportunity to observe her character. She has been confined to her house by indisposition most of the time since her marriage, has not appeared at court since the Drawing Room held on that occasion, and is *said* to have met with an unpropitious accident. But to what the French call the

[1] Rev. E. Tuckerman of Chelsea is named by Abigail Adams as the person, but it was more probably Rev. Joseph Tuckerman.

on dits about her, or any of the royal family, I make it a rule never to believe any of them. It is *fashionable* to talk about them, fashionable to tell strange stories about them, and the stranger the story the more fashionable, because it gives the person telling it the air of being a knowing one, initiated in all the mysteries of high life. The lies, therefore, concerning them are innumerable, the truths excessively few. The Princess Charlotte is popular, because she is presumptive heiress to the throne, because she is young, because she is thought to have been harshly treated, and because she has given some indications of sense and spirit. But she and her husband set out upon the principle of having nothing to do with public affairs. That may be politic. The question is how they *spend their time.* Elizabeth lost no time while she was living in the shade and precarious safety. The Princess Charlotte may think she must now be insignificant. But if she thinks she must be idle, she will never restore the golden days of good Queen Bess. All well. Ever affectionately yours.

TO LORD CASTLEREAGH

The undersigned Envoy Extraordinary and Minister Plenipotentiary of the United States of America has the honor of submitting to the consideration of his Majesty's government the enclosed copy of the information of Thomas Avery of the Borough of Tavistock, taken before R. V. Willesford, Clerk, a Justice of the Peace for the County of Devon, relating to the treatment experienced during the late war by the American prisoners at Dartmoor in regard to the provisions furnished to them.

This paper was transmitted to the undersigned by Philip

Thorne of Tavistock, a person unknown to him, but who declares himself able and willing to support by other testimony the charge contained in it, as well as others of a similar and no less aggravated character, and affirms it can be proved that the damaged flour and biscuit mentioned in the information were purchased by Gill and Hornbrook [1] at the Plymouth victualling office, sold by order of government, it being damaged and unfit for his Majesty's service.

The undersigned feels it his indispensable duty to make known these circumstances to Lord Castlereagh, and to request that an immediate solemn and effectual legal investigation of these transactions may be directed which shall ascertain the foundation of these charges, bring to light all the accomplices of such atrocious practices against the health and lives of the American prisoners of war, and inflict upon those who have been guilty of them exemplary punishment.

The undersigned prays Lord Castlereagh to accept the renewed assurance of his high consideration.

Craven street, 19 August, 1816.

TO ABIGAIL ADAMS

EALING, 24 August, 1816.

MY DEAR MOTHER:

I shall send you by the earliest opportunity the newly published numbers of the *Edinburgh* and *Quarterly Reviews*, but unless you read Cobbett's *New York Register*, you will

---

[1] John Gill and Saunders Hornbrook. The charge implied that damaged biscuit had been ground down and mixed with meal, for the supply of the American prisoners at Dartmoor. This practice led to an outbreak among the prisoners, when many were killed and wounded by the guards.

not have the key to the secret history of those works. There are now three very distinct parties in this country—Tories, or the ministerial party, Whigs, and Reformers. The *Quarterly Review* is the literary instrument of the first; the *Edinburgh Review* of the second; and Cobbett's *Register* of the third. This party, still deeply depressed, and having no leader but Sir Francis Burdett, who seems at this moment to shrink from the post, will, however, if events should continue to follow their present impulse, rise upon the ruins of both the others. The taxes are breaking the back of the nation. The revenue itself has begun to show symptoms of decay. They are not yet unequivocal, but if they continue and increase, the funding system cannot stand the shock that will soon ensue. The nation must compound with its creditors. The Tories still hold out stoutly against this, and struggle for further taxation. The Whigs faintly resist the idea of a national bankruptcy, and vaguely talk of economy, retrenchment, reduced establishments, and the necessity of a general sacrifice, to bear equally upon the funds and the lands. The reformers alone speak out boldly, that the interest of the debt must be reduced. But then they add that the sinecures, pensions, and rotten boroughs, must go too. Of the three parties the Whigs are now the weakest. Their principles give them no plausible remedy for the evils of the day. They offer nothing but palliatives. The reformers call aloud for the knife. The patient shudders at the thought of the operation, but as the mortification spreads and approaches the vital parts, he begins to feel that the alternative is life. You will see the resolutions, passed unanimously last Wednesday by the people of the City of London. Neither Whigs nor Tories dared to raise their voices at that meeting. A petition to the Regent was voted which it is well known he will not receive. But if similar meetings take place in other parts of the country, they will tend to manifest and to increase the strength of the reformers. There will probably be serious occurrences at the next session of Parliament.

I have no time to enlarge. We are all well and ever faithfully yours.

TO THE SECRETARY OF STATE

No. 53.   [JAMES MONROE]

LONDON, 24 August, 1816.

SIR:

. . . .

On Wednesday last I had an interview with Lord Castlereagh, in which he informed me that this government declined entering upon any negotiation relative to the commercial intercourse between the United States and the British colonies in the West Indies. That they were averse to any discussion relative to blockades and the other conflicting pretensions of neutral and belligerent rights. And that they were willing to receive any proposals that we may wish to offer respecting the intercourse by land between the United States and the British continental colonies respecting seamen, but there was a manifest reluctance to negotiate even upon these points. With regard to the West Indies he said it was understood by this government that the United States would be perfectly free to adopt any countervailing regulations, either of prohibition or of additional duties, that they might think advisable. That Great Britain would have no right to complain of them. That the determination in this instance arose altogether from that of adhering to their colonial system, of the wisdom of which he spoke as being in his own mind not unquestionable, but from which it was not thought expedient now to depart. He renewed at the same time the assurance of the pacific and friendly dispositions of this government.

Since the commencement of this month the government advertised for transports to carry five thousand two hundred tons of ordnance stores to Canada. This advertisement, appearing immediately after the publication in the newspapers of Governor Cass's letter to the commander of the *Tecumseh*, produced an alarm among the commercial people in the city of London which it might perhaps have been intended to produce in another quarter. But it occasioned a depression of the funds which was probably neither intended nor expected. A part of these stores lately sailed, together with officers to command some of their vessels on the lakes. At the beginning of the summer they had stripped a number of their merchant vessels at Quebec of their crews, to the heavy damage of their owners and the ruin of some of the voyages, for the purpose of manning their armed vessels on the lakes, and now they send out ordnance and officers at a season of perilous navigation, and too late for service if they arrive. Far from being alarmed at these measures, I rather infer from the ostentatious publicity given to them some alarm on their part. They are the precipitances of imaginations haunted with terrors of a sudden invasion of Canada from the United States. I believe there is no intention here of an immediate war with America, but there may be a policy of exciting frequently a public expectation of it. I spoke to Lord Castlereagh of the improper conduct of the officer from the *Tecumseh*, and told him I should send him a note concerning it and copies of the affidavits. He said he wished me to express in the note the conviction that this government would take the promptest measures to repress any misconduct of that nature, and to mark their disapprobation of it. His Lordship also communicated to me the instructions to Lord Exmouth on his present expedition to Algiers. They are dated the 18th of July, and they direct Lord Exmouth to offer peace to the Dey upon three conditions: 1. That the Dey shall sign a declaration similar to that lately obtained from Tunis and Tripoli never more to reduce Christian prisoners to slavery. 2. That he shall immediately liberate, and in the first instance deliver up to Lord Exmouth, all the Christian slaves of whatever nation now in his possession. 3. That he shall repay all the money paid for the Sardinian and Neapolitan slaves under the treaties of 3 April last. No modification of either of these three conditions is to be accepted. He is to prescribe a reasonable time within which the Dey's answer is to be given, and in case of refusal of either of the conditions he is to commence hostilities against the Algerine fleet. In concluding the peace he is to admit no stipulation for any consular present in future. These instructions are founded upon the formal undertaking of Great Britain to break up the whole system of Barbary piracy, an enterprise worthy of her power and among the noblest purposes to which it could be applied. Nothing is left but for the execution to correspond with the design.

I am, etc.

TO ABIGAIL ADAMS

EALING, 30 August, 1816.

George says that his writing master has forbidden him to write letters for the present, because it will retard the improvement of his handwriting. I do not understand this theory, and suspect it will not meet the approbation of George's correspondents at home. The consequence of it is, that I am called to write the weekly letter that is to go with the newspaper almost every week myself.

The present Lord Mayor of London, Matthew Wood by name, and a fishmonger by profession, that is a member of the fishmongers' company, has taken the fancy to show extraordinary civility to the American Minister, and has manifested it from the time of his election. You remember perhaps that the annual day of the Lord Mayor's induction to office is the 9th of November. That is always a day of ceremony, and there is a great entertainment at Guildhall to which all the foreign ministers are invited. I received accordingly an invitation to it from Mr. Wood, then Lord Mayor-elect; but I was then confined to my chamber with the inflammation in my eyes, and was obliged to send an excuse. In February he gave a splendid dinner and ball to the Austrian Archdukes, John and Louis, the two youngest brothers of the Emperor of Austria, who were then in England upon a visit. To this all the foreign ministers were likewise invited, and many of them attended. I went a total stranger to the Lord Mayor and to all the company, excepting the Archdukes, to whom I had been presented the day before, and the foreign ministers whom I had met at the Regent's levee and occasionally elsewhere. It was at this dinner that I was suddenly and most unexpectedly called to answer a complimentary speech with which the Duke of Kent, who sat next to the Lord Mayor, introduced the toast of the President of the United States. I answered of course in a very few words, concluding with that toast which was published in the newspapers, then copied into some of those in America, and which is mentioned in one of your letters.[1] He invited me within ten days afterwards to another great entertainment which he gave to the wardens and officers of his fishmongers' company. I was the only foreigner invited to that party, and there I met the Duke of Kent again, and the Duke of Sussex, whom I had formerly known at Berlin.[2] Not long afterwards these royal brothers were made members of the fishmongers' company, upon which occasion the company itself gave a dinner to which I was invited.[3] Then there was the Easter Monday dinner and ball.[4] Then a dinner given by the Lord Mayor to the Duke of Wellington,[5] and lastly a water party upon the Thames last week—a voyage from Westminster Bridge to Richmond, and a dinner there on board a new city barge.[6] Will you not be ashamed for me, when I tell you that the first return I have made to the Lord Mayor for all these more than polite hospitalities, has been by having him to dine with us this day in company with the Duke of Sussex, Lord Erskine, Sir Robert Wilson (who has just returned from his honorable imprisonment in France), your and my father's old friend, the Chevalier de Freire, and two or three other friends.[7] But if my returns have not been as

[1] Adams, *Memoirs*, February 19, 1816.
[2] *Ib.*, February 27, 1816.
[3] *Ib.*, May 23, 1816.
[4] *Ib.*, April 15, 1816.
[5] *Ib.*, August 8, 1816.
[6] *Ib.*, August 22, 1816.
[7] *Ib.*, August 30, 1816.

prompt, and frequent, and sumptuous, as his kindness to me, you know the reason why. I have not refused his invitations, because I thought a sulky reserve in return for frank and open civility would be worse than no return at all. The Lord Mayor of London who, as you know, never serves in that office but one year, receives from the city twelve thousand pounds sterling for discharging the duties of it. They usually exceed this sum by an expenditure of six or eight thousand pounds, and the present Lord Mayor, who has a large fortune of his own, and has been magnificent in his entertainments beyond example, will not get through his year at less than double his salary. His year is now drawing to a close, and he is to be succeeded by a person who has no partialities for anything American. We shall not be much embarrassed by his civilities.

The weather still continues cold and damp, though having for the last ten days had an occasional sight of the sun, and the temperature of the air only cool, it passes for fine weather, and has revived the hopes of an abundant harvest, which I think will be disappointed. Accustomed as I have been all my life to observe the workings of party spirit, I have been surprised to find that from the beginning of this month, it has been here a great party question whether the harvest of this present year would be good or bad. Cobbett, who is the literary representative of the reformers, very early in the month announced that it would be scanty. Mr. Hunt [1] another ardent reformer, at the city meeting last week, pledged his honor that it would be bad. But all the newspapers, ministerial and oppositionist, Whig and Tory, have opened in full cry against these predictions, and foretold a plentiful or at least an average harvest. The *Morning Chronicle*, which seldom ventures to encounter Cobbett,

[1] Henry Hunt (1773–1835).

has felt in this case so confident, that it has opened a battery of ridicule upon him for his foresight, and says it was a ghost who told him it for a joke, and he took it in earnest. ·Cobbett himself, alarmed for his prophetic fame by this universal concurrence of all the legitimates against him, or by the improving prospects of the last ten tolerable days, has partially recanted, and now, 31 August, *begins* to think there will be an average harvest. It is, to use an expression much in vogue here, a fundamental feature of Cobbett's character and the source of almost all his errors, that he always overleaps many of his premises to get at his conclusion. He was overhasty in pronouncing the first week in August that the harvest would fail, and he has been premature in his recantation. My own belief is that there will be a considerable deficiency of all the crops, and especially of the wheat. But to account for the fact seemingly so whimsical, that this question is made a subject of acrimonious party discussion, you must know that all the ruling parties in this country, Whigs and Tories, Lands and Funds, all but the reformers, have agreed that most of the distresses now weighing down this country are owing to excessive plenty, to the cheapness of wheat. This they all continue to say, while no small part of their population are nearly perishing with famine. Near two years ago, when this excessive plenty was at its height, Parliament enacted a law for the express purpose of keeping up the price of grain. But why this portentous symptom of aggravating the burthens of the poor? This struggle to give scarcity to the staff of life? Because, if the farmer who raised the corn could not sell it at a high price, he could no longer pay his taxes to the government, his rent to the landlord, his tithes to the parson, and his rates for the poor. If the landlord could not collect his rent, nor the parson his tithes, they too would no longer be able to pay their taxes. If the taxes could not be collected, the revenue would fail, and the public creditor could not be paid. Now the cheapness of corn was then attributed to its excessive plenty, and Cobbett alone, I believe, insisted that there was no superfluous plenty; but that the fall of price was owing entirely to the calling in of the Bank paper. The corn-bill occasioned violent and dangerous riots in London when it passed, but it did pass, and its full effects will be disclosed only when the scarcity shall be felt. The scarcity is coming, but it has not yet brought relief to the public distress, and as it has dangers of its own, all the parties but the reformers seem inclined to disguise the fact even to themselves. I am yet doubtful what its effect, and that of the removal of the property tax, will be upon the revenue. Yet that is the all important question. If the revenue does not fail, the machine, ponderous and complicated as it is, will get along. If it falls off the present quarter, even in proportion as it did the last (I think it will not), there will be a serious struggle to tax the funds, and perhaps compulsively to reduce the interest of the national debt at the next session of Parliament. In the meantime the popular feeling is getting sore and irritated to such a degree that fears of commotion are entertained by the sober people of all parties. The City of London have voted a petition to the Prince Regent which they know will not be received. Westminster is to have a meeting soon. But petitioning will not become general until the meeting of Parliament. The next winter may produce serious events.

With my duty to my father I remain, etc.

TO LORD CASTLEREAGH

The undersigned Envoy Extraordinary and Minister Plenipotentiary from the United States of America has the honor of renewing to Lord Castlereagh the proposal which he has been instructed to make on the part of the government of the United States, for the negotiation of a treaty of commerce embracing all the principal objects most interesting to the friendly and commercial intercourse between the two nations. He has already exhibited to his Lordship the authority with which he has been furnished by the American government for that purpose, and has fully stated to him the motives which induced this proposal. They are all founded in the anxious desire of the American government to cultivate the harmony between the two nations, and to concert by engagements of mutual accommodation such arrangements of the points, from which differences have unfortunately arisen heretofore or which might have a tendency to produce them hereafter, as may be satisfactory to both parties, guard against future misunderstandings, and promote that amicable temper and disposition which can alone perpetuate the peace and friendship dictated by the clearest and highest interests both of Great Britain and of the United States.

It will be recollected by Lord Castlereagh that the commercial convention of 3 July, 1815, was not considered at the time of its conclusion as the ultimate or definitive arrangement of the commercial relations between the high contracting parties. Other objects besides those upon which the agreement was completed were discussed in the course of that negotiation. Others yet, including all or most of those upon which Great Britain is now again invited to treat, were presented to the attention of the British plenipotentiaries, but postponed in consideration of peculiar circumstances then operating and which have happily since been done away. On bringing them again to the view of the British Cabinet the undersigned has the honor of distinctly specifying the several objects upon which the American government repeats the proposal to enter into further reciprocal commercial stipulations, of suggesting the urgent additional motives for desiring them which have arisen since that period, and of exposing the liberal principles upon which they propose that this supplementary treaty should be founded.

1. The commerce between the United States and the British colonies in North America and in the West Indies.

From the relative geographical position of those countries, from the nature of their respective productions, and from the wants on either side which may be most advantageously, if not exclusively, supplied by the other, this commerce is not only of the greatest convenience to both parties, but in some respects, and on many occasions, it is of the first necessity to the colonies. At the time when the commercial convention of 3 July, 1815, was negotiated, this commerce was open to vessels of the United States. The ports of the British colonies in the West Indies are still accessible under certain restrictions to French, Spanish, Dutch, Danish, and Swedish vessels, and while the ports of every nation in the West Indies, Great Britain alone excepted, are in like manner accessible to American vessels, they have been and still are by new regulations enforced since the conclusion of that convention rigorously excluded from the British ports. This exclusion of all participation in the advantage of carrying between the two countries the articles of commerce mutually beneficial to both parties has not only the aspect of a policy peculiarly pointed against the United States, but it defeats in a great degree the principle of equalizing the advantages of the commerce between the two countries, by equalizing the duties and charges upon the vessels of both in the direct intercourse between them. For while British vessels, after performing a direct voyage from Europe to the United States, are there received upon terms of equality with those of the United States, they now enjoy the exclusive benefit of resorting to an intermediate market in the West Indies, while the vessels of the United States are restricted to the direct interchange to and from Europe. The result of which is that British vessels enjoy in the ports of the United States important advantages even over the vessels of the United States themselves. It must be obvious that this cannot long be tolerated, that if the commerce with those parts of the British dominions is not placed on a footing of reciprocity, similar restraints will become indispensable on the part of the United States. Such countervailing restraints were proposed at the last session of Congress and postponed, in the hope that satisfactory arrangements might be made before the next meeting to prevent a recurrence to a system of commercial hostility, inconsistent with the interests of both nations, inauspicious to the amicable relations now existing between them, and repugnant to the most earnest wishes of the American government. In the arrangements proposed they do not contemplate any interference on their part with the colonial monopoly of Great Britain. It is not asked that she should renounce the right of prohibiting the importation into her colonies from the United States of whatever articles she may think fit, but that the commerce, which for their and her own advantage Great Britain allows between them and the United States, should be placed on the same footing of reciprocity as the direct trade between Great

Britain and the United States was intended to be placed by the convention of 3 July, 1815.

While on this subject the undersigned cannot but remark the extraordinary measures relating to the commercial intercourse between the United States and the British colonies in North America and in the West Indies, adopted since the conclusion of the commercial convention of 3 July, 1815. In all of them very heavy duties have been imposed upon the importation of American produce, even when carried in British ships. A heavy duty of exportation has been laid in the Province of Nova Scotia upon plaster of Paris, an article for which there is no other market than the United States. And in the Province of Upper Canada an act of the Provincial Legislature, having first vested in the Lieutenant Governor and Council the power of regulating the commercial intercourse between that province and the United States, that body did on the 18th of April last issue an order imposing heavy duties upon many articles of the growth or manufacture of the United States, with an addition of twelve per cent on all those duties upon importation in American vessels, and a tonnage duty of twelve shillings and six pence per ton upon every vessel exceeding five tons burthen entering any port or harbor of the Province and belonging to citizens of the United States.

The inland commerce between the United States and Upper Canada is believed to be of paramount importance to the Province; but were it equally important to the United States, measures like these can be received in no other light than as efforts to engross exclusively the whole of the trade on one side. It would be far more agreeable to the American government to settle this intercourse by amicable concert than to be left under the necessity of meeting a system of exclusion by counteracting regulations.

2. Seamen.

It is proposed to stipulate that neither the United States nor Great Britain shall employ in their naval or merchant service native citizens or subjects of the other party, with the exception of those already naturalized, of whom the number is very small. From the well known fact that the wages of seamen in time of peace are invariably higher in the American service of both descriptions than in the British, it is apparent that the advantage of this stipulation will be almost entirely on the side of Great Britain. Although obviously proper that it should be reciprocal, it is offered not as an engagement from which the United States expect to derive any advantage in itself, but as the means to Great Britain of reserving to herself the services of all her own native seamen, and of removing forever the necessity of resorting to means of force, either by her naval officers to take men from the vessels of the United States, or by the United States to resist the renewal of that practice in the event of any future maritime war to which they may be neutral. In adopting the principle proposed the American government are prepared to secure its faithful execution by any reciprocal regulation which may be deemed necessary consistent with their Constitution and the spirit of their laws.

3. Neutral and belligerent rights.

It is equally desirable in the view of the American government to arrange at this time every question relating to neutral rights, particularly those concerning blockade, contraband of war, visits at sea of merchant vessels by ships of war, the trade with the colonies of enemies, and between them and the parent country, and the trade from one port of an enemy to another. The tendency of discordant principles upon these points to embroil neutral and belligerent states with each other has been shown by the melancholy experience of ages. The frequent departure during the most recent wars from all acknowledged principles founded on the general usages of nations have still more unsettled whatever reliance might heretofore have been placed upon their authority. A time of peace when the feelings of both parties are free from the excitement of any momentary interest, and when the operation of the principles to be sanctioned by mutual compact depends upon contingencies which may give either party the first claim to the stipulated rights of the belligerent or of the neutral, must be more favorable to the amicable adjustment of these questions than a time of actual war under circumstances, when the immediate interests of each party are engaged in opposition to those of the other. Whether Great Britain or the United States will be first engaged in a maritime war with any third party cannot now be foreseen; but it is of the deepest interest to the permanency of the peace and friendship between them that they should come to an explicit understanding with each other upon the points here referred to, before the recurrence of any such event on either side. It is not the desire of the American government to propose upon these subjects any innovation upon principles often recognized by Great Britain herself in her treaties with other powers. They wish only by a mutual compact now formed to guard against collisions which the recollection of the past so forcibly admonishes the rulers of both nations to obviate, if possible, for the future.

4. Slaves carried away from the United States by British officers after the peace.

As the construction given by his Majesty's government to the first article in the treaty of Ghent in reference to the slaves carried away from the United States by British officers after the ratification of the peace is so directly at variance with the construction which the American government think alone applicable to it, the undersigned has been further instructed to propose that this question should be submitted to the decision of some friendly sovereign. This reference is suggested by provisions in the treaty of Ghent itself applicable to the contingency of differences in other instances, and it is conceived that when such differences exist, no better mode can be adopted for settling them in a satisfactory manner.

Should his Majesty's government think proper to accept this proposal for a negotiation upon the points with regard to which the general wishes of the government of the United States have been frankly exposed, the undersigned will be ready to enter into further communication with any person who may be authorized to confer with him for the purpose of such a negotiation. If the offer should not be deemed acceptable, he requests the honor of as early an answer as may be convenient.

The undersigned prays Lord Castlereagh to accept the assurance of his high consideration.

13 Craven street, 17 September, 1816.

TO THE SECRETARY OF STATE

No. 55.   [JAMES MONROE]

LONDON, 18 September, 1816.

SIR:

. . . .

On the 14th instant I received your letter of 13th August. You will perceive by all my late dispatches that there is no prospect of doing anything here in the way of a negotiation upon objects of commerce. I addressed yesterday to Lord Castlereagh a note renewing the proposal to negotiate, the object of which is to have the refusal explicitly signified in writing. In my last interview with Lord Castlereagh he did unequivocally decline negotiation upon the trade between the United States and the British colonies in the West Indies, and upon all the questions relating to neutral rights in time of maritime war. He said they were willing to receive any proposition respecting seamen, and respecting the inland intercourse between the United States and the British colonies in North America. I told him I should repeat the proposal for treating in a note. He expressed a wish that I would not mention in the note the neutral questions at all. I was somewhat surprised at the objection, but promised him I would give it full consideration before I sent in the note. I did accordingly take ample time for reflection and have concluded that I ought not only to include them in the note, but to urge with earnestness the reasons which make it peculiarly desirable that the two governments should come to an understanding upon those points before the recurrence of a maritime war.

With this dispatch I have the honor of enclosing the

Gazette Extraordinary sent from the foreign office, containing Lord Exmouth's dispatches from Algiers, with the account of his attack upon that place on the 27th of last month, the result of which was the complete success of the expedition under his command—the redemption of all the Christians who were detained in slavery, the abolition stipulated by the Dey of all such slavery for the future, and the repayment of the money which had been paid for ransom of Sardinians and Neapolitans by virtue of Lord Exmouth's previous treaties in April. The issue, both of the hostile operations and of the negotiations of the American squadron in the Mediterranean in the summer of 1815, had sufficiently shown to the Christian world what was the only proper method of treating with the Barbary States, and the perfect ease with which Algiers has now been reduced to terms, including the gratuitous deliverance of prisoners and the repayment of tribute money, amply proves how inexcusable it would have been to have endured any longer that system of tribute and servitude which has been hitherto the disgrace of modern Europe. I had indulged the hope that we ourselves were destined to wipe off this disgrace from the face of Christian society; but as the British government did finally undertake it, I rejoice that they have been so easily and so completely successful. The precise tenor of the treaties is yet to be published, and as they will effect a total revolution of the external policy of Algiers, perhaps some time may elapse before all the internal consequences of this event will be disclosed as they may affect the government of the country. What the situation of our affairs there may be I am altogether ignorant, not having heard from Mr. Shaler since his letter of 21 May.

.   .   .   .

I have the honor, etc.

TO ABIGAIL ADAMS

EALING, 20 September, 1816.

MY DEAR MOTHER:

My wife's brother, T. B. Johnson, has written from New Orleans to his sister and me, requesting us to send him our portraits, and we are accordingly sitting for them to a young American named Leslie,[1] who is working hard to make a reputation as a painter. This is the second time that, according to a melancholy joke of poor Sheridan's, I have undergone the *operation* of sitting for my picture within these two years. The first was at Ghent, where the President of the Academy of Fine Arts of that place, Mr. Van Huffel, prevailed upon me to allow him to paint me, when I fancied it was much against my will, and so it is now. But these are cases in which one yields compliance as the least of two evils. Be that as it may, I went yesterday to town *to sit*, and upon alighting at my office, No. 13 Craven Street, I found the cards of Mr. S. C. Thacher [2] and Mr. A. Bigelow,[3] with a whole budget of letters from the *fireside* (in

---

[1] Charles Robert Leslie (1794–1859). He makes no mention of the portrait in his *Autobiography*.

[2] Rev. Samuel Cooper Thacher (1785–1818), who had been editor of the *Monthly Anthology*.

[3] "Mr. [Andrew] Bigelow has been out here and dined with us. His father, the Speaker [Timothy Bigelow], was one year before me at the University, where I had a pleasant, though short acquaintance with him. He was then as sociable as you find him now, and an excellent scholar. I remember his telling me then that his mother [Anna Andrews] had been one of your pupils at Worcester. Since he left college, I have scarcely seen him, but have ever heard of him as an estimable man in everything but his Hartford Convention politics. He was John Lowell's chum at college, and you who know so well how to combine causes and effects, may trace to that source the channel both of his political advancement and his political errors. He is one of those well meaning and sensible men who followed the *ignis*

July and August) at Quincy, for two of which, dated 18 July and 7 August, I am indebted to you, my own dear and honored mother. I could not call upon Messrs. Thacher and Bigelow yesterday, but I hope we shall see them here.

I have long been of opinion that there were too many sympathies of various kinds between New and Old England, but the sympathy of chilling frigidity, of a cold, ungenial, unprolific and churlish summer, must now be added to the ungracious list. We have had lately a few barely comfortable days, but not one evening and scarcely a day in 1816, when a fire would have been superfluous. In one respect there has been a difference, for while you complain of dry weather, I have been listening every Sunday until the last for more than two months, to a prayer that we might be released from the *plague of waters*. Last Sunday it was changed to a thanksgiving for fair weather, but the cold still continues. There were several sharp frosts in July and August, and the newspapers are filled with accounts of snow in harvest, and of ice an inch thick in dog-days within a hundred miles of London. What agency the spots upon the sun have had in all this, is more than I, or perhaps anybody else is astronomer enough to know. In Europe, as you must have heard, the spots on the sun portended the end of the world until the 18th of July, and since then there has scarcely been seen enough of the sun to know whether it was spotted or not. It is pretty certain, however, that the harvests have been much affected by the weather in a great part of Europe, though not so much as by your account they have been with you. The oddity of the thing here is, that it is a rancorous party question between the Jacobins and the Legitimates, who pledge their words and their honor, on one side

fatuus of juntoism, till they and their country were sinking in the bottomless quagmire of disunion." *To John Adams*, October 12, 1816. Ms.

that there will be a great failure in the harvest, and on the other that there will be no failure at all.

You mention some of our forefathers who figure in Mather's *Magnalia*. I begin to feel something of the genealogical maggot myself, and want to know something more about my ancestors than I have ever yet discovered. I remember the round robin of that great genius, Cousin Elijah Adams, Esquire, of Medfield, and hope you have it in safe keeping. Perhaps that and Willard's *Body of Divinity* contain as much of the *Adams* annals before my father, as is to be gleaned after the harvest old Father Time has reaped of them. It traces them back to England, which for us is going back to Noah's flood. But of the female branches of the ascending line I should be glad to know more. For example, who were my father's grandmothers, paternal and maternal. I suppose my father knows; but if I ever heard, I do not remember. Again, who was your grandmother Smith, and who was the wife of the said Thomas Shepard, whose daughter was your grandfather's mother? When you have leisure I wish you would write me all the family history that you can remember.

The rage of royal matrimony seems to be spreading beyond its natural bounds. According to the rumors in circulation here, it has even reached his Royal Highness the Prince Regent of England. Although I have satisfied myself that very little of what is said about him ought to be believed, yet his design of obtaining, if he can, a divorce from his present wife has become so notorious that it will no longer admit of a doubt. The Princess of Wales [1] has been living these two years abroad, with his consent, and scandal, which had always been nibbling at her reputation,

[1] Caroline Amelia Elizabeth (1768–1821), daughter of Charles William Ferdinand, Duke of Brunswick Wolfenbüttel.

has been gorging upon it since she left England, like an Alderman upon *high* venison. All the English ladies who accompanied her when she first went, have left her and returned to England, and she is now travelling about, living publicly with an Italian adventurer,[1] in such utter contempt of all decorum, that some of the captains of English men of war have refused to admit the paramour with her at their tables. These are the stories about her now in circulation; and it is further said that the Regent has now in his possession positive proof against her, such as by the Ecclesiastical laws of England will entitle him to a divorce. When he first proposed it to his Ministers, the Chancellor and the Earl of Liverpool are said to have been so averse to the measure as to tender the resignation of their offices; but since the return of Mr. Canning, and his re-installation into the Ministry, he has become the manager of the transaction, and there is now little question that it will be brought before Parliament at their next session. The public take very little interest in the Princess of Wales herself; the appearances are so much against her, that it is universally taken for granted the proof in the Regent's possession will be ample to warrant a divorce, but the multitude inquire *why* he wants it, and the attorney's clerks ask *how* he is to obtain it? As if a husband was bound to find a justification of his wife's frailties in the supposed conspicuousness of his own; or as if the Parliament of George the Third had ever shown themselves less omnipotent, or less complaisant to the personal wishes of *the Sovereign*, than the Parliaments of Henry the *Eighth*. Opposition to the measure there will undoubtedly be, and if Ministers should find their power in Parliament staggering upon other and national objects (which is not probable), they may take this opportunity

[1] Bartolomeo Bergami.

to go out at a good door, as Pitt when he got frightened in 1801 went out upon the Catholic question. That the Regent wishes a divorce for the sake of a second marriage there is nothing as yet but conjecture and the fears of the Princess Charlotte's partisans to indicate. The Princess Charlotte had a show of popularity at the time of her marriage, but she has few if any friends, and after more than four months of marriage, it is a question as unsettled as that about the harvest, whether she is in the way of increasing the family or not. Those who assume as a fact that the Regent is bent upon a second marriage, suppose that he looks to the Princess Sophia of Gloucester, who is in her forty-fourth year, but much the handsomest of all the females of the royal family.

The bustling season of London, the levees, drawing rooms, dinners, routs, balls, etc., are over for this year. The fashionable world are all gone to bustle in the country, or at the watering places, and since the close of the last month we have been altogether quiet. I wish it were possible we could expect to remain so through the next winter. We found so much inconvenience in residing so far distant from London, while we had such frequent and indispensable calls there, that we determined, perhaps inconsiderately, to remove to town for the ensuing winter. We have not yet, however, found a house to suit us, and it is scarcely possible that at double the cost we should find one in London, half so agreeable or comfortable for a residence as this. My wife's health for the last six weeks has been affected by a troublesome cough and pain in the side, and George frequently gives us great uneasiness. His growth continues as rapid as ever, and it is attended with great debility and with a continual recurrence of complaints which alarm us. The other two boys enjoy much better health.

I am happy more than I can express to learn that yours has been so much restored, and that my father's is so generally good. What with your Independence day, your Neponset Bridge Hotel, and your parties at Mr. Quincy's, Mr. Marston's, and my brother's, you have had as gay a summer of it as we have, and I hope without any occasion for such a remark as was made to me by one of the guests at the Mansion House dinner to the Duke of Wellington: "It is very well for us to be here dining upon turtle and venison, but the country is ruined!" Happier be the lot of ours!

I remain, etc.[1]

TO THE SECRETARY OF STATE

No. 56.   [JAMES MONROE]

LONDON, 27 September, 1816.

SIR:

I have the honor of enclosing herewith a copy of the note which I have addressed to Lord Castlereagh renewing the proposal for the negotiation of a treaty of commerce. From the determination of this government, as communicated to me in my personal interview with him on the

---

[1] "I have at last succeeded in making a visit to our old friend and countryman, Mr. [Benjamin] West. He is at the age of seventy-eight as deeply engaged in his art, and as enthusiastically fond of it, as at any period of his life. He is now employed upon a picture which he thinks will surpass all his former works. The subject is Death upon the Pale Horse from the Book of Revelations. He was at work upon it when I called to see him. But allegorical personages, creatures of the imagination embodied into human shape, do not appear to me the happiest subjects for exhibition upon canvas. The two pictures of Christ healing the sick, and Christ rejected, are more to my taste." *To Abigail Adams*, September 28, 1816. Ms.

21st of August, it is to be expected they will decline treating upon the subject of our trade with the British colonies in the West Indies, and upon the questions relating to neutral interests during maritime war. They may profess to be willing to receive specific proposals relative to seamen and to our inland intercourse with their colonies in North America; but it is not probable that upon either of those subjects they will agree to anything that can be satisfactory to you. Nor shall I think it expedient to conclude any separate arrangement concerning them excluding the others without further instructions to that effect. In the conversations that I have had with Lord Castlereagh he has given me very distinctly to understand that with regard to seamen, if they shall even agree to the proposed stipulation of excluding from the respective naval and merchant services the native citizens and subjects of each other, they will not understand it as implying or intending an engagement to renounce the practice of taking men from our vessels in the event of a future maritime war. In the instructions hitherto transmitted to me it is not insisted that such a renunciation should be included in the article, yet I cannot but suppose it was expected that if the article should be agreed to, it would be with at least a tacit understanding that the practice of impressment shall be abandoned. Under the present composition of the Cabinet I believe that the only advantage to be derived from the repetition of proposals to negotiate will be to multiply proof of refusal, or of expedients having all the features of refusal except its candor. An example of this has occurred in relation to the proposal for disarming, or at least for limiting armaments upon the lakes. When conformably to your instructions I made that proposal on the 25th of January last, from the manner in which it was received I was convinced it would not be accepted. Afterwards in April I was assured by Lord Castlereagh that this government was disposed fully to meet the proposition, and that Mr. Bagot should immediately be authorized to enter into a formal stipulation for the purpose. From your letter of 13 August I am apprehensive that Mr. Bagot's power will terminate in a reference back to his own government; and in the meantime, while Mr. Bagot was negotiating and receiving your specific proposition to be transmitted here, five thousand two hundred tons of ordnance stores have been dispatched to Canada, with the avowed purpose of arming their new constructed forts and new built ships upon the lakes. So in respect to the fisheries, the course of proceeding which they have adopted so evidently manifests the disposition to amuse the government of the United States with propositions which they know will not be accepted, that I am persuaded that the only effectual means of protecting the right of the coast fisheries the ensuing year will be for Congress to authorize the President to employ an adequate portion of the naval force of the United States to that service.

A change of ministry might possibly bring into power persons more favorably disposed towards the United States, or at least individually less inveterate against them. But there is less prospect of such a change at present than there was believed to be some weeks since. Much of the agricultural distress which pressed upon the country has been removed by the rise in the price of corn. Wheat has now been more than a month above the standard of eighty shillings a quarter, and the other grains have risen in proportion. The release from the property and malt taxes begins to be felt in the ease it has given from a very oppressive part of their burthens. Manufactures and commerce are reviving, and the revenue itself is understood to be improving. There will be, it is said, no deficiency in the produce of the quarter now about closing, and the prospects of the future are still more promising. The success of the expedition against Algiers has given a new strength to the Ministers, and notwithstanding the strong petitions and violent resolutions voted at the late popular meetings in London and Westminster, their example has not been followed by any other city or by any country in the kingdom. There has indeed been within the last six weeks a depreciation of the funds, probably from the effect of the falling off of the revenue of the last quarter. But it has not been equivalent to the property tax from which they are disburdened, and the prospect now is that the Ministers will meet Parliament with the view of the finances so much more advantageous than was expected, that they will have no material difficulty in carrying through the measures they may have to propose. It has been for some months rumored that the Prince Regent is desirous of obtaining a divorce, and that proceedings to that end are in a train of preparation for the approaching session of Parliament. It will doubtless occasion some debate, but no change, at least no important change, in the Ministry.

I am very respectfully, sir, your most humble and obedient servant.

TO THE PRESIDENT OF THE UNITED STATES

[James Madison]

London, 28 September, 1816.

Sir:

I have lately had the honor of receiving your favor of 10th May last, accompanied by letters for Sir John Sinclair, which I immediately delivered in person to him; for Mr. Bentham, which I left at his house; and for Dr. Eustis, which was forwarded by post to The Hague. Sir John Sinclair then put into my hands the printed paper which I now enclose, requesting me to forward it to you; and Mr. Bentham has since sent me two small volumes lately published by him under the title of *Chrestomathia*, Parts 1 and 2, with a similar request. They will be sent in a packet with this letter.

You will perhaps think there is something like desperation in the remedies proposed by Sir John Sinclair for the calamities which an insupportable debt and intolerable taxes have brought upon this nation. But the only practical problem for the British financier to solve is, how to accomplish a national bankruptcy or a composition with the public creditors without appearing to make it. When the distress, about which so much has been and yet is said, and which I believe to have been much exaggerated by almost all parties, when it comes to pinch as it has hitherto only threatened, the remedy will present itself as unequivocally as the disease, and the most decisive proof to my mind of the exaggeration in all the representations of general distress which have been spreading over the world for so many months, has been the arrant trifling of all parties in the character of remedies they have administered or proposed. While wheat was at six shillings a bushel, the farmers must certainly have found it difficult to pay their taxes, tithes, and poor rates, and subsist themselves and support their families. Had it continued long at that price, they would have found it impossible. But it has now risen again to ten shillings and upwards. At that price the farmers can yet stagger along with their load. The streams of the revenue which had begun to fail are again filling up, the cry of distress is still continued, but the symptoms of suffering have much abated. The present paroxysm has evidently passed its point of greatest severity, and a great portion of those who were really distressed are relieved for the moment. It will, however, be scarcely possible to raise a revenue of sixty millions sterling a year upon this people for any considerable length of time, without occasioning frequent renewals of the pressure which they will not always be in a humor to endure with equal patience and resignation.

You will perceive by my correspondence with the Secretary of State that the proposal of negotiating a treaty of commerce has been declined with a profession of readiness to receive and consider any specific proposition upon two of the points suggested under your instruction. Upon the point most immediately interesting, our commerce with their colonies in the West Indies, the refusal to treat is positive and unqualified. Lord Castlereagh, with the utmost courtesy and politeness in point of form, observed that with regard to any regulations which might be contemplated on our part, the whole subject was in the hands of the American government; they might prohibit the trade in British vessels, or they might impose aggravated duties upon it, as might best suit their view of the policy of the United States, and Great Britain would have no right and feel no disposition to complain of it. He appeared to intimate that the British Cabinet had anticipated the effect of anything that could be done by Congress, and were prepared for it. He said it was merely an adherence to their colonial system, and acknowledged that he had some personal doubt whether it was for their own advantage. I am indeed inclined to think that this inflexibility upon colonial subjects proceeds rather from the Colonial Department than from Lord Castlereagh.

When the first proposal in relation to the ships at Venice was made, I was apprehensive that there would be objections to the agency of the person through whom it was proposed. It was afterwards renewed through a regular and unexceptionable channel, and I had hopes that it would then have been found acceptable. I have lately been asked from the official source of the last proposal whether I had received any answer to it. I had none from the Secretary of State, and it was a few days before I had the honor of receiving your letter. The terms upon which the ships may be obtained are so advantageous, and the ships themselves are so good, that another opportunity to decide upon the proposal may be offered.

Some months since I received a letter from a person [1] in the Danish Province of Jutland requesting me to propose to the government of the United States the purchase from Denmark of the Nicobar Islands in the East Indies. The writer of the letter intimates that the Danish government would readily dispose of them to the United States, but that there were particular and satisfactory reasons for making the proposal in this indirect and unaccredited manner. I answered the letter and declined the negotiation as having no authority to treat upon the subject. The proposal was, however, repeated and urged in a second letter which I have

[1] O. C. Kellermann.

not answered. I knew nothing of the writer of the letters, but they were transmitted to me through the medium of the Danish Consul. There is no inconsiderable alarm prevailing here at this moment in consequence of rumors circulating in the newspapers that an object of Mr. Pinkney's negotiation at Naples is to obtain a cession of the Neapolitan island of Lampedusa to the United States. Some of the public journals are for ordering Lord Exmouth's whole fleet immediately to the Bay of Naples to anchor, yard arm and yard arm, along side of the American seventy-four, and give courage to the Neapolitans to reject the ridiculous American demands. If you will send a Minister in a line of battleship to Copenhagen, with instructions to claim indemnity for the Danish spoliations upon our commerce, and let it be circulated that he is negotiating for the Nicobar Islands, I will answer for its working the British Cabinet and Parliament up to another year of a thirty millions peace establishment, and shall not be surprised if it rearms the whole body of the militia, and remounts all the yeomen cavalry of the British Isles.

I have the honor, etc.

TO ABIGAIL ADAMS

LITTLE BOSTON, 5 October, 1816.

MY DEAR MOTHER:

As I am not yet enabled to write the threatened long letter to my father, I must replace it by the weekly short one to you.

Last Sunday Mr. E. Brooks,[1] Mr. Bigelow,[2] and a few

---
[1] Edward Brooks (1793–1878), son of Peter Chardon Brooks.
[2] Andrew Bigelow.

other of our American visitors, came out and dined with us. Two days afterwards Mr. Brooks sent me your letter of 2nd May, enclosed with Mr. Norton's funeral sermon upon our venerable friend and kinsman Dr. Tufts, and a letter of 3 May from my dear and honored father.[1] I supposed Mr. Brooks had kept these letters considering them as merely introductions. He had already some weeks since delivered at my office in town the watches for George and John.

You were no doubt surprised at the remark in Mrs. Tarbell's[2] letter upon your son's neatness, surprised at least enough to underscore the word. But I should be sorry to disappoint you with any delusive hopes of his radical reformation. Well does he remember your ever affectionate admonition to him thirty years ago. "Careless at twenty is a sloven at thirty, and intolerable at forty." But what then of fifty? for that is the question now. Alas! Mrs. Tarbell saw him at a lucky minute. He hopes he has not verified your proverb of progressive viciousness, but he is certainly at fifty what he was at twenty, at thirty, at forty, careless, excessively careless of personal appearance, and utterly incapable of ever rising to the dignity of a *dandy*.

Our boys have contrived to eke out their Michaelmas holidays till next Monday. Enclosed are letters from John and Charles. George has gone with his namesake Mr. G. Joy to Cambridge, and has had at the same time the opportunity of seeing the Newmarket races. He is to give you a full account of it in his Journal. We expect him home this evening.

We are all in comfortable health, and all in duty and affection ever yours.

[1] Jacob Norton (1764–1858). The sermon was delivered at Weymouth, December 11, 1815, on Cotton Tufts.
[2] Lucy Tufts, wife of Thomas Tarbell of Groton, Mass.

TO THE SECRETARY OF STATE

No. 57.   [JAMES MONROE]

LONDON, 5 October, 1816.

SIR:

Lord Castlereagh left London this week upon a visit to Ireland. Previous to his departure I received from him a letter of which a copy is herewith enclosed. Although the absence of several of the Cabinet Ministers is alleged as the motive for postponing the answer to my note of 17 September, and although his Lordship promises to lay the subject suggested in it before his colleagues immediately after his return, there is no reason to expect that any departure from the policy already determined upon will take place. It is probable that you will receive this dispatch about the time of the meeting of Congress. Any measures in the spirit and with the object of those proposed at the last session and then postponed may be now adopted without hesitation. My own entire conviction is that the operation of such measures, if successful, will be the only possible means of convincing this government of the expediency of relaxing from the rigor of their exclusive colonial system. It is and uniformly has been my opinion that the result of the equalization of duties will be to the advantage of Great Britain and to our disadvantage. But the principle was sanctioned by an act of Congress before the convention of 3 July, 1815, was negotiated. The benefit of the convention to us, if any, is in the India trade; but as its duration is to be so short, the only chance of having it renewed at the end of its four years with additional articles of more liberality will be effective counteracting regulations in respect to the commerce with the British Colonies in the West Indies.

I am, etc.

TO THE SECRETARY OF STATE

No. 58. [JAMES MONROE]

LONDON, 12 October, 1816.

SIR:

With my letter of 27 July were enclosed copies of my occasional correspondence with this government upon various subjects of secondary interest which had then recently occurred. I now transmit copies of the notes which have since passed between us on similar occasions, chiefly concerning the execution of the commercial convention of 3 July, 1815, and the acts of Parliament respecting the conveyance of passengers.

By the first section of the act of Parliament of 24 June, 1803, it was provided that British vessels should take no more passengers than in the proportion, including the crew, of one person to every two tons of the vessel's burthen, deducting all the tonnage occupied by a cargo.

By the eleventh section of the same act it was prescribed that vessels other than British should take no more passengers including the crew than in the proportion of one person to every five tons of the vessel's burthen, but they were not restricted to the unoccupied tonnage.

In December last I received representations from Ireland that under this act British vessels were taking passengers in the proportion of one person for every two tons, while American vessels were allowed to take only one for every five tons. My correspondence and conversations with Lord Castlereagh on this subject were then reported to you. Much reluctance was discovered to any alteration of the law, the real object of which was admitted by Lord Castlereagh to be a check upon emigration. As, however, these regulations manifestly infringed the stipulation of the commercial convention that the vessels of the two nations should be placed on the same footing as to duties and charges, it was soon determined that the discrimination between them established by this act should be removed. This was done for all the ports of the island of Great Britain by a mere order from the Lords of the Treasury, dated on the 27th of April, directing the officers of customs to apply to American vessels only the same restrictions with regard to the number of passengers to which British vessels were subjected by the act of Parliament. This order, however, did not extend to Ireland, but there the British vessels continued to enjoy their advantage over those of the United States until the new act of Parliament passed on the first of July last. This act relates exclusively to British vessels conveying passengers from the United Kingdom of Great Britain to the United States of America, and it enacts that all the regulations and restrictions contained in the act of 1803, with respect to foreign vessels carrying passengers and *no other*, shall be made applicable to such British vessels.

The first effect of this law was to break up and ruin the voyage of the *Independence*, an American vessel at Glasgow, which on the faith of the ordinance of 27 April from the Treasury had contracted to carry out passengers in the proportion of one person for every two tons, when every preparation and expense for the voyage had been incurred, and when the agents for the vessel were utterly ignorant of the existence of the law until upon their application for a clearance it was produced by the Collector to stop them. They immediately applied through their correspondents in London for my interposition with this government. The peculiarity of the case induced me to address not only an official note to Lord Castlereagh, but also an informal one to the Earl of Liverpool concerning it. Copies of both these notes and of the answers to them are enclosed. Lord Castlereagh verbally assured me that he would recommend that the vessel should be allowed to clear out without being subjected to the new restriction. Of the grounds of the decision by the Lords of the Treasury you may judge, by considering that the new act of Parliament has no operation whatever upon foreign vessels, but leaves them precisely where they were, and that the order from the Treasury of 27 April was directly in the face of the act of Parliament then in force, of June 24, 1803.

The next difficulty that occurred was experienced by Colonel Aspinwall, the consul, in contracting for a vessel to convey to the United States upwards of one hundred destitute American seamen. My application to Lord Castlereagh was in this instance more successful as you will perceive by the copies of my note and of his answer. This case was also noticed in my informal note to Lord Liverpool.

Since then Colonel Aspinwall has endeavored to contract for the passages of other destitute American seamen with the masters of American vessels bound from London to the United States. Besides the number which by the law of the United States they are required to take for ten dollars each, they are sometimes willing to take others at the rate of ten pounds per man for passage money, which is as low as it has been found practicable to contract for the conveyance of large numbers by special vessels. But the Custom officers in the port of London have counted these destitute seamen as composing part of the number of passengers limited to the act of Parliament, and still further, they have without any authority from the act extended the restriction of *unoccupied tonnage*, which was applied only in the first section of the act of 1803 to British vessels when allowed to take a passenger for every two tons; and they now apply it both to British and American vessels, though permitted to take only one passenger for every five tons. I have received no answer from Lord Castlereagh to my note respecting the destitute seamen, and have not yet written to him respecting the unauthorized restriction of unoccupied tonnage. But since his departure I have had a conversation upon both the points with the under Secretary of State, Mr. Hamilton. With regard to the destitute seamen he told me he thought there could be no question, and that the order would go to the Customs to cease counting them as a part of the limited number. But as to the restriction of unoccupied tonnage, although he appeared convinced by his own view of the two acts of Parliament which I showed him that the present practice at the custom house is not warranted by the law, yet he intimated that it was merely owing to an inadvertence in drawing up the last act, which if I should press the subject, would only produce an amended act to warrant the restriction at the next session of Parliament.

The subject of emigration is one of those upon which all parties here are under the influence of irritable feelings. The government are deterred, more perhaps by shame than by the want either of inclination or of power, from enacting open and explicit laws to prohibit their people from deserting the country, and thus they resort to such indirect and skulking expedients to [place] obstacles in the way of their removal. The disposition, or rather the necessity for emigration has been growing stronger from hour to hour since the conclusion of the general peace. It would be much more supportable if the emigrants would go anywhere but to the United States. I have lately sent you a pamphlet probably issued from official sources, the object of which is to prove how much more eligible it would be for emigrants to resort to the British Provinces in North America than to the United States. The ministerial papers are constantly filled with paragraphs to the same purport. Anonymous letters are published announcing the application by thousands of British emigrants at New York to the consul there to be sent back to England. A letter from the consul himself, declaring that he has great numbers of such applications and containing a reflection upon the United States not very becoming in the situation that he holds, has also gone the rounds of publication, and lastly as a decisive fact to set the question forever at rest, an affidavit before a notary public and magistrate of one Irish linen weaver attests that he has returned from New York because he could procure no employment in America. Notwithstanding all this the propensity to emigrate even to the United States continues and increases, so that instead of relaxations from the passengers act, it is not improbable that the power of removal may, as Mr. Hamilton suggested, be further shackled at the next session of Parliament.

With regard to the execution of the commercial convention I have had occasion to address Lord Castlereagh twice. First, by a note on the 5th of August, relative to the extra duty of five per cent upon merchandise sold at auction; and again, on the 7th of September, upon the refusal of the officers of the customs at the port of London to return the extra tonnage duties levied upon American vessels arriving from or clearing for any port other than of the United States. I have received no answer to either of these notes. But I was informed verbally that the order relative to the extra duty upon sales at auction had been issued, and from what was said to me by Mr. Hamilton at my last interview with him, as well as from the reason of the thing, I have no apprehension that the other will be withheld.

I am, etc.

TO ABIGAIL ADAMS

EALING, 15 October, 1816.

MY DEAR MOTHER:
The quiet season has at length arrived. For the last six weeks I have had no occasion to go into London except upon business, and there is some relaxation of that. Almost all the Cabinet Ministers are absent upon excursions, and Lord Castlereagh has gone to Ireland to see *his father*. The *Morning Chronicle* gives a shrewd hint that it is the sign that Parliament will be dissolved, and that his Lordship has gone upon an electioneering campaign. The *Courier* says Parliament will *not* be dissolved, and that the visit of a son to his father is amply sufficient to account for Lord Castlereagh's journey. On this occasion I agree with the *Courier* in opinion, and oh, that I could make a visit to my father!

You will learn from the newspapers that the Lord Mayor of London, of whose polite and friendly attentions to us I have more than once made mention to you, is as popular among his constituents, as he is at Little Boston House. The Livery of London by a commanding majority and a spirit which the Court of Aldermen did not venture to resist, have reëlected him for the ensuing year, an honor which for more than a century no other Lord Mayor has enjoyed. This is attributed, partly to the uncommon ability and vigor with which he has filled the office, and partly to the political dispositions of the people in the city. There is a certain dissatisfaction spreading, not only among the citizens of London, but throughout the kingdom, occasioned by what are called the distresses of the country, that is, by the load of taxes.

Mr. Russell, our Minister to Sweden, passed through London last week on his way to Liverpool to embark for the United States. It is rumored that he proposes shortly to return with a fair partner from Boston.

George says that he sends you a copy of his journal by the month. He will give you an account of his visit to Cambridge. Your ever affectionate Son.

TO P. VAN HUFFEL

Londres, le 21 Octobre, 1816.

Monsieur:

J'ai depuis long temps reçu la lettre qui vous m'avez fait l'honneur de m'écrire en date du 13 Juin, et j'ai attendu pour y repondre l'occasion de pouvoir me faire parvenir mon portrait peint par vous. Cette occasion se presente maintenant par mon ami Monsieur Connell, qui est dans l'intention de passer par votre ville et qui aura la bonté de vous presenter cette lettre. Il compte sous peu revenir ici, et il a bien voulu se charger d'apporter mon portrait avec lui. Je vous prie de vouloir bien le lui remettre. Votre lettre parle de plusieurs copies comme en ayant été faites. Je vous serai obligé si vous voulez bien me faire savoir si c'est vous même qui les avez peints et à qui elles appartiennent.

J'ai l'honneur d'être, Monsieur, avec la plus haute considération votre très humble et très obéissant serviteur.

TO JOHN ADAMS

LITTLE BOSTON HOUSE, EALING, 29 October, 1816.

MY DEAR SIR:

I have acknowledged the receipt of your seven letters dated in July and August, received by Mr. Thacher and Mr. Bigelow, and also of one dated 2 May, but very lately delivered by Mr. Brooks. It is more than time for me to reply to their contents.

I never had much relish for the speculations of the first philosophy. In that respect I resemble your eels in vinegar, and your mites in cheese, more than you do. For with proper deference to your opinions I venture to suggest that this inquiry into the why and the wherefore of all things is precisely that which constitutes the difference between your transcendental philosophers and the eels and the mites. They never inquire *why* or *wherefore*. You say, trust the Ruler with his skies, and do as you would be done by. I say so too. The first we must do, willing or reluctant; as to the last, all the philosophers join in the chorus. All say, do as you would be done by. But not so do they all do. Whether Frederick recollected where he had passed his first nine months when he stole Silesia from Maria Theresa, may be questioned; but then, and throughout his life, he never ceased to say, do as you would be done by. I have heard it said that when Charles Fox was a boy his father gave him a watch. The first thing he did was to take it to pieces *to see how it was made.* His father should have said to him, Charles, trust the watchmaker with his watch. It was a foolish curiosity in Charles, and he lost his watch by it, for the watchmaker himself could not put it together again. But if Charles had been one of the mites or eels in human shape, he never would have taken his watch to pieces. As for you, my dear and ever honored father, though you never like Frederick stole anything from anybody, and although you have been all your life doing as you would be done by, yet your theory and your practice do not always coincide. Your great example does not strengthen all your laws. You inquire into the why and wherefore as curiously as any man, whether pious Christians like Sir Isaac Newton, or reprobate atheists like Diderot and the Baron d'Holbach. Now my theory is more like your practice, and my practice more like your theory. I never took much delight in reasoning high upon

    Fix'd fate, free will, foreknowledge absolute;

but I have always thought that they are favorite contemplations of the brightest human intellects, and independent of revelation, it is only by such researches that the mind of man can arrive at the idea of a God. All reasoning upon such subjects leads to that, and that is the foundation of all morality.

For the present my principal inquiries are not after the inside but the outside of heaven. I have got Bode's *Uranographia*, and with the help of it am taking lessons every starlight night of physical astronomy with George, and an amiable young lady of eighteen who is here on a visit to my wife. I think you were the primary cause of all this. Some five or six years ago Mr. Van der Kemp gave you a hint that Turgot's famous Latin compliment to Dr. Franklin was stolen from the astronomics of Manilius; upon which you wrote to me making some inquiries about the book. The consequence was that I procured and read it, and was much diverted with it. But although it was rather a book of astrology than of astronomy, still it contained such an account of the principal ancient constellations that I was ashamed to find I could not understand much of it, for want of knowing the constellations as they appear in the heavens. I therefore borrowed Bode's charts, and with an opera glass for my only telescope made my acquaintance with all the constellations which the few clear wintry nights and mornings of St. Petersburg would discover. After leaving Russia my attention was too much absorbed by the affairs of the earth to be wandering over the firmament; but since I have resided here I have sent to Berlin for a set of Bode's charts, and with the benefit of their introduction take occasionally tickets again for the concerts of the sphere. The mystical seal upon this letter is one of the fruits of my profound studies into the necromancy of Manilius, and the motto is from him, from whom I have as good a right to *borrow* as Mr. Turgot, though, in the practice of doing as I would be done by, I think proper to acknowledge the debt.

Your advice to me with regard to my children must in all cases have the greatest weight. That of returning them soon to complete their education in our native country accords entirely with my own sentiments and intentions. I hope George will be prepared here to enter one or two years in advance at Harvard. He is making his principal proficiency in the Latin and Greek languages, and I hope will become a scholar. He has a fault which always attended his father, that of being slow in learning precisely those things for which he has the assistance of a teacher. As to the performance of Terence's plays, I have formed a much higher opinion of the usefulness of that exercise than I entertained before I had witnessed its effects. Its great advantage is in familiarizing the language, and forming a habit of speaking naturally in public. It compels all the performers to understand the whole play, gives them the correctest idea now obtainable of the colloquial language of Rome; and the manners and plots of these comedies are so remote from everything they witness around them, that I think there is not much to be apprehended of an unfavorable influence of them upon their morals. The spur to emulation is sharper than in the performance of tasked studies. The part in a play is not a task, but a reward; not a burden, but a prize. The voluntary student applies to it with double ardor, and the idler buckles to it from the dread of shame. Then the language is elegant; the taste pure simplicity, and the sentiment, though as you have observed to the children rather scanty, generally correct, often ingenious, occasionally profound, and in some instances sublime. You have indeed skimmed the cream of Terence and sent it to my boys. I trust they will preserve it, and that it will aid them in drawing all the solid benefit from the amanuensis of Laelius and Scipio which he can afford to their future lives.

Mr. Thacher is gone, by the advice of the physicians whom he consulted here, to the Cape of Good Hope. They flatter him with hope which I wish may prove well founded. I saw him only once and for a short half hour, and regretted much that I could not enjoy more of his society. Mr. Bigelow is gone or going to Edinburgh.

Since beginning this letter I have received yours of 26 August and 5 September, and am highly gratified by your and my mother's account of your social party at Judge Otis's.[1] Among the lights and shades of that worthy Sena-

---
[1] Morison, *Harrison Gray Otis*, I. 222.

tor's character, there is none which shows him in brighter colors than his hospitality. In the course of nearly thirty years that I have known him, and throughout the range of experience that I have had in that time, it has not fallen to my lot to meet a man more skilled in the useful art of entertaining his friends than Otis; and among the many admirable talents that he possesses there is none that I should have been more frequently and more strongly prompted to envy, if the natural turn of my disposition had been envious. Of those qualities Otis has many. His person while in youth, his graceful deportment, his sportive wit, his quick intelligence, his eloquent fluency, always made a strong impression upon my mind; while his warm domestic affections, his active friendship, and his generosity always commanded my esteem. This tribute is due from me to him, after the remarks which I made to you in a former letter upon some of his less estimable characteristics. I think his politics have never been founded upon steady principle. I believe he has countenanced and supported measures of the most fatal import, which his conscience did not approve, from the want of mental energy; and I know that from a very early date he has personally been afflicted with the feelings of a rival towards me. A vague and general feeling of rivalry, for I never stood in the way of his wishes for any particular object. It was so with poor Bayard, in a much greater degree and with less reason. Mrs. Otis is and always has been a charming woman, and I am very glad you have seen them both in the place where of all others they appear to the greatest advantage—their own house.

The peace of Europe is and will continue for the present to be undisturbed. There is in this country some distress, considerable discontent, much grumbling, efforts to stir up the people to petition for a reform of Parliament; but hitherto with very little success. Occasionally a riot among the workmen, which is immediately suppressed. The revenue still yields abundantly. Parliament will not meet before February. Faithfully yours.

TO ABIGAIL ADAMS

LITTLE BOSTON, EALING, 4 November, 1816.

MY DEAR MOTHER:

Since I last wrote you, I have received your kind letters of 27 August and of 10 June, which I mention in the order, not of their dates, but of their reception. That of June enclosed a printed copy of Judge Story's biographical eulogium of our late excellent friend Dexter,[1] whose loss is a calamity to our country, and especially to our native state, which with all her errors and follies I do most faithfully love. Colonel Aspinwall had already received and obligingly sent me Judge Story's sketch, which is very good, but which would have been much better had the judge not been manacled and fettered by his situation. He is thereby precluded from paying the deserved tribute to that which was precisely the brightest part of Dexter's character — his political firmness, independence, and intrepidity, his contempt of the shackles of party politics, and the vigor of mind which enabled him to break from them as easily as Sampson in his strength broke from the cords of the Philistines. Now a panegyric upon Dexter which slurs over this his first and most glorious characteristic, is like a life of Columbus which should skip over his discovery of America. I readily admit the judge's apology that these are hot ashes,

[1] *Sketch of the Life of Samuel Dexter*, Boston, 1816.

over which it would have been dangerous for him to tread; but then it must in return be admitted that neither the time, the place, nor the speaker, *could* do justice to the highest merits of Mr. Dexter. I am, nevertheless, very glad that this tribute was paid to him, and trust his memory will in due time be honored by an estimate in which no sacrifice will be necessary to the passions and prejudices of a discordant auditory.

I am ever yours.

TO GEORGE WILLIAM ERVING

EALING, 15 November, 1816.

MY DEAR SIR:

My last letter which had been delayed until I was much conscience smitten was scarcely gone to the Post Office, when your two favors of 30 September and 7 October were brought to me, and I reply to them without delay, rejoicing that you have received maps so far satisfactory to yourself that you could dispense with that which I found it impracticable to procure for you here. My first application upon receiving your former letter had been to Faden, and from him I received the first assurance that no such thing as a separate map of Louisiana was to be found in London. The *Examiner*[1] was ordered to be forwarded according to your directions immediately after your request was received, and I marvel that none of its numbers had reached you before October. It cannot, I think, have been delayed much longer, and you will find in him an auxiliary who would be almost equal to Cobbett, but for his occasional anxiety to be taken for a gentlemen and a man of taste, as if his business was to

[1] The paper established by John and James Henry Leigh Hunt.

write a story of Rimini about them; and he thinks that millions of money squandered in sinecures and millions of paupers starving in the midst of plenty are not in *good taste*. You have other auxiliaries beginning to show who, if they should increase and multiply, may in due time make something of your cause. The Cornwall meeting has brought forward at least two men of eloquence on your side, and Phillips,[1] the rising orator, has been hurling electrical thunderbolts at Liverpool. The progress of affairs, however, is slow, the spirit of reform is sluggish, and Cobbett's prediction of it within one or two years is ridiculous. Hitherto all is children's play.

The case of the *William and Mary* is here before the Admiralty Court, which its judge last week told me had become the "Castle of Indolence." The Spanish Ambassador, at my request and by the order of his court, has twice demanded restitution of the property, and twice been referred to the aforesaid court of Admiralty. I do not imagine there would be anything obtained by your interference at present, though it might do no harm to suggest an instruction to the Ambassador occasionally to refresh the memory of Lord Castlereagh with information that there is such a case.

I remain, etc.

[1] Charles Phillips (1787?–1859).

TO THE SECRETARY OF STATE

No. 61.   [James Monroe]

London, 16 November, 1816.

Sir:

I now enclose the reply received from Lord Bathurst to my last note on the subject of the shipment of destitute American seamen by direction of the Consul in American vessels,[1] and upon some other particulars connected with the execution of the commercial convention of 3 July, 1815. The anxiety to check emigration, especially to the United States, is so great that additional measures of restriction may be expected at the next session of Parliament rather than any relaxation from the present system. The ministerial papers continue to be stocked with almost daily paragraphs and extracts of letters attesting the wretchedness and ruin which awaits all emigrants from this country in the United States.

The clamor of distress is still continued in this country, but in the districts where it was some weeks since most

[1] "I am aware of the frequent impositions which must be attempted to obtain relief from you in the guise of destitute American seamen, and of the necessity you are under of using precautions against such frauds; and I am perfectly satisfied that every proper attention will be paid by you to those whom you consider entitled to that relief. Perhaps in ordinary times, slight misconduct, or even long voluntary service in British or foreign vessels might be held to operate as a forfeiture of the right to relief as an American seaman; but in the present state of this country, if an American, unquestionably such, is found in a situation *needing* relief, perhaps it may be better to allow it (always including the passage home as a *sine qua non*), even though his conduct may have been in some degree improper, rather than throw him back upon the multitude of starving vagrants in the metropolis." *To Thomas Aspinwall*, November 18, 1816. Ms.

severely felt it is said to have lately much subsided. A few popular meetings have been held in various places, where resolutions and petitions for retrenchment and parliamentary reform have been adopted; but the spirit has been held in check by the loyalty of the great mass of the nation. All the meetings held have been in places where the same sort of opposition has for many years predominated. The revenue of the last quarter was more productive compared with the corresponding quarter of the preceding year than that which ended in July, had been. There have been symptoms of riots in various places, owing to the diminution of laborers' wages, or the rise in the price of bread; the ministry, however, appear to enjoy the most perfect security, and Parliament is not expected to meet until late in January, perhaps not till February. The stocks are rising. . . .

TO ABIGAIL ADAMS

LITTLE BOSTON HOUSE, 19 November, 1816.

MY DEAR MOTHER:

Last week I sent you with a letter from my wife the newspaper containing the account of the Lord Mayor's day feast at Guild Hall, where you will find again some mention made of the American Minister.[1] The singularity of the feast did not, however, consist in his being there, but in the circumstance that no other minister, either home-bred or foreign, was present, and in the phenomenon still more extraordinary, that it was the second installation of the same person in the office of Chief Magistrate, in immediate succession after the first.

[1] Adams, *Memoirs*, November 9, 1816.

A Mr. Aspland,[1] an Unitarian clergyman, called upon me not long since, and gave me two copies of a late periodical publication, one of which I now enclose to you.[2] It will be particularly interesting to my father and you as containing a letter from Mr. Van der Kemp, and one to him, as I take it from Mr. Jefferson, with a syllabus for a comparison between the doctrine of Jesus and that of the Grecian philosophers, and that of the Jews before the time of Jesus.[3] I possess a work of this kind, much more comprehensive, including a parallel between the doctrines of Jesus, and those of the Jews and Greeks, but [also] those of Mahomet, of the Persians, Egyptians, Hindoos, Chinese, and indeed with all the systems of religion and morals that have ever been promulgated upon earth. It is in five large quarto volumes, and at St. Petersburg where I had some leisure hours I did occasionally dive into it. But it would require an uninterrupted leisure of years even to read the book, and I must therefore at least postpone the subject, satisfied that I shall find no doctrine that will stand the test of Jesus.

. . . .

Yours as ever.

TO ABIGAIL ADAMS

LITTLE BOSTON, 26 November, 1817.

MY DEAR MOTHER:

Last week I sent you a number of the *Monthly Theological Repository*, containing some speculations of Mr. Van der Kemp and Mr. Jefferson. With this letter I enclose to my

---
[1] Rev. Robert Aspland, of Hackney Road.
[2] *Monthly Repository of Theology and General Literature*, October, 1816.
[3] The "syllabus" is printed in *Writings of Jefferson* (Ford), VIII. 223.

father the numbers just published of the *Edinburgh* and *Quarterly Reviews*. Presuming that you know the history and character of these publications from Cobbett, you will sufficiently understand them to be in the nature of lawyers' arguments in support of their respective factions. The superiority of talent continues to be greatly on the side of the Scottish critics, but the Quarterly gentlemen are backed by the heaviest purse. I know not how my father will feel at seeing how the Scots have belabored the reputation, political, literary, and *amatory*, of the Dean of St. Patrick's; but it seems to me they rave at him like madmen. If his ghost could rise up in judgment against them, he would give them a severer scourging than that they received from Lord Byron. In the last week's *Observer* you will find a speech made at Liverpool by a young Irish orator, whose fame is in the blossom. The Edinburgh Reviewers did their best to blast it in the bud, but it lives and will flourish in spite of them. His name is Phillips, and I think he is destined to make a splendid figure in this country. At the next general election for Parliament it is expected he will be set up in opposition to Mr. Canning at Liverpool, and although a President of the Board of Control may be too much for him at the first heat, he cannot fail of obtaining a seat in Parliament before long; and once there he will soon make them feel the force of eloquence, which is now at a lower ebb in the House of Commons than it has been for a century.

I dined last Saturday with a gentleman by the name of Frend,[1] in the very focus of Unitarianism. I was almost in as much danger of conversion as I had been at St. Petersburg by the Father General of the Jesuits. To aggravate

---

[1] In a letter of December 20, he is described as "a unitarian, an astronomer, and an actuary of an insurance company." He was William Frend (1757–1841), who had become a convert to unitarianism in 1787.

my danger there was a Jew there who gave me a pamphlet upon the constancy of Israel. But my favorite constancy is of duty and affection with which I am yours.

TO JOHN ADAMS

LITTLE BOSTON, 3 December, 1816.

DEAR SIR:

Mr. Cobbett whose political opinions, as you know, have undergone some changes since he was battling it in favor of the British government in Philadelphia, has become the great champion of Parliamentary reform; and in order to increase the number of his readers among the laboring classes of the people, he has lately had recourse to the expedient of reprinting particular numbers of his weekly *Political Register* in a cheap form, upon open sheets. I enclose you those that have been thus published, in which you will find *his view* of the present situation and prospects of this country; and you will know what deductions are to be made on account of his ardent temper, his violent prejudices, his bitter animosities, his overbearing self-sufficiency, and his gross partialities. The distressed state of the country, which from different and opposite motives is exaggerated by many of all parties, has revived his popularity, which he had almost entirely lost. As he attacks indiscriminately Whigs and Tories, and as most of his predictions relative to the war with France were refuted by the event, he was quite out of credit and had lost most of his readers. The ministerial and opposition papers took no notice of him. But now they are all assailing him again, and he is rising in the popular opinion. But he and a few of the disciples of his school have in great degree driven the Whig leaders from the hustings of the popular meetings, and thus far he is essentially serving the cause of the Ministry. The Whigs would most gladly take advantage of the present times, but Cobbett has cried them down so that they scarcely dare show their heads. Cobbett boasts of the meetings all over the country; but there have been as yet very few. How it may be when Parliament meets, which is to be on the 28th of January, I undertake not to say; but I expect the next session will pass like the last in making long speeches, very moderate and very excellent sense-less, and in doing nothing. They will feed as many as they can by subscriptions, let the rest starve, and keep the soldiers to shoot down rioters. They will get along with the revenue, and set all else at nought.[1]

Very faithfully yours.

[1] "The difficulties of this country are maturing, not with anything like the rapidity that he [Cobbett] announces, but hitherto with a slow and regular progress. The numbers of people perishing by famine are not yet great, but the cases occasionally occur in every part of the country. The discontent scarcely keeps pace with the distress, for much of it is kept down by the terror of the bayonet and gibbet on one side, and the allurement of the soup basin on the other. But this only formidable symptom is just now disclosing itself, *a falling off in the revenue*. The first appearance of this was in July last, and it is already so considerable, that there is no doubt the income of the present year will be ten millions sterling less than that of the last. In the temper of the people new taxes cannot be imposed. The easiest resource of the ministers will be new loans, which they will perhaps disguise under the name of exchequer bills. This expedient will be easy, and will put off the evil day. But they will not materially reduce their national establishment; they will reject with contempt all the petitions for parliamentary reform, and the national debt in 1817 will be not diminished but increased. The storm is brewing, but by no means ready to burst." *To John Adams*, January 14, 1817. Ms.

TO ABIGAIL ADAMS

LITTLE BOSTON, 11 December, 1816.

Last week I enclosed several numbers of Cobbett's *Register* as they are republished in open sheets. Here are two additional numbers, with an *Observer*, where you will find an account of the late riots in London, and an extract from a recent publication containing some interesting particulars about Napoleon at St. Helena.

The ministerial daily, weekly, monthly, and quarterly publications, the ministers, and the government, make so very light of the distresses of the country, and treat with so much contempt and defiance all the manifestations of popular feeling on the subject, that I have hitherto believed the representations of them much exaggerated. There is no essential deficiency of the revenue, and the evil as yet seems to resolve itself merely into an increase of paupers rather greater than usual. The only resource to which the friends of government have judged it necessary to have recourse is voluntary subscriptions, to feed the starving and clothe the naked. The Spa fields meeting and the riots [1] have given a new spur to benevolence, by bringing motives of charity closer home. But there does not appear to exist in any part of the country a degree of distress beyond that which the very moderate subscriptions of the affluent are competent to remove. The Parliamentary reformers do not gain ground upon the mass of the nation; and notwithstanding the urgent call of the City of London, the town or county meetings to petition for reform have been very few.

[1] November 15, and December 2, 1816.

From Warden's pamphlet [1] it would appear that Napoleon bears his confinement at St. Helena with dignity and composure, if not philosophical tranquillity. A speech of Lord Castlereagh's at Belfast betrays a deep anxiety to keep up the sentiment of fear and hatred against the ex-Emperor in this nation. This will be a hard but not impracticable task.

Our latest letters from you are of 1 October. We hope to hear soon from you again. Mr. J. Winthrop [2] lately brought an old letter from my father.

Ever yours.

TO WILLIAM SHALER

LONDON, 19 December, 1816.

DEAR SIR:

On the 23rd of last month I had the pleasure of writing to you, and then explained to you the causes which had delayed until that time the replies which were due to your very interesting and most acceptable communications from Algiers.

Since then I have received your favor of 28 October, dated off Gibraltar, and the joint letter from you and Commodore Chauncey announcing your appointment as Commissioners to treat for a renewal of peace with Algiers. It is very true, as you remark, that fame both military and diplomatic is to be obtained from that quarter, and it might be added that in the present condition of the world they are to be acquired in no other. You have my most earnest good wishes that you may again extract from it a full share

[1] William Warden, *Letters written on board his Majesty's Ship the* Northumberland *and at St. Helena,* 1816.

[2] John Winthrop, son of John, and grandson of the Professor of the name.

of the latter, and without being under the necessity of recurring to the former. I have copies of your instructions and of the President's letter to the Dey. The abominable trick of foisting into the Dey's Turkish of your former treaty two articles which you had not agreed to, and which were not in the treaty sent for ratification to the United States, deserved exemplary punishment, and I should have been gratified to learn that it had been inflicted by our naval heroes. But the moderation of the President's final determination is so exemplary that I hope it will not fail to produce a suitable effect upon the Dey's councils, and that it will render any further resort to hostile measures unnecessary.[1]

Mr. Russell has returned to the United States upon a matrimonial negotiation. Hughes is here, going to Stockholm as chargé d'affaires in his absence. G[eorge] Boyd has been here, and is now in France upon some business for the War Department. I sent your letter for Mr. Russell under cover to the Secretary of State, and immediately forwarded those to the Ministers in France and the Netherlands. Mr. Pinkney was at Vienna on his way to St. Petersburg about the last of November.[2]

Hoping to hear from you still as your leisure shall serve, I am with great esteem, etc.

[1] See *Messages and Papers of the Presidents*, I. 575.
[2] *Life and Correspondence of Rufus King*, VI. 35, 67, 683.

TO WILLIAM TEMPLE FRANKLIN

EALING, 24 December, 1816.

SIR:

I beg leave to return you my warmest thanks for your very obliging and acceptable present of a copy of the private correspondence of Dr. Franklin which you have just published. Among the earliest of my recollections is that of the happy days which I passed under the same roof with your venerable grandfather and yourself at Passy, and I very cordially reciprocate the sentiment of regret which you are kind enough to express, that the circumstances which have since almost constantly placed us at a distance from each other have deprived me of the opportunity of cultivating that acquaintance which I had there the pleasure of forming with you. The private correspondence of Dr. Franklin will be in a very high degree interesting to the country of which he was one of the brightest ornaments, and in particular to me who, besides sharing in the general tribute of gratitude due from his countrymen to his memory, am under additional obligations of my own to him for the kind and condescending notice that he was pleased to take of me in my days of childhood, and which have left an indelible impression upon my heart. I shall take great pleasure in forwarding to Mr. Monroe the copy of a correspondence destined for him, and pray you, sir, to be assured of the respect with which I have the honor, etc.

TO CHRISTOPHER HUGHES

EALING, 25 DECEMBER, 1816.

DEAR SIR:

The enclosed list will more than suffice for eighteen months or two years, reading. Many of them will prove by no means attractive. To Smith, Montesquieu, Grotius and Ward, I would recommend your particular attention for the development of the *principles* which are generally recognized in the intercourse of nations. Vattel is the author most commonly resorted to in practical diplomacy, and his work being written in a popular and easy style is among those that you will find the least tedious in reading. If your object were to form a diplomatic library, the list should be much larger, and would include many books in other languages than the English; several voluminous collections of treaties, particular as well as general histories of the European nations, and numerous dissertations and treatises upon special questions of national law. The enclosed list contains only books of a general nature and all published in Europe which I thought most conforming to your request. They will sufficiently absorb your time for two years. But as you have a *career* before you, and do me the favor to consult my opinion, I would suggest to you the utility of preparing your mind for application when you return home to the *history*, the internal *interests*, and the external *relations* of our own country. In the history of the several colonial establishments united together by the war of our independence, you will find the source of the various and in some respects conflicting interests which it is the first duty of an American statesman to conciliate and unite. In the collections of American state papers and the Journals of Congress under the confederation you will find the best key to the interests and rights of our country in her internal administration and in her intercourse with foreign powers. But all the books upon these subjects are to be procured in America, and many of them are not to be found elsewhere.

Wishing you success in your studies and in your negotiations, I remain with great esteem, etc.

List of authors in general, modern history, national law and diplomatic intercourse.
  Robertson's History of Charles the fifth
            History of America
  Watson's History of Phillip the second
                  Phillip the third and
  Roscoe's Life of Lorenzo de Medici
            Leo the tenth
  Coxe's History of the House of Austria
  Russell's Letters on Ancient and Modern History
  Raynal's History of the East and West Indies
  Edward's History of the West Indies
  Brougham's Colonial Policy
  Annual Register from 1758 to 1815
  Jenkinson's or Chalmer's collection of Treaties
  Smith's Wealth of Nations
  Montesquieu's Spirit of Laws
  Grotius' Rights of War and Peace with Barbeyrac's Commentary
  Puffendorf, Law of Nature and Nations with   do
  Vattel's Law of Nations
  Marten's Summary of the Modern Law of Nations
  Burlamaqui, Law of Nature and Nations
  Ward's History of the Law of Nations.

TO JOHN ADAMS

LITTLE BOSTON, EALING, 3 January, 1817.
MY DEAR SIR:
Your favor of 23 September and 3 October was brought to me by my old friend and classmate J. M. Forbes,[1] and that of 13 November by General Boyd,[2] who both came fellow passengers in the same vessel. Mr. Everett has since arrived, by whom I received a letter of 26 November from my dear mother. I have briefly replied to my mother upon the advice which you and she have given me, to return to the United States. It may be proper for me to say something further upon the subject to you, for whose constant solicitude and kindness, as for my mother's, I can never be sufficiently grateful, and for whose approbation not only of my conduct but of its motives I am earnestly anxious.

I am and have been well aware, that in consulting only personal views of political ambition, my plainest and most obvious course would have been to return home immediately after the conclusion of the peace at Ghent. I knew that I could then return with some *éclat*, and that while neither honor nor profit of any kind was to be acquired in a mission to England, it was at home alone that I could be in the way of advancement, for the prospect of which I should never again have so favorable an opportunity of presenting myself to the notice of my country. Upon the appointment of the first mission for the pacific negotiation, it had been officially notified to me as the President's intention, in the event of the conclusion of a peace, to place me as the representative of the United States in this country. I accepted the appoint-

---

[1] John Murray Forbes (1771-1831). He died at Buenos Ayres.
[2] John Parker Boyd (d. 1830). See *Mass. Hist. Soc. Proceedings*, XVIII. 347.

ment, because I have made it the general principle of my life to take the station assigned to me by the regular authority of my country, and because I perceived no decisive reason for declining it; and having accepted it, I have thought that a term of three years was as short as I could with propriety hold it, before asking to be recalled. My expectation and intention was to return to private life, not from any settled purpose of relinquishing the service of the public, but from the knowledge that in my native state my services are not held in much estimation by those who could alone exercise, at least for the present, the power of calling them forth; and with regard to the government of the Union, although very shortly after my arrival in this country I had received an intimation, through a stranger, that it was the intention of the administration to *reserve* as long as might be compatible with the public convenience an important office for me, yet, as the person who made me this communication did not profess to have been authorized to make it, I neither understood precisely what it meant, nor paid much attention to it. From that time until within these six weeks I thought no more of it. About the middle of November last Mr. George Boyd arrived here, and among the rumors of news circulating at Washington at the time of his departure, told me it was said by some that the State Department would be offered to me by the next President. Since then numerous suggestions to the same effect have reached me, and the report has finally been distributed throughout this country by the paragraphs of newspapers, extracted from those of the United States. Although these circumstances have been sufficient to induce me very seriously to deliberate in my own mind upon the determination which it may be proper for me to come to, if the proposal should really be made, yet nothing has yet occurred which would justify me in taking any step on the presumption that it will. No direct communication, either from the present President, or from his expected successor, has made it necessary or proper for me to inform either of them what my decision would be upon it, and I think it due both to them and to myself to reserve my answer and my resolution upon the offer, until it is made.[1]

[1] "Your J. Q. A., it is said, is to be recalled to be made Monroe's Secretary of State, either to disgrace, or to promote him. But rather any southern or western democrat than J. Q. A. for President; rather Cheves or Clay. If J. Q. A. become President, all of New England that is virtuous or enlightened, will be persecuted and degraded; manners, laws, principles will be changed and deteriorated." *Rufus King to Christopher Gore*, November 22, 1816. *Life and Correspondence of Rufus King*, VI. 36. On January 1, 1817, he repeated this report and added: "I hear that Mr. Clay says this must not, and shall not be." (*Ib.*, 45.) Gallatin and Crawford were said to have been considered (*Ib.*, 49), and even Clay, rumor said, was to be the man (*Ib.*, 56). "Nothing seems to be agreed on as to the next cabinet. Crawford, it is said, wishes to be retained. If so, he must be gratified for a short time; but the sins of a competitor for the diadem can never be forgotten or forgiven. I think it probable Mr. Monroe is inclined to make J. Q. Adams Secretary of State, believing there is no danger of finding in him a dangerous rival four years hence. But Clay, with his western people, will oppose that project. If Adams is brought in it will not be with any intention of his final advancement to the presidency. I rather expect he will remain in his present situation, where he seems in no danger of acquiring too much reputation." *Jeremiah Mason to Christopher Gore*, December 30, 1816. Memoir of *Jeremiah Mason*, 148. "Within a day or two, the report that J. Q. Adams is to be Secretary of State has gained more credit. I have had it from a source that convinces me it is seriously thought of. The inducement is said to be to lessen the jealousy against Virginia, and conciliate New England. Some think there is a *bona fide* intention to designate him for the next presidency, and that Colonel Monroe believes this the best way of securing his next four years term. Others suppose the only object is to afford A. a fair chance of hanging himself, which they say he will certainly do in a short time. Mr. Clay gives no credit to the latter supposition. He with all his western friends are clamorously opposed to A. Crawford is said to be sulky, and to talk of retiring. I think better of Mr. Adams's prospect than I have heretofore." *Jeremiah Mason to Christopher Gore*, January 25, 1817. *Ib.*, 149. By February 17 the selection of Adams was looked upon as certain. Crawford wrote to Gallatin, March 12, 1817, of his own interests in Cabinet appointments, and added: "Mr. [Jonathan] Russell

You caution me against commencing to be the champion of orthodoxy, without first reading more than would consume all the leisure of the remnant of life which I have any reasonable prospect of enjoying, even if it were to be all leisure. I think I shall neither commence champion of orthodoxy, nor as your old friend Franklin used to say, of any man's *doxy*. If after sixty years of assiduous study and profound meditation you have only come to the result of trusting the Ruler with his skies, and adhering to the sermon upon the mount, I may be permitted to adopt the same conclusions by a shorter and more compendious process. But you observe again that mosquitoes are not competent to dogmatize "περι τόυ παντος." I have in a former letter contested the application of this remark to our own species. To compare *man* with a mosquito, an eel in vinegar, or a mite in cheese, shoots as wide of the mark of reality, as to suppose him an angel. You and I are competent to *dogmatize*, taking the sense of its derivation, that is, *to hold opinions* about the "το παν." To hold opinions, but not to obtain perfect knowledge. Mosquitoes hold no opinions. Now in the sermon upon the mount much is said about the kingdom of Heaven, and those who alone

made a deliberate effort to prevent the appointment of Mr. Adams, and had the address to enlist Crowninshield in the exertion. How far he felt interested in his exclusion is difficult to decide. There is much reason to believe that he also urged the appointment of Mr. Clay to the State Department. I believe Mr. Monroe's confidential advisers from Virginia were laboring the same vocation, some from proper and others from interested motives, which you will be able to conceive. After the explanation of his views to me, he could not for a moment have thought of Mr. Clay for the State Department without having previously made up his mind to lose my good opinion and, of course, my services; because every reason assigned against my going into the State Department operated stronger against Mr. Clay than against me. These reasons, as you will conceive, were all of a political nature, and existed in a stronger degree against him than any other person brought into view for that office." *Writings of Gallatin* (Adams), I. 26.

shall enter it. The preacher of that sermon announced himself as a being superior at least to human nature. If you say that he was a mere ordinary man, you include him also in the class of those who are not competent to dogmatize upon the system of the universe. You, or at least I, can by no possible process of reasoning consider him as a mere man, without at the same time pronouncing him an *Impostor*. You ask me *what* Bible I take as the standard of my faith—the Hebrew, the Samaritan, the old English translation, or what? I answer, the Bible containing the sermon upon the mount—any Bible that I can read and understand. The New Testament I have repeatedly read in the original Greek, in the Latin, in the Genevan protestant, and in Sacy's Catholic French translations, in Luther's German translation, in the common English protestant, and in the Douay English Catholic (Jesuitical) translations. I take any one of them for my standard of faith. If Socinus or Priestley had made a fair *translation* of the Bible, I would have taken that, but without their comments. I would also give up all the passages upon which any sound suspicion of interpretation can be fastened. But the sermon upon the mount commands me to lay up for myself treasures, not upon earth, but in Heaven. My hopes of a future life are all founded upon the Gospel of Christ, and I cannot cavil or quibble away, not single words and ambiguous expressions, but the whole tenor of his conduct, by which he sometimes positively asserted, and at others countenanced his disciples in asserting that he was *God*. You think it blasphemous to believe that the omnipotent Creator could be crucified. God is a spirit. The spirit was not crucified. The body of Jesus of Nazareth was crucified. The Spirit whether eternal or created was beyond the reach of the cross. You see my orthodoxy grows upon me, and I still unite with you in the doctrine of toleration and benevolence. You will marvel perhaps that with these sentiments I have been recently falling in with some of the broadest Unitarians, such as Mr. Frend and Mr. Aspland, who has obligingly presented me several sermons and tracts of his own upon the Unitarian faith.

I shall send you by the *Galen* or some other opportunity a work of a different kind. I mean the private correspondence of Dr. Franklin, one quarto volume of which has at last been published by his grandson. I have not seen this gentleman since my present residence in England, though we have more than once exchanged visits. But he lately sent me a copy of the book with a very polite letter in which he speaks in the most respectful terms of you. The first volume containing the memoirs of the Doctor's life has not yet been published.

We have just received the President's message at the opening of the session of Congress. It has extorted a few sentences of unwilling and sulky approbation from the ministerial papers. Its contents are in a high degree gratifying to the friends of our country. Mr. Madison has the happiness of leaving the Union in a state of prosperity and of tranquillity which did not accompany the retirement of either of his predecessors. For that very reason he leaves a more doubtful prospect to his successor. In the political as well as in the physical world the tempest must always alternate with fair weather. Hitherto, blessed be God, all our pilots have succeeded in weathering the storm. There are breakers ahead and all around us, however, and I hope your letter to the perpetual peace-mongers will give a lesson of useful instruction to our countrymen. By the returns for Congress I perceive that Hartford Convention Federalism is still upon the decay in Massachusetts, though I hear the

Roman Senators are still firm and vigorous in their resistance against the factious tribune of the people.

May the blessings of Heaven attend you and my dear mother, and the friends around you, through this and many succeeding years, prays your affectionate son.

TO WILLIAM EUSTIS

LITTLE BOSTON, EALING, 13 January, 1817.

DEAR SIR:

The American newspapers have announced and some private letters have given countenance to the rumor that I am to be recalled from the mission here upon the entrance of the new President into office, and I perceive by your favor of 28 December that you also give credit to the report. My principal reason for entertaining any doubt upon the subject is the silence hitherto both of the present chief, and of his apparent successor in their direct communications to me. Thus far I have no ground for expecting to be recalled until I shall ask it, which is my intention at the close of the present year. Should the proposal which you anticipate be made to me, I shall have several strong personal motives for accepting it, with others both of public and private consideration for declining it. Whether the latter will have the weight upon my mind which they ought, I can scarcely promise myself, for on consulting my own feelings and opinions I find the *pro* and the *con* so nearly balanced that I willingly postpone the decision until there shall be a certainty that it will be called for.

The change of public sentiment in our section of the Union, and particularly in our native state, is evidently though slowly progressive. The party which as you justly observe had of late years degenerated into a faction, still however control the legislature of the Commonwealth, although the good sense and integrity of their governor has in a great measure extricated him from their hands. The most violent men are dropping off from the representation in Congress, and the trimmers are preparing to step to windward while the ship is in the very act of tacking. If the separation of Maine should not be consummated before the next election for the legislature, I should hope the majority in both branches will be friendly to the national government. The leaders and instigators of the faction are incorrigible, because their errors are errors of principles, and because they are honest in the belief that all the wisdom of the nation is in their heads, and all its virtue in their hearts. They have erected their whole political system upon the perverted axiom that a part is greater than the whole. They see nothing in the American Union but New England. They have no country distinct from their party. As soon as they have sunk into a minority, they will fall into hypochondriac fits, and fancy the world is coming to an end for want of putting its trust in them.

Mr. A. H. Everett and his wife are here, having arrived not in the *Telegraph* but in the *Galen*. They are to proceed to Bruxelles in the course of this week. He has concluded not to go to St. Petersburg, being apprehensive that the journey at this season would be too severe for the state of Mrs. Everett's health. If no preferable mode of conveyance should occur, he will forward the dispatches from Bruxelles by the post.

The contingent charges upon our foreign missions are the payments for postage, stationery, yearly fees to court servants, and in this country for office rent, a charge that I never made elsewhere, because I never had occasion for a separate office but here. I should think there ought to be an allowance for the expense of your removing, and that you would do well to ascertain what the allowance is to the other foreign ministers respectively, and state it to our government. There was formerly something similar to your case in Spain, where the court had four residences to which they removed in the course of every year, and to all of which the foreign ministers were obliged to follow them. Perhaps Mr. Erving can inform you whether our ministers there were allowed to charge for the expense of those removals. If they were I should think the precedent decisive.

I am with the highest respect, etc.

TO WILLIAM PLUMER

EALING, near LONDON, 17 January, 1817.

MY DEAR SIR:

I am yet to acknowledge the receipt of your two obliging favors of 6 March and 30 July last, the latter enclosing a copy of your speech to the legislature. During the whole time that I have enjoyed the happiness of an acquaintance and friendship with you, there has been so general a coincidence of sentiment between us upon all the objects of concernment to our country, which have successively arisen, that I can ascribe it to no other cause than to the similitude, or rather the identity, of our political and moral principles. It was therefore not possible for me to read your excellent speech without great pleasure, and I was much gratified to see that its merits did not escape public notice even in this country. It was republished entire in one of the newspapers of most extensive circulation, not as during our late war some of our governor's speeches were republished, to show the subserviency of the speakers to the bulwark of our holy religion and to the press gang, but professedly for the pure and patriotic and genuine republican sentiments with which it abounded. It has been a truly cheering contemplation to me to see that the people of New Hampshire have recovered from the delusions of that unprincipled faction, which under the name of Federalism were driving to the dissolution of the Union, and under the name of Washington to British reconciliation; to see them returning to the counsels of sober and moderate men, who are biassed by no feelings but those of public spirit, and by no interests but those of their country. Such a person I well knew they had found in you, and such I hope you will find in your present and future coadjutors. Although the progress of reformation has not been so rapid and effectual in our native state as it has been with you, yet the tendency of the public opinion has been steadily since the peace in that direction, as it has been throughout the Union; and as that faction cannot fail to sink in proportion as the country prospers, I do not despair of seeing the day when the policy of all the state governments will be in union with that of the nation.

We have lately received what may be termed President Madison's valedictory message to Congress, and grateful indeed must it be to his feelings to compare the condition of the country at the close of his administration, with the turbulent and perilous state in which it was at the period of his first election. It will be the great duty of his successor, and of the Congress with which he is to coöperate, to use diligently the days of peace to prepare the nation for other trials which are probably not far distant, and which sooner or later cannot fail to arise. Your speech most justly remarks that the late war raised our public character in the estimation of other nations; but we cannot be too profoundly impressed with the sentiment that it has by no means added to the number of our friends. In this country more particularly, it is impossible for me to disguise to myself that the national feeling of animosity and rancor against America and the Americans is more universal and more bitter than it was before the war. A considerable part of the British nation then despised us, and contempt is a feeling far less active in spurring to acts of hostility, than hatred and fear which have taken its place. No Briton of any party ever imagined that we should be able to sustain a contest against them upon the ocean. Very few among ourselves expected it. Our victories both by sea and land, though intermingled with defeats and disasters which *we* ought to remember more studiously than our triumphs, have placed our character as a martial nation upon a level with the most respectable nations of Europe; but the effect here has been to unite all parties in the conviction that we are destined to be the most formidable of the enemies and rivals of their naval power. Now the navy is so universally the idol of this nation that there is not a statesman of any description or party who dares befriend anything opposed to it, or look with other than hostile eyes to anything that threatens its glory or portends its downfall. The opposition party and its leaders before the war were much more liberally disposed towards America than the ministerialists; but after the war commenced they joined the ministers in full pack, and since the peace their party tactics have constantly been to cavil against any liberality or concession of the ministers to America. The issue of the late European wars has been to give for the moment (though it will not last long) to the British government an ascendency of influence over the whole continent of Europe which they will naturally use to inspire prejudices and jealousies against us. There is already in all the governments of Europe a strong prejudice against us as Republicans, and as the primary causes of the propagation of those political principles, which still make the throne of every European monarch rock under him as with the throes of an earthquake. With Spain we are and have been on the verge of war. Nothing but the impotence of the Spanish government has hitherto prevented the explosion, and we have so many collisions of interest as well as of principles with Spain, that it is not only the Court but the nation which hates and fears us.[1] In France the government, besides being in tutelage under Britain, have feelings against America more venomous even than the British. The mass of the French nation have no such feelings; but they have no attachment to us, or friendship for us. Their own condition absorbs all their feelings, and they would delight in seeing us at war with Great Britain, because they flatter themselves that would operate as a diversion in their favor, and perhaps enable them to break the yoke under which they are groaning. We have claims for indemnification against the governments of France, Spain, the Netherlands, Naples, and Denmark, the justice of which they do

[1] At this time Bagot, the British minister at Washington, wrote that the differences between the United States and Spain were on the eve of adjustment by the sale of the Floridas to the United States; that Erving had been instructed to present the American claims against Spain, and should payment be refused, to abandon the whole claim, upon being permitted to purchase the Floridas for five millions of dollars. "Mr. Onis, the Spanish Minister in this country, is said to be ignorant of this negotiation. I repeat to your lordship that, deriving this information from one source only, I can form no judgment as to its accuracy; but the distressed state of the Spanish finances makes it not improbable that this government should have thought it worth while to make such an offer; and it is certain that the high tone which was held some months ago by this government against Spain, and which had all the appearance of being given for the purpose of preparing the people for a war between the two countries, has suddenly and greatly subsided." *Charles Bagot to Castlereagh*, January 7, 1817. *Letters and Dispatches of Lord Castlereagh*, XI. 345.

not admit, and which nothing but necessity will ever bring them to acknowledge. The very pursuit of those claims has a tendency to embroil us with those nations, as has been fully exemplified in the result of Mr. Pinkney's late mission to Naples; and yet as the claims are just they ought not to be abandoned. The states of Barbary owe us a heavy grudge for the chastisements we have inflicted upon all of them, and for the example first set by us to the European nations, of giving them battle instead of tribute, and of breaking up their system of piracy. We have therefore enemies in almost every part of the world, and few or no friends anywhere. If there be an exception it is in Russia; but even there the shameful misconduct of the Russian Consul General at Philadelphia,[1] and the infamous manner in which he has been abetted by the Minister Daschkoff, have produced a coldness on the part of the Emperor which endangered at least the harmony of the relations between the two countries. Add to all this, that there is a vague and general sentiment of speculative and fomenting jealousy against us prevailing all over Europe. We are considered not merely as an active and enterprising, but as a grasping and ambitious people. We are supposed to have inherited all the bad qualities of the British character, without some of those of which other nations in their dealings with the British have made their advantage. They ascribe to us all the British rapacity, without allowing us the credit of the British profusion. The universal feeling of Europe in witnessing the gigantic growth of our population and power is that we shall, if united, become a very dangerous member of the society of nations. They therefore hope what they confidently expect, that we shall not long remain united. That before we shall have attained the strength of national

[1] Nicolas Kosloff.

manhood our Union will be dissolved, and that we shall break up into two or more nations in opposition against one another. The conclusion from all which that we must draw is, to do justice invariably to every nation, and at the same time to fix our military naval and fiscal establishment upon a foundation adequate to our defense and enabling us to obtain justice from them.

I have not yet been able to procure for you Adair's *History of the Indians*, but I have found at a very moderate price a complete set of the *Remembrancer*, including the *Prior Documents*, all in eleven volumes, which I purpose to send you by the *Galen*, to sail about the first of March. I remain, etc.

TO THE SECRETARY OF STATE

No. 68.   [JAMES MONROE]

LONDON, 21 January, 1817.

SIR:

I have the honor of enclosing copies of two notes which I have addressed Lord Castlereagh, one respecting the revenue bonds taken at the capture of Moose Island,[1] and the other on the case of the Sloop *Mary* and cargo belonging to Clark and Kempton of Philadelphia, seized and confiscated in the island of Jamaica.

Parliament are to assemble on the 28th of this month, and the session is by all parties here anticipated as likely to be

---

[1] These bonds, given by citizens of the United States to the government, fell into the hands of British officers, were taken to Halifax, and "by a procedure unprecedented in the usage of civilized nations, put in suit in the British Vice Admiralty Court and were then condemned as prize of war."

of the highest importance. But the opposition to the ministry in that body stands upon a foundation so different from that which exists among the people, and separated from it, is so essentially weak that I cannot even now divest myself of the opinion that the session will pass over without any essential change. A distinguished member of the opposition has very lately said that the difficulty will be not to turn the Ministers out, but to keep them in; and this sentiment discloses at once that much of the ministerial strength lies in the weakness of their Parliamentary opponents, and that both parties have an external opposition to encounter which may be found equally unmanageable to both. At the last winter session the whole amount of parliamentary opposition was concentrated in the effort to throw off the property tax and in objections to petty items of expenditure. Many speeches were made about the distresses of the country, but so little were any of the members disposed to probe the wound to the bottom, that when Lord Castlereagh confidently asked if wheat should rise to eighty shillings a quarter *where would be the distress?* not a man was found in the House of Commons to answer him. There had been to that time no deficiency in the revenue, and so long as that state of things continued the ministry might be quite easy at the effect of opposition speeches. At the July quarter appeared the first falling off in the receipt of the taxes. In October they seemed to be recovering, but the January quarter has been again largely deficient, and that which is to terminate on the 5th of April will probably be still more so. The Ministers will have no difficulty in providing for this deficiency, either by loans or by issuing exchequer bills; and although this, while affording momentary relief, will ultimately but aggravate the distemper, yet the parliamentary opposition will have no other effectual remedy to propose.

The plain state of the fact appears to me to be that the load of taxation to pay the interest upon the national debt is greater than the nation can bear, and that the only possible remedy will be a composition with the public creditors, or an authoritative reduction of the debt in one form or another. But this neither the ministers nor the opposition in Parliament are yet prepared to admit. One member the last session distinctly hinted that a reduction of the interest of the debt might in the end become necessary, but he found no supporters and the very suggestion was deprecated by the Chancellor of the Exchequer as dishonorable.

At the meeting of Parliament an amendment to the address is to be moved by the opposition, and a circular from the Treasury to the ministerial members has been issued, earnestly calling for their attendance the first day of the session avowedly on that account. This amendment will doubtless contain the pledges of the opposition and will give the measure of what they are willing to do for the relief of the nation; but there is not a man possessed of any weight or influence in either house who is not already pledged to the *principles* of the present system, and neither the condition of the country nor the temper of the people will admit at this time of an opposition merely of detail.

The external opposition is of character altogether different from that which will be seen in Parliament. Among the people the party attached to the support of the government is almost universally ministerial. The Whig party so called is almost a nullity—that portion of the people who, dissatisfied with the ministers, are in general still more dissatisfied with the leading parliamentary members of opposition. The discontented part of the nation have been led to the conclusion that the great source of their calamities has been the defective representation in the House of Commons, and that their only effectual remedy will be a parliamentary reform. This opinion has evidently gained ground within the last year. The meetings to petition for reform have already been [called] and the object is assuming a consistency which it has not had certainly for these twenty years, if ever. Some correspondence between different meetings has been established, and there has been even a delegated meeting of deputies from several popular meetings with a view to concert the future measures to be adopted in the pursuit of their object. In this cause of parliamentary reform there are out of Parliament three men at this time peculiarly conspicuous: Major Cartwright, whose principal weight arises from the steadiness with which he has adhered to this particular pursuit for the last forty years; Cobbett, who notwithstanding that he has successively defended almost every possible change of opinion, is now beyond all question and spurning all comparison the most popular writer in the British Islands; and a Mr. Henry Hunt, who has distinguished himself by the violence of his speeches at the public meetings on various places. The most powerful and most active person of this triumvirate is Cobbett who, having declared open and inveterate hostility to both the Parliamentary parties, and having attacked indiscriminately individuals of every description, is equally hated and dreaded by all the prominent political characters, but has acquired by his weekly political *Registers*, which he has lately published in a cheap form accessible to all classes of the people, an influence over the indigent and suffering multitude possessed by no other person in the kingdom.

But while the general impulse of the external opposition is towards a reform of Parliament, there are in Parliament itself not more than two or three noted members of the

House of Commons, and perhaps not one of the Peers, cordially friendly to the cause. Cobbett says that the petitions for reform have been signed by more than half a million of people. They will be presented at an early period of the session and may prove embarrassing to both parties. They will probably be most so to the opposition, because the resistance on the ministerial side will be open and explicit, and consistent with the system they have always pursued; while the only ground upon which the opposition can assail the ministers is a reform of some kind, and they cannot withstand the great and essential reform from which alone all others can proceed without disabling their own argument, and at the same time sinking themselves still further in the estimation of that part of the people, without whose support they could not maintain themselves in power, even if they could drive the present ministers from their seats. This view of things will explain the apprehension expressed by a leading opposition member, that the difficulty would be not to turn the ministers out but to keep them in.

On the whole it is scarcely to be doubted that the established political system of this kingdom and of all Europe depends on the single question of the productiveness of the British revenue. The symptoms of the year just expired have indicated that in this country taxation has overstepped its practicable boundaries, and that a revenue *cannot* during peace be raised sufficient to defray the interest of the public debt and the current expenses of the government. That the deficiency in the revenue will be permanent and progressive is, however, by no means ascertained. Cobbett in his strongest tone of confidence predicted that the revenue of the year 1816 would not yield forty millions sterling. It has yielded more than fifty-seven millions. He now says that 1817 will not yield thirty-five millions. If it should fall even as low as fifty, it will not defray all the charges of the year and the distress of the country will be greater than it is now. But if, as is probable, the revenue of this year should be more rather than less productive than that of the last, the system may still hang together a little longer. There is no prospect that the burthen of the public debt will be lessened this year, but expedients to get through the year will be found with perfect ease. The payment of nearly forty millions yearly to the public creditors forms a great mass of capital, a large portion of which is constantly seeking employment. The government might borrow money to any amount they should want, and upon terms more advantageous than those of these late war loans. So great is the tendency of this capital to find employment that the French government have succeeded in negotiating a loan here, it is said, of twelve millions sterling or 300 millions of francs. How far this measure has had the sanction of the British government is not fully known. The agents of it are the Houses of Baring, Hope, Parish, and La Fitte. The terms are understood to be very burdensome to the borrowers. The British ministers disavow all connection with it on their part, but it probably could not have been accomplished without at least their tacit approbation. The first application for it was declared to have been unsuccessful because they declined affording the guarantee to it. Immediately afterwards the Duke of Wellington very suddenly and unexpectedly made an appearance here of three or four days only, and then returned to Paris. The general impression is that he came to show the indispensable necessity that this loan should be accomplished and it has accordingly been effected. The experiment may perhaps hereafter be repeated, and it affords an additional and a striking proof how indissolubly the present establishment of politics throughout Europe is connected with the state of British revenue.

I am, etc.

TO ABIGAIL ADAMS

LITTLE BOSTON, EALING, 25 January, 1817.

MY DEAR MOTHER:

Scarcely a day passes without the arrival of vessels from the United States, but they are principally from New York or more southern ports. The failure of the harvests in this country has much contributed to their frequency. Two years ago the British Parliament made a law to raise the price of bread, having discovered that if that first necessary of life should be cheap, the country would be irretrievably ruined. This act prohibited the importation of grain from foreign countries until wheat should for six weeks successively be at an average price throughout England and Wales of ten shillings sterling a bushel. From the time of the passing of the bill this event did not occur until last November. Since then wheat has constantly been above the price which admits of importation. It is now about at thirteen shillings sterling and likely to be higher. The importations have already commenced, and many vessels laden with flour have arrived from America. We have accounts from New York almost to the close of the year, but I have nothing from you later than your letter of November 26.

I am reading at once two Unitarian pamphlets—steering from grave to gay, from lively to severe, tragedy and comedy, my very good friend the Reverend Robert Aspland's plea for Unitarian dissenters, and that most laughing and laughable philosopher *Basanistes*,[1] recommended to me by my father. The project of putting down the Trinity by a joke amuses me much. Voltaire wrote two huge volumes to put down the whole Bible by jokes, and the hundred volumes of his works are a sort of joking encyclopedia against the Christian religion, which nevertheless, strange to say, flourishes in despite of them. And now I remember me the imperial philosopher Julian cracked his joke upon the Trinity too. "Εἰς τρίον, τρίον ἐν!"

But Plato says that *one* implies *another*. Now if God is *one*, who is the *other?* A profound question, which I leave for Unitarian solution, being ever faithfully yours.

TO FRANCIS FREELING

LONDON, 28 January, 1817.

SIR:

I am informed by Mr. James Maury, Consul of the United States at Liverpool, that a parcel of books, being a printed copy of the Laws of the United States addressed to me, but to be delivered to the care of the American consul at Liverpool, was sent to him from the post office charged with £19. 16. 8 postage, and that by the advice of the postmaster at Liverpool he had forwarded this parcel by the mail to London of the 20th instant.

This parcel was sent by a bookseller at Philadelphia on board of an American vessel bound from that port at Liverpool, certainly without the expectation or idea that it would be chargeable with postage. A dispatch from the government of the United States, bearing the seal and superscrip-

---

[1] A name attached to a volume entitled Αιρεδεων: *a New Way of deciding Old Controversies*. London, 1815.

tion of the Department of State, and addressed to me with my official character marked on the direction, was taken from the gentleman who had been intrusted with it and who came as a passenger in the vessel, and was sent to me by the post office charged with eleven shillings and ten pence postage.

I have on various occasions paid charges of postage from three to four pounds on parcels of newspapers thus taken and sent by the post office, and some months since I declined taking one packet of newspapers marked as such on the superscription, but charged with postage as letters. It was sent back to the General Post Office, where I presume it still remains.

I consider it as a breach of the privilege of my public character that any letter or dispatch addressed to me should be taken from the bearer of it by any officer of this government to be put into the post office.[1] And I now have the honor of writing to you, not for the purpose of complaining with regard to any of the cases in which it has been done, but to inquire whether you consider it within the extent of your authority to give such instructions as may prevent the recurrence of such accidents in future. They are necessary principally at the port of Liverpool, where most of the dispatches and letters which I receive from the United States are sent. I do not know that the case has occurred to bearers of letters for me landing at any other port. If you have the authority and think proper to give such instructions, I shall deem it unnecessary to give his Majesty's government any trouble by a further application in the case. With respect to the parcel of books the postage upon them may, I presume, be remitted at your discretion. I have the honor, etc.

[1] Freeling replied that the letters were probably taken by officers of the customs in forgetfulness of Adams' office.

TO THE SECRETARY OF STATE

No. 69.   [JAMES MONROE]

LONDON, 29 January, 1817.

. . . .

The newspapers now forwarded will give you an account of the opening of the session of Parliament yesterday, and of the extraordinary circumstances with which it was attended. A window of the Prince Regent's carriage was broken by bullets or stones thrown by persons among the crowd upon his return from the House of Lords, but he sustained no personal injury. The proceedings in the House of Commons upon the address in answer to the speech were interrupted by this incident, and the debate was adjourned to this day. The amendment was moved by Mr. Ponsonby,[1] and from the speeches on both sides that were made, it is apparent that the Whigs in Parliament will persevere in their opposition of detail as they did last year, and as then, it will probably come to nothing.

A delegation of deputies from various popular assemblies of petitioners in various parts of the kingdom have held several meetings, to concert the principles of a bill to be proposed for a reform of the Commons House of Parliament. They agreed to ask for annual Parliaments and the elective franchise for all persons paying taxes. Major Cartwright presided at these meetings, and Mr. Cobbett and Mr. Hunt were among the members. But the city reformers have had their meetings, too, and have pronounced themselves in favor of triennial Parliaments. The Whigs in Parliament

[1] George Ponsonby (1755–1817).

may perhaps support this project, but not with any intention or expectation of its being adopted.

It is the policy of the ministerial party to confound together as much as possible the Whigs, the reformers, and the desperate and riotous parts of the populace. The Whigs, though highly indignant at these imputations, and excessively anxious to repel them, practise the same sort of tactics against the reformers, who in their turn allow of no discrimination of merit between the ministerialists and the Whigs.

The ultimate object of the Whigs appears to be merely to get into power, but they have no system of policy that can possibly extricate the country from its difficulties. Their panacea is to reduce the army, but they are for maintaining everything which makes the army necessary. They would enjoy the good and cavil the conditions. They will not see that the incurable evil of the nation is a debt the interest of which they *cannot* pay, and that the only possible remedy is a composition with the public creditor. The reformers see this most distinctly, and Cobbett in particular has proved it in a manner to which nothing but events could reply. Cobbett's calculations have indeed been too rapid for the progress of events. The confirmations of his argument are slower than his anticipations, but they are now disclosing themselves with evidence more and more luminous. This I take to be the reliance upon which the reformers now reject all communion with the Whigs and bid defiance to them no less than to the Ministry. They conclude that the debt must ere long break down both these aristocratic parties, and that the government must finally come to the hands of those who will reduce at once the interest of the debt and the taxes. But the reformers are no more to be confounded with the rioters than either of the other parties. The rioters are people perishing by famine.

The deficiency is admitted in the Regent's speech, but he trusts it is to be ascribed to temporary causes, and he intimates that the public service of the year may be provided for without additional taxes and without touching the sinking fund. The resource is understood to be an issue of exchequer bills, which is a loan in disguise.

It is now about one year since the clamors of distress in this country began to be heard which I have repeatedly been assured, if real and sufficiently extensive to be called national, will be discovered in symptoms very different from those under which they arose. The great symptoms to which I alluded were a deficient revenue and popular petitioning meetings. These are now presenting themselves to an alarming degree, the political prospects of the country are assuming an aspect highly interesting, and which may be followed by results important to Europe and the world.

It has been suggested to me that the Board of Control, the President of which is now Mr. Canning, intend to pass a bill to levy an export duty of thirty per cent on all articles exported from a British India in foreign bottoms, with a drawback of fifteen per cent upon the goods when landed in England.

I am, etc.

TO GEORGE WILLIAM ERVING

EALING, 30 January, 1817.

DEAR SIR:

I am sorry to learn by your letter of 30th ultimo the trouble in which you find yourself involved, and congratulate you upon those from which you have been extricated. It seems to be a maxim with European ministers of state in their relation with the United States to transfer the negotiation *there*, whenever they intend to do *nothing*. When they mean to do anything they treat themselves; but for a mere interchange of notes and diplomatic altercation they empower and instruct their plenipotentiaries beyond sea. It may be sometimes for our advantage as much as theirs to talk and write about it, and as the measure and sum total of the Chevalier's [Onis] vivacities are now pretty well understood, I hope there will be nothing lost by transferring the pourparleys thither.

I think you have no cause to be alarmed at the other pourparleys which you mention. You will see the Regent's speech at the opening of the session of Parliament, and will find that the continuance of *external* peace is expected and intended. That the revenue is deficient, but that the supplies of the year are to be provided without loan, without additional taxes, and without touching the sinking fund. Exchequer bills will suffice. The Regent's carriage window was broken by bullets or stones on his return from the House of Lords, but mark the universal burst of loyalty that this outrage will bring forth from all parts of the kingdom. The *Huntsmen* muster strong, but as they have the Blues and Greys all against them, they will not be in at the death this year. I am sorry the *Examiner* has fallen into disgrace with you; he has too much taste exactly to suit mine. But then the two penny trash![1] Surely you have no relish for the two penny trash.

Wishing you patience and composure to await the signs of the times, I remain ever faithfully yours.

[1] A term applied to Cobbett's pamphlets, which were suppressed in 1817 by extending the stamp duty to all pamphlets.

TO ABIGAIL ADAMS

EALING, 12 February, 1817.

. . . . . .

There is an old vulgar saying that misery loves company, and the people of this country have in the midst of their distresses great consolation in being told, as they are with great assiduity, that all Europe, and especially that the people of the United States, are as wretched and much more wretched than themselves. There is, however, one very remarkable difference in the consequences of *Peace*, on the two sides of the water. For while on your side it has allayed the discontents and cooled down party spirit to such a degree that even the presidential election could not stimulate excitement, its effects here in the short compass of a year have been to spread disaffection and treason abroad, and to compel the government to resort to means of defense like those which marked the most inflammatory periods of the French revolution. But as the government here assure the people that their distress will be merely temporary, and as their resources for present purposes are abundant, the system will get along undoubtedly some time longer. There are many symptoms of its decay; but it has lasted so much longer than reasonable men ever thought it would, and recovered from a condition seemingly so desperate, that I cannot yet venture to affirm that it will not recover again. In the meantime I rejoice as an American, that we have no such indications of distress as I am witnessing here. . . .

TO THE SECRETARY OF STATE

No. 72.   [James Monroe]

London, 20 February, 1817.

Sir:

Although since I had the honor of writing you last I have received no communication of an official nature, either from this government, or from your Department, the situation of this country is already sufficiently interesting and is apparently drawing towards a crisis sufficiently momentous, to require an assiduity of observation and a frequency in the transmission of the notice of passing events, more particular than might be necessary in times of ordinary tranquillity.

The most prominent occurrences of the last ten days have been: 1. The notice given by the Ministers to Parliament that the Prince Regent had made the sacrifice of £50,000, being a fifth part of his annual establishment, to alleviate the distresses of the people. The example was followed by the Cabinet Ministers, who give up a tenth part of their salaries, being the amount which was deducted from them by the property tax while that was in force; by Mr. Ponsonby, an opposition member of the House of Commons, formerly Chancellor of Ireland, who gives up a like proportion, ten per cent of his pension of £4,000 a year; and by the Marquis of Camden, the holder of the mammoth sinecure yielding by common repute more than thirty thousand pounds a year,[1] which he gives up, with the reservation of a

---

[1] John Jeffreys Pratt, first Marquis of Camden (1759–1840). In 1780 he was appointed one of the tellers of the Exchequer and held the position for sixty years. The emoluments, originally £2,500 a year, had increased to £23,000 in 1808. An effort to limit them failed in 1812.

stipend of £2,700 a year. 2. The committal of four persons, Preston, Watson, senior, Hooper and Keen, or Kearns, by an order of the Privy Council to the Tower upon a charge of high treason. A proclamation has also been issued offering rewards of £500 each for the apprehension of two others, Watson, junior, and Thistlewood,[1] both implicated in the same charge of high treason. 3. The continual discussions in the House of Commons on the presenting of petitions for a reform of Parliament. 4. The report of the secret committee of the two Houses, setting forth the existence of an extensive conspiracy to effect a revolution and to overthrow the government.[2] 5. Meetings and counter-meetings among the people, some to petition for relief, retrenchment, and reform; and others to address the Prince Regent upon his providential escape from the traitorous assault upon his carriage, to protest of their own loyalty, and declare their abhorrence of the popular demagogues and instigators of reform. 6. A prayer and thanksgiving ordered to be read two Sundays successively in all the churches: the thanksgiving, for the Prince's escape from the base and barbarous assaults of a lawless multitude; the prayer that he may be protected from the secret designs of treason and from the madness of the people. To which is added a supplication to God that the people may "not seek relief where relief is not to be found," understood to mean in a reform of Parliament. The peculiar character to be remarked in the combination of all these proceedings of the government of Parliament and of the people is the disjointed state of public opinions and the violent effervescence of the public feelings. The very elements of the political system seem to be breaking up. The Regent and his government are unpopular.

[1] James Watson, the younger, and Arthur Thistlewood.
[2] Printed in *Annual Register*, 1817, 6, 12.

The opposition in Parliament are still more so. The people are in great distress, looking on every side for relief, resorting, some to a reform of Parliament, some to schemes for a new distribution of the land throughout the kingdom, and some to riot and insurrection; but all without the concert either of views, or of expedients which can lead them to any result useful to themselves. In the proceedings of the government there is a mixture of rigid inflexibility, of transparent artifice, and of tardy and reluctant concession, which indicates an internal struggle between exulting pride and incipient fear. When the Prince Regent's carriage was stoned by the populace, it was believed by himself and his attendants that he had been shot at with bullets. The difference is material, because the shooting with the bullets imports conspiracy, assassination and high treason; while stones and potatoes would prove only the spontaneous excesses of an exasperated mob. Nothing has occurred to confirm the supposition that bullets were fired, but it appears on the contrary to have been proved that the glass was broken in a place where it was scarcely possible it should have been done from a gun of any kind. The Ministers themselves have not ventured to pledge their credit to the shooting part of the affair; but the police magistrates and other loyal personages, at some of the meetings assembled to address the Prince upon his escape, have labored to establish the treasonable feature of the transaction with an earnestness of zeal bordering upon the ridiculous, and which has had a tendency to make the whole matter a subject of derision among the people.

It was some days after this event that the Ministers announced in Parliament the Prince's intention to apply £50,000 of his annual establishment to relieve the public distress. This measure in itself was highly popular, but would have been more approved at an earlier period. It is observed that if it had been determined upon before the meeting of Parliament, it would certainly have been announced in the speech, and that in that case the populace, far from committing outrage against him on his return from the House of Lords, would have cheered him with shouts of applause. The time for the sacrifice was not judiciously chosen; among those who are not predisposed to a favorable estimation of the acts of the government there is little confidence in its reality. It is doubted whether the Regent's establishment will be found to endure the retrenchment of expenditure which would be necessary to leave so large a sum unapplied at the end of the year, and the most prevalent anticipation is that its ultimate consequence will be to occasion a debt of the establishment itself, to be hereafter provided for by Parliament. The ministerial free gift of ten per cent upon their salaries for this year is deemed more than patriotic by their partisans, who insist that all the great offices of state are quite underpaid; and is not much admired by others, who think the salaries too high, and that they ought to be permanently reduced more than the ten per cent. The only real and considerable sacrifice yet made is that of the Marquis of Camden, and although that is considered as having been extorted by the extreme odium which in this time of public distress the mere possession of such a sinecure had drawn upon him, yet as he was the first to make the surrender, and as the example hitherto remains solitary, there appears a general disposition of all parties to give him credit for it as a voluntary and public-spirited act. But while these partial, equivocal, and ungracious concessions are yielded as peace offerings to the spirit of discontent, the government and all parties in Parliament are proceeding to the highest and most violent measures against the people. Two of the persons now confined in the Tower upon charges of high treason have already been tried for their lives for the same acts of which they are now accused, upon indictments for capital offences but not amounting to treason. They are apparently men all of the humblest condition of respectable life, rendered desperate by extreme want. In the depth of their wretchedness they resorted to the speculations of a writer named Spence,[1] who some years since had published pamphlets proposing a community not absolutely of goods but of lands throughout the kingdom, books which had probably derived their only importance from the prosecution and harsh treatment which had befallen their author. He is dead, but his doctrines have survived and famine has given them a new impulse to obtain proselytes. The Spafields meetings were called by some of these persons, and they had connected with them some wretchedly concerted and absurd plan of insurrection, the utter impotence of which was manifested by the feeble and despicable riot which ensued upon the meeting of the 2d of December. But the great and anxious object of the government, in which they have hitherto been not merely countenanced but encouraged and stimulated by the opposition in Parliament, is to confound these ravings of hunger with the petitions for a reform of the House of Commons. Major Cartwright, Cobbett, and Hunt have organized the pursuit of Parliamentary reform with so much ability and success that the opinions and wishes almost unanimous of the reformers are decidedly in favor of annual Parliaments and representation co-extensive with taxation. But this, although rigidly conformable to the theory of the English Constitution, suits the views of no

[1] Thomas Spence (1750-1814).

party in Parliament, and instead of putting it down by argument and deliberation, the Whigs in both Houses have outstripped the ministerial party in crying it down as wild, impracticable, absurd, mischievous, and even *treasonable*. The reports of the secret committee are elaborate attempts to fix the stigma of treason upon petitions for Parliamentary reform, and they are to be followed by a suspension of the habeas corpus act, and by restrictions upon the right of meeting to petition. It is probable that the Whigs in Parliament, or at least a part of them, after having in a manner *driven* the Ministers to these desperate measures, will desert them, or shrink from their share of the responsibility attached to the support of them. These statesmen may probably return to their declamations about the rights of Englishmen, and to their clamors for retrenchment and *practicable* reform, when they must be perfectly aware that all they can say will be a mere waste of words. The practicable result will be the silence or indefinite imprisonment of the great reforming triumvirate, perhaps the execution for treason of some poor wretches who, if left to their fate, would have perished by want, and ultimately renewed congratulations between the Prince Regent and his faithful Lords and Commons upon their enjoyment of the "most perfect system of law and government that has ever fallen to the lot of any people."

The measures now to be adopted have been heretofore found effectual to suppress discontents, similar and perhaps even greater than those that now prevail. Whether they will be equally efficacious now will depend upon the single question of revenue. As long as the ways and means hold out the government will be safe, whatever may be the distresses of the people, and from the conduct of the opposition in Parliament, they will have none of that difficulty which one of their leaders suggested that they would find of keeping the Ministers in.[1]

I am, etc.

TO THE SECRETARY OF STATE

No. 73.   [JAMES MONROE]

LONDON, 4 March, 1817.

SIR:

I have received letters from Mr. Shaler and Commodore Chauncey with the information of the renewal of the treaty with the Dey and Regency of Algiers, with the modification authorized by the instructions of those gentlemen. But from Commodore Chauncey's account it appears that the Dey gave them explicit notice that he should abide by this treaty no longer than he should find it expedient. The transactions both of the United States and of Great Britain with all the Barbary States have so clearly demonstrated the policy to be observed in all political relations with them that it is earnestly to be hoped that neither the disgrace of tribute nor the scandal of Christian slavery will again be submitted to or endured. It is evident that their military energy both by land and sea has been greatly overrated, or is in a stage of deep decay; that they are quite as vincible as other men, and that they are not equal to a contest with the boldness or the skill of European war with its recent improvements. But the gross and clumsy fraud of foisting into their copy of a treaty articles never agreed to, and the

[1] Castlereagh's account of the measures of this session of Parliament may be seen in his letter to the Duke of Wellington, March 31, 1817, in *Supplementary Dispatches . . . of the Duke of Wellington*, XI. 660.

open avowal of intended future perfidy to engagements subscribed to from present necessity, leave no possibility of doubt that the only guarantee for the permanency of our peace with them will be our own force.

Since I had the honor of writing you last the bill for suspending the habeas corpus act has passed both Houses of Parliament by large majorities. Three other bills, to prevent seditious meetings, to give more security to the person of the Prince Regent, and to guard against the seduction of the soldiers, are in progress with little opposition. There is a pretty general impression of the necessity of these measures throughout the country; their principal object is undoubtedly to break the concert of operations among the votaries of parliamentary reform. The opposition in Parliament concur with or feebly resist these repressive [measures], and spend all the fire of their patriotism in motions to save £2,000 a year to the nation by reducing the number of the Lords of the Admiralty from seven to five, and to cut off £220 from the salary of their Secretary. The Ministry have obviously gained strength since the meeting of Parliament and the funds continue rapidly rising.

I am, etc.

FROM JAMES MONROE

WASHINGTON, March 6, 1817.

DEAR SIR:

Respect for your talents and patriotic services has induced me to commit to your care, with the sanction of the Senate, the Department of State. I have done this in confidence that it will be agreeable to you to accept it, which I can assure you will be very gratifying to me. I shall communicate your appointment by several conveyances to multiply the chances of your obtaining early knowledge of it, that, in case you accept it, you may be enabled to return to the United States, and enter on the duties of the office with the least delay possible. This letter is delivered to Mr. Cook, a respectable young man from Kentucky, who is employed as a special messenger for the purpose.[1]

JAMES MONROE.

[1] "On full consideration of all circumstances, I have thought that it would produce a bad effect to place anyone from this quarter of the Union in the Department of State, or from the south or west. You know how much has been said to impress a belief on the country north and east of this, that the citizens from Virginia, holding the Presidency, have made appointments to that Department to secure the succession from it to the Presidency of the person who happens to be from that state. . . . It is not sufficient that this allegation is unfounded. Much effect has been produced by it, so much indeed that I am inclined to believe that if I nominated anyone from this quarter (including the south and west, which in relation to such a nomination at this time, would be viewed in the same light) I should embody against the approaching administration, principally to defeat the suspected arrangement for the succession, the whole of the country north of the Delaware immediately, and that the rest [north?] of the Potomack would be likely to follow it. My wish is to prevent such a combination, the ill effect of which would be so sensibly felt on so many important public interests, among which, the just claims, according to the relative merit of the party of persons in this quarter ought not to be disregarded. With this view, I have thought it advisable to select a person for the Department of State from the eastern states, in consequence of which my attention has been turned to Mr. Adams, who by his age, long experience in our foreign affairs, and adoption into the republican party, seems to have superior pretensions to any there." *James Monroe to Thomas Jefferson*, February 23, 1817. In a letter to Andrew Jackson, March 1, he said: "I shall take a person for the Department of State from the eastward; and Mr. Adams' claims by long service in our diplomatic concerns, appearing to entitle him to the preference, supported by his acknowledged abilities and integrity, his nomination will go to the Senate. . . . After all that has been said I have thought that I should put the administration more on national grounds by taking the Secretary of State from the eastward than from this quarter, or the south or west. By this arrangement there can be no cause to suspect unfair combination for improper purposes. Each member will stand on his own merit, and the people respect us all according to our conduct. To each I will act impartially, and of each expect the performance of his duty. While I am here I will make the administration, first, for the country and its cause; secondly, to give effect to the government of the people, through me, for the term of my appointment, not for the aggrandizement of anyone."

TO THE SECRETARY OF STATE

No. 74.   [JAMES MONROE]

LONDON, 20 March, 1817.

SIR:

The day before yesterday I had an interview with Lord Castlereagh, when he informed me that the British government had come to a determination respecting the commercial part of the proposals for the negotiation of a further treaty which I had made last September.[1] That they were yet not prepared to abandon their ancient colonial system, but they were willing to extend to the United States the benefits of the free port act to the same extent that they were now enjoyed by the vessels of European nations, and to give a partial admission of our vessels to the island of Bermuda and to Turks Island. And with regard to the intercourse between the United States and the adjoining British provinces, they would renew a proposal heretofore made founded altogether upon the principle of reciprocity. Which proposal he read to me from a paper, which he said was not quite finished, but which would be sent me in the course of the next day. Last evening I received a note from Mr. Hamilton, the under Secretary of State in the Foreign Department, with a draft of four articles, a copy of which hastily made I now enclose, as Mr. Everett leaves town this morning. The part read to me by Lord Castlereagh was the fourth article, excepting the last paragraph.[2]

I do not think it possible to make anything out of these articles to which I can under my present instructions agree.

[1] Adams, *Memoirs*, March 18, 1817.
[2] *Ib.*, March 19, 1817.

I therefore enclose copies of them with the request of immediate further instructions. Lord Castlereagh informed me that they had received information that the act of Congress prohibiting the clearance for ports to which vessels of the United States are not admitted had passed, and he renewed the assurance that this government considered it as perfectly proper and as giving them no cause of complaint or dissatisfaction. It seems to me, however, that the very slight and partial concessions in the enclosed articles are intended to counteract its effects, and this opinion contributes to caution me against subscribing to them without your further orders. Lord Castlereagh offers to make them supplementary to the convention of 3 July, 1815, and to be in force for the same time.[1]

I am, etc.

TO JOHN ADAMS

LONDON, 31 March, 1817.

. . . . . .

To mingle a little amusable matter with these grave and solemn disquisitions, I send you a couple of drolleries that have just started from the press, and are now administering food for the public curiosity. One is a short summary of the life and reign of Napoleon, purporting to have been written by himself, though generally believed here to be spurious.

[1] In sending a copy of these articles to Bagot, Lord Castlereagh wrote: "Whether Mr. Adams may think it necessary to take this project only ad referendum; or whether he may feel himself justified in accepting or modifying it without reference home, I have thought it advisable that you should be in possession of the views of the government upon the subject, although I do not wish you to make any further use of it, nor indeed to mention that it is in your possession, unless Mr. Monroe opens the subject." March 21, 1817. Ms.

It has many internal marks both of authenticity and of imposture; and if not written by himself, is at least the composition of some person who understands his character and has the art of assuming his style. I incline to think it genuine.[1] Several of the servants who accompanied him to St. Helena have lately left him, and arrived in this country. Among them one was in some degree a confidential person. He has published a letter from Montholon to Sir Hudson Lowe, the present governor of St. Helena, remonstrating against the ill-treatment experienced by the ex-emperor, and an additional narrative of his own, which represents that ill-treatment as extending to the denial of the necessaries of life. Lord Holland made a motion in the House of Peers for the production of papers to show whether these complaints were well or ill-founded. The ministers admitted and undertook to justify some of the alleged facts and contradicted others; but refused to produce the papers. It is remarkable, though perhaps according to the ordinary workings of human nature and human passions, that the enemies of this man grow more inveterate against him, and his partisans more enthusiastic in his favor, as the term of his captivity lengthens, and as the prospect of its being perpetual acquires probability. Chained to his rock, he is at this moment more dreaded and detested, and at the same time more admired and beloved than when he was at the summit of his power.

The other enclosed pamphlet is by the Poet Laureate Southey. It is a bundle of combustibles, of materials the most worthless—mere stubble, fit for nothing but to kindle a blaze, without substance enough in itself to burn longer than time enough to light up other inflammable matter. But the *piquant* of the matter is, that the same Southey is

---

[1] See Adams, *Memoirs*, April 27, 1817.

the author of an article in the last number of the *Quarterly Review*, in which he inveighs against the reformers with a spirit of a grand inquisitor, and calls upon the government to put them down by halters and hurdles. It was notorious that Southey had begun his career as a furious Jacobin; but even then he had not been able to find a publisher for his *Wat Tyler*. He had given a copy of it to a clergyman named Winterbotham,[1] who was in prison for seditious writings, and it had lain *perdue* from that time until after the publication of the article urging political persecution in the *Quarterly Review*. Winterbotham has been some time dead, and after his decease the manuscript of *Wat Tyler* fell into the hands of a bookseller, who sent it forth as a ghost to haunt Southey for his political prostitution and apostasy. It has answered its purpose so well in this respect, that Southey applied for an injunction from the Lord Chancellor to suppress his own book. And the Lord Chancellor refused the injunction, because the book is of so atrocious a character that no action for the property of it could be maintained at law. And so Southey, the very tool employed to stimulate literary political persecution, stands the avowed author and publisher of the most incendiary book upon which the crown officers could fasten their fangs. 'Tis sport to see the "engineer hoist with his own petard."

As Southey has become one of the most useful, because one of the basest literary scavengers of the party in power, they cannot prosecute him for *Wat Tyler*, nor with their hands thus tied, can they with any remnant of decency prosecute any other person for the publication of it now.

[1] William Winterbotham (1763–1829) author of the *Historical, etc., View of the American United States*, London, 1794. He was released from prison in 1797, and from 1808 to his death lived at Newmarket.

And while they are thus forced to let that book pass unnoticed, and circulate among the people, it compels them to pass over many other publications which they would most willingly prosecute, but which are harmless in comparison with it. Yet as they are not overburdened with delicacy, and as with the aid of their new laws they are sufficiently sure both of their judges and juries, they have commenced already their persecutions for libels, and probably would very soon have laid hold of Cobbett had he not shrunk from the crisis, and taken his departure for America.[1] They have thus succeeded in driving him off the ground, and have broken up in him the main pillar of parliamentary reform. They have also probably succeeded in silencing the itinerant orator of the same cause, Hunt; and by rejecting all printed petitions they have disqualified the third great member of the reforming triumvirate, Major Cartwright.[2] Lord Cochran also appears to have found it expedient to seek another field for his active energy, and is going upon some project not fully disclosed to South America. The parliamentary campaign hitherto has been consumed in one laborious effort to suppress the reformers and their projects. Both parties in Parliament have substantially joined in this effort, and they have bound the people hand and foot so that apparently they will be unable to move. They have adjourned for a fortnight over the Easter holidays, and at the last moment the opposition members started up and said that as they had done as yet nothing but coerce the people, they hoped the ministers would *in the recess* do something to relieve the people. What the ministers could do in the recess of such high importance, they did not explain. It is very obvious to all the world that during a

[1] In March, 1817.
[2] Adams, *Memoirs*, May 18, 1817.

recess of fourteen days, the ministers can do little or nothing to remedy evils for which the tried wisdom of parliament has effected nothing in as many months. But now the reformers are down I suppose the Whigs are planning to stand forth again as the champions of *the people*. . . .

TO LORD CASTLEREAGH

The undersigned Envoy Extraordinary and Minister Plenipotentiary from the United States of America has the honor of enclosing to Lord Castlereagh sundry papers relative to the case of William Bedlow Crosby, a citizen of the United States, from whom an estate in the island of Jamaica was, by the process of escheat and under the sentence of the highest Court of Jurisdiction in that island, taken in the name of the Crown and by the prosecution of the Attorney General of the island, on the single ground that the said Crosby and his brother John Player Crosby who devised the estate to him were aliens born.

It has been universally understood both in the British dominions and in the United States that by the treaty of peace which succeeded the war of the American Revolution, neither the titles of British subjects who held at that time real estate in the United States, nor those of citizens of the United States who held such estates in the British territories, became in any manner liable to escheat upon the principle of alienage. By the ninth article of the treaty of November, 1794, those titles were recognized as existing, and it was stipulated that persons thus holding lands should continue to hold them, according to the nature and tenure of their respective estates and titles therein, and that neither they, nor their heirs or assigns, should so far as might respect the said lands and the legal remedies incident thereto be regarded as aliens.

There has been no decision by any court of judicature in Great Britain that lands held by citizens of the United States within the British territories are by the laws of England liable to escheat to the Crown by reason of alienage of the tenant. The decision of the courts of Jamaica in this case is believed to be the first and only one of its kind that has occurred in the British dominions. From that decision made in October, 1811, an appeal in behalf of William Bedlow Crosby, the party suffering under it, was regularly entered, but which he was prevented from prosecuting within the term of one year by the unfortunate rupture between the two countries which in that interval took place. No instance has ever occurred of land held by British subjects in the United States having been taken from them by process of escheat for the cause of alienage. On the contrary, the legislature of the state of New York, of which both the Crosbys were native citizens, have repeatedly interposed by special acts to preserve the titles and the succession by inheritance or devise to such estates to the heirs or devisees of their owners, and to foreclose all claim of the state to them by escheat.

The undersigned has been instructed to support by a candid representation to the British government of the circumstances of this case the claims of Mr. Crosby to the restitution of this estate. Whether by the laws of England it was liable to escheat is in the highest degree questionable. Even if it was rigorously so liable, the undersigned is persuaded his Majesty's government will feel the harshness of the application of the law in stripping an unoffending individual of his estate on the single circumstance of his birth. The application of the same rule to British subjects holding lands in the United States would doubtless be far more extensive in its effects in impairing the possessions of individuals than its extension even to all American citizens holding lands in British territories. It is perhaps desirable, at least, as promotive of a friendly and harmonious disposition between the two countries, that no such precedent should be established as would seem to call for reciprocal rigor, which in its turn might produce further instances of asperity towards individuals without any proportionate balance of advantage to the government on either side. The restitution of this property would not only remove the precedent, but doubtless prevent the recurrence of similar cases on either part, and relieve both governments from solicitations and complaints of their citizens and subjects which could not fail to arise from the frequent enforcement of the principle of escheat for alienage.

The Undersigned, etc.[1]
Craven street, 31 March, 1817.

TO THE SECRETARY OF STATE

No. 76. [JAMES MONROE]

LONDON, 10 April, 1817.

SIR:

. . . .

The Spanish ambassador at this Court, Count Fernan Nuñez, Duke of Montellano, has been recalled and appointed ambassador at Paris. The object of his new mission, he intimated to me, is a negotiation to which the Portuguese invasion of the Buenos Ayres territory has given

[1] Adams, *Memoirs*, April 30, May 5, 1817.

rise. This incident happening so immediately after the marriages of the King and Prince of Spain with the Portuguese Princesses [1] has occasioned the supposition that there was some understanding between the two governments on the subject. The Count assured me there was none. That the Spanish government felt itself deeply injured at this unprovoked invasion of their territory from Rio Janeiro, and would have been fully justified in retaliating the same measure upon Portugal. But in the pursuit of a policy altogether pacific, they had preferred appealing to the good offices and mediation of the allied powers, and that this was the object of his mission to Paris. He spoke of this as indicating also a pacific disposition on the part of Spain towards the United States, and in the course of the same conversation he asked me, if the American government were now satisfied with the personal deportment of the Spanish minister at Washington.[2] I told him I had received no late advices to the contrary, though at a former period and about this time last year I had been informed his conduct had not been unexceptionable. He did not suggest that there was any intention of recalling Mr. Onis. By this appeal to the allied powers for their mediation to settle the question as between Spain and Portugal, Spain may possibly have it in contemplation to engage the allies on her side upon the question as between herself and the insurgents of the disputed territories. There is a perpetual tendency to interference against the insurgents in all the councils of the allies, and in none more than in those of this country, upon the principle of legitimacy. The public feeling throughout Europe, and especially here, corroborated

---

[1] Ferdinand VII. married in 1816, Isabel of Braganza. The wife of Don Carlos was Maria Francisca of Braganza.

[2] Onis.

by a powerful commercial interest is on the other side. From something that fell from Mr. Brougham in the House of Commons the other day the opposition appear apprehensive that the Ministry are about to take decided part against the South Americans. I think they dare not. They would however, willingly undertake the office of mediators. In the meantime Lord Cochrane and perhaps Sir Robert Wilson are following upon the track of Sir Gregor McGregor,[1] and are going to offer the insurgents a mediation of their own.

Parliament have adjourned for the Easter holidays, after adopting all the measures proposed by the Ministry for suppressing sedition and putting down the reformers. Those measures have for the present very effectually answered their purpose. The voice of the complaining part of the people is already almost stifled, and the murmurs which were so menacing and the clamors which were so noisy are dying away into silence. Cobbett is gone, and you will doubtless hear of him at New York before this will reach you. Of the reforming triumvirate little more will henceforth be heard. Between five and six hundred of Major Cartwright's petitions have been rejected because they were printed, and the popular meetings will for the future be limited to householders, and dissolvable at the discretion of every Justice of the Peace. The three per cents have risen from 61 to 73, and are still rising. The revenue is improving and has yielded more during the quarter just expired than in the corresponding quarter of the last year. As the favorable aspect of affairs is attributed to the vigorous measures of the government, they will probably be prolonged in their operation as long as may be found expedient.

I am, etc.

[1] See *Dictionary of National Biography*, XXXV. 95.

TO THE PRESIDENT OF THE UNITED STATES

[JAMES MONROE]

London, 17 April, 1817.

Sir:

I had the honor of receiving yesterday [1] the quadruplicate of your favor of 6 March, informing me that you have been pleased with the concurrence of the Senate to commit to me the Department of State. For this distinguished mark of your confidence, and for the obliging terms in which you have the goodness to communicate it, I pray you to be assured of the grateful sense which I entertain. I accept it with no other hesitation than that with which I cannot but be affected in contemplating the arduous duties assigned to me by this appointment, and the consciousness of needing your indulgence and that of our country in the endeavor faithfully to discharge them.

I hope to be able to embark for the United States in the course of the next month, and have the honor to remain with perfect respect, sir, your very humble and obedient servant.

TO LORD CASTLEREAGH

The Undersigned Envoy Extraordinary and Minister Plenipotentiary from the United States of America has received the four projected articles for a supplement to the commercial convention of 3 July, 1815, sent him by direction of Lord Castlereagh, and has transmitted them for the consideration of his government.

[1] Adams, *Memoirs*, April 16, 1817.

By a letter of instruction from the Secretary of State of the United States of the 5th of February last, the undersigned is informed that the negotiation between him and Mr. Bagot in relation to the fisheries on the North American coast had not been brought to the desired result. That it is yet to be hoped that it may be satisfactorily settled. That with this view it was the President's intention to renew the negotiation as soon as he could obtain the information necessary to ascertain what arrangement would be best calculated to reconcile the interests of both parties, which he hoped to do in the course of a few months. That in the meantime he relied that no measures would be taken by his Majesty's government to alter the existing state of things, and particularly that the order to the naval officer commanding on that station, not to interrupt or disturb the American fishermen during the approaching season, would be renewed.

The Undersigned, etc.
28 Craven Street, 25 April, 1817.

TO ABIGAIL ADAMS

LONDON, 23 April, 1817.

MY DEAR MOTHER:

Your kind letters of 12 and 17 March, the latter enclosing one (copy) from Mr. H. G. Otis to my father, reached me on the day with a letter from the new President of the United States, informing me that with the concurrence of the Senate he had appointed me to the office just vacated by himself. I had never received from him any previous intimation that it was his intention to make this nomination, although from various sources, and among others the public newspapers, suggestions had found their way to me that it would probably be made. I am duly sensible of this mark of his confidence, and devoutly wish that he may never have occasion to regret that it was misplaced. The only hesitation that I could feel with regard to my duty on the occasion arose from a very serious doubt of my competency for the place. You will give me credit when I assure you that this doubt has weighed more heavily upon my mind than it ever did upon the occasion of any former appointment with which I have been honored. You may not be aware, and it is not necessary for me to set forth the array of all the incidents that contribute to the pressure of this doubt, because I have nevertheless overstepped them all and accepted the trust. The dispenser of every good gift can alone enable me faithfully and acceptably to discharge it.

Your imagination travelled upon the wings of your affection when you allotted the month of May for the period of our arrival in the United States. It will at the utmost be that of our embarking. The letter that I have received from the President was a fourth copy, and a mere notification of my appointment. The official letter of recall and the instructions how and with whom to leave the affairs of the mission here have not reached me. We are making in the meantime preparations for our departure, and next Monday we are finally to quit the mansion at Little Boston, one of the most delightful spots upon which I ever resided. If we land upon my native soil as early as the first of August, it is the utmost that I can expect.

16 May, 1817.

You will scarcely think it possible that this letter should have lain nearly a month unfinished for want of an hour of time at my disposal. We took final leave of our residence at Little Boston on the 29th of last month. On the 3d of the present I received the letter of recall from the mission here, which I delivered the day before yesterday to the Prince Regent.[1] I have engaged passage for myself and family on board the ship *Washington*, Captain Forman, to sail the first week in June from this port for New York. My books, together with the portrait of my father painted by Copley, and that of my sister, which I have procured for you, I shall send to Boston, perhaps by the Brig *Lion*, to sail about the last of this month. My son George has just returned from his tour to Paris, Bruxelles, and Ghent.

I received yesterday your kind letter of 13 April on the subject of my new appointment. I can add nothing to what I have said on the other side. The manner in which the President has thought proper to nominate me was certainly honorable to himself, as it was without any intimation from me, or, as far as I know, from any of my friends, which could operate as an inducement to him. His motives were altogether of a public nature, and I trust I shall be duly sensible of the personal, as well as of the political duties which this unsolicited and spontaneous confidence imposes upon me. As to the popular favor with which you observe the appointment has been attended, I well know how to appreciate its stability as inherent in its own nature but that is the smallest of my concern. I have no fear of injustice from my countrymen. For through the whole course of my life I have experienced from them favor far beyond my deserts. They have always over-estimated, not the goodness of my intentions, but the extent of my talents; and now when *their* anticipations go so far beyond what I have the consciousness of being able to realize, *mine* have too much reason to apprehend that they will terminate in disappointment. I have no anxious forecast but of my

[1] Adams, *Memoirs*, May 14, 1817.

inability to justify the President's choice by active, efficient, and acceptable assistance to his administration, and the expectation of the public by solid and useful advice to my country.

You observe that among the various public speculations there have been some expressing apprehensions that my public opinions and feelings would not harmonize with those of the President. It is certain that our sentiments upon subjects of great public interest have at particular periods of our public life been much at variance. That they may be so again is as certainly not impossible. If I had any present reason for expecting it, I should deem it my duty to decline the office which he has tendered to me; but I have none. Ever since his appointment to the Department of State has brought me into official relations with him, I have known few of his opinions with which I did not cordially concur, and where there might be shades of difference, have had ample reason to be satisfied with the consideration which he has given to the candid expressions of mine. I am aware, however, how much more delicate and difficult a task it will be to conciliate the duties of self-respect and the spirit of personal independence, with the deference of personal obligation and the fidelity of official subordination, under the new station assigned to me than it has hitherto been in those which I have held. I am aware that by the experience of our history under the present constitution, Mr. Jefferson alone of our four Presidents has had the good fortune of a Cabinet harmonizing with each other and with him through the whole period of his administration. I know something of the difficulty of moving smoothly along with associates, equal in trust, justly confident of their abilities, disdainful of influence, yet eager to exercise it, impatient of control, and opposing real, stubborn resistance to surmises and phantoms of encroachment, and I see that in the nature of the thing an American President's Cabinet must be composed of such materials. For myself I shall enter upon the functions of my office with a deep sense of the necessity of union with my colleagues, and with a suitable impression that my place is *subordinate*. That my duty will be to *support*, and not to counteract or oppose, the President's administration, and that if from any cause I should find my efforts to that end ineffectual, it will be my duty seasonably to withdraw from the public service, and to leave to more competent persons the performance of the duties to which I should find myself inadequate. The President, I am sure, will neither require nor expect from me any sacrifice of principles inconsistent with my own sense of right, and I hope I shall never be unmindful of the respect for his character, the deference to his sentiments, and the attachment to his person, due from me to him, not only by the relative situation which he has placed me to himself, but by the gratitude with which his kindness ought to be requited.

I am obliged to close my letter and remain ever affectionately yours.

TO WILLIAM EUSTIS

LONDON, 20 May, 1817.

DEAR SIR:

I received a few days since your two letters of the 10th instant. Having had no communication on the subject from the President or the Department of State, I am not acquainted with the motives upon which your instructions to return home the next autumn were founded; but I cannot imagine any which would interfere with your preference to undertake the voyage at a more comfortable season of the year. So far as my opinion or voice can have any influence in the case, it will be at your option to return in the autumn or the ensuing spring, as may best suit your own convenience. Colonel Aspinwall's arrangements here are, I believe, already much better suited to his interests than anything *diplomatic* in the service of the United States could afford him. His prospects are certainly better. He is preparing for an establishment for several years which I should not think it advisable to disturb. When you conclude to return, whether in the autumn or next spring, if Everett declines to be chargé d'affaires, there are other candidates already in the career to whom the office may be desirable and well qualified for it.

Mr. Winthrop has suggested to me his wish to be authorized by you to act as your Secretary of Legation till an appointment. I told him I had never conceived myself authorized to appoint a Secretary of Legation *pro tem*, and believed you would have the same scruple, but advised him to write about it to yourself.

Mr. George Joy applies for the appointment of Consul at Amsterdam, and among his reasons in support of the pretension alleges a letter from you proposing to him to go over to Holland about a year since when there was a prospect of Mr. Bourne's immediate decease. He has twice written to you recently stating his views and expectations in this respect, and I believe proposes to make a further direct application to the President for the office. . . .

TO JOHN GRAHAM [1]

London, 31st May, 1817.

Sir:

On the 14th instant I delivered to the Prince Regent my letter of recall. I took the occasion to repeat to him the assurance which I had previously given to Lord Castlereagh of the President's earnest desire to cultivate the best understanding with this government and the most friendly relations between the two countries, and I also mentioned the motives which had induced the President to postpone the immediate nomination of a minister to his court, assuring the Prince that the appointment would be made at a very early period. The Prince expressed his entire satisfaction at this and gave the strongest assurances in return of the reciprocal desire of his government to continue upon the most friendly terms with the United States.

The assistant master of the ceremonies made me the offer of the customary present made to foreign ministers upon their departure, which I declined as being prohibited by the Constitution of the United States. I afterwards suggested to Lord Castlereagh that as the United States had not adopted the custom of giving presents to foreign ministers, consistency and delicacy required that they should not permit their own minister abroad to receive such presents from other sovereigns.[2]

The Queen having been lately in an infirm state of health it was intimated to her Majesty at my desire that, however desirous of paying my respects to her in person to take leave of her by a private audience in the usual form, I should

---

[1,2] Of the Department of State.

Adams, *Memoirs*, May 14 and 23, 1817.

prefer to forego that privilege if it would put her to the slightest inconvenience. She was pleased to approve of this arrangement and of the motives upon which it was proposed.

I have presented Mr. Smith to Lord Castlereagh as charged with the affairs of the legation until the arrival of a minister, and he was presented in that capacity to the Prince Regent at his levee on the 28th instant.[1]

. . . . . .

TO RICHARD RUSH

Private. QUINCY, 21 August, 1817.

DEAR SIR:

The day after my arrival [2] here I had the pleasure of receiving your favor of the 14th instant. As a truant I believe I must bring a writ of error from your black letter decision before the Supreme Court of the United States, where common law is of no authority. Feeling nevertheless the force of considerations which your kindness and friendship have forborne to urge, I shall abridge as much as possible my visit here, and as far as anticipation may be allowed to the instability of human events, you may depend upon seeing me at Washington upon this day month. As the learned are agreed that the world began at the autumnal equinox with the sun entering upon the sign of the balance, I hold it the most auspicious time for commencing existence upon my new world; and although the season is apt to be tempestuous, if I am entering upon it to ride in the whirl-

---

[1] Adams embarked at Cowes, June 15, on the *Washington*, Captain Jacob Forman, and landed at New York, August 7, after a passage of fifty days.

[2] He had arrived on the 18th. Rush was in charge of the Department of State, and to succeed to the English mission.

wind, I shall have the consolation of looking to a steady spirit in our chief who will know how to direct the storm.

I have heard here with great satisfaction that you are destined to the pilgrimage from which I am just returned. You will find the time and the place both critical in a high degree. I reserve for the time when we shall meet full and free communication with you upon the subject.

I enclose a letter for the President, and remain, etc.

TO JOSEPH ANDERSON

QUINCY, 1 September, 1817.

DEAR SIR:

Accept my warmest acknowledgments for your very obliging favor of 23rd ultimo, and your kind congratulations upon my return with my family to our beloved country. As the recollection of the friendship which I had the happiness of forming with you at an interesting and critical period of my life had been a frequent source of gratification to my mind during my long absence, so the hopes of a renewal of that confidence and intimacy which formerly subsisted between us has been among the most pleasing anticipations of the prospect now before me.

I have given the President and Mr. Rush reason to expect me at Washington in three weeks from this day, and I hope to be punctual in the performance of that promise. You had justly concluded that I could make no definite arrangement concerning the vacancies in the Department with which I am to be connected until my regular introduction to it. Your friend's [1] pretensions shall be candidly estimated with

[1] This proved to be Alexander Anderson, son of Joseph Anderson. Adams, *Memoirs*, December 6, 1817.

those of other applicants, already numerous, and whatever the result may be I trust you will not doubt the weight of your recommendation as well upon my opinions as upon my inclinations.

I am with respect, etc.

TO FRANCIS CALLEY GRAY

Quincy, 5 September, 1817.

Dear Sir:

I am duly sensible to the delicacy of sentiment and generosity of spirit which have induced you to consider yourself as my debtor, and to offer me the enclosed bills, which I must, however, explicitly decline accepting.

When you accompanied me to Russia it was with the knowledge and consent of the government of the United States in the capacity of my private secretary. As you was at the same time a student at law, the gentlemen at the Suffolk bar, of which I was and am yet a member, very properly allowed you the time during which you was with me as a part of the period of study required by their rules previous to their recommendation for admission to practice. Had I been keeping an office and in professional practice at the time, I should have received from you the usual fee. But as you performed for me the services of a private secretary without compensation, and living at your own expense, I consider those services as an equivalent for any benefit you may have derived from my advice in the pursuit of your law studies, and pray you to set them down as a balance to any sums which your liberality may think me entitled to on that account.

While you actually resided in my family at St. Petersburg

I received from you the amount of about fifty dollars a month as repayment of the additional expense which we estimated your board and lodging might occasion. When in the summer of 1811 I took a house in the country, I offered you an apartment in it on the same terms; but as you eventually concluded to keep your lodgings in the city, and only came out occasionally to dinner or to pass a night, the expense which it was intended should be repaid was in fact not incurred, and I have no pretension to any demand upon you for that time.

I cannot conclude without assuring you of the great satisfaction which I experience from the reports which have come to me of the fair and honorable reputation which you have established and sustain, and of the warm and cordial interest in your welfare which I shall never cease to take. Being with sincere and faithful attachment, etc.[1]

TO ABIGAIL ADAMS

WASHINGTON, 21 September, 1817.

MY BELOVED MOTHER:

An alternation of six stages and six steam boats finally landed us here yesterday afternoon, being the very day upon which I had promised to be here. The President had arrived here on Wednesday[2] and occupies the official mansion, where I had an interview with him last evening. But the walls are fresh plastered, and the wainscoting is new painted, and they render it so insalubrious for present residence, that the President proposes immediately to

---

[1] On Gray's career see *Mass. Hist. Soc. Proceedings*, XLVII. 529.

[2] He had just returned from a tour of four months in the east and west. See Waldo, *Tour of Monroe*, 1817.

leave it again and to pass some time at his estate in Virginia.

To-morrow I expect to enter upon the arduous duties of my office.[1] Mr. Rush has obligingly offered to remain here a short time longer, until I can be properly launched upon the ocean of business before me. His family are at Annapolis where his lady has just been confined.

We found our family connections here all well, excepting Mrs. W. S. Smith, who was in the midst of the affliction of having lost her second child.

The weather is so intensely warm that I have not yet been out of the house this day. We are lodging at the house of my wife's sisters, Mrs. Frye. We have a house engaged for us, into which we expect to enter on or before the first of October.

Dearest mother, my spirits will often want the cordial refreshment of a letter from you and from my dear father. Let me not thirst for them in vain. How long or how effectually I shall be able to discharge the duties of my trust is in higher hands than mine. Instead of your praises, let me have your prayers.

My wife is well and joins me in assurances of duty and affection.[2]

---

[1] It was by a circular letter of September 24 that his entrance upon the discharge of the duties of the office of Secretary of State was officially notified to foreign ministers.

[2] September 20 Bagot had an interview with the President and gave "expressions of the satisfaction which his Royal Highness [the Prince Regent] had derived from the conciliatory conduct of Mr. Adams during the period of his mission in England, and of the constant desire of his Royal Highness the Prince Regent to preserve and strengthen those friendly relations between the two countries which had been so auspiciously commenced. The President in a short reply, which he delivered in a tone of some earnestness, expressed his satisfaction at learning that Mr. Adams had done so much justice to the friendly sentiments which actuated the American government, and he enjoined me to convey to his Royal Highness

TO HYDE DE NEUVILLE [1]

WASHINGTON, 24 September, 1817.

SIR:

I have been directed by the President of the United States to acknowledge the receipt of your written communication to the Department of State of the 12th instant, accompanied with copies of certain documents indicating the existence in America of an association organized under the name of a Napoleonian confederation; [2] from which documents you conceive it results that a very considerable levy of men is on the eve of taking place in some of the western states or territories of the Union, for objects prohibited by the laws of the United States and hostile to France.

From the nature of the institutions and laws of this country you will be aware that the repressive powers of the government, in their application to the freedom of individuals, are limited to cases of actual transgression, and do not extend to projects which, however exceptionable in their character, have not been matured at least into an attempt or a commencement of execution. The vigilance of the government will, however, be peculiarly directed to every object of information disclosing designs illegal in their character, or tending to disturb the public tranquillity by menacing the peace of friendly nations. In this view your communication has not failed to meet the special atten-

the Prince Regent the assurance, that so long as he continued to hold his present situation, he should make it his constant endeavor to cherish and promote them." *Bagot to Castlereagh,* October 6, 1817. Ms.

[1] The French Minister.

[2] Concerning a project for invading Mexico from the United States, and declaring Joseph Bonaparte king of Spain and the Indies. Neuville permitted Bagot to take copies of these papers.

tion of the President, and I am directed, in answering it, to repeat the assurances which you have received personally from him, that every measure within the competency of the government, and compatible with the rights of individuals, shall be adopted, that may be necessary to maintain or to vindicate the honor of the laws, and to manifest the friendliness of its disposition towards your government. Should any further information reach you, tending to establish the fact of illegal combinations, whether of citizens of the United States or of strangers amenable to their laws, to invade the territories bordering upon those of the United States, or for any other purpose forbidden by the laws of this Union, you are invited to a free communication of it to this Department, and assured that it will be received with all the interest which its importance will inspire, and acted upon with an earnest desire of evincing the determination of this government to cause the laws to be inviolably respected, and at the same time to fulfil the good offices of a disposition sincerely friendly towards France.

Be pleased to accept the assurances, etc.

TO THE PRESIDENT

[JAMES MONROE]

WASHINGTON, 25 September, 1817.

SIR:

. . . . . .

I should have been desirous of submitting in like manner the answer to Mr. de Neuville, particularly as it refers to assurances which he received personally from you. But as he had been earnest in the request of an immediate answer to be transmitted to his government, I acquiesced in the opinion of Mr. Rush, to whom the paper was communicated, and who thought advisable that it should be sent immediately.

After it was prepared, I had occasion to see Mr. de Neuville and had some conversation with him on the subject;[1] in which he expressed the wish for a publication of his letter to the Department, of the documents by which it was accompanied, and of the answer he should receive from me; and observed that no other measure on the part of this government would be desired by him, as he supposed that alone would be sufficient to break up the whole project. At the same time he intimated that his government might perhaps demand the arrest of Joseph Bonaparte, and the seizure of his papers. I understood from Mr. Rush, who was present at this conversation, that the idea of publishing the papers had been thrown out at the audience you had given to the minister, and that it had obtained your assent. To this, the draft of the answer to the Spanish minister refers, and although Mr. de Neuville had admitted that the arrest of Joseph Bonaparte and the seizure of his papers would be inconsistent with the spirit of our institutions (which, he added, he was far from disapproving), yet, as he did suggest that such a demand might be made, and as there is in the Spanish minister's letter, a sort of precursory hint to the same effect, it seemed to me a suitable occasion for meeting such intimations at the threshold, and for giving to the governments of those gentlemen, as well as to themselves, a warning, that as arbitrary seizures must not be expected from this government, it will be, to say the least, useless to require them. . . .[2]

[1] Adams, *Memoirs*, September 26, 1817.
[2] "The reply to the Minister of France appears to be sound in principle and

TO JOHN SPEAR SMITH

WASHINGTON, 26 September, 1817.

DEAR SIR:

Your very obliging and friendly letter of the 24th instant came to hand yesterday. Mrs. Adams and myself regretted much being deprived of the pleasure of meeting you at Baltimore. But we had had the happiness of seeing your father at Philadelphia the day before, and having learnt from him that you were residing a mile or two out of town, my engagements to be here permitting us to pass only the night at Baltimore, we were obliged to postpone the hope of seeing you, and now rejoice that we have that prospect so soon as the time promised us in your letter. We both pray you to accept and to make acceptable to your lady our warmest thanks for your kind invitation to your house, of which we hope to have at some future day the opportunity to avail ourselves.

It gave me pleasure to be informed by your father that you had the immediate prospect of becoming a legislator, and it is still more gratifying to find that you are not to have a competitor in Mr. Breckinridge; but if you enter upon that career, the first lesson you must learn is that to suffer pinching without wincing.

---

guarded in its terms. There is a feeling in this country favorable to revolutionary men in France, proceeding from the interest which was taken in the success of the revolution, which although the cause has long ceased, still has influence with many. It is well not to excite this feeling, and I think that your reply will avoid it. The publication will, however, attract attention, and the only question likely to be made is, whether a charge, which is supported by no movement of any kind in the country, and presumably so unfounded merited such notice. The soundness of the principle on which we rest cannot fail to sustain the measure with so enlightened and virtuous a people as our fellow citizens are; and in Europe it will, I think, do us good." *Monroe to Adams*, September [29], 1817. Ms.

The son of Alnomack must never complain.

There are roses as well as thorns in the paths of public life, and if you are gifted with a tolerable portion of good conscience and of self-confidence, the best defense against abuse is to take it as a testimony of merit. So I advise you to consider every slander circulated to defame you as a certificate of past and a summons to future good conduct; and if the batteries of your political enemies annoy you, only resolve to take them and melt them down into a triumphant column to your country's glory and your own.

I am, etc.

TO WILLIAM CRANCH

WASHINGTON, 26 September, 1817.

DEAR SIR:

I cannot forbear to offer you my thanks for your kind and affectionate letter of the day before yesterday, and to assure you how much I feel myself affected by the expression in it of that sentiment of which, as you remark, even friendship is inadequate to convey the idea.

Next to brothers, as we are by the ties of blood, brothers as we were by the habits and intimacies of childhood and of youth, we have passed the period of active manhood for the most part remote from each other, and deprived in a great measure of the comforts of each other's society. But that sentiment which was among the first that took root in my heart has never been eradicated from it, and during the long and repeated absences from our country which have been my portion in life, I have never ceased to feel the warmest interest in your welfare and that of your family, nor to derive heartfelt satisfaction from the knowledge that you also was devoting your life to the public service, and discharging duties of the highest order with honor and reputation of the highest degree.

Among the enjoyments which I have anticipated as to result from the new station to which I am called, was that of meeting you again, not in a ceremonious visit, which I trust can never happen between you and me, but as we met when classmates at college, as we met at the cottages and on the rocks of Braintree and Weymouth, as we met at the north end in Boston before memory could draw a lasting trace upon either of our minds. Come then and see me entirely at your convenience, not to pay your respects but to take once more by the hand one who has never ceased to bear you in his heart.

TO THE PRESIDENT

[James Monroe]

Washington, 27 September, [1817].

Sir:

I have the honor of enclosing a copy of a letter received the evening before last from the French Minister, in reply to that which I had addressed to him the preceding day. Yesterday morning I received a note from him, stating that he found himself obliged to leave the city sooner than he had expected, and requesting to see me before his departure. I received him immediately, and he recurred again to the idea of seizing upon the person and papers of the writer of the papers communicated by him,[1] or if that was

[1] Lakanal, a member of the convention who came to the United States early in 1817, and was suspected by the French Minister of being an agent of Joseph Bona-

impracticable, at least he urged the immediate publication of the documents, with an introductory commentary descanting upon the wickedness and the absurdity of the conspiracy. He remarked upon the turn of expression in my letter to him, as importing that *he conceived* the levies of men, etc., were about to take place, and said that he had the most perfect certainty of it—that they were recruiting the men; that they were marching; *that he had men of his own among them*, and was perfectly informed of their movements. That he knew individual American citizens who were engaged in the plot, but could not make known who they were; and that after the verification of the writing by the comparison of hands, the existence of the conspiracy and of its real motives could be no subject of question. He also much insisted upon the opinion that this was a subject much more interesting to the government of the United States than to that of France. I observed that the fact of the levy of men and of its motives had been mentioned as his allegation and not as a positive fact, because this government could not hold itself pledged to the reality of the facts, or to the authenticity of the papers. That even admitting the papers to contain, if authentic, evidence of criminal actions, this government had no evidence of their authenticity, but comparison of handwriting, which in the judicial tribunals upon criminal prosecution would not be admissible. That the individual whose signature appeared to the papers might in the event of their publication deny publicly that he had written them, and perhaps even prosecute the

parte. "Le plan est à peu près celui du colonel Burr; c'est l'insurrection de l'Ouest ayant pour but caché de faire de Joseph un roi du Mexique." Hyde de Neuville, *Mémoires et Souvenirs*, II. 319. The fear of a "Confédération Napoléonienne" had been expressed to Monroe by Hyde de Neuville in January, 1817, and remained with him through the year. His notes to Adams of September and the Secretary's "evasive reply" are given *Ib.*, 322.

printer of them for a libel; in which case the government could not escape the censure of having assumed and published as authentic, papers deeply affecting the character of an individual, without possessing evidence which could legally establish their authenticity. He then said that if this was a consideration of weight to this government, it ought to be still more so to him. That of his own authority he could not publish these papers consistently with the respect due from him to the government. That he had no other evidence to prove the writing of the individual than the comparison of hands, and that he could not compromit the dignity of his own government by entering into a controversy with that individual in the public prints. He asked me how this government would under these circumstances make the publication of the papers. I told him that my opinion was that they might be published with an introductory notice as papers, copies of which had been transmitted to the government by him. That although by the comparison of the handwriting they had every appearance of authenticity, the projects which they disclosed were at once so wicked and so ridiculous that the hope might yet be entertained that they were spurious. He said he should be satisfied with this; but with the further caution and notice that the original papers, together with other indisputable writings by the same person, should be deposited in the hands of some public officer, open to the inspection of anyone disposed to contest or to verify their authenticity. It was therefore agreed between us that the publication should be suspended until I can receive your further directions concerning it.[1] This delay was proposed and

---

[1] The introductory notice, conformably to the directions of the President, read as follows:

"The following documents cannot fail to attract the public attention. They

even urged by him; for upon my observing that I foresaw no inconvenience in it, except that his letters appeared to apprehend the explosion to be so near at hand that, unless the publication should be immediate, it might come too late to answer its purpose of breaking up the whole conspiracy, he replied, that there was yet time; that he had, *by his frigates* and by other measures that he had taken, given them the alarm and put a check upon their progress. In the meantime, I think it necessary to suggest to you that indications are coming in from various quarters that projects are in agitation among some of the emigrants from Europe to which it will be necessary for the government to put a stop as soon as possible.

I had also an interview yesterday with Mr. Bagot at his request. He referred to several communications from him to the department to which he was expecting definite an-

consist of a letter from the French Minister to the Secretary of State, and of his answer; with the translation of copies transmitted by M. de Neuville with his letter, of several very extraordinary papers. Of their authenticity we express no opinion; the originals, apparently in the handwriting of the individual whose name is subscribed to the principal of them, are in the possession of the French Minister, and will be deposited in the hands of [blank] for the inspection of any person who may be desirous of verifying them. The projects which they disclose are of a nature to excite in no common degree the merriment as well as the indignation of our readers. That foreigners, scarcely landed upon our shores, should imagine the possibility of enlisting large numbers of the hardy republicans of our western states and territories in the ultra-Quixotism of invading a territory bordering upon their country for the purpose of proclaiming a phantom king of Spain and the Indies, is a perversity of delirium, the turpitude of which is almost lost in its absurdity. If it be true that attempts are making to engage citizens of these states in projects like that which appears to be the ostensible object held out as the purpose of this confederacy, it will be sufficient to warn them that the ostensible object itself is no less contrary to the laws than the supposed real object is to all their habits and feelings. Nor may it be unseasonable to remind the foreigners who are enjoying the hospitality which our country ever delights to extend to the unfortunate, that the least return which that country has a right to expect from them, is an inviolable respect for her laws."

swers. One of them related to a question upon the construction to be given to the term *country*, in the first section of the navigation act passed at the last session of Congress and to go into operation the first of next month. Mr. Crawford had already mentioned the question to me and asked my opinion of it, which coincided with his own, that the expression included the colonies. Mr. Bagot was anxious to receive the answer on this point in time for making up his dispatches to go by the packet. He spoke also of the proposal to be made respecting the fisheries, which I assured him should be communicated to him as soon as possible after your return. He likewise alluded to the project of four additional articles for the commercial convention; upon which I told him my apprehension was that they could not be matured into anything that would meet the concurrence of the two governments. There were some other objects of minor importance upon which he touched, but with which it is not necessary to trouble you at present.

The commission of governor of the Alabama territory has been made out and forwarded to Mr. Bibb;[1] and the instructions for Mr. Prevost have been prepared from minutes drawn up by Mr. Rush.

I have the honor, etc.

[1] William Wyatt Bibb, governor of Alabama Territory to November, 1819, and of the state of Alabama, to July, 1820, dying in office.

TO ALEXANDER HILL EVERETT

WASHINGTON, 28 September, 1817.

DEAR SIR:

During the few days that I passed at Boston I called several times both at your house and at your office for the purpose of having some conversations with you, as well upon the subjects referred to in your letter of the 23rd instant, which I received yesterday, as upon some others. My last visits were on the day before I left Boston to come here, when I found at your office door a notice that you were out of town, and were informed at your home that you and your lady were gone upon an excursion to Portsmouth. I seriously regretted the circumstance, as I was desirous of communicating with you more fully and more confidentially than either my time or some other considerations will admit of in writing. This, however, is now the only remaining expedient of intercourse between us, and I take the hour before the dawn of the day of rest for the purpose.

I arrived here on Saturday the 20th instant and saw the President the same evening. He was obliged to leave the city again on Monday morning for his seat in Virginia, and the only conversation that I had with him was upon objects concerning which he had instructions to leave with me. Upon his return I will not fail to mention your letter to him, and ascertain if he received it. . . .

With regard to your return to the diplomatic career, I consider the prospect of your services to the public in that line as so favorable that I shall not hesitate to recommend you to the President for employment, if any situation should present itself in the class of those which would be acceptable to you.

From the correspondence of Mr. Eustis it appears to be his intention to return next spring to the United States, unless in the meantime a Minister of rank corresponding to his should be appointed by the king of the Netherlands to reside here. Should he return, a chargé d'affaires will, I presume, be appointed to reside at that court, and as the President in anticipation of such an event had already offered you the situation, I suppose, and so far as I may expect to be consulted in the selection, intends that it shall be offered to you again. I am not inclined without a clear and obvious propriety to multiply the diplomatic agents of the United States in Europe, and probably the next Congress will be as little disposed as I am to aggravate unnecessarily the public expenses in that department. But before I left England I was informed that the king of Prussia had appointed a chargé d'affaires to the United States, and I was led to expect that he would before now have arrived in this country. Should such an event take place the appointment of a person in the same character may be judged advisable, and may perhaps meet the sanction of Congress. In that case, or in any other that may occur of a similar nature in which I can with propriety present your name to the President, you may be assured I shall neither be backward nor cold in recommending you.

I have read all the numbers upon the present state of England that have been published since I landed at New York, and am sure I shall take great pleasure in reading the remainder.[1] That they have been received by the public with more attention than they deserve is by no means my opinion. That they should have been ascribed to me would

---

[1] The numbers appeared in the *Independent Chronicle and Boston Patriot*, beginning June, 1817. Much revised and extended they were published in a book entitled *Europe*, Boston, 1822.

have been one of the highest compliments that could have been paid me, if I could have recognized as mine many of their sentiments. But the argument against the theory of the checks and balances would scarcely have been decent from my pen, if I had ever been convinced of its correctness, which I am not. It would have been inconsistent too with the opinions which I have always avowed, and particularly with a series of papers which in the year 1795 I published in the *Boston Centinel* under the signature of Publicola. They encountered instead of flattering the prevailing prejudices of the time, and were very unpopular. They are now and have been long since forgotten by the public; but I am not conscious of having changed any important opinion contained in them. Their view of the British constitution is altogether different from yours, and although I do ample justice to the ingenuity of your argument against Montesquieu, I have not been convinced by it. I cannot compress into this short letter an argument that would exhaust a volume, and probably leave you on your side "of your own opinion still"; but to deal with you in perfect candor, your view of the British constitution, of its operation, and I might perhaps add of the present state of England, is not impartial. If you and Walsh were painters and had to take the portrait of a one-eyed man, you would both paint him in profile, but your picture would show the blind and his the seeing side. He would conceal the loss of the eye, and you would represent the man as blind. You know it is a trite maxim in natural philosophy that a mathematical truth is a physical falsehood. The practice of no machine ever corresponds precisely with its theory. What would you say to an Englishman who should aver that the constitutions of the United States are all impostures, and that we have nothing but a government of caucuses? There are engines unknown to our constitutions and laws, but not less operative upon the administration of our governments than what Cobbett calls the borough-mongering faction is upon that of England. As to the general state and condition of the country, I must say that no country or people that I have ever visited present more solid, more numerous or more noble topics for panegyric than England. That she presents at the same time numerous topics for the severest and most indignant reprobation is equally true. Your papers are admirably calculated to eradicate from the minds of our countrymen every prejudice in her favor. To do her entire justice would require another series of essays, an age more upon the search for the forms, and a hand more ready for the delineation of beauty. The eye and the hand are your own, and why should the disposition be wanting? You have a heart not insensible to beauty, physical, moral or intellectual—why should you hide its feelings from itself? You know that the agriculture of England is superior to that of every other country; that the learning, literature, and science equal, if they do not exceed, those of any other nation; that in arms she stands at least upon a level with the first military nations of the age by land, and that she reigns but too triumphant and unrivalled upon the ocean. Is all this the result of despicable or pernicious institutions? If England had no other claim to reverence than that of having founded the colonies which are now your country and mine, her solid and unquestionable glory would transcend all Greek, transcend all Roman fame. France, Spain, Portugal and Holland have founded colonies as well as England—look at them, and look at the United States, and what is the cause of the difference between them? English institutions, principles, and manners. Milton tells us that the very spirits reprobate lose not all their virtue, and has accordingly endowed his fallen angels with virtues of the highest order. He has given the devil his due, and I think you should do the same with England. . . .

TO THE PRESIDENT

[James Monroe]

Washington, 29th September, 1817.

Sir:

In my last letter I had the honor of stating to you that indications from various quarters were coming in, that there were projects on foot among the emigrants from Europe, which I apprehended were of a nature requiring the interposition of this government to prevent their further progress or execution.

Of the enclosed papers one is a copy of a letter which has been confidentially transmitted to me from Boston [1]— the character of the projects alluded to had been obscurely

[1] "I thank you for the confidential extract from the letter. You wished to know my opinion of the *projets* in question. I can now assure you that I disapprove them *de fond en comble*. I entreat you, as your friend, to have no concern with them. I shall be obliged to you for any further information you may be enabled to give me, of the *real* and entire projects, for I have reason to believe that what you disclosed to me was but a small part of them. If there is yet time, and you have any influence over the writer of the letter persuade him to break off entirely from all such adventures." *To Peter Paul Francis de Grand*, September 28, 1817. Ms. To the same correspondent he wrote on November 13, 1817: "I have seen the elder general Lallemand here, and have had the opportunity of observing and admiring his talents. He has given me the strongest and most satisfactory assurances that he will engage in no project of military adventure forbidden by the laws of this country. I am very happy to learn that schemes of that character which had been entertained are abandoned. Lallemand's brother has got into better quarters than he would find in Mexico—or Peru." For his interview with Charles Lallemand, see Adams, *Memoirs*, November 9, 1817.

and partially disclosed to me before I left that place. They were described as a plan for assisting the patriotic party, so called, in Mexico, for reorganizing their military and political system, and for consolidating their struggle for independence into a regular and legitimate form of government. Another is a statement drawn up by Mr. Lee,[1] of information derived from the conversation of several persons connected with these projects who have recently been here.

The papers present the subject under an aspect altogether different from either of those in which it is exhibited by Mr. de Neuville. It is neither to conquer Mexico, nor to proclaim a king of Spain and the Indies; but whatever the purpose may be, it is evidently not warranted by nor compatible with our laws. As Mr. de Neuville avowed to me, that he had some of his own people among the conspirators, and as he also intimated that most if not all the principal exiles were endeavoring to make their peace with the existing government of France, it has occurred to me as a surmise that the writer of the documents furnished by Mr. de Neuville might himself be acting in concert with him, or with his government, unknown to him, and endeavoring to obtain his own pardon, by entrapping or implicating in criminal transactions a more important personage.

After I had prepared upon the minutes furnished me by Mr. Rush the new instructions for Mr. Prevost, a question was started by Mr. Brent, whether it had not been your intention to associate Captain Biddle [2] with that gentleman, in the authority to assert the claim of territorial possession at the mouth of Columbia river. He said that Captain Morris [3] had been formerly appointed to perform

---

[1] William Lee.
[2] James Biddle (1783–1848).
[3] Charles Morris (1784–1856).

a similar service at the same place, and that Captain Biddle might expect when ordered to coöperate in the performance of the act, to appear not merely in a subordinate character, but as sharing the authority by which it should be performed. On consulting Mr. Rush he informed me that the intention to give the joint authority to Captain Biddle had not been expressed by you, but he thought it might be merely because the idea had not occurred to you at the time—adding to the consideration of the precedent referred to by Mr. Brent, that of the association of the naval commanders with the civil officers in the commissions for negotiating with the Barbary powers. Perceiving a propriety in the thing itself, and not being aware of any objection which might induce you to give a different direction, I have ventured to join Captain Biddle in the authority for taking possession, and to make it joint and several to meet the possible contingency that either of them should by any accident be prevented from assisting at the ceremony.

Dispatches have been received, since your departure from this place, from the legations at St. Petersburg, Paris, Madrid and London. Their contents not requiring your immediate orders or attention are reserved with all other objects of similar nature in the business of the department for communication to you upon your return.

I have the honor, etc.

The copy of the letter first mentioned will be sent tomorrow.

TO THE PRESIDENT

[James Monroe]

Washington, 30th September, 1817.

Sir:

The confidential copy of an extract of a letter which I had received from Boston, and which an accident prevented from being transmitted to you yesterday, is herewith enclosed.

Mr. Rush sent me last evening your letter to him respecting Mr. de Neuville's communication. I was very desirous of sending the draft of the answer to his letter for your examination; but as he was obliged to leave the city immediately and urgent to receive the answer before his departure, by the advice of Mr. Rush to whom I communicated the draft, it was sent without waiting for your approbation to the minister. I am happy that the result of it, of his reply, and of the last conversation that I had with him was so far conformable to your intentions that the publication of the documents was suspended, even at his own desire, until your further orders should be taken.

This will of course render necessary an alteration in the answer to the Spanish Minister, of which the draft was sent to you with my first letter. And perhaps another alteration in it will be equally necessary, in regard to the reference to the letter from the department to him of 22 May. By the enclosed dispatches from Mr. Erving you will perceive that Don José Pizarro proposes to *discuss* and adjust the terms of a treaty with him, and at the same time to send instructions to Mr. Onis to conclude one here. Although the object of his letters is very obviously procrastination, yet in his last letter he is completely pledged to send Mr. Erving the project for a treaty. That it will be of such a character as Erving's instructions will not authorize him to agree to, is almost equally clear; but the language of Mr. Pizarro's letters is moderate and conciliatory. Count Fernan Nuñez, the Spanish Ambassador in London, who was removed in the same capacity to Paris shortly before I left England, assured me with the most earnest protestations that his government had come to a full and frank determination to adjust all their differences with the United States, *however disagreeable that adjustment might be to some others.* But I suppose that Florida for the boundary line on the Mississippi was the basis of their project, and it would be curious if that should be disagreeable to *others.* I was very happy to learn that upon your arrival home you found your family in good health and with the tender of my respects to your lady, remain, etc.

TO JOHN ADAMS

WASHINGTON, 5th October, 1817.

DEAR SIR:

Yesterday your kind letter of 29 September came to hand. I thank you for your congratulations upon my arrival here. My wife and our family relations at this place are well. I was happy to meet the President here, but had the pleasure of seeing him only once before he departed for his seat in Virginia.

I am breaking in to the business of my office. I find it even now as burdensome as I had expected, and how I shall be able to get through the winter is yet a problem for solution. The *moral* difficulties have not yet begun to present themselves.

George no doubt was as much delighted as you were to find your Fanning,[1] and I hope will derive great instruction and benefit with your assistance from it. Let me entreat you to keep John and Charles strictly to the rule of returning to Boston on Sunday evenings, so that they may lose no school time. Their voyages and travels have thrown them so much in arrear in their classical studies that I am anxiously hoping they will now endeavor to retrieve the time lost.

Your political calm will not last long. Even now two of the principal states in the Union, Pennsylvania and Kentucky, are in violent fermentation upon electioneering questions. The fever as yet is confined to them, but will be very likely to spread before long throughout the Union. There are several questions relating to our foreign policy in embryo which will be likely to produce heats and dissensions, and you well know that in our country the passions, always at work, will never suffer opinions for any length of time to harmonize. . . .

Ever faithfully yours.

7 October. I have received your letter of 30 September.

TO ANDRÉ DE DASCHKOFF

DEPARTMENT OF STATE, [6] October, 1817.

The undersigned Secretary of State has had the honor of, and has submitted to the President, the note of his Imperial Majesty the Emperor of Russia's Envoy Extraordinary and Minister Plenipotentiary, announcing that he has been

[1] Described by John Adams as "my old friend of sixty-five years." Probably some book.

officially notified by his court that the relations of the Imperial government with Mr. Harris, the representative of the United States near the Emperor, have been reëstablished as heretofore, and that the conduct of his Majesty's Minister here in his relations with the government of the United States must henceforth be regulated accordingly.

The undersigned is directed by the President in answer to this communication to assure Mr. Daschkoff that it has been received by him with a satisfaction proportioned to the solicitude which has been invariably felt by this government to cherish and cultivate the most friendly relations with that of his Imperial Majesty.

The undersigned prays the Minister of his Imperial Majesty to accept his congratulations upon this happy restoration of that entire harmony and good understanding between the two governments, to which it will ever be as it ever has been among his most earnest wishes to cultivate and to maintain which he is happy to rely with confidence upon the warm and effectual coöperation of Mr. Daschköff.[1]

[1] The last phrase was omitted at the suggestion of the President, who did not wish Daschkoff to receive a commendation which might advance his personal interests with his own government. Monroe was Secretary of State when Daschkoff presented a protest against the arrest of the Russian Consul General in Philadelphia. He believed that Daschkoff wished to use the incident against the United States and transferred all discussion and explanation to St. Petersburg. "The opinion entertained of Mr. D.'s views was confirmed by the first letter which was received from Mr. Harris on that subject. From that moment it was perceived that as whatever weight Mr. D. might possess with his government would be turned against the U. S., it would be improper to allow him to derive any from a supposed good understanding between him and our government. He had been very hostile to us through the war with England, and rendered us in many ways essential injury. Mr. Harris was therefore, instructed to place his conduct here, and the President's view of it, in a just light before his government, which he accordingly did, and in my letter to Count Nesselrode I stated facts which made it apparent that Mr. D. did not possess the confidence of the President." *Monroe to Adams*, October 11, 1817. Ms.

He prays Mr. Daschkoff to accept the assurance of his high consideration.

TO JOHN ADAMS SMITH

WASHINGTON, 8 October, 1817.

DEAR SIR:

. . . .

From the latter end of May until the middle of September the President was absent from this place on a tour through the eastern and part of the western states. He was everywhere received with the strongest demonstrations of respect, and met with the most assiduous attentions from that part of the country which has been conspicuous for the violence of its opposition to the administration of his immediate predecessor. Party spirit has indeed subsided throughout the union to a degree that I should have thought scarcely possible. It re-appears indeed in the states where elections are depending, but with a virulence so much diminished that its effects are imperceptible beyond the limits of those states. On my arrival at Philadelphia I was surprised to find that Pennsylvania was in a state of extreme agitation upon the question whether General Hiester or Mr. Findlay should be the governor;[1] while at New York I don't believe there was one person in ten who knew who the candidates to be governor of Pennsylvania were. In Connecticut the federal party have had a complete downfall; while at New York there has been a coalition of all parties in favor of Mr. Clinton so entire that the newspapers' combatants have nothing upon which they can make a bustle and call hard

[1] The question was settled in favor of William Findlay, but Joseph Hiester became governor in 1820.

names, but the projected great canal. The political calm will probably not be of long duration; individual ambition must have some great and durable question of public interest, upon which to exercise its faculties which are essentially controversial. The great European question of the last twenty-five years has been solved, at least for the present; but another cannot fail to offer itself. In the meantime the general prosperity of our country, and the contentment which pervades every part of it, are delightful to the patriotic feelings of an American, and most especially of an American arriving from Europe. After his return from his long tour the President remained only five days in this city; he then went to pass five or six weeks at his seat in Virginia. As I arrived here on Saturday evening and he departed on Monday morning, I saw him only once. He is expected here about the end of this month.

You know that Mr. Rush has had the superintendence of the Department of State from the commencement of the present administration until my arrival. You have doubtless also been informed of his appointment as envoy extraordinary and minister plenipotentiary to Great Britain. He is to take passage with his family in the *Franklin* and may be expected to embark about the middle of next month. You are to continue in the office of Secretary of Legation under him, and according to the established usage you will be authorized to charge in your accounts an outfit of $4,500 as chargé d'affaires, and a salary at the rate of $4,500 a year from the day of my departure from London until that of Mr. Rush's arrival there. He has expressed himself to me with much satisfaction at the punctuality and frequency of your communications to the department, and as I know that he will find you a faithful, industrious and discreet assistant, so I am persuaded you will meet in him a courteous and pleasing companion, and a liberal minded and friendly principal.

. . . .

And believe me, etc.

TO THE PRESIDENT

[JAMES MONROE]

WASHINGTON, 8 October, 1817.

SIR:

. . . .

The question by what right Mr. de Neuville addressed the government of the United States on the supposed Napoleonian confederacy, occurred to me on the first perusal of the papers, and I particularly stated it to Mr. Rush. On further reflection there appeared to me to be reason sufficient to warrant his procedure in that respect.[1] His letter to the department indicates that he was aware that question might arise—it professes to proceed from a motive of friendship to this government itself; as considering the United States

---

[1] The President had suggested the doubt. "A question will probably be made, what had he [de Neuville] to do with the business? The establishment of a monarchy in a Spanish province is a Spanish (it may be said) and not a French concern. The consideration that the agents are French, the association said to be Napoleon, and that the acquisition of power by these emigrants, with Joseph Bonaparte at their head, might prove in its immediate consequences of great importance to France, will, I think, justify the notice of the representations of the minister of France; but independent of these and such like considerations, the movement and projects complained of are of deep interest to the United States, and the notice of them, by whomsoever communicated, seems on that account alone, to be proper. I mention these circumstances as having had their weight in what had passed in the affair before your arrival, and which I do not recollect to have adverted to, when we were together." *Monroe to Adams*, October 6, 1817.

more deeply interested in arresting the progress of the conspiracy than France. It refers to the character of the alleged conspirators as subjects of France; in a state of exile indeed, but not irrevocably banished from their country. It alludes to the general interest felt by all the European allies to suppress every political enterprise connected with the name of Napoleon. And besides all this, I think the representative of a Bourbon sovereign may fairly claim to be indulged in an extraordinary degree of solicitude with regard to any project in which the Bonaparte family are concerned.

My own principal hesitation with respect to the publication was in its probable bearing upon the situation and personal condition of Joseph Bonaparte. I see nothing in the papers, though Mr. de Neuville thinks he does, that tends to prove *his* being accessary to any part of the project; and it seems hardly equitable that *he* should be made responsible before the public for any schemes by which madmen or desperadoes use his name without his knowledge or consent. Add to which that I could not altogether avoid the suspicion that the whole of this affair of the Napoleon confederacy has been somehow or other gotten up for that purpose; or to countenance the allied governments in their arbitrary detention of Lucien by refusing him passports to come to this country.[1] I am unwilling to extend this suspicion to Mr. de Neuville himself; but if the papers purporting to be signed by Lakanal are genuine, the question still remains whose cause they were intended to serve, and by what *real* motive they were dictated? Upon the whole, however, the publication may eventually elucidate the facts, whatever they may be.

I am, etc.

[1] *Mass. Hist. Soc. Proceedings*, XLVII. 301.

TO THE PRESIDENT

[JAMES MONROE]

WASHINGTON, 9 October, 1817.

SIR:
Of the enclosed letters, one is from Mr. Johnston, who I believe is already known to you as one of the candidates for the office of consul at Amsterdam; an appointment which he with many others prefers to one without a salary, like that of Calais, to which I am informed he has been appointed. The others are the recommendations of and letters from G. Hughes, also of Baltimore, soliciting the appointment of marshal for the district of Maryland.

I should have informed you that upon assuming the duties of my office I appointed Mr. Daniel Brent chief clerk of the Department. There remained then two vacancies of the usual clerkships; that which had been held by Mr. Pleasanton [1] at a salary of 1,500 dollars, and that which had been vacated by Mr. Brent [2] at 1,350.[3] Upon a suggestion that the former of these would be acceptable to the elder of your brothers,[4] and on the presumption that he was in all respects suitably qualified for the office, I held it in reserve for him until it could be ascertained from you whether the appointment would be agreeable to him and satisfactory to you. Mr. Rush informed me that he would write to you on the subject, but I understood him the day before he left the city that he had not then received your answer. The

---

[1] Stephen Pleasanton.
[2] Daniel Brent.
[3] Adams, *Memoirs*, September 22 and 23, 1817.
[4] Joseph Jones Monroe.

other vacancy I offered to Mr. John Bailey of Massachusetts, a person unknown to me, but who applied to me for the office of chief clerk, and was most earnestly recommended by General Dearborn, Judge Story, and many other characters of the highest respectability. He has been several years a tutor at the Providence University, and is now a member of the Massachusetts legislature. In his answer to my letter he acquiesces in the reasons which I had alleged to him for appointing Mr. Brent to the office of chief clerk, and accepts the place offered him, though with some hesitation at the tender of a third place, instead of the first for which he had applied. If the second should be occupied by your brother, I presume Mr. Bailey will be fully reconciled to the propriety of the appointment, as he is to that of Mr. Brent. Should the place which was held by Mr. Pleasanton not be suitable to the views of your brother, I shall immediately assign it to Mr. Bailey, and select from the numerous other candidates a person for the office now reserved for him.

The enclosed letter from Princeton, Indiana, which I must request you after perusal to have the goodness to return to me, is from Mr. Morris Birkbeck, and it covered copy of an application from him to you dated 9 of August last, which I conclude you must before this have received. Mr. Birkbeck was well known as one of the most intelligent and respectable farmers in England and, as the author of a tour through France in the year 1814, has been distinguished in the literary world.[1] He has had an independent fortune, but emigrated with a part of his family to this country last spring, and his statement is perfectly correct, that there are numbers of persons in England of the same condition with himself, some with and others without property, who are anx-

[1] He also printed in 1818, *Notes on a Journey in America*, and *Letters from Illinois*.

iously waiting for the result of his undertaking to follow his example and join the settlement that he shall make. I consider him as a valuable acquisition to this country, and believe it will be extensively useful to the public if facilities such as those for which he applies can be afforded to him by the government.

I am, etc.

TO THOMAS JEFFERSON

WASHINGTON, 11 October, 1817.

SIR:

I received a few days since from my father the enclosed pamphlet, with directions, after availing myself of the opportunity of perusing it, to return it to you to whose kindness he was indebted for the loan of it.

I have found in it no material fact with which I had not been before acquainted, unless it be the authentication by his own narrative of the author's treachery to his master, and of that time-serving obsequiousness to the Bourbons, which his morality as well as his religion has ever found him ready to bestow upon the *powers that be.*

The Abbé de Pradt makes a conspicuous figure in the Dictionnaire des *Girouettes,* a work in which a multitude of the characters which have made themselves notorious at the various stages of the French revolution by the versatility of their principles and talents, are displayed in all the colors of the iris with which they have decorated themselves. Napoleon, who had formed a just estimate of his character, employed him in negotiations where his ecclesiastical profession would contribute, together with the vivacity of his wit, the suppleness of his address, and the unprincipled looseness of his morals, to ensure success and to invest him with an imposing dignity in the eyes of the pious Catholics with whom he employed him to treat, had made him archbishop of Mechlin. So long as Napoleon was the spoilt child of victory, his archbishop was ready for all his work, whether at Bayonne, at Dresden, or at Warsaw. Talleyrand, the ex-bishop, might have scruples when Napoleon was at the summit of his fortune; but de Pradt, the archbishop, had none till the hero was so far down in his descent as to lead the prelate's sagacity to the conclusion that he was never to rise again. He saw that the counter revolution would remove him from the archiepiscopal see, and it behoved him by an early prostration to the Bourbons to assume the appearance and claim the merit of having anticipated their good fortune by his devotion. He took care, therefore, to be among the foremost to bow the knee to them upon their reappearance, and now affects to have been the very fly upon the wheel at the restoration. They have known, however, how to appreciate him at his real worth, and have left him to make his future way in the world as a political pamphleteer. He writes for the booksellers and has had the sagacity to perceive the most profitable topic upon which he can publish. Besides this pamphlet, and another upon the affair at Bayonne, and a third upon his own embassy to Warsaw, he has been vehemently suspected of being the author of the manuscript from St. Helena, a book professing to be from Napoleon himself, but now generally considered as a forgery. It is possible that this suspicion may be not well founded; but its mere existence shows the equivocal character of the Abbé's reputation. He says it was at his instance that the Emperor Alexander in his declaration for himself and his allies upon entering Paris, after announcing that he would never again treat with

Napoleon, added, "nor with any of his family." This was doubtless an ingenious stroke of address in the archbishop to ingratiate himself with the Bourbons; but it was superfluous and worse than useless as part of the declaration of the allies, for they would never the more have treated with Napoleon's family or any part of it had that passage been omitted; and considering that the Empress Maria Louisa's father, who had made her a member of Napoleon's family, was a party to the declaration, it would have been more decent to have spared her the insult and humiliation which it must necessarily cast upon her.

But enough of the Abbé de Pradt, whom I ought in justice to thank for the opportunity now offered me of recalling myself to your recollection, and of assuring you of the respect and veneration which I entertain for your character. I have besides a selfish motive, though connected with the public service, for addressing you at this time. The Senate of the United States have thought proper to assign to the Secretary of State the same task which the House of Representatives in the year 1790 required of you, and which was then so faithfully and ably performed—a report upon weights and measures. The resolution of the Senate is indeed more extensive than that upon which your report was formed, as it requires an account of what has been done by foreign nations for establishing uniformity in weights and measures; and a statement of the regulations and standards as established in the several states of this union, together with such propositions as *may be proper to be adopted* in the United States.

This last of course is merely matter of individual opinion, and I find in your report an alternative of two plans; one, importing great, and the other smaller deviations from the existing state of things presented to the consideration of the house for *their own* determination, an example which I shall certainly deem it my duty to follow.

The *great* deviation which I have it in contemplation to propose is an implicit adoption of the new French meteorological system as already established in France. My motives for taking it as it stands are: 1. Because it presents not only the best and most perfect system that ever has been attempted to be carried into execution, but one in itself so good that probably the subject is not susceptible of any *material* improvement upon it, and certainly no system constructed upon other principles could be made preferable to it. 2. Because the work is already done—done at immense expense and by the labors of many of the most ingenious and profoundest men of the age. 3. Because the adoption of it would extend the principle of *uniformity* to the intercourse between different nations, and ultimately might lead to the adoption of it by all the commercial nations. We have now only the weights and measures of England with all their varieties and confusions. We should then have a system not only uniform in itself, but uniform with that of France. The men who understand the most of the subject in England, strongly incline to the adoption of the French system. The late Lord Stanhope was particularly known to favor it. Should we set them the example, they would probably fall in with it perhaps at no distant day. Yet when I look at the other side of the question, and observe the obstacles and resistances of every kind which stand in the way and make the practicability of so great a change questionable, I shall have some hesitation even in disclosing the opinion that I entertain. I shall feel myself particularly obligated to you if your leisure and convenience will permit to be favored with your ideas on the subject and with the loan of any work or treatise upon meteorology which you may possess. I have made some unsuccessful search for the reports of the committees of the House of Commons in 1758 and 1759, and for the report of Mechain and Delambre on their measurement of the arc of the meridian between Dunkirk and Barcelona. I have as yet been unable to procure them either in England or France. I have found in the library which was yours a valuable collection of tracts on the general subject which I have no doubt will prove useful to me.

Apologizing for the length of this letter I have only to conclude with assurances of my perfect respect.

TO ALEXANDER HILL EVERETT

WASHINGTON, 15 October, 1817.

DEAR SIR:

The pressure upon my time will not permit me to reply to your letter of the 7th instant at the length which its various and important subjects would deserve, and might require. I am expecting the return of the President to this place in the course of a week, and shall soon have occasion to mention you to him. The return of Mr. Eustis next spring is rather more uncertain than it has been; for, as Mr. Gallatin and he have probably negotiated before this a commercial treaty with the Netherlands, the chance of an appointment of a minister from that country to this becomes greater. If a Prussian diplomatic character should come, it will be for Congress to decide whether they will provide for a mission to Berlin, and in the case of that or any other opening that may occur, I shall not be forgetful of you. But as the President usually reserves the appointments abroad for his own selection, and as there may be other candidates to whom he may give the preference, I would recommend it to you to pursue your profession with as much ardor and assiduity as if you had renounced public life altogether.

I send you back the statement of your account with the public for two reasons. First, because it should be presented in regular forms, like merchants' accounts, and signed at the bottom. And secondly, because you have omitted two charges in your own favor, which having been usually allowed of late to other Secretaries of Legation will I presume be by the accounting officers allowed to you. One is a quarter's salary for an outfit, and the other a like sum for the expenses of returning home. These two charges will reduce the balance due from you to 900 dollars, which for your own interest, as well as for the attention indispensably due to the public, I earnestly advise you to pay over immediately, as your account cannot be settled without it. You have likewise omitted the dates and the names of persons from whom you received the money on the credit side. These are essential, because on the public accounts what one person charges as credit, another charges as debt, and the accounts serve as mutual checks and vouchers for each other. You observe that you have an inattentive habit in pecuniary concerns which requires correction. I pray you to set aside entirely the occasion on which you make this remark, and to make the settlement of your account with me an affair of convenience to yourself. But with regard to the public, indulge me with a few remarks dictated by the sincerest and most faithful friendship for you.

For a public officer of the United States abroad punctuality is a quality as essential as integrity, and in the general estimation of the people of this country inseparable from it. Delinquency in regard to public money fixes irretrievable ruin almost always upon a man's fortune, and universally upon his reputation. It never fails to shed a portion of his disgrace upon his friends, and to cast obloquy upon the administration which employed him. I will not attempt to show you its effects upon the *moral* character, but you may perhaps not be unaware of its operation upon the powers of the mind. When I was first in Russia, in 1785, I knew at St. Petersburg a French Ambassador, a man of the most amiable manners and the most generous temper, far from being deficient in understanding, possessing a private fortune of at least sixty thousand dollars a year, and the liberal salary allowed by the Court of France to all their Ministers in foreign countries. He had a Secretary of Legation named Calliard, a man without show or pretension, but of sound sense, worldly prudence, and perfect integrity. The Minister, however, was a man inattentive to pecuniary concerns and the Secretary was not. The Minister had immense wealth, and the Secretary had nothing but his place. In the year 1798 I met Calliard again at Berlin, where he was Minister Plenipotentiary from the Court of France. I inquired of him after his former principal at St. Petersburg. He said he was at Paris "dans la misère," living upon a pension of 200 ducats a year allowed him by the Emperor of Russia, the sovereign *at* whose predecessor's court he had been the representative of France. I asked him if he had lost his fortune by the Revolution. No! Had he squandered it by ruinous vices? No; but he was careless of his pecuniary concerns. I expressed my astonishment that with such an ample fortune he should have been so foolish. "Monsieur! said Caillard, il est impossible qu'un homme qui n'a pas d'ordre dans ses affaires, en ait dans sa tête." My dear Everett, Rochefoucauld and La Bruyère together cannot yield you a sounder and wiser maxim than that. As you value your reputation, your integrity, and your *understanding* correct your habit of inattention to pecuniary concerns.

And if you cannot roughly, inflexibly, permanently correct it, let me advise you for your own account and entreat you for mine, to renounce all thoughts of entering again upon the career of public life. If you must travel the road to ruin, take at least a private path and not the thoroughfare, where your fall will be the blush of your friends, the triumph of your enemies, the scorn and derision of the public, and the bitter disappointment of your country.

The impression that your letters in the *Patriot* on the present state of England have made in the public sentiment of the country, while it discloses to the country and to yourself the extent of your powers, I am rejoiced to see has suggested to you the importance of observing caution and prudence in the promulgation of your opinions. Your doctrine with regard to the balance is, and always has been, very popular in this country—so popular, that the whole nation in their *confederations* and several of the states in their first constitutions totally discarded the balance, and tried the experiment of single assemblies and invisible executives, just as the ladies now wear invisible petticoats. It is strange, but it is certain, that although this experiment failed in every instance of its being tried, although the Union and all its states have adopted the balance, and are so well satisfied under it that every new state as it rises adopts it without opposition, yet the people everywhere still love to be told that there is nothing in it, and still incline to the suspicion that it is anti-republican. Your declaration and argument against it will be among the most popular parts of your letters. That you will change your opinion, as experience and a more thorough examination of the system may give you the occasion, I am by no means certain; but that you have not thoroughly examined it I infer from the remark in your letter, that if the theory of balances is correct you think the British Constitution must be superior to ours. This observation does not discriminate between the properties essential to the balance and the accessaries incidental to it. You might as well say that if the theory of steam engines is correct, an engine of 100 horses power must be superior to one of a five horses power. The balance in the English Constitution is applied to one state of society, in ours it is applied to another. The engine necessary to move that machine would blow ours to atoms. The engine that moves ours would itself shiver into atoms if applied to that. The British Constitution will be destroyed not by any defect inherent in itself, but by the national debt, the same cause that destroyed the French monarchy—inattention to pecuniary concerns.

It is impossible for me to do justice to this subject in a letter. And upon the closing topic of yours I could say nothing with propriety that would suit the purposes of either party. As a new candidate there is not a man in the Commonwealth for whom I should more readily vote than the person you mention,[1] but I am not enough of a partisan to be willing to displace the present incumbent, and I am too much of a partisan to desert a candidate once fixed upon. I have and always had a fixed aversion to displacing a man without substantial reason. On the subject of your election, therefore, I wish to take no part whatever, a course which my situation would enjoin upon me, even if I had otherwise motives for interfering. This much only can I say. If the Republicans would have the government of the state, let them concentrate their efforts upon the elections for the legislature.[2]

I am, etc.

---

[1] Jonathan Mason.
[2] "The President has but within these few days [on the 20th] returned from

TO ALEXANDER HILL EVERETT

WASHINGTON, 29 October, 1817.

DEAR SIR:

I reply immediately to your letter of the 25th instant, to assure you that in the warm and earnest remarks of my last I had not the slightest idea of considering the statement of your accounts with the public as a case of delinquency; but the proposal to leave the balance against you standing, when the settlement is made, as an advance upon the contingency of a future appointment, I conceived I could not consistently with my own public duties accede to; and although I was perfectly sure it had not occurred to your mind as in any degree irregular, its tendency as a precedent, together with my sincere friendship for you, and my earnest desire to serve you, led me to express myself with so much freedom and force upon the subject. I had also the additional motive in the apprehension that the very existence of this balance, after the adjustment of the account in the Treasury, might operate as an objection to any future appointment; and if it should be started I know would be insuperable until removed. I was very desirous that no possibility of making such an objection should exist. If therefore there was heat in the manner of pressing my argument upon you, it was

---

Virginia; and the cabinet, as it is sometimes called, is not yet fully constituted. That in the views which the President may take of measures to promote the public interest there may be cordial and harmonious coöperation among those whom he has called and may call to the executive departments is my earnest desire, and as far as can depend upon me, my intention—coincidence of opinion even between four or five persons upon all great political questions is not to be expected. I hope there is no danger that differences of opinion will lead to dissensions detrimental to the public interest." *To William Plumer*, October 27, 1817. Ms.

kindled altogether by the ardor of my good wishes in your favor. . . .

I shall as soon as possible speak to the President upon the subject of Ebeling's library.[1] In the meantime, if five or six thousand dollars will purchase it, there shall be no danger of its being lost to this country for want of the money. I pray you to write immediately to your brother, if it can be procured entire at or under six thousand dollars, to purchase it for me; to have it packed up carefully and sent out in the spring to New York, and to give me as early notice as possible, if he obtains it. . . . My object is at all events to secure the books; and the public Library of Congress shall have them at their cost to me, if Congress think proper to make the purchase. If not, as I cannot afford to keep them myself, I shall dispose of them elsewhere, which I have no doubt of being able to do without eventual loss. . . .

TO ABIGAIL ADAMS

WASHINGTON, 2 November, 1817.

MY DEAR MOTHER:

Your kind letter of 15th October was received by me on the 20th, from which time the only possible choice that has been left me with regard to my employment has been what necessary act of duty I should postpone for the sake of attending others still more urgent. On that day (the 20th) the President returned to the city. There is a routine of the ordinary business of the Department where I am stationed which requires nothing but my signature; yet even that occasions no trifling consumption of time. But there is business enough which cannot be committed to clerks or

[1] Christopher Daniel Ebeling (1741-1817).

performed by them. The only possible means of transacting much business of complicated character is by some methodical course of arrangement, and as every one's method must be his own, it can only be formed as the result of his own experience. As yet my experience is not sufficient to enable me to organize the method. Business crowds upon me from day to day requiring instantaneous attention, and in such variety that unless everything is disposed of just as it occurs, it escapes from the memory and runs into the account of arrears. I am endeavoring gradually to establish a regular order in the course of business for my own observance; but the session of Congress is at hand, which will greatly increase the load of business already so burdensome, and until I shall have gone through that ordeal it will be impossible for me to ascertain whether my strength will be equal to my task, or will sink under it.

I return you Mr. Jefferson's letter according to your directions. I sent him back the Abbé de Pradt's pamphlet on the Restoration of the Bourbons, and took the occasion of writing him a long letter, to which I am expecting his answer.

Mr. Rush is yet here, but will I hope be dispatched in the course of the week. His family are at Annapolis where they are to embark in the *Franklin* 74, going to the Mediterranean to relieve Commodore Chauncey. Rush prefers going in this *bulwark of our holy religion* rather than in a merchant vessel. I think I should not. But I expect we shall be amused with the speculations of John Bull upon seeing an American minister landed upon his shores from a line of battle ship—a 94 gunship as he already calls our 74's. And I hope these speculations will all be of the amusing kind—like the late grave and solemn resolution and order of the Lords of the Admiralty, that henceforth no ship in the British Navy shall ever be *rated* lower than the actual number of guns she has on board. The Duke of Wellington in some official paper boasted that the allied powers were giving *a great moral lesson* to France by plundering the National Museum. It is but fair that Mr. Bull should show his readiness to take great moral lessons as well as to give them. He discovers all of a sudden, under the discipline of Yankee teachers of morality, that rating ships lower than their actual number of guns, though always practised by him in the innocence and simplicity of his heart, became instantly fraud and duplicity when practised by his schoolmasters. So he begins by reforming himself for the sake of setting a good example to them. John has also another very prudent motive for this amendment of his life. Namely, that of authorizing in future his naval heroes to run away from an equal *American* force, without disgrace and without breach of admiralty regulations.

.   .   .   .

Ever faithfully yours.

TO GEORGE JOY

WASHINGTON, 4th November, 1817.

DEAR SIR:

On the very day of my arrival from Europe at New York, which was the 6th of August, Mr. Coles likewise arrived there from Liverpool, whence he had sailed about a week after our departure from Cowes; and he delivered to me your letter of the 14th of June, and a large packet containing your letter of the 8th of May, 1812, which I then saw for the first time, at least as a whole. Some small and disconnected parts of it I had indeed received at St. Petersburg, but in shreds and patches from which it had been impossible for me to collect its argument or its purport. . . . I have made known to the President your wish to obtain the appointment of the consulate at Amsterdam, but such is the multitude of applications which have been made to him from all quarters of the union for that identical office, that I am scarcely able to conjecture upon whom his choice will fall. The length of time which you have held the commission of consul at Rotterdam without going there will undoubtedly operate as an objection against your appointment to the larger port. The President is not well satisfied at observing persons, commissioned as consuls of the United States, constantly residing at a distance from the place of their appointment. The motives which you have assigned for not repairing to Rotterdam on receiving your last commission for that place are no doubt humane and benevolent, as referring to Mr. Bourne; but it is considered that the first duty of a public officer is to the government, and consists in the discharge of the trust committed to him, and that kindness to a brother officer can be indulged only in subordination to it. I do not mean to say that any express disapprobation has been manifested by the President to your remaining two years in London with the commission for Rotterdam in your pocket, but it takes off from your application for another and a better office the very strong claim to consideration which would have resulted from prior services in the immediate vicinity of the place to be filled. Mr. Eustis has also alleged your absence at the time of Mr. Bourne's decease, as the motive upon which he made the provisional appointment of another person at Amsterdam, and this circumstance will doubtless operate with more weight, as he had invited you about a year before, on the prospect of the same event, to go over for the very purpose of being at hand to receive the provisional appointment when it should become necessary. The opinion of Mr. Eustis will undoubtedly have great influence in determining the final appointment, which the President has concluded not to make until the meeting of Congress; and I think it due from me in candor to say, with a view to relieve you from that suspense which would only aggravate a future disappointment, that probably the President's choice will be fixed upon another person. With the same motive, and from a disposition, the friendliness of which towards you I hope you will not doubt, I feel myself bound to say that if you have ultimate views to any consulate office other than that of Rotterdam, your most effectual expedient will be to go immediately there and enter upon the exercise of the duties of the commission which you hold. After residing there for some years, if another vacancy should occur of a consulate more advantageously situated for purposes of emolument, you might be presented as a fair candidate for it; but with regard to your exertions in behalf of American property at Copenhagen, you are doubtless aware that the impression upon the public mind in this country with regard to them is rather, so far as they are known, disadvantageous than favorable to you; and that this impression has chiefly been made by the representations of the very persons whom you there attempted to serve. This objection as I understand it is this: that to the Danish government you presented yourself as an agent authorized by the government of the United States and bearing a public though informal character, while you charged commissions for your services to the master or owners of every individual vessel or cargo, in behalf of which you applied to the government, or to the tribunals. You observe in your letter of 8 May, 1812, that you had stipulated with Mr. Pinkney to make no charge against the government, but to derive all your compensation from the individuals who might employ you. But Mr. Pinkney probably did not consider his letter to you as so much in the nature of a public commission as you did. No authority was ever given you by the government to act as a public agent, and the appearance which you had of acting as such, while you were charging individuals with commissions and selling licenses of the Danish government, gave considerable dissatisfaction to most, if not all of the Americans there, which upon their return home naturally made its way to this country. As to your friend Pulsford's speech about Mr. Erving, I shall only observe that it was not very respectful towards the American government, and that they have much better evidence upon which to estimate Mr. Erving's talents than any opinion of Mr. Pulsford. You rather insinuate than assert that Erving received commissions from individuals, for business for which he was paid by the public. I presume you were misinformed on that subject. His execution of the special mission to Copenhagen was entirely satisfactory to Mr. Madison, as is apparent from his subsequent appointment to Spain.

I have thought it necessary to be thus explicit on these subjects with a view to dissuade you from the encouragement of any expectation of further appointments, which would probably not be realized, and because you intimate the wish in your letter of May, 1812, that your conduct at Copenhagen might be approved by the then President, Mr. Madison, by Mr. Pinkney and by me. For the opinions of those two persons I cannot answer; but Mr. Madison, by his renewal of your commission to Rotterdam, has at least shown that he thought there had been nothing strongly exceptional in your previous proceedings. As to your writings in England during the controversies that led to the late war, they were considered as friendly in their intention, but not as maintaining the whole of the American ground.[1] They were published as the lucubrations of a British subject, and as such were marked with great liberality towards the United States; but there was more concession in them to the British pretensions than the supporters of the American cause could admit, and every concession was the more detrimental to that cause from the *appearance of impartiality* which it gave to the general argument with which it was connected. It bore the character rather of a neutral or common friend to both parties, than of an ardent and zealous partisan on our side.

I conclude with assurances of sincere and faithful personal regard and consideration.

TO RICHARD RUSH [2]

DEPARTMENT OF STATE, November 6, 1817.

SIR:

The relation in which you have for several years stood to the executive government of the United States, and particularly the superintendence which you have some time exercised over this Department, have made you extensively and familiarly acquainted, as well with the general external concerns of the Union, as with the present state of our political intercourse with Great Britain. In committing to your charge the office of Envoy Extraordinary and Minister Plenipotentiary to that Court, the following objects

---

[1] *American Question: Letter from a calm Observer.* London, 1812.

[2] These instructions are printed from the original manuscript written by the Secretary himself. This applies to all of the dispatches and instructions while he was Secretary of State, for they were prepared without the assistance of a secretary or Department clerk.

are those which the President thinks proper to recommend in a particular manner to your attention.

The treaties unquestionably subsisting at present between the United States and Great Britain, are two: the treaty of peace concluded at Ghent, and the commercial convention signed at London the 3d of July, 1815, the duration of which is limited to four years from that time. Both these compacts have given rise to several questions yet in discussion between the two Governments, some if not all of which will call for your assiduity and active exertions to bring them to a satisfactory result.

The several commissions under the 4th, 5th, 6th, and 7th articles of the treaty of Ghent, are organized and in progress of execution. That under the 4th article, the object of which is to ascertain the title to the islands in Passamaquoddy Bay, will very shortly be closed. The commissioners have agreed upon their report, which is to be declared on the 24th of this month at New York.[1] It is proper, however, to anticipate the possibility of a different result to the other commissions, and that a consequent necessity may arise of resorting to the other expedient for settling the difference stipulated by the treaty; namely, the arbitration of a sovereign, the common friend of both parties. A proposal has been made by this government to that of Great Britain to refer in like manner to the decision of a third party, the question concerning the slaves carried away by the British naval and military commanders, after the ratification of the peace, contrary as we have contended to the express and positive stipulation of the treaty. To this proposal no answer has yet been received. It is hoped, however, that it will not be rejected by the British government, and under

[1] In the first draft of these instructions this sentence read: "There is some reason for apprehending that the two commissioners will not agree in their opinions."

that expectation it may be proper to prepare for carrying it into effect. To this end it may be advisable to sound the disposition of that government with regard to the sovereign, who may be requested to perform the part of the arbitrator, and to the manner in which the arbitration is to be carried into effect. Various considerations appear to indicate the Emperor of Russia as the sovereign to whose decision it is desirable that this trust may be committed, and of whom this good office may be asked.

By the terms of the commercial convention of 3 July, 1815, its operation for the term of four years was to commence, not according to the usual precedents from the exchange of the ratifications, but from the day of the signature. The discriminating duties, however, which by the laws of both countries had been previously levied upon the navigation and commerce of each other; and which it was the object of that convention reciprocally to remove, continued to be levied on both sides to various times, and in Great Britain without uniformity, in respect to duties of different descriptions. The first act of equalization was an order of the British Council, issued the 17th of August, 1815, by which the discrimination was removed from that time, and only with respect to duties of import. The duties of tonnage, for light money and port charges, of various kinds, with which the navigation of foreign nations is more heavily burthened in England than that of the country itself, continue still to be levied, in point of form; but by an order from the Lords of the Treasury to the collectors of the customs, are, in the case of American vessels, *returned* to the masters of the vessels or other parties concerned. The same course is pursued in relation to Portuguese vessels, and to carry into effect a similar treaty stipulation. The reason assigned for it is, that the produce of the duties having been, by previous acts of Parliament, pledged and appropriated to certain public charitable corporations, has become to them a species of property which cannot, consistently with good faith, be diverted from them. That the duties must therefore be levied; and, to fulfil the engagements of treaties, repaid from the general funds of the Treasury. But the order from the Lords of the Treasury to that effect indicated the 22d of December, 1815, the time from which the revocation of discriminating duties here had been fixed by the act of Congress, as the time from which the return of that description of duties should also commence in Great Britain. There was in that country likewise an export duty of one per cent upon the value of all goods, wares and merchandise shipped from British ports to any part of North America, and the West Indies, while it was only half of one per cent upon articles shipped for any part of the continent of Europe. This discrimination was removed only by an act of Parliament passed on the 30th of June last; but it directs the payment back of the one-half per cent extra duty levied upon exportations in American vessels from the 3d of July, 1815, the day of the signature of the convention. This is the rule, which by the terms of the convention itself, ought to apply to all the extra duties levied in either of the two countries upon the navigation and merchandise of the other, since that day, and the operation of which would, it is believed, be, on the whole, to the advantage of the United States. You will therefore take such measures as may be necessary to induce the British government to give it full effect. The act of Parliament last referred to contains a full admission of the principle, and the British government is otherwise known to be well disposed to apply it to all the cases in which it is applicable. To many citizens of the United States it is an object of great pecuniary importance; particularly in relation to the extra impost levied upon the importations into the British ports between the 3d of July and the 17th of August, 1815. The amount of extra duty paid in that interval upon the article of cotton alone is an object deserving of national attention.

The commercial relations between the United States and Great Britain, incident to the state of peace, are regulated by the commercial convention of 3 July, 1815, and by the respective legislative enactments of the two governments. The convention will expire by its limitation on the 3d of July, 1819, and it will at least be very questionable whether a renewal of it, unless with great and important modifications, will be found to comport with the interest of this country. The advantages of the commercial convention to us, are, the participation which it secures to us of the trade with the British possessions in India, and the exemption from the extra duties payable by the shipping of foreign nations in Great Britain. Its disadvantages are the loss to the revenue of the extra duties upon British ships and merchandise imported in them into the United States, and the unequal competition which our navigation is compelled to hold with that of Great Britain, while their ships are admitted into our ports upon equal terms with our own, and have at the same time access to the British colonies in the West Indies, from which our vessels are excluded. Should it be found inexpedient on our part, or should the British government be disinclined to renew the commercial convention, it will probably be necessary for Congress, at the session after the next, to adopt some legislative measures, to commence their effect from the time of its expiration. It will then be very desirable that the executive should be enabled to furnish Congress with all the information that may be necessary or useful to enlighten their judgment, and to present the subject to them in all its bearings. You will therefore direct your immediate and constant attention to obtain exact statements of the extra duties, whether of import, export, tonnage, light money, port charges, or others, which have ceased to be paid in the British ports upon shipping and merchandise, in the commercial intercourse between the United States and the British dominions, and which will revive at the expiration of the convention. The consuls of the United States, and particularly those at London and Liverpool, will give you much of the information desired upon this head, and to their reports you may find it useful to add the result of inquiries, made of intelligent merchants in those places connected with the American trade. You will probably find it not difficult to ascertain from these sources the amount of duties actually repaid in conformity to the terms of the convention, after having been levied under the revenue laws existing before its commencement. This and all other information analogous to it which you may collect you will from time to time communicate to this Department, with which it is hoped that your correspondence will be as frequent and regular as your convenience will permit.

A question of no small moment has arisen between the two governments, how far the general principle of international law, by which the obligations of treaties are considered as dissolved by the event of a war between the parties to them, is applicable to the peculiar character of the treaty of peace of 1783, by which the independence of these states was acknowledged by Great Britain. The general validity of the treaty of 1783, notwithstanding the intervening war, is indeed not contested by the British government. It is tacitly recognized and expressly referred to in almost every article of the treaty of Ghent. It is only to a part of one article that they have determined to apply the principle of abrogation, namely, to that part of the 3d article, by which the right of fishing, and drying and curing fish on the northeastern coast and shores of this continent, which had always been enjoyed by the people of these states, was reserved and secured to them for the future, in places which were left within the territorial jurisdiction of the British colonies. In the discussions upon this subject at Ghent, the British plenipotentiaries, while they gave notice and insisted that their government would thenceforth consider that part of one article of the treaty of 1783 as annulled by the war, at first claimed, by virtue of another article of the same treaty, a right for the British nation of navigating the Mississippi, a river upon which it is now ascertained that they possess not one foot of ground. The inconsistency of their pretensions with each other was so flaring, that they found it impossible to adhere to them both. The offer was made to them, of recognizing the validity of the treaty of 1783, in respect to both the articles, which they declined, proposing, in return, a recognition that both the articles were annulled. This last proposal clearly indicated at once the indifference which their government felt with regard to the right of navigating the Mississippi, and their want of confidence in the soundness of their own doctrine, that our fishing privilege within their jurisdiction was forfeited by our declaration of war. After the conclusion of the peace, the discussion was renewed, both in personal conferences, and by an official correspondence, between Earl Bathurst, then acting as the British Secretary of State for Foreign Affairs, and your predecessor in London. In the summer of 1815, sundry fishing vessels of the United States were arrested and interrupted in the pursuit of their occupation by a British armed vessel, warned against fishing within *twenty leagues* of the coast. This act was unequivocally disavowed by Earl Bathurst, who in conversation verbally stated that the intention of the government was to exclude the American fishermen only from drying and drying fish on the shores, and from fishing within one marine league of the coast of the British provinces. Copies of the correspondence on this occasion are in your possession. It resulted in a proposal on the part of the British government to settle the conflicting pretensions of the two parties on this subject, by some conventional arrangement. The British Minister here has received powers and instructions for that purpose, and the negotiation is in progress. You will be duly informed of the steps that may be taken in it here, and your attention will be constantly awake to obtain and communicate to this Department the knowledge of any measure in relation to it that may be adopted by the British executive government or Parliament.

The numerous and dangerous collisions of commercial interest between the United States and Great Britain, in times of general peace, and the conflicting claims and pretensions of neutral and belligerent States in times of maritime war, have been so severely felt, and the latter so unavoidably led to the late war between the United States and Great Britain, that an earnest wish has been entertained by the President that the British government might be prevailed upon, by a liberal and comprehensive treaty, to place the commercial intercourse between the two nations upon a footing of general reciprocity, and to settle, by positive and definite agreement, the principles with regard to the search of neutral vessels, to the list of articles of contraband, to the neutral right of trading with the enemies of a belligerent party and with their colonies, to the doctrine of blockades, and, above all to the pretensions upon which, in the late wars, the British naval officers followed the practice of impressing men from American merchant vessels on the high seas, upon which the rights of the respective parties should in future be understood to rest. For this purpose the American plenipotentiaries, who concluded the peace of Ghent, were authorized on the contingency of that event to negotiate such a treaty of commerce, and after it was found that all they could accomplish under that authority was confined to the commercial convention of 3 July, 1815, a new authority was given to your predecessor to negotiate such a general treaty of commerce, and an instruction to press it upon the attention of the British government. Having had access to all the correspondence on this subject also, you are well acquainted with the reluctance manifested by the British government against contracting any further engagements with regard to the commercial part, and their uniform refusal even to treat upon the political part of this proposed negotiation. A draft of four articles was, however, ultimately sent to him by Lord Castlereagh as the whole extent of what the British government were willing to add to the convention of July, 1815. These articles have been submitted to the President, and are now under his consideration. It is not probable that either of them will form even the basis of an article, which will prove acceptable to both governments.

The hope is, however, not abandoned, that the British government may, during the period of your mission, find occasion to take different views of these subjects. And there are some considerations which may be presented to them, as inducements to that end, perhaps rather in occasional and informal conversations with individual members of the Cabinet, than by regular official communications;

always observing to offer them as arguments of what may be naturally expected on the contingency supposed, and not as implying any change in the principles which have constantly been asserted by this government, or even any present intention of resorting to other principles in case they should be involved in a new maritime war.

From the present situation and circumstances of the political world, it is by no means improbable that the next maritime war that may arise will be one, to which the United States will be a belligerent, and Great Britain a neutral party. If the nature of our constitution and laws should in that event make it impossible for our naval commanders to adopt the practice of impressment from British merchant vessels to the extent which the British officers have carried their impressments from ours, there will undoubtedly be many cases in which they may exercise it, without violating any individual rights. The case of deserters from their ships is an obvious instance, and others might easily be adduced. They would suffice at least to warrant the practice of searching British merchant vessels for men, and of taking them out, on the responsibility of the officer who should take them. It may be suggested that the British government cannot expect that the United States, after suffering nearly twenty years in succession this pretension as practised by the British officers against us, will forego entirely the exercise of the principle, should it come to operate in their favor.[1] That while the United States are anxiously desirous of making such an arrangement as shall secure to each of the two nations the services of its own mariners, and, at the same time, forever abolish the pretension of impressing more from neutral merchant vessels, if

---

[1] "It is proper then that the British government should have fair and timely warning," was in the original draft at this point, but was struck out.

their long and unwearied efforts to obtain such an agreement continue to be unavailing till a moment when the application against British merchantmen, of the principles of their own government may become convenient to the United States, it is not to be supposed that they will allow their *rights of war* to be less extensive than those of Great Britain, or that they will submit to the abridgment of any power against her which she has inflexibly persisted in exercising against them.

This consideration ought to operate with still greater force in leading the British Cabinet to an adjustment of the principal objects of collision between neutral and belligerent interests. The unexampled outrages upon all neutral rights, which were sanctioned during the late wars, both by Great Britain and France, were admitted by both to be unwarranted by the ordinary laws of nations. They were, on both sides, professed to be retaliations, and each party pleaded the excesses of the other, as the justification of its own. Yet so irresistible is the tendency of precedent to become principle, in that part of the law of nations which has its foundation in usage, that Great Britain, in her late war with the United States, applied against neutral maritime nations almost all the most exceptionable doctrines and practices which she had introduced during her war against France. The maritime nations were then, too, so subservient to her domination, that in the kingdom of the Netherlands a clearance was actually refused to vessels from thence to a port in the United States, on the avowed ground that their whole coast had been declared by Great Britain to be in a state of blockade; while the British commerce upon every sea was writhing under the torture inflicted by our armed vessels and privateers, issuing from the ports thus pretended to be in blockade. The dereliction of the rights of maritime neutrality by *all* the allied powers at the Congress of Vienna and at the subsequent negotiations for settling the affairs of Europe at Paris, have so far given a tacit sanction to all the British practices in the late wars, that none of them would have a right to complain, if the United States on the contingency of a maritime war in which they should be engaged, should apply to the neutral commerce of all those allies the doctrines which they thus suffered Great Britain, without remonstrance, to apply against it, in her late contest with the United States.

Put the case of a rupture between the United States and Spain, to which Great Britain and the other allies should be neutral. All the British doctrines and practices of search, of blockade, of contraband, and of *accustomed peace trade*, not to mention impressment, would be of the highest importance and utility to the United States; and if the war should break out while they are free from any engagements favorable to neutral interests, none of the European powers, and least of all Great Britain, can suppose that we shall indulge their commerce with privileges of neutrality, which, while we ourselves were neutral, were denied to us; and when we were the weaker belligerent, were allowed to none of those who had commercial intercourse with us. Upon this view, even the present state of our relations with Spain, might justify this government in pausing before they contract engagements so favorable to the interests of neutrals, but which in a proportionate degree certainly do trammel the operations of a maritime belligerent party. We can scarcely imagine indeed the possibility of a war between the United States and any European power, of which the ocean would not be the principal theatre; and there is no nation upon the globe, which in contracting conventional engagements to enlarge the rights of maritime neutrality would make so great and real a sacrifice of their particular interests to the principles of general justice, and progressive civilization, as this.

Some of these ideas have already been thrown out, in the freedom of inofficial conversation, with individual members of the present British Cabinet; but apparently with little effect. Circumstances may occur which will give them, and other arguments which your reflections may suggest, more weight with them or with others who may succeed them. A full power to conclude a commercial treaty is therefore furnished you, together with your commission and credential letters, and in your earliest communications with the British Secretary of State for Foreign Affairs you will give him notice that you have such a power. Should he then or at any subsequent time, *while the United States are at peace*, manifest on the part of his government a disposition to enter upon the negotiation and be provided with similar powers, you will recur to the instructions given to the American plenipotentiaries for the negotiation of the peace. In them all the views of this government in relation to the proper regulation of maritime neutrality are developed at large, and the President, still convinced that the principles there recommended are the best adopted to promote the great and permanent welfare of all mankind, and the preservation of peace upon earth, is yet willing that the United States should be bound by them, when their occasional and temporary operation may be to their disadvantage, provided they can secure the benefit of them when they shall hereafter be under circumstances to operate in their favor. With regard to the strictly commercial part of the treaty the principles for regulating trade between the two countries during peace, you will recur to the same instructions to the plenipotentiaries for the peace; to the commercial convention of

3 July, 1815, and to the instructions given to your predecessor, in reference to the negotiation of a commercial treaty; particularly with regard to the intercourse between the United States and the British colonies, in the West Indies and upon this continent.

It is the practice of the European governments, in the drawing up of their treaties with each other, to vary the order of naming the parties, and of the signatures of the plenipotentiaries in the counterparts of the same treaty so that each party is first named, and its plenipotentiary signs first in the copy possessed and published by itself. This practice has not been invariably followed in the treaties to which the United States have been parties; and having been omitted in the treaty of Ghent, it became a subject of instructions from this Department to your predecessor. The arrangement was therefore insisted on at the drawing up and signing of the commercial convention of 3 July, 1815, and was ultimately acquiesced in on the part of the British government, as conformable to established usage. You will consider it as a standing instruction, to adhere to it in the case of any treaty or convention that may be signed by you. A custom prevails also among the European *sovereigns*, upon the conclusion of treaties, of bestowing presents of jewelry or other articles of pecuniary value upon the minister of the power with which they were negotiated; the same usage is repeated, upon the minister's taking leave at the termination of his mission. In Great Britain it is usual to offer the minister at his option a sum of money, graduated according to his rank, or a gold box, or other trinket of equal value. The acceptance of such presents by ministers of the United States is expressly prohibited by the constitution; and even if it were not, while the United States have not adopted the custom of *making* such presents to the diplomatic agents of foreign powers, it can scarcely be consistent with the delicacy and reciprocity of intercourse between them, for the ministers of the United States to receive such favors from foreign princes, as the ministers of those princes never can receive from this government in return. The usage, exceptionable in itself, can be tolerable only by its reciprocity. It is expected by the President that every offer of such present which may in future be made to any public minister or other officer of the government abroad, will be respectfully but decisively declined.

Besides the subjects immediately interesting to the relations between the United States and Great Britain which will naturally form the principal topics for your correspondence with this Department, you will be aware of the importance at all times, and of the momentous consequence at particular periods, of observing with an attentive, and impartial eye, the political condition of the country where you are to reside; and of noting with accuracy the actual state and the occasional changes of its policy towards the other principal European powers. It will be advisable even to extend your views to the general state, and foreign policy of those nations themselves. Besides the general connection subsisting between the European states, their present condition exhibits them in aspects very different from those of ordinary times. Europe may be said to have been recently new modeled, and its principal governments are leagued together for the purpose of maintaining through all its borders the state of things which they have established. The operation of this system in all its parts, the resistances which it has to encounter, as well in the internal struggles of each of the allied nations, as in the elements of discord never extinguished between the parties to the compact themselves, its effects upon the civil liberties of the individual subjects, and upon the political independence of each of the nations thus associated, are deserving of the most careful and scrutinizing observation. An active though discreet correspondence with the other ministers of the United States abroad, and a friendly intimacy with the diplomatic representatives of the European powers at the court where you reside, will give you great facilities for acquiring this kind of information.

It is a common practice for citizens of the United States having claims of any kind upon the British government, to apply for the interposition of the minister of their country to support them. This cannot always be afforded in any manner. Sometimes he may be of service to them by inofficial suggestions and a personal influence, when a formal and official interference would be ineffectual, and perhaps offensive. Much of the power of rendering assistance of this nature depends upon the disposition of personal esteem and consideration which a conciliatory deportment will inspire. There are other cases in which the official aid of the minister is proper and warranted by common usage as well as by the nature of his functions. The papers of several cases of this description now pending are in the possession of Mr. J. A. Smith, and will upon your arrival be delivered over by him to you.

It is known to you that a number of fishing vessels belonging to citizens of the United States were in the course of the last summer captured by the British armed vessel, the *Dee*, Captain Chambers, and carried into Halifax, where by a decree of the Vice Admiralty Court they were liberated and restored, but upon payment of costs. From which sentence the king's advocate having appealed, the masters of the vessels were compelled to give bottomry bonds pledging their vessels for the defence of the prosecution upon the appeal to the High Court of Admiralty in England. Most of these fishermen being destitute of the means of prosecuting their defence, applications in their behalf have been made to the government to authorize the employment of counsel in the High Court of Admiralty for that purpose at the public expense; and the object being of a public nature, the President directs that such counsel be employed conformably to precedents of cases similar in principle during the operation of the Orders in Council of November, 1807. The doctors at Doctors Commons, Slade, Bedford and Slade, are considered of the persons heretofore employed as those most deserving of this confidence.

Copies of the papers, in two cases, involving the interests of individual citizens of the United States, and in which the interposition of this Government is desired, are also furnished to you; one upon the application of Mr. Jared Ingersoll of Philadelphia; and the other concerning the Brig *Paul Hamilton*. You will make to the British government in these cases such representations as you shall judge best adapted to obtain the objects desired in the respective applications.

The expenditures for the relief of destitute American seamen, are made by the consuls of the United States under the direction and superintendence of the minister. They are of so serious amount that some such control upon the discretion of the consuls is indispensable. The accounts of the consuls at London and Liverpool for this object will be regularly transmitted to you, with their vouchers, from quarter to quarter, and their payment will be made by your orders upon the Brothers Baring and Co., the bankers of the United States in London. These accounts have been hitherto kept with perfect regularity by Colonel Aspinwall and Mr. Maury, the consuls at those two principal ports, and I am happy to have this opportunity of recommending both those persons to your particular kindness, and of assuring you that you will receive from them every assistance for the discharge of your duties, for which you may have occasion to call upon them, and which it may be in their power to bestow. The expenditures of the other consuls upon the same object are of comparatively trifling amount; but you may find it necessary to repress, at least by declining the al owance of unusual charges, a perpetual tendency to universal expense, which you will soon discover in most of the consular accounts. You will be careful to transmit at the end of every quarter together with your own accounts, a statement of all the drafts you have made upon the bankers of the United States during the quarter, specifying the amount of each draft, the person in whose favor it is drawn, and the fund from which you will have directed it to be paid.[1]

TO DANIEL SHELDON

DEPARTMENT OF STATE,
WASHINGTON, 11 November, 1817.

SIR:

Since I entered upon the official duties of this Department I have received the dispatches from Mr. Gallatin,

---

[1] After Rush had held his first conference with Castlereagh, of which he gives an account in his *Memoranda of a Residence at the Court of London* (1833), he records (p. 68) his opinion of the Secretary of State: "First of his [Monroe's] cabinet as regarded everything foreign stood Mr. Secretary Adams; a statesman of profound and universal knowledge. He had received the best education that Europe and his own country could bestow, and from early life been practised in public affairs. Minister at several of the courts of Europe, favorable opportunities were before him of studying their policy, and a superior capacity enabled him to improve his opportunities. Thus gifted and trained as a statesman, he was accomplished as a scholar, fervent as a patriot, and virtuous as a man."

Numbers 35 to 40, and duplicates of Numbers 35, 36, 37, 39, and 40. Also your dispatch No. 41, dated 20 August, and its enclosures. The books forwarded by Mr. Barlow have likewise been received.

It is presumed that before this letter can reach you, Mr. Gallatin will have accomplished the business upon which he went to the Netherlands and returned to Paris.[1] Should it prove otherwise you will please to forward to him the letter for him which is left open for your perusal. If he should be absent your attention is requested to procure and forward the books. I also take the liberty of recommending to your care another letter herewith enclosed.

One of the seamen charged as an accomplice of the murders and piracy committed on board the Schooner *Plattsburg*, named Nils Petersen, alias Fogelgren, has upon the application of Mr. Hughes at Stockholm, been delivered up by the Swedish government, and sent to Boston, where he has arrived and is now confined for trial before the Circuit Court of the United States in the District of Massachusetts. Six others are in confinement at Copenhagen, because Mr. Forbes has been unable to find the means of conveying them to the United States. With regard to the man taken up in France, Lemolgat, you are aware that by the principles of our administration of justice, no proof conclusive against him can be produced here, *in his absence*. The last letter of the Duke de Richelieu, to Mr. Gallatin on the subject of 25 July seems therefore to have placed the delivery of the men, upon a condition which cannot be complied with. The proof of his guilt cannot precede his trial.

If the French government will direct him to be tried by their own tribunal, there will be no necessity for pressing his delivery for trial in the United States. The crime of which

[1] See Adams, *Writings of Gallatin*, II. 41.

he is accused, murder and piracy committed upon the high seas, as an offence against all mankind, within a jurisdiction common to them all, may be tried and punished, wherever the criminal is found; and as this might on the one hand furnish a motive for delivering over a person thus charged from one nation to another, so it may present a motive equally cogent for declining the extradition, in cases where the culprit may conveniently be tried in the country where he is first arrested. We are perfectly sensible that we cannot demand the delivery of the man as a right; but as the Duke of Richelieu most justly observes, the crime is of so heinous a character, and it would be so repugnant to every idea of justice and good order that the man if really guilty should escape with impunity, that we think it incumbent upon the government of France, either to deliver him over for trial by the competent court in this country, or to try him by a competent court of their own. The motive upon which the delivery of all these men was requested from the governments, as well of Denmark and Sweden, as of France, was because the proof essential to their conviction was supposed to be producible *only* in this country. If the proof against Lemolgat, existing or obtainable in France, is sufficient for his conviction there, we have ample confidence in the justice of the tribunals, and shall be well satisfied if they will relieve us from the task of inflicting vengeance upon the "hostis humani generis," by assuming it upon themselves. These observations may be submitted to the consideration of the French government, and we shall readily acquiesce in their determination upon them. If they should conclude to deliver up the man, it will be desirable that he should be sent to Boston, where the trial of his supposed accomplice will be, or has already been had. You will recollect that by the laws of the United States persons charged with crimes committed upon the high seas, must be tried in the district into which they are first brought.

I am with much respect, etc.

TO JOHN STUART SKINNER

WASHINGTON, 14 November, 1817.

SIR:

I have the honor of writing to you, by direction of the President of the United States, and in consequence of a private letter which he has received from you of the 9th instant, of which the following is an extract:

"I heard the editor of the Weekly Register (Mr. Niles) say at a large dinner party at the Mayor's not long since, that a friend of his had assured him that for the sum of FIFTY DOLLARS he had last winter procured information from the State Department by which he made a large sum of money." As this allegation evidently involves a charge both of venality and breach of trust committed by some person officially connected with the Department, the President considers it extremely desirable that, if possible, the assertion may be traced to its source. That the names both of Mr. Niles's informant, and of the person from whom he obtained the information, and to whom he paid the money may be ascertained and made known to the President. If by any proper means you can obtain and communicate these means to him or to me, you will render him an essential and very acceptable service, the application of the remedy depending upon the means of ascertaining the precise seat of the evil. You will of course perceive that this letter is in its nature entirely and exclusively confidential, and your reply as well as the measures you may take for detecting the offender will be of the like character.[1] I am, etc.

TO ALEXANDER HILL EVERETT

WASHINGTON, 16 November, 1817.

DEAR SIR:

Mr. Eustis has given regular notice to the government that he does not now intend to return home to the United States until next spring; and also that, having now occasion for the services of a secretary of legation (being engaged in the negotiation of a treaty of commerce), he has provisionally appointed Mr. Appleton,[2] son of Mr. John Appleton of Cambridge, a young gentleman of very respectable character and suitable qualifications. This appointment has of course been approved by the President, but now mark the consequences. When Mr. Eustis next spring takes leave at Bruxelles to return home, unless expressly otherwise ordered he leaves of course his secretary of legation as chargé d'affaires, and where is Mr. Everett? Mr. Everett, after an absence from his post for very good and sufficient cause, returns to his station at Bruxelles, remains forty-eight hours (I believe I have doubled the time) secretary of legation, for which he charges the public *only one quarter's salary* besides 1,000 dollars as bearer of dispatches which he did not carry, and then returns home, charging another quarter's salary for returning, resumes his office of secretary of legation, and four months afterwards informs his friend at

---

[1] No names could be obtained, but Niles intimated that the information obtained from the Department concerned a proposal which enabled a contractor to gain advantage over his rivals.

[2] J. J. Appleton.

Washington that he is willing to go abroad again, provided he can be accommodated with a place where he is to act independently of any other person—that is he is willing to be a chargé d'affaires, but cannot afford to be a secretary of legation. Very well; but now another person has stepped into the place which was not good enough for Mr. Everett, and will be on the spot to fall naturally into that which would have been allotted to him if he had waited for it, and which he is yet willing to accept. Mr. Everett, after less than three years' service as secretary of legation, and with an interval of half a year's absence, would have found himself promoted without an effort and without displacing any other person to the office of chargé d'affaires and *to its emoluments.*

Now, it becomes necessary to thrust another person out of the way in order to reinstate Mr. Everett where he could in due time have been, if it had suited his convenience to wait at the post where he was stationed.

Be it so. I have written Mr. Eustis by direction of the President that the provisional appointment of Mr. Appleton to perform the duties of secretary of legation is approved, but that it is the President's intention when Mr. Eustis returns to appoint Mr. Everett chargé d'affaires at the court of the Netherlands, that Mr. Everett has been apprised of this intention. Mr. Eustis is therefore requested on taking leave of the court to give them notice of Mr. Everett's appointment, and when he fixes the time for his own departure to come home, to give early notice of it to the Department of State, that Mr. Everett may be enabled without unnecessary delay to repair to the place of his destination. All this was done several days before I received your last letter. And I am thinking what your reflections will be when informed of it, to find that while the President was doing this for *you*, you was charging him with an inquisitorial mode of proceeding with punishing you without trial or hearing, and with half a page of such respectful and civil language respecting the Chief Magistrate of the country, used to me, his confidential Minister and friend, at the very moment while I was soliciting and obtaining from him for you this mark of his distinguished favor.

I wrote you that the President was well disposed towards you, but that some vague and general insinuations to your disadvantage had come to him from a quarter which I supposed your own sagacity would easily discover.[1] That he felt it his duty to ascertain what these vague and general insinuations alluded to before employing you again in a highly important public trust, and that there would be ample time for obtaining this explanation before the opportunity would occur of giving you the appointment which he intended for you. And this you call an inquisitorial mode of proceeding, punishing you without trial or hearing—injustice of the President, and what not. It never was the President's intention to do you any injustice whatever. If when the expected explanations come they are found to be of a nature to require explanations or refutation from you, they will not only be explicitly stated to you, but the person from whom they came shall be named to you, and every possible means of justification shall be allowed you to disprove them. But suppose they should amount to no more than this: that Mr. Everett has not a sufficient control over his own temper to have the interest and the peace of his country committed to his charge in a mission to a foreign country; or that Mr. Everett has a habit of inattention to pecuniary concerns which makes it dangerous to trust him with a discretionary power to draw public money; that

[1] Monroe had derived some doubts of Everett from letters of William Eustis.

he has afterthoughts of forgotten and inadmissible charges against the public to wipe off balances against him which he has acknowledged to be due, you will doubtless acknowledge that these are charges very proper for the President to weigh and consider before he appoints Mr. Everett to a new office of great trust and importance. But how will you go to work to prove these charges of "unprovoked and wanton malice," and to "bring them to open shame"? . . .

You will justly conclude that I do by no means advise you either to come to Washington yourself, or to write to the President, unless it be to atone to him for the injustice you have done him in your last letter to me, an injustice which I feel the more keenly, because while my duty to him would urge me to make it known to him, my friendship for you still more imperiously constrains me to withhold the knowledge of it from him. I pray you never again to indulge your angry feelings in such reflections upon *him* while writing to *me*—to consider the relation in which I stand to him as well as to the kindness that I feel for yourself. I advise you, as you still look to a diplomatic career, to acquire a little diplomatic phlegm—to bear a little contradiction with coolness, to meet momentary and necessary delays with patience, to exercise a little of your discernment in distinguishing your friends from your enemies, and in your just abhorrence of ingratitude to reserve a little of your kindness for those to whom it is no more than kindness in return.

I have neither room nor heart to speak now of the *library*.
Farewell.

TO JOHN ADAMS, JR.

WASHINGTON, 17 November, 1817.

MY DEAR JOHN:

I have received three letters from you since I have been here, all grumbling letters, and all very badly written. The first was of the 16th of September, the second of the 17th September, and the last of the 24 October. This last I disapprove of the most, and request you to write me no more such letters. You conclude by saying that you hope I will forgive anything rash in my son, but I shall do no such thing. If my son will be rash, he must take the consequences; and if my son speaks or writes to me anything disrespectful of his uncle, as you have done, he must not expect to be countenanced by me.

You boast of your studying hard, and pray for whose benefit do you study? Is it for mine, or for your uncle's? Or are you so much of a baby that you must be taxed to spell your letters by sugar plums? Or are you such an independent gentleman that you can brook no control, and must have everything you ask for? If so, I desire you not to write for anything to me.

You say I know that in England the more I indulged you the more you studied, and the better you behaved; but that is not my opinion. But this I know, that the more I indulged you the more you encroached upon my indulgence. The consequence is that now when you come to enter at Mr. Gould's [1] you were as far behind the boys of your own age, and even what I expected, at the same school. If you want more indulgence you must deserve it not only by constant and close application to your studies, but by good

[1] Benjamin Apthorp Gould (1787–1859), principal of the Boston Latin School.

conduct, by a cheerful temper, and by respectful demeanor to your uncle and to all my friends who have charge of you. Now you see I have answered your letter as soon as possible as you required, and I hope you will enable me to answer your next letter with more pleasure, being always your affectionate and, whenever you deserve it, Your indulgent father.[1]

[1] "Among these purposes [of the commission to South America] is that of explaining where it may be necessary the views of this government, and its policy in relation to the contest between Spain and the South American provinces. In this respect they will enable you to give, it is presumed, a satisfactory answer to the note of 19 March, from the late Count de Barca, founded on a complaint from the governor of Madeira, unless you shall before their arrival have given already an answer. From the communications received from you it would seem that the note itself of 19 March partook of the infirmities of the minister from whose office it issued, and which were not long afterwards terminated by his death. The administration of Count Palmella, there is every reason to hope, will be marked by no such infirmities. To that administration you can have no difficulty in urging anew the various subjects in which the United States or their citizens have an interest, and upon which your representations heretofore have been ineffectual; nor in convincing the government that the transaction complained of by the governor of Madeira is one for which the government of the United States are in no wise answerable. That the system of *neutrality* between Spain and the South Americans is only just in itself and sanctioned by the universal law of nations, but that it is in like manner pursued by all the European nations, and particularly by the most intimate of the allies of Spain, by France and Great Britain. That for the faithful preservation of this neutrality the United States have adopted stronger measures than either of those nations; that by two laws, one enacted in 1794 and another on the third of March last, adopted with a special reference to this contest, heavy penalties are annexed to the violation of this neutrality by any citizen of the United States. That by an article of amendment to the constitution of the United States every citizen of the United States who accepts a commission from a foreign government forfeits thereby his rights and character as a citizen. That those laws are carried into faithful execution by the government; but that neither they nor any other government, can be responsible for the acts of their citizens committed without the bounds of their jurisdiction, and unknown to and disavowed by them." *To Thomas Sumter*, November 19, 1817. Ms.

TO ALEXANDER HILL EVERETT

WASHINGTON, 23 November, 1817.

DEAR SIR:

I congratulate you very cordially upon your success at the election. I certainly know not a man in our district more calculated to represent it with dignity to the nation, with honor to himself and with advantage to his constituents than Mr. Mason.[1] I was also highly gratified with the moderation, the conciliatory spirit and the good management which the Republican party at Boston have so remarkably manifested on the occasion, and am not a little amused with the anti-climax of address and temper with which the *Wise Men of the East* have contrived to put themselves in a minority at a place where they have for several years had majorities of two to one for whatever and whomsoever they pleased. It has given me great pleasure to see the influence of your personal exertions in this affair, and I had already recognized your hand in the two pieces in the *Patriot and Chronicle* before you sent them to me.[2] The decorum and moderation, the recurrence to sound principle, and at the same time to popular topics of persuasion, in the neat and easy style so well suited to the temper of the times and to newspaper discussion, are not very common in the five hundred daily newspapers "that our goodnatured" countrymen are content to read. The view of parties has already been transplanted at least into other newspapers—a distinction rare indeed for political speculations written merely

---

[1] Jonathan Mason (1752–1831), elected a member of Congress.

[2] One signed "American" on "Hon. Jonathan Mason" and the other, without signature, "Brief Review of the Origin, Progress and Present State of Parties, in reference to the Election."

to bear upon a local election. It is succinctly in the main just, and peculiarly suited to produce the proper impression at the time. A federalist might perhaps insist that with all the extravagancies, and intolerances, and absurdities, and almost treason of his party, they have nevertheless rendered the most important and durable services to the common country. That if at one period they drove headlong to the dissolution of the Union, they saved it from the assaults of their opponents at another. That the Constitution of the United States is peculiarly theirs. That the navy and its glories are in a peculiar sense theirs, and that if in the late stages of the French Revolution the horror of its excesses and the terror of its gigantic despotism drove them into a delirium of subserviency to England, the delirium of their antagonist in favor of that same Revolution in its earlier stages was equally extravagant and of a tendency not less pernicious. A faithful and impartial and philosophical history of our *parties* from the formation of our Union would be a most desirable, valuable, and instructive work, and the time is now come when it might be written without danger to the author. Carey's *Olive Branch* is an imperfect attempt at such a work, and is already at its tenth edition. But one great defect of that work is that Carey, born an Irishman, has always been himself in this country a violent partisan of the Democratic party, and that all his acknowledgments of faults on that side are apologies, while all his enumerations of faults on the other side are charges. The essential spirit of all confessions is palliative, that of all accusation is aggravating. Carey's book would be a proof of this, if it were not in proof from almost everything else. And as to philosophical speculation, reference to the general principles of human nature, or comparison with the operations of party in other free nations, or delineations of individual characters, no such thing is to be found in the book. It is an old joke that a good historian ought to have neither religion nor country; but it is hardly to be expected that an impartial historian of a struggle between two parties should have been an actor in one of them.

I regret very much not having seen the printed vote of the Central Committee to which you allude, but after the accession of two such members as Gen. Welles and Major Russell, I can scarcely conceive the blindness of the rest in pushing their candidate against Mr. Mason. This, however, appears to me clear. That it has *broken their line*, and if the Republicans continue their party management in the same spirit, they cannot fail to have the very next year the majority in both branches of the legislature, the selection of the Council, and with regard to the town of Boston from henceforth the full weight to which they are entitled by their numbers.

I should think the second of the two plans suggested by you as likely to be adopted at the next spring election as in every point of view the best, and particularly since this election of Mr. Mason to Congress.[1] First, because I trust he will be a very weighty and influential member of the House of Representatives, and should exceedingly regret the loss of his services there so soon. I have understood that Mr. Brooks serves with some reluctance in the office of governor, and would probably not choose to continue in service long.[2] He would have no better successor than Mr. Mason, whose service in the meantime in Congress would I trust be as

---

[1] "Either the Republicans will put up Mr. Mason as candidate for governor, as the Federalists now seem to anticipate, or will unite in support of Gov. Brooks and a union ticket of senators." *A. H. Everett to John Quincy Adams,* November 17, 1817. Ms.

[2] John Brooks was governor from 1816 to 1823.

useful even to the state as it would be in the governor's chair. Secondly, I doubt whether the Republicans could split hairs of principle with sufficient accuracy to find a distinction upon which they could justify themselves in turning out Mr. Brooks to put Mr. Mason in his place. If during the late war Mr. Brooks was in some degree implicated in the misconduct of the Massachusetts state government by his official situation, his sentiments were undoubtedly the same as those of Mr. Mason. His situation may have prevented from expressing them so freely, but what censure upon the policy of his predecessor could have been stronger or more keenly felt, than his silence concerning it, and the totally different policy that he announced in his first speech to the legislature? Nor can I forget that in that very war he had a son who died in the cause of this country. Thirdly, I think you would still fail in carrying the election against Brooks. By adopting him they, the Republicans, would make another and a most effectual step towards conciliation and harmony, and would scarcely fail to carry a majority into both branches of the legislature. I can scarcely imagine how this should be more difficult to accomplish throughout the state, than it would be for the Republicans to set up another federalist, merely for the sake of displacing Brooks.

Enough upon a subject which, as you observe, is out of my sphere. From a conversation that I have had with the President I am apprehensive that when Ebeling's library comes I shall have it left upon my hands. I should be glad of this if I could either afford the prime cost of it, or a place where it could be safely kept, till I shall have leisure to make a suitable use of it myself. But as my means are not adequate to this I expect to be under the necessity of disposing of the books, or of the greater part of them, upon the best terms that I can obtain. My determination to purchase them was founded upon the confidence that I reposed in your brother's judgment, and a feeling of shame that such a collection, so peculiarly interesting to this country in a national point of view, should be lost to it, and scattered over Europe for the want of a few thousand dollars. But the President is of opinion that 150 volumes would comprise all the books relating to America worth having in the Library of Congress, and probably three-fourths of them are already there. My deference to his judgment has very much staggered my confidence in my own, and a little damped the sanguine temper with which I had entered into yours and your brother's feelings. I will yet, however, not countermand the order which I authorized you to give him for the purchase, but must request you in writing to him to enjoin upon him not upon any consideration to exceed the limits which I prescribed in regard to the cost, either by any addition to the sum or by deduction from the books. I shall find it hard enough to carry the thing through as I have undertaken it, but am still bent upon securing the whole collection to ourselves. Ask your brother also to have the goodness to forward to me as soon as possible a catalogue of the library. I would write to him, but am uncertain where he is. Can you inform me? I understand it was his intention to pass the next, or rather present, winter in England. I am faithfully yours.

P. S. I give you joy of the opponent [1] that your letters upon England have found. Such an antagonist is worth ten panegyrics.

P. S. 2 November 25. I have received your letter of the 20th which was already answered by mine of the 16th. Mr. Eustis has got a secretary, and if there should be any mis-

[1] John Lowell.

sion to Russia it will not be sooner than next summer and then—how many candidates!

TO JOHN ADAMS

WASHINGTON, 24 November, 1817.

DEAR SIR:

I have to answer two letters from you, one of 28 October, and the other of 13th November. *Tant va la cruche à l'eau qu'à la fin elle se casse,* was an old French proverb long before Washington's mother was born. *Tant va la cruche à l'eau qu'a la fin elle s'emplit,* is the variation of Beaumarchais's Basile in the *Marriage of Figaro.* But whether the pitcher is broken or whether it is filled, it was made to go to the water, and go to the water it must. Break it also must, a little sooner or little later, and pitchers when they come from the hands of the potter would be very unreasonable if they should refuse going to the water, because they may thereby be brought a little sooner to the end to which they must come at last. I have heard of a highway robber who, upon going to the scaffold, was asked, why he had not been deterred from leading such a life by the fear of the halter, answered, "It is only *one more disease* that we are subject to than others." Now under every form of government a man who devotes his life to the public must have a little of the philosophy of that highwayman. He must be sensible that his calling is subject to one more disease than others, and when it comes, must bear its sufferings and its consequences with what patience and resignation he can.

You know that in my own person I am not without experience of the vicissitudes of public favor and displeasure. That I have once gone through the process of being discarded with signal marks of disapprobation by those whom I had most faithfully served, and of being abandoned at the critical hour by those upon whose friendship I had the strongest claims. In a situation more conspicuous, and therefore more perilous, and the fall from which must be in every probability irrecoverable, without a single friend upon whose aid or support I can with any confidence rely, you may be assured that I am not blind to the real circumstances of my situation; and that with the sense of my obligation to devote all my faculties and all my time to the public service in which I am engaged, the result as it may affect my family or myself must be left to my countrymen and to heaven.

The choice of a representative to Congress for the Boston district has been a circumstance indicating the temper of the time and of the place more curiously than I could have imagined it to be possible. But there is a *dessous des cartes* of which I doubt whether you have heard. Dean Swift, or some other wiseacre, has said, that in political arithmetic two and two do not make four, and on the same principle it may be seen that in party logic the conclusion does not follow from the premises. What difference of principle is there, for instance, between Mr. Mason and Mr. Lloyd? And why should those who were so ardent for the one, be so frigid for the other? This of itself would appear sufficiently strange. But that the very same party which first nominated Mr. Mason should take an antipathy to him the moment he was adopted by their opponents, is like Othello's adventures—"passing strange and wondrous pitiful."

The town of Boston for the last two years has been spellbound. The talisman is at length broken. The portion of the federal party who for two years have suffered themselves to be browbeaten and bullied, and juggled into the support of men and things disapproved by their consciences, have at length burst their bands and determined to be Americans in deed as well as in name.¹ The spring elections however must pass before it can be seen whether this is merely a momentary struggle against the excessive servility required of them, or whether they will find it possible to coalesce with the party hitherto in the minority, so as to redeem them from the thraldom to which they have so long submitted. In geometrical progression the product of the extremes you know is equal to that of the intermediates. Something like this often occurs in politics. I am therefore not at all surprised to hear that the Austins at the late election should have favored, if not have voted for, Mr. Ritchie.² And I have seen an extract from the *Daily Advertiser* using quite a flattering and coaxing style towards two or three of the ultra-Republicans, who in caucus made speeches against voting for Mr. Mason.

Mr. J. T. Austin ³ is one of the rising and promising char-

---

¹ "I congratulate you upon the return of the golden age, especially as at Boston it takes the place of the age of lead—the fine Saturnian age, for which iron was too precious a metal. The republicans have one step more for conciliation to make, at the next spring elections, and then they may be sure of having the majority in both branches of the legislature.

"Here in Congress, after two weeks of session, a stranger could not have discovered from the debates, that there had ever been such a thing as party divisions. If it were not for Spain, South America and Amelia Island, there would scarcely be diversity of opinion enough to take the yeas and nays. There are however great pains taking in the public out of Congress to make parties upon South American affairs, and it is impossible to say how they will end. . . .

"Your manifesto for the *Patriot* is very good; but you will have extremes at both ends which will equally endanger your balance; especially as those extremes have manifested on their part no very equivocal symptoms of a propensity to unite too. When the serpent of faction coils himself up to sleep, his head and tail will always come together." *To P. P. F. de Grand*, December 16, 1817. Ms.

² Andrew Ritchie (1782–1862), described as a young man who had acquired a large fortune by marrying the only child of Cornelius Durant.

³ James Trecothick Austin (1784–1870).

acters in our state. He has been employed as the public agent for the commission under the 4th Article of the treaty of Ghent, and has distinguished himself in that service. The Commissioners have just made known their report. It is *suum cuique*—the *status ante bellum*. We get back Moose Island, and the British keep Grand Menan. All this might have been done without the trouble and expense of a commission, but John Bull has a marvellous propensity to "cavil with us for the ninth part of a hair."

Since I began this letter I have received yours of the 18th instant, enclosing one from Captain Riley[1] to you. Mr. Simpson had written to me stating that he had authorized Captain Riley to act as his agent for the settlement of his accounts at the Treasury, and I had answered him that the accounting officer would readily admit him in that capacity. I am afraid from what I see in the newspapers that Captain Riley deals too largely in invective as well as in flattery. Some strong documents to discredit his book have just been published at New York, but it will be proper to wait for his reply.

Mr. Rush, as you have seen, has sailed from Annapolis in the line of battleship *Franklin*, going on a mission of peace. The cabinet is full and the session of Congress commences on next Monday. The new Secretary of War, Mr. Calhoun, has not yet arrived. I have not the pleasure of his acquaintance, but his reputation here is high. Mr. Wirt, the Attorney General, is already here. He has recently published a life of your friend and early coadjutor Patrick Henry, of which I have seen some interesting extracts. I have had an excellent letter from Mr. Jefferson about

---

[1] James Riley (1777-1840). The volume mentioned was *Authentic Narrative of the Loss of the American Brig "Commerce" on the Western Coast of Africa*, prepared from Riley's journals by Anthony Bleeker.

weights and measures and the Abbé de Pradt. We have just dispatched a triumvirate to South America.[1] Yours dutifully and affectionately.

26 November, [1817.]

TO ALEXANDER HILL EVERETT

WASHINGTON, 30th November, 1817.

DEAR SIR:

If you have satisfied yourself, either that your remarks upon the conduct of the President in some of your letters, or the new charges in your second account, were warranted by anything that I had written to you, there can be no benefit to yourself or me in protracting a discussion which has always been painful to me, and which would only become more so by being continued. With regard to the sentiment at the close of my letter of the 16th, very explicitly given and intended as *advice*, but which your feelings have construed into reproach, I wish you distinctly to understand that its allusion was intended specially in reference to the President, and not to myself. I have in the feeling of very

---

[1] Cæsar Augustus Rodney, John Gaham and Theodorick Bland.

Writing to the French Minister of Foreign Affairs, December 11, 1817, Hyde de Neuville described the administration as divided on the South American question: "Mr. Adams, homme calme, très instruit, et l'Américain qui, présentement, connait le mieux l'Europe, penche pour les mesures sages. Je sais même qu'il a osé se prononcer assez fortement, dans plusieures occasions, contre des idées indiscrètes et purement spéculatives. Le Président met beaucoup de soin à ménager sa popularité; d'un autre coté, comme il est homme d'État et qu'il appréhende de se laisser entraîner par des tribuns irréfléchis au delà d'une sage politique, il tâtonne, examine, envoie des commissionaires dans le Sud pour bien s'assurer du véritable état des choses, mais avec le désire prononcé, il n'en faut pas douter, que leurs rapports soient favorables à la seule cause ici populaire." Hyde de Neuville, *Mémoires et Souvenirs*, II. 329.

sincere friendship and entire confidence given you my sentiments—always with reference to what I deem important public principle. Their operation must be left to your own mind.

In my efforts to secure to our country the great advantages which I have hoped she might derive from your talents, I have been governed, if not exclusively yet in so great a degree, by my zeal for her interest and welfare, that I have no claim of pretension to your gratitude on that account. It is in the earnestness of my exhortations, and even in the severity of my expatiations, that I have performed the acts of friendship which constitute my only claim to your gratitude. It is by them that I have proved my anxious desire to see you acquire two qualities, without which the most brilliant talents would make you rather a curse than a blessing to your country—accuracy of accountability and self-control. You do not feel the want of them, and satisfied with yourself as you are, ascribe your own misconceptions and the tempest which they excited to ambiguity or defect of expression on my part, and receive as unkindness what was meant for necessary and faithful admonition.

While you are under these impressions it would be real unkindness to press the subject any farther. I would therefore close it with the assurance of my most ardent wish that in your future life, neither your country, your friend nor yourself may have occasion to feel the want in you of any qualities essential to the patriot and statesman.

Remaining with the truest regard your friend.

TO JAMES MADISON

WASHINGTON, 15 December, 1817.

DEAR SIR:

In the summer of 1816 I received under cover from you a letter addressed to Jeremy Bentham, of Queen Square Place, Westminster, a person then known to me only by reputation. I called at his house to deliver the letter, but he was then absent in the country and I left the letter to be forwarded to him. A few weeks afterwards a friend of his who resides with him, a Mr. Koe, came to my residence which was a few miles out of the city, with the compliments of Mr. Bentham who was still absent, and a packet addressed to you, containing the first and second parts of a work which he was then publishing entitled *Chrestomathia*, which packet I soon after forwarded with my dispatches to the Department of State; and which was I hope duly received by you.

I heard no more of Mr. Bentham until last spring, when about two months before I left England, I found it necessary to remove into London to make the preparations for my departure.[1] Mr. Bentham, who had in the meantime returned to his town residence, then called upon me, and from that time I saw him three or four times a week, and had frequent conversations with him upon the subjects of political economy, legislation, Chrestomathic instruction and other topics, with which his mind was over occupied, but upon which the singularity of his humor, and the cheerful benevolence of his disposition, afforded an inexhaustible fund of entertainment, as the accumulated mass of his knowledge furnished a store no less copious of instruction.

[1] Adams, *Memoirs*, April 29, 1817.

He soon communicated to me your letter to him, of which I had been the bearer, and I saw with regret that it had not produced the effect to which it appeared to me so well adapted, of convincing him that his proposal to you in his letter of 1811 was an impracticable undertaking. He had determined to renew to the governors of each of the states of this Union the offer in reference to each separate state, which he had first made to you when presiding over the whole confederate body, and which you had declined accepting. His mind was so steadfastly made up to the measure of making this proposal that I found it useless to attempt eradicating the *mentis gratissimus error*, and I saw no justifiable motive for withholding my compliance to his only request, that I would take charge of the books and pamphlets which he destined for the governors of the respective states, and transmit them upon my arrival in this country.

I had received a printed circular letter from Mr. Nicholas [1], then governor of Virginia, as president of the directors of the literary fund, requesting a communication of any ideas tending to promote the excellent objects of that institution, and particularly that of digesting and reporting a system of public education embraced in the views of the legislature; and from a perusal of the first part of Mr. Bentham's *Chrestomathia*, being persuaded that this work would more fully respond to the invitation in the circular than anything that my own information could then suggest, or my leisure admit of being prepared, I showed Mr. Bentham the circular letter, and requested of him copies of both parts of his *Chrestomathis* (the second part not having been published) to send to the governor of Virginia. He gave me the copy accordingly, and printed in a pamphlet his correspondence with

[1] Wilson Cary Nicholas (1757–1820).

you, the circular of Mr. Nicholas, and a circular from himself to the governors of the states, to accompany his papers upon *codification*, as he calls it, and upon public instruction. And since I left England he has printed eight letters to the *people* of the United States, copies of which he has sent to me to be distributed in such a manner as to give them extensive circulation.

I take the liberty of enclosing to you copies of these late publications, in which besides the general interest of the subjects to which they relate, you have a special property, as one of the immediate parties to the correspondence, and as having in some sort given rise to the whole. Mr. Bentham having sent you copies of most of his former works, you are already well acquainted both with his personal character and with his style.

The enclosed letters from the governor of New Hampshire [1] and his son (which after perusing I must request the favor of you to return) are upon a very different subject. I send them to you at the suggestion of the President, who thinks that a compliance with the request that a copy of the journal of the convention [2] should be allowed to be taken for publication ought to be subject to your opinion that it may be done without public inconvenience.

I am happy to avail myself of this opportunity of expressing to you the high respect and veneration that I entertain for your character, and of renewing the personal acknowledgments which I feel to be due from me for the repeated instances of trust and confidence with which I was honored by you in the course of your public administration.

I beg to be respectfully remembered to your lady, and remain, etc.

[1] William Plumer.
[2] Of 1787, which framed the Federal Constitution.

TO JOHN ADAMS

WASHINGTON, 21 December, 1817.

DEAR SIR:

Your letters of 25 and 26 November, and of the 8th instant, have been received. Of Mr. Mason, the bearer of the first, I have seen much less than I could have wished; and of Mr. Barrell,[1] who brought the second, a little more; for coming not only with your recommendation but with a volume of others all highly respectable, he pushed his importunity to such an excess that I lost my temper with him, for which he was really more to blame than I was. He will get the place that he is soliciting, although there are at least three other candidates as respectable, and two of them nearly as importunate as himself. I remember laughing heartily at the description in one of Quincy's speeches, of the sturdy beggars for office here at Washington,[2] and I am sometimes strongly tempted to have it reprinted in the form of a sheet almanack, and hang over the mantlepiece of my chamber at the Department, for the amusement of those gentlemen, while I "sit with sad civility and read" the quires of vouchers and testimonials and pathetic narratives with which they support their claims to office, which they have no sooner got than it becomes in itself a new machine for complaint and lamentation and crying claims for more. Of the whole tribe of those door-bursters of public confidence with whom I have yet had to deal, Mr. Barrell was I think the most intrepid and pertinacious, until I found myself in mere self-defence compelled to give him a downright scolding. Upon

---

[1] George Barrell, who desired to be appointed United States consul at Malaga.

[2] Delivered in the House of Representatives, January 30, 1811, and printed as a pamphlet at the time, and in *Speeches of Josiah Quincy*, 225.

which he affected to apologize to me, as being unacquainted with the *etiquette*, and began to bedaub me with flattery, which brought me quite to the end of my patience. I believe he has been as unsparing of etiquette with the President as with me, for when I mentioned his name and showed his papers, the President smiled and directed me to have the nomination of him *immediately* made out, that he might hear no more about it. As this is a piece of secret history, I must ask you to receive it as confidential; for notwithstanding all this, I dare say Mr. Barrell was fully deserving of your recommendation and will be a very good officer.

Mr. Mason and Mr. Otis have once done me the honor to call at my office for a quarter of an hour, and it was the only time I have yet been able to see them. Neither of them has yet taken much part in the debates of their respective houses this session. But there has been indeed very little debate.

There are, however, several subjects of no small importance upon which opinions are not well settled, and some upon which the divisions will soon awaken the *antagonizing* [1] feelings of party spirit. The Abbé de Pradt, whose pamphlet on the Bourbon restoration you have read, has since published, in July last, another pamphlet called *Les trois derniers mois de l'Amérique Méridionale*, in which he says that South America has now taken in the world the place which the French Revolution had held for twenty years before. It is very much so here. The republican spirit of our country not only sympathizes with people struggling in a cause, so nearly if not precisely the same which was once our own, but it is working into indignation against the relapse of Europe into the opposite principle of monkery and des-

---

[1] I think the Yankee philologists have at last forgiven me for the use of this word, and admitted that it is legitimate *king's English*.—*Note by Adams.*

potism. And now, as at the early stage of the French Revolution, we have ardent spirits who are for rushing into the conflict, without looking to the consequences. Others are for proceeding more deliberately, and for waiting to ascertain what the nature and character of the governments in South America are to be, with whom we are to associate as members of the community of nations. Spain, on the one hand, by her mode of negotiating provokes us to take a part against her; and the colonies, by the irregular and convulsive character of their measures, and by their internal elements of the exterminating war between black and white, present to us the prospect of very troublesome and dangerous associates, and still more fearful allies. Such are the ingredients of the caldron, *which will soon be at boiling heat.*

I have given a letter of introduction to you to Mr. Nathaniel Pope, the delegate in Congress from the Illinois Territory, and brother to Mr. John Pope of Kentucky, who married Eliza Johnson. He is going with Mr. Crittenden, one of the Senators from Kentucky, to pay a visit to New York and Boston.

The political fever in the states of Kentucky and Pennsylvania has not subsided. The contest against the election of Governor Findley continues, even after he has been sworn into office; and what is yet more curious is that they are making an effort to impeach the governor, for his conduct while he was State Treasurer. These turbulent movements are not altogether disconnected with each other. They form part of a plan with more extensive objects which time and the course of events will unfold. . . .[1]

Your ever affectionate son.

---

[1] A note to Hyde de Neuville, dated December 23, 1816, on the treatment of French vessels in the ports of Louisiana, is in *American State Papers*, Foreign Relations, V. 152 and 641.

TO JOSEPH HALL

WASHINGTON, 23 December, 1817.

DEAR SIR:

I have received your favor of the 15th instant and shall be very happy to see Mr. and Mrs. Sears, Mr. Codman,[1] all of whom I have already the pleasure of knowing, and every other person, whether previously known to me or not, who shall bring a letter of introduction from you.

I very heartily share in the satisfaction which you express at the election of Mr. Mason to Congress, because first, of the personal respect and friendship which I have entertained for him, even from the years of childhood. Secondly, because of the character and consideration which his talents and experience bring with them, and from him will be reflected upon our district represented by him. Thirdly, because the choice of a man of his sound political principles and sentiments indicates the prevalence of them among his constituents; and fourthly, because his election, as it was the effect, so it will prove in turn a cause, of conciliatory and harmonizing dispositions among fellow citizens whose interests are the same, but who have been spurred and fretted into hatred and contempt for one another. I have seen only one extract from the *Brighter Views* which the highly democratic newspapers have circulated with great alacrity for the amusement of *their* friends. What amused me in it principally was the characteristic consistency of the writer in imputing to his own party the violent and detestable turpitude of conduct in the same breath that he proclaims them the most exalted and sublime patriots that ever adorned the earth.

[1] Charles Codman of Boston.

I hope the Republicans of Massachusetts will at the spring election give another signal proof of their conciliatory temper, and that the national Federalists will meet them with a similar spirit. The seers of *Brighter Views* may thus pursue their visions beautiful across the ocean without interruption, till they are absorbed in the effulgence of their glory.[1]

I am, etc.

TO GEORGE WASHINGTON ADAMS

WASHINGTON, December 26, 1817.

MY DEAR GEORGE:

I have but one moment of time to answer your letter of the 2nd instant, and to direct you at the close of the winter vacation to offer yourself and pass examination for admission to the present freshman class, and I hope you will assiduously employ the interval in preparing yourself for it. I cannot but acknowledge my surprise and mortification to learn that you have been wasting your time with Mr. Gilman[2] upon the Greek Testament and *Collectanea Minora* and other books with which you are already perfectly acquainted, instead of applying yourself to those particular studies in

---

[1] "It is reported here that Mr. Monroe intends *bona fide* to make his Secretary of State his eventual successor, and that he will in due time give evidence of such intention. Of course we are all to give our utmost aid to secure the inheritance to the present occupant, during his lawful term of eight years, in hopes thereby to obtain the reversion to ourselves. In confirmation of this, it is said the Secretary is very desirous of keeping New England quiet. That he has advised his friends in Massachusetts not to set up a candidate, nor make any opposition to the reëlection of Governor Brooks. I believe the latter report to be true, and that his advice will have good influence." *Jeremiah Mason to Rufus King*, January 27, 1818. *Memoir of Jeremiah Mason*, 187.

[2] Samuel Gilman, of Cambridge (1791–1858).

which you was deficient. It has been as I infer from his letter by your own choice, and notwithstanding your boast of hard study, I can attribute it to nothing but a propensity to skulk from real study and idle many hours upon what was no study at all. I regret that he has indulged you in this subterfuge of laziness, and now most explicitly desire that you would devote the remnant of your time till the examination to the books which you have not studied before.

Instead of writing for any of the Bowdoin prizes of the year 1818 I advise you to write a dissertation upon the good old maxim "Mind your business." But to be consistent with your theme, take for writing it none of your hours of study. Send it to me, and if I am satisfied with it, and with the comment upon it in your conduct till this time next year, I may then consent to your writing for one of the prizes of the next summer afterwards.

Mr. Motte was here about a fortnight since and delivered to me your letter No. 3 of 16 November. He spoke of you very kindly.

George, my dear George, let another praise you and not your own lips. Let me hear from others and not from yourself that you apply yourself closely and STEADILY to your *proper* and necessary studies. Beware of frivolous pursuits. Beware of all seductions to company, and give comfort to the anxious hearts of your affectionate parents.[1]

---

[1] A letter of this date to Don Luis de Onis, on the case of Richard W. Meade, is in the *American State Papers*, Foreign Relations, IV. 153. In February, 1821, all the papers relating to Meade's case were communicated to the Senate, and printed. They were accompanied by a report by the Secretary of State, dated February 13. See *Ib.*, 704.

TO ALEXANDER HILL EVERETT

WASHINGTON, 29 December, 1817.

DEAR SIR:

Your letter of the 16 has been a full week unanswered upon file, and I am obliged now to answer it very imperfectly. The newspapers mention that Mr. Eustis has gone to pass the winter at Paris, and has left Mr. Appleton chargé d'affaires at The Hague. I suppose this is true, though we have no notice of it. My last letter from Mr. Eustis is of 4th October, from The Hague, and its symptoms instead of indicating an intention of speedy departure rather disclose a willingness to be detained even beyond the period of the ensuing spring. No necessity for any such detention is supposed here to be likely to arise; but if circumstances should occur to render the homeward voyage inconvenient next spring, it may perhaps be postponed for another year. I have no particular reason for this surmise other than that gentlemen abroad who have projects of returning home do not like to be hurried.

I have not seen the article upon Peace Societies in the *North American Review*,[1] nor the review itself; but if our Peace Societies should fall into the fashion of corresponding upon the objects of their institutions with foreign Emperors and Kings, they may at some future day find themselves under the necessity of corresponding with attorney generals and petit juries at home. Philip of Macedon was in very active correspondence with a Peace Society at Athens, and with their coöperation baffled and overpowered all the eloquence of Demosthenes. Alexander of the Neva is not so near nor so dangerous a neighbor to us as Philip was to the

[1] Vol. VI. 25.

Athenians, but I am afraid his love of peace is of the same character as was that of Philip of Macedon. Absolute princes who can dispose of large masses of human force must naturally in applying them be aided by all the pacific dispositions that they can find or make among those whom they visit with the exercise of their power. In the intercourse between *power* and *weakness,* peace in the language of the former means the submission of the latter to its will. While Alexander and his Minister of Religious Worship, Prince Galitzin, are corresponding with the Rev. Noah Worcester upon the blessedness of peace, the venerable founder of the Holy League is sending five or six ships of the line, and several thousand promoters of peace armed with bayonets to Cadiz, and thence to propagate good will to man elsewhere. Whether at Algiers, at Constantinople, or at Buenos Ayres, we shall be informed hereafter.

The mention of Buenos Ayres brings to my mind an article that I have lately seen in the *Boston Patriot* and which I concluded was from your pen. Its tendency was to show the inexpediency and injustice there would be in our taking sides with the South Americans in their present struggle against Spain. It was an excellent article, and I should be glad to see the same train of thought further pursued. As for example by a discussion of the question in political [*blank*] by what *right* we could take sides? and who in this case of civil war has constituted us the *judges* which of the parties has the righteous cause? Then by an inquiry what the cause of the South Americans is, and whether it really be, as their partisans here allege, the same as our own cause in the war of our Revolution? Whether for instance, if Buenos Ayres has formally offered to accept the Infant Don Carlos as their absolute monarch, upon condition of being politically independent of Spain, their cause is the same as ours was?[1] Whether if Bolivar, being at the head of the republic of Venezuela, has solemnly proclaimed the absolute and total emancipation of the slaves, the cause of Venezuela is precisely the same as ours was? Whether in short, there is any other feature of identity between their cause and ours, than that they are, as we were, colonies fighting for independence? In our Revolution there were two distinct stages, in the first of which we contended for our civil rights, and in the second for our *political independence*. The second, as we solemnly declared to the world, was imposed upon us as a necessity after every practicable effort had been made in vain to secure the first.

In South America civil rights, if not entirely out of the question, appear to have been equally disregarded and trampled upon by all parties. Buenos Ayres has no constitution, and its present ruling powers are establishing [themselves] only by the arbitrary banishment of their predecessors. Venezuela, though it has emancipated all its slaves, has been constantly alternating between an absolute military government, a capitulation to Spanish authority, and guerillas black and white, of which every petty chief has acted for purposes of war and rapine as an independent sovereign. There is finally in South America, neither unity of cause nor unity of effort, as there was in our Revolution. Neither was our Revolution disgraced by that buccaneering and piratical spirit which has lately appeared among the South Americans, not of their own growth, but I am sorry to say chiefly from the continuation of their intercourse with us. Their privateers have been for the most part fitted out and officered in our ports, and manned from the sweeping of our streets. It was more effectually to organize and promote their patriotic system that the expeditions to

[1] Adams, *Memoirs*, December 24, 1817.

Galveston and Amelia Island were carried into effect, and that the successive gangs of desperadoes, Scotch, French, Creole, and North Americans, that no public exertions have been constituting the republic of the Florida. Yet such is the propensity of our people to sympathize with the South Americans, that no feeble exertion is now making to rouse a party in this country against the government of the Union, and against the President, for having issued orders to put down this host of freebooters at our doors.

Your preparations for the next spring elections in Massachusetts appear to be judicious, and I hope they will be successful. I neither see nor hear anything more of Brighter Views [1] nor of Old North [2] than what you tell me, and there is at present not much to be apprehended from the authors of either of them.

We have the prospect of a troublesome Indian war in the South, and its bearings upon our political affairs may be more extensive and important than is expected.

I am, etc.

TO CHARLES COLLINS

WASHINGTON, 31 December, 1817.

SIR:

Your letter of the 24th instant,[3] with the enclosed paper has been laid before the President, who has directed me to thank you for the information which it contains, and to request you to obtain from the same source any such fur-

[1] Lowell?
[2] Benjamin Austin.
[3] Collins' letter is found on p. 10 of the papers accompanying the message of the President of March 25, 1818, laid before the House on March 26, and printed as document 175. This document does not appear in the *American State Papers*.

ther intelligence of the designs and proceedings of the various parties who successively occupied Amelia Island in the course of the last summer, as the situation of your friends at the place may have enabled them to acquire, and as they may be willing to give. With this letter I forward to you a printed copy of the message and documents communicated to Congress relating to Amelia Island and Galveston.[1] In page forty-three you will find a letter from Mr. Wayne, purser of the *Saranac*, the statements which perfectly coincide with those of your friends and with the paper enclosed in your letter. As your informants left the island at the same time with McGregor, I conclude they know nothing of Aury or his party who arrived there afterwards, or of the contentions between him and Hubbard which terminated in the death of the latter. You will see it stated in the pamphlet, page twenty, that Aury insisted upon having the Mexican flag hoisted, because "McGregor never had any commission whatever." Perhaps your friends can give you some further particulars upon that point. As they took a commission for their vessel from McGregor, it is to be presumed they then *believed* he had some authority to grant it. But did they ever require of him to exhibit to them his authority? Did he ever exhibit any authority? And if he did from whom was it derived? And what was its extent? Was it an authority merely to grant commissions to privateers, or did it also authorize him to make territorial conquests and establish independent republics? As your friends can have no further use for the commission which they received from him, and which you say you have seen, perhaps they may be willing to put it into your hands or to furnish a copy of it. If their own names are in it, and they are unwilling to disclose them, they may be erased. Of

[1] Message of December 2, 1817.

course no information received from them would in any case be used against him.

You will probably see in the newspaper accounts of what has most recently passed at Amelia Island—that a professed attempt has been made to proclaim a republic of the Floridas there, and to form a constitution. That a provisional government has been vested by a semblance of popular election in nine persons whose names are, *P. Geral*, *V. Paros*, Murden, Comte, *Irwin*, Lavingnac, Forbes, Mabrity and Chapelle; of the underscored names we have some knowledge; of the others we know nothing. As four of them are French names, it is probable they are of Aury's companions; but if your friends know anything of them, and who they are, whatever they may be disposed to communicate will be acceptable, and may contribute to the public service. It has frequently been surmised that if McGregor had any real authority after he came to the United States, it was rather of *European* than of South American origin. He certainly did at times himself countenance conjectures to that effect. Your friends must have had opportunities to observe how far such a suspicion might be well founded. It can scarcely be supposed that in September last he should have projected an expedition from New Providence to be carried into effect next April or May, and chiefly with *British* materials, if the British government, either at home or in the colony, should be very intent upon obstructing or defeating him. In fine these suggestions, together with a perusal of the documents in the enclosed printed report, will point out to your own reflections such inquiries to your friends as may lead them to give you such further information relating to the transactions at Amelia as it may be interesting to the government to be made acquainted with. Your letter has according to your desire been received as confidential, as will any future communications on the subject which you may wish to have kept secret.

I am, etc.

SUPPRESSION OF PIRATICAL ESTABLISHMENTS [1]

[January, 1818.]

8. That the resolution and the act of 15 January, 1811, fully empower the President to occupy any part or the whole of the territory lying east of the Perdido and south of the state of Georgia, in the course of an attempt to occupy the said territory, or any part thereof, by *any* foreign government or power, and by the same resolution and act he may employ any part of the army and navy of the United States which he may deem necessary for the purpose of taking possession and occupying the territory aforesaid and in order to maintain therein the authority of the United States.

Among the avowed projects of the persons who have occupied Amelia Island was that of making the conquest of East and West Florida, professedly for the purpose of establishing there an independent government; and the vacant lands in those provinces have been, from the origin of this project and down to the latest period, held out as lures to the cupidity of adventurers, and as resources for defraying the expenses of the expedition. That the greater part of West Florida, being in the actual possession of the United States, this project involved in it designs of direct hostility against them, and as the express object of the resolution

---

[1] On December 31, Henry Middleton, chairman of the House Committee on Foreign Relations, sent to the Secretary of State the draft of a report on the piratical establishment on Amelia Island, and asked for suggestions. The above paper was prepared and was embodied in the report. *American State Papers*, Foreign Relations, IV. 132.

and act of 15 January, 1811, was to authorize the President to prevent the province of West Florida from passing into the hands of any foreign power, it became the obvious duty of the President to exercise the authority vested in him by that law. It does not appear that among those itinerant establishers of republics, there is a single individual inhabitant of the country where the republic was to be constituted. The project was therefore an attempt to occupy the said territory by a foreign power. Where the profession is in such direct opposition to the fact, where the venerable forms by which a free people constitute a frame of government for themselves are prostituted by a horde of foreign freebooters, the refuse of civil society, for purposes of plunder, if under color of authority from any of the provinces contending for their independence, the Floridas, or either of them, had been permitted to pass into the hands of such a power, the committee are persuaded it is quite unnecessary to point out to the discernment of the House the pernicious influence which such a destiny of the territories in question must have had upon the security, tranquillity and commerce of this Union.

That the immediate tendency of suffering such armaments in open defiance of our laws would have been to embroil the United States with all the nations whose commerce with our country was suffering under these depredations; and if not checked by the use of all the means in the power of government would have authorized claims from the subjects of foreign governments for indemnities at the expense of the nation, for captures by American citizens in vessels fitted out in our ports, and as could not fail of being alleged, countenanced by the very neglect of the necessary means for suppressing them.

That Spain, one of the powers with which the United

States have formally thus stipulated to prohibit under the penalties of piracy, the acceptance by their citizens of any commission from any prince or state for privateering against her subjects, was precisely the nation against whose subjects these privateers have been commissioned to cruise; though in fact they have respected no flag when plunder was to be obtained—not even that of our own country. That the issuing such commissions, as it was an offence against the United States on the part of those who issued them, was on the part of those who accepted them, a forfeiture, by the 13th amendment of the constitution, of their characters and rights as citizens of the United States. That the possession of Amelia Island as a port of refuge for such privateers was a powerful encouragement and temptation to multiply those violations of our laws, and made it the duty of the government to restore the security of our own commerce, and that of friendly nations upon our coasts, which could only be done by taking this refuge from them.[1]

[1] A letter to Don Luis de Onis, dated January 7, 1818, asking for information concerning American citizens imprisoned at Santa Fê, is in *American State Papers*, Foreign Relations, IV. 208. Also a letter to Onis, January 16, 1818, on the negotiations between the United States and Spain, is in *Ib.*, 463.

Writing to Hyde de Neuville, July 21, 1817, the Duc de Richelieu gave instructions on the question of boundary between the United States and Spain under the Louisiana treaty:

"Le territoire dont la France avait obtenu de l'Espagne la rétrocession en 1801, était borné à l'ouest par le Mississippi. L'Espagne n'avait jamais entendu comprendre dans cette rétrocession aucune partie de la rive orientale du fleuve; elle s'y était même formellement refusée durant tous les cours de sa négociation. Quand la France a ensuite cédé cette province aux États-Unis, elle l'a cédée telle qu'elle l'avait reçue elle-même, et elle n'a pu transmettre que ses propres droits. Voilà la règle à laquelle nous devons nous attacher dans cette question. Si les États-Unis ont sur les limites de la Louisiane des prétentions plus étendues que celles que nous avions nous-mêmes, nous ne devons pas les appuyer; il s'agit ici de la vérification d'un point de fait sur lequel mon opinion ne peut pas changer."

TO PETER PAUL FRANCIS DE GRAND

WASHINGTON, 21 January, [1818].

DEAR SIR:

I received yesterday your letter of 14 December, and three of the 15th of this month, one of which being marked confidential; and the perusal of it being by that in which it was enclosed proposed to me on a particular condition, I hesitated for some time whether I should open it, or return it to you unsealed. I had no doubt of the subject to which it related, because, to be candid with you, we have other information concerning the same projects, and as it may become my indispensable duty to act against the *really* contemplated plans, I was at first not quite sure that I could give the pledge which you required. On reflection, however, I concluded that you certainly had not intended to exact a condition from me which would imply a violation of, or a forbearance to perform my own public duties and in that confidence opened the confidential letter. There is nothing in the project disclosed in it which my duties enjoin upon me to oppose, but if the contemplated projects should be altogether different from those represented to you, and I should be called to act against them, it will of course not be in consequence of information received from you. But the view of the subject presented by your communication is in some particulars new and important. If you can give me any information how far, or in what manner the Germans [1] are connected with a certain Count de Galvez, the project may be opened more fully to our inspection. I am

---

[1] Two generals L'Allemand, leaders of some French military emigrants, who had it was stated, been invited by the Spanish minister to settle in Texas, to protect that province from attacks from the United States.

not without suspicion that the disclosures made to you were only of *colorings*.

You have seen in the newspapers the proceedings of this government, and the message of the President concerning the Amelia Island. You have observed that Commodore Aury talks very loudly about the rising republic of the Floridas, and being at war with Spain, and entering into all the rights of his enemies. But do you know that Aury is all the time acting in concert with the Germans, and by consequence with the Spaniards here? There is so much double and treble treachery in the speculations of these auxiliaries to the South American revolutions, that the principal difficulty is to discover on which side the chief acting personages are.

There is a notification first published at New York by one of the persons from Amelia Island, that McGregor is preparing an expedition at Nassau, New Providence, against the Spaniards, with an invitation to the *friends of liberty* to join him. It is called an extract of a letter from an officer of rank in the patriot service, dated at Fernandina, 20 December, and is republished only in part in the Boston *Patriot* of the 16th of this month. The German solemnly protested to me that he had refused to have any concern with McGregor, and never would have any; but Aury has certainly been connected with McGregor, and Aury, if we are rightly informed, is connected with the present designs of the German.

You say that the invitation to the Germans by the Spaniard here was *obtained* by a *coup de maître*, and afterwards that it was his own personal act which may be disapproved by his master. If it was his own act, how was it *obtained?* But the most essential inquiry I have to make is, *when* was it obtained? Was it for example before you spoke to me of the German's projects, when I saw you at Quincy?

Any further particulars that you can give me consistently with your obligations to your friends will be very acceptable, may be very useful; and you may rest assured shall be used without violating your confidence in me, or that of your friends in you.

Your letter of 14 December was received too late. The appointment was made and I believe the political misconduct of the man [1] was not known—it certainly was not to me. The policy of this government between Spain and South America continues to be fair and honest neutrality; but the adventurers, and the enthusiasts, and the intriguers from the school of *Ferdinand the Catholic*, are all combining their frenzies and their treacheries to push us from our stand, or to worm us out of it. The only word for our pilot at the helm is—Steady!

It is also the word with which I subscribe myself

Your friend.

P. S. I will thank you, if you have my last letter to you to send it to me. It shall, if you wish it, be returned to you again.

TO HYDE DE NEUVILLE

DEPARTMENT OF STATE,
WASHINGTON, 27 January, 1818.

SIR:

Your notes to this Department of 20 November, and of 15 and 22 December, and of 17 January, have remained until this time unanswered, only with the view of communicating to you the result of the measures taken by the govern-

[1] Charles Bulfinch, who was charged with British sympathies in the war of 1812.

ment of the United States in regard to the subjects to which they relate.

In the civil wars which for several years past have subsisted between Spain and the Provinces heretofore her colonies in this hemisphere, the policy deliberately adopted and invariably pursued by the United States has been that of impartial neutrality. It is understood that the policy of all the European powers, and particularly that of France, has been the same.

As a consequence from this principle, while the ports of the United States have been open alike to both parties to this war for all the lawful purposes of commerce, the government of the United States, both in its legislative and executive branches, have used every exertion in their power, warranted by the laws of nations and by our own constitution, to admonish and restrain the citizens of these states from taking any part in this contest, incompatible with the obligations of neutrality. If in these endeavors they have not been entirely successful, the governments of Europe have not been more so, and among the occupants of Amelia Island for the piratical purposes complained of in your notes, natives or subjects of France have been included no less than citizens of those states.

It is known to you, Sir, that the leader of the party which first occupied Amelia Island in the course of the last summer, was a British subject. From the time when that event was first made known to this government, it was perceived that its immediate consequences would be very injurious to the laws, commerce and revenue of this country; and measures of prevention adapted to the circumstances were immediately taken, the effect of which was partially to give the protection necessary to the commerce of nations at peace with the United States, endangered by that establishment as well as our own. Those measures, however, not proving effectual while a port in the immediate vicinity of the United States, but not within the reach of their jurisdiction, continued to be held by the persons who had wrested the island from the possession of Spain, this government, after having seen the total inability of Spain, either to defend the place from the assault of the insignificant force by which it was taken, or to recover it from them, found it necessary to take the possession of it into its own hands; thereby depriving these lawless plunderers of every nation and color of the refuge where they had found a shelter, and from whence they had issued to commit their depredations upon the peaceful commerce of all nations, and among the rest upon the French vessels mentioned in your notes—the *Confiance en Dieu*, the *Jean Charles* and the *Maby*. . . .

By your letter of 22 December it appears that the captain and another man belonging to the crew of the privateer which had taken the *Maby*, were at the instance of the French consul arrested upon a charge of piracy; but that the consul has thought proper to desist from the prosecution of this charge upon the advice of legal counsel, founded upon a supposed defect in the eighth section of the law of the United States in which the crime of piracy is defined. I have had the honor of observing to you that the opinion of this defect has not received the sanction of the Supreme Court of the United States, the only authority competent to pronounce upon it in the last resort. That the crime of piracy has been more than once prosecuted and punished under the section of the law to which your letter refers, and that if the consul has thought proper in deference to the advice given him to abandon the prosecution of the persons who had captured the *Maby*, it cannot be inferred that he would have failed to obtain their conviction, if he had persisted in his pursuit for the execution of the law.

Be pleased, Sir, to accept, etc.

MEMORANDUM ON THE BRITISH OFFER TO MEDIATE BETWEEN THE UNITED STATES AND SPAIN [1]

2 February, 1818.

It is proposed in answer to the communication from the British government of the proposal made to them by that of Spain, to interpose their mediation for the adjustment of the differences between the United States and Spain, and of Lord Castlereagh's answer to that proposal, verbally to state to Mr. Bagot:

1. That the President has received the communication with the full conviction of the frankness and candor with which it was made. That he is justly sensible to it as a manifestation of friendship towards the United States, as well as Spain, on the part of Great Britain, and that he has peculiarly noticed the delicacy of the proceeding of Lord Castlereagh, in suspending the decision upon the Spanish proposal, and making the acceptance depend upon the expression of a like request for the good offices of Great Britain from the United States.

2. That the character of the subjects in dispute between the United States and Spain, though they have been of

[1] On January 27, 1818, Bagot, acting under instructions of his government, made their offer of mediation to settle the differences between the United States and Spain. Adams, *Memoirs*, January 27, 28, 31. When the offer was considered by the President and his cabinet "the sentiment against accepting it was unanimous, but more earnest in all the others than in me. I had doubts whether we should ultimately be able to avoid European interference in this affair, and therefore whether we ought now absolutely to decline that of Great Britain."

long standing and of considerable importance, is not, however, such that the United States either intend or expect to result in immediate war. The United States have shown no disposition to proceed to that extremity for them; nor do they suppose that Spain has such an intention.

3. That they are, nevertheless, subjects in which the people of the United States feel a deep interest, and feeling a perfect conviction of the justice of their cause, they have an equal confidence of an ultimate result entirely satisfactory to themselves.

4. That the general sentiment, having never been turned to the prospect of the interposition of any third power in this controversy, would consider it probably with strong disapprobation in the first instance; and that the tendency of this disapprobation would be to awaken jealousy and revive animosity against the mediating power. They would be still more aggravated, if in the course of such a mediation, any concession should be suggested or recommended to the United States to which they would not readily agree by the means of a direct negotiation with Spain alone. That the public opinion would in that case attribute the concession to the interference of the third power, and the strong censure which would fall upon the American government for having asked the interposition of any third power, would be mingled with irritation against Great Britain, who would be represented as influenced by motives unfriendly to the United States, even though conscious herself of performing the office of an impartial mediator.

5. That if the government of the United States were of opinion that their differences with Spain might be more readily adjusted with the aid of any mediator, there is no European power to whose friendship they would with more confidence resort for that good office than Great Britain.

Fully confiding in the friendly sentiments expressed in the dispatch from Lord Castlereagh, and earnestly desirous of cultivating them by a course of policy equally friendly to Great Britain in return, they believe that the result of the interposition of Great Britain in this case, *requested* by Spain, would be of an opposite and unpropitious character, to the harmony between Great Britain and the United States. It is evident that the *national feeling* of England and this country is, and has been from the conclusion of the late peace, tending towards reciprocal good-will. We see this effect with pleasure, and wish to promote it to the utmost of our power. We will not suppose that the object of Spain in asking for the mediation of England between her and us is to counteract this friendly spirit between us and England; but we say that even if Spain should, while in the very act of asking the good offices of England on one side, make overtures to us on the other, manifesting a disposition unfriendly to England, we should decline listening to them, as frankly as we now decline asking in concert with Spain for the mediation of England.

6. That while fully convinced that Great Britain would act a part of perfect impartiality as a mediator, the government of the United States would be peculiarly liable to the animadversion of public opinion in asking for her mediation, from the circumstance that heretofore, but during the administration still in power, England has expressed an opinion unfavorable to the United States upon the most prominent points of the controversy between them and Spain. This opinion was unfolded with much force in the course of the negotiation at Ghent, particularly in the notes from the British to the American plenipotentiaries of the 4th and 19th of September, and 8th October, 1814. It had already been manifested in the public declaration of Great Britain at the

commencement of the late war; and at a still earlier period by the note of Mr. Foster to the Secretary of State, on the occupation by the United States of the part of West Florida included in the cession of Louisiana.[1] The American government are very sure that the British cabinet would not now accept the office of mediating upon these very subjects of contest, without discarding all the prepossessions upon which the opinions formerly expressed by them on those differences had been formed. We should even expect from their magnanimity that they would be the more earnest in the determination to do us complete justice now, from the wish to disclaim any erroneous opinion adopted perhaps from the *ex parte* representations of Spain, at a moment of irritation heretofore. But if in the ordinary litigation of individuals before the judicial tribunals the previous expression of an opinion upon the question at issue is regarded as a disqualification for sitting as a juryman to decide it, would not the people of the United States have just reason to complain of their government in asking as the arbitrator of their cause, a power which had already more than once loudly pronounced its opinion against it? Could they possibly be satisfied with the result of such a mediation, unless it should be on every point in their favor? And in that case would not the mediating power give equal dissatisfaction to the other party, and be liable to the further reproach of deciding against Spain points which they had long before, so far as opinion could have weight, decided in her favor?

7. That the communication from Mr. Bagot, having been verbal and confidential, the President thinks proper that the answer should be of the same kind. Considering it not as an offer of mediation from Great Britain, but as a proposal of Spain upon which Great Britain consults our

[1] Henry Adams, *History of the United States*, VI. 37.

sentiments, before making up her definitive answer, we expose in perfect candor and sincerity our reason for not acceding to it. We suppose it may be most agreeable to Great Britain that the whole subject as between her and us should rest upon these verbal conferences; but if it will be more satisfactory to Mr. Bagot to treat it further in writing, and he will address to me a note concerning it, we shall very readily acquiesce in that course of proceeding, and give him in substance the same answer.

8. That as Mr. Pizarro in making the proposal to the British government appears to have sent at the same time an extended statement of the points in controversy, according to the views entertained of it by Spain, if Great Britain takes any interest in possessing our views of them, they will shortly be disclosed in a communication from the President to Congress which will undoubtedly be made public, and which it is hoped will satisfy the world that these differences may be adjusted without difficulty and without mediation, whenever it may suit the purpose of Spain to bring them to an amicable termination.[1]

---

[1] This offer of mediation determined the President and his advisers to make a full reply to the notes of Onis, as Adams had desired. This reply was the note to Onis, March 12, printed in *American State Papers*, Foreign Relations, IV. 468. See Adams, *Memoirs*, February 11 and 27, and March 3, 1818.

Bagot sent a summary of his interview with Adams to Castlereagh, February 8, and informed Onis of the rejection of the offer. He added that Onis "seemed rather to congratulate himself upon being furnished with a fresh evidence of the injustice of the American government, than to experience any serious disappointment."

TO PETER PAUL FRANCIS DE GRAND

1st March, 1818.

DEAR SIR:

Your letter of 28 January was duly received, and I trust I need not tell you with how much concern and regret I received Mr. Copeland's [1] letter of the 18th of last month, containing the account of that ugly accident that has befallen you.[2] How much of that regret arose from the mistake which the accident made in befalling you instead of your adversary, I shall not say; and as I suppose this letter will find you not in a humor to listen to homilies upon the duties of Christian forbearance and forgiveness of injuries, I shall only assure you of my anxious wish for your speedy and perfect restoration to health and exhort you to "go and sin no more."

On the faith of your confidence in friendship, I am willing to believe that the German project has nothing in it unfriendly to this country. As to the suggestion with regard to a supply of money, that might not be inadmissible—on one positive preliminary condition. We must know distinctly, clearly, and minutely the whole plan—what has been done with the Spaniard, and what he has done, what his project has been, and how far the Germans have embarked in it, before we can authorize the advance of a dollar. In fine, we must have details and proof. In which case, if the occasion will warrant it, money might perhaps be found. If they are to go to Texas, it will be ostensibly for annoyance to us. With that aspect, we must know very specially that other purposes are intended, what

[1] E. Copeland, Jr.
[2] A duel with one Bremand, in which De Grand was wounded.

they are, and the ways and means of execution. We can give nothing blindfold. We may be liberal with sufficient cause. To be candid with you we have reason to distrust semi-confidences. If assistance or even forbearance is expected from us we must know the whole.

Adieu mon cousin. Portez vous bien.

TO RICHARD RUSH

WASHINGTON, 9 March, [1818].

DEAR SIR:

Your despatch No. 1, and your letters of 17th December from Cowes and of 25 December from London, have been received. That which you had written from Annapolis, with the statement of your conversation last summer with Mr. Aguirre, came likewise duly to hand.

You will find herewith enclosed a letter from Doctor Thornton, stating the substance of a conversation which he had with you, at the time of Sir Gregor McGregor's visit to this city.[1] The President, who has no recollection that this was ever made by you a subject of communication to him, wishes you would have the goodness to make a statement of this conversation between you and Mr. Thornton as it remains upon your recollection.

McGregor sailed from Nassau, New Providence, for Liverpool, the 28th of December last, professedly with the intention of coming back in the spring. He left his family behind, and wished to be understood as still persevering in a project upon Florida. You will do well to watch his movements, and let us know if he really comes back, of

[1] Adams, *Memoirs*, February 7, 13, 1818.

which we entertain some doubts. We know he has varied his plans two or three times since he left Fernandina.

Our new negotiation with Spain, like those which preceded it, is not likely to result in any agreement. The late correspondence between the department and Mr. Onis will be immediately communicated to Congress.

I am, etc.[1]

REPORT ON SOUTH AMERICAN INDEPENDENCE [2]

DEPARTMENT OF STATE, March 25, 1818.

The Secretary of State, to whom has been referred the resolution of the House of Representatives, of the 5th December, has the honor of submitting the documents herewith transmitted, as containing the information possessed at this Department, requested by that resolution.

In the communications received from Don Manuel H. de Aguirre,[3] there are references to certain conferences

[1] "Already there is considerable stir and whispering as to who is to be the next President. It is thought here that J. Q. Adams will not be a successful candidate. It seems that the great objection to him is, that he is retiring and unobtrusive, studious, cool, and reflecting; that he does nothing to excite attention, or to gain friendships. He contents himself with doing his duty without seeking any reward. I suspect that he is not calculated for popularity; the old proverb asserts that 'God helps them who help themselves.'" *Joseph Story to Ezekiel Bacon*, March 12, 1818. *Life and Letters of Story*, I. 311. See Adams, *Memoirs*, March 18, 1818.

"I hear little and see nothing of Adams. He declines calling on Senators, I understand, and his wife refuses to return the visits of the ladies. He however gives parties, and is, I am told, quite splendid. Of his political course nothing is said, except once in a while it will be gently suggested that it is out of the question as to his being President." *David Daggett to Jeremiah Mason*, March 18, 1818. *Memoir of Jeremiah Mason*, 200.

[2] Transmitted by the President to the House of Representatives, March 25, 1818. Printed in *American State Papers*, Foreign Relations, IV. 173.

[3] Manuel Hermenegildo de Aguirre.

between him and the Secretary of State, which appear to require some explanation.[1]

The character in which Mr. Aguirre presented himself, was that of a public agent from the government of La Plata, and of private agent from that of Chili. His commissions from both simply qualified him as agent. But his letter from the Supreme Director, Pueyrredon,[2] to the President of the United States, requested that he might be received with the consideration due to his *diplomatic* character. He had no commission as a public minister of any rank, nor any full power to negotiate as such. Neither the letter of which he was the bearer, nor he himself, at his first interviews with the Secretary of State, suggested that he was authorized to ask the acknowledgment of his government as independent; a circumstance, which derived additional weight from the fact that his predecessor, Don Martin Thompson, had been dismissed by the Director Pueyrredon, for having transcended his powers; of which the letter, brought by Mr. Aguirre, gave notice to the President.

It was some time after the commencement of the session of Congress, that he made this demand, as will be seen by the dates of his written communications to the Department. In the conferences held with him on that subject, among other questions which it naturally suggested, were those of the manner in which the acknowledgment of his government, should it be deemed advisable, might be made? And what were the territories, which he considered as forming the state or nation to be recognized? It was observed, that the manner in which the United States had been acknowledged as an independent power by France, was by a treaty concluded with them, as an existing independent

[1] Adams, *Memoirs*, October 29, December 24, 1817; January 13, 22, 1818.
[2] Juan Martin de Pueyrredon.

power; and in which each one of the states, then comprising the Union, was distinctly named. That something of the same kind seemed to be necessary in the first acknowledgment of a new government, that some definite idea might be formed, not of the precise boundaries, but of the general extent of the country thus recognized. He said the government, of which he desired the acknowledgment, was of the country which had, before the revolution, been the viceroyalty of La Plata. It was then asked, whether that did not include Montevideo, and the territory occupied by the Portuguese; the Banda Oriental understood to be under the government of General Artigas;[1] and several provinces still in the undisputed possession of the Spanish government? He said it did; and observed, that Artigas, though in hostility with the government of Buenos Ayres, supported, however, the cause of independence against Spain; and that the Portuguese could not ultimately maintain their possession of Montevideo. It was after this that Mr. Aguirre wrote the letter offering to enter into a negotiation for concluding a treaty, though admitting that he had no authority to that effect from his government. It may be proper to observe, that the mode of recognition by concluding a treaty, had not been suggested as the only one practicable or usual, but merely as that which had been adopted by France with the United States, and as offering the most convenient means of designating the extent of the territory, acknowledged as a new dominion.

The remark to Mr. Aguirre, that if Buenos Ayres should be acknowledged as independent, others of the contending provinces would, perhaps, demand the same, had particular reference to the Banda Oriental. The inquiry was, whether General Artigas might not advance a claim of independence

[1] Josê de Artigas.

for these provinces, conflicting with that of Buenos Ayres, for the whole vice-royalty of La Plata? The Portuguese possession of Montevideo was noticed in reference to a similar question.

It should be added, that these observations were connected with others, stating the reasons upon which the present acknowledgment of the government of La Plata, in any mode, was deemed by the President inexpedient, in regard as well to their interests as to those of the United States.[1]

TO ALEXANDER HILL EVERETT

WASHINGTON, 6 April, 1818.

DEAR SIR:

. . . . . .

A letter from your brother of 23 January, at Paris, has informed me that he was in treaty for the purchase of the Ebeling library for me; that while he was in treaty for the purchase for me, with a prospect of obtaining it though the price demanded for the whole was somewhat beyond the sum that I had limited, he received another order to purchase it for the Harvard University without limitation of price.[2] He therefore justly considered mine as superseded, as the only object which I could propose to myself was that the possession of the treasures to this country should at all events be secured, while my limited means would neither

---

[1] The South American questions formed the basis of Clay's opposition to Monroe's administration, and the resolution to which this report was a reply was one of the means sought to strengthen his attack. On March 30 his proposition to send a Minister to the United Provinces of Rio de la Plata was rejected in the House by a vote of 115 to 45.

[2] It was Israel Thorndike (1755-1832) who made the gift.

admit of my keeping them myself, nor of my making a donation of them to one of our public institutions.

I rejoice that another person has undertaken to carry into effect that which I could only have partially accomplished, and most especially that our dear Alma Mater will receive the precious deposit.

A joint resolution of the two Houses of Congress has passed for adjourning on the 20th of this month, and they are to meet again on the first Monday of November. The present session will stand remarkable in the annals of the Union for showing how a legislature can keep itself employed when having nothing to do. It has been a session of breaking ground, more distinguished as a seed time than as a harvest. The proposed appropriation for a minister to Buenos Ayres has gone the way of other things lost upon earth, like the purchase of oil for light houses in the western country.

From the moment that the Massachusetts Republicans resolved to be in a minority upon the choice of governor, there would be no hope of an effective coalition of the choice of senators. The completion of the legislature for the ensuing year is of more importance to this interest of the Commonwealth than to those of the Union. Perhaps at the end of the next *political* year, as it is the fashion in this country to call it, the disposition of parties will be more favorable to harmony and good feelings than it is now.

Mr. Eustis by the last accounts we had from him was at Marseilles. His health much improved. He was to return to The Hague in March, and to embark upon his return home in April or May.

Very faithfully yours.

TO GEORGE WILLIAM ERVING

DEPARTMENT OF STATE, 20 April, 1818.

SIR:

Your despatches to number 59, inclusive, have been received. The pressure of indispensable business during the session of Congress has prevented the regular acknowledgment of the receipt of them as from time to time they came to hand.

Mr. Onis finds himself under the necessity of sending a messenger (Mr. Pizarro) to Spain, for more ample instructions. The printed documents which will be transmitted to you by this occasion will give you a full view of the manner in which the negotiation has been conducted by him since the return of Mr. Noeli [1] from Spain, and the situation in which it now stands. If in the inflexible perseverance with which Mr. Onis insisted upon going again over the whole detail of discussion, which had been exhausted at Aranjuez in 1805, the procrastinating temper and disposition of Spain were fully disclosed, they are still more eminently displayed in the motive which he now alleges for sending again a special messenger to Spain for further instructions, and enlarged powers. He now alleges that in all the offers which on our part have been made to assume the Colorado River for the westward boundary, the Spanish government have invariably understood that we meant the Red River of Natchitoches, instead of the river that falls into the gulf of Mexico. How this mistake should have been made is inconceivable to us, inasmuch as we know of no maps which call the Red River of Natchitoches the Colorado, the usual name by which it passed being Rouge, or Roxo. Mr. Onis has inti-

[1] Don Luis Noeli.

mated verbally that his government might after all prefer to conclude the negotiation at Madrid. And as this conjecture appears to be countenanced by some of your late communications, I have only to state that the President will be well pleased if Spain should seriously come to that determination. Your authority and instructions are amply sufficient for the conclusion of a treaty and no alteration of them is deemed necessary. It is, however, to be remarked that the impression upon the public opinion of this country, of our unquestionable right to the Rio Bravo as the western boundary, is from day to day becoming stronger, and you will give it very distinctly to be understood, that in offering now to agree by treaty to the substitute of the Colorado, the United States will not hold themselves bound to abide by the same offer at any future period.

On the 27th of January, Mr. Bagot showed me the copy of a despatch from Lord Castlereagh to Sir Henry Wellesley, dated 27 August last, and being in answer to one from him, which had enclosed a detailed statement of the Spanish minister Pizarro of the state of the controversies between the United States and Spain, *with a request on the part of Spain of the mediation of Great Britain.* The answer of Lord Castlereagh declined the offer of mediation, unless it should be requested by both parties.[1] In making this communication Mr. Bagot expressed the willingness of Great Britain to mediate, if we should concur with Spain in requesting it. Our motives for declining are generally set forth in my letter to Mr. Onis of 12 March.[2] But in reflecting upon these

[1] "And also hinted a refusal to mediate, unless Spain would first give satisfaction to Great Britain upon certain complaints of her own."—*Original draft.*

[2] Monroe suggested that instructions be prepared for Gallatin, Rush, and Erving on Spanish and South American affairs and the British offer of mediation, on which he now accepted Adams' position. The instructions to Gallatin, dated May 19, are on p. 312, and those to Rush, May 20, on p. 319, *infra*.

transactions, it could not escape observation: 1. That this overture from Mr. Pizarro to Sir Henry Wellesley must have been made early in August last, between the 1st and 15th, and precisely while Mr. Pizarro was professing an intention to conclude immediately a treaty with you. 2. That no notice was given to you, either by Mr. Pizarro or by Sir Henry Wellesley of this very important incident in a negotiation to which the United States were a party, and in which the step ought not to have been taken, without first consulting you.¹ Mr. Onis, however, privately insinuates that the offer of mediation did really first come from Great Britain; that it was not requested by Spain, but resulted from an intimation by Spain that she had resolved to cede the Floridas to the United States, to which she requested the assent of England; having been as he further hinted, under previous engagements to England that she would not cede any of her territories to them.² Instead of acquiescing in the pretended cession, Great Britain now, according to Mr. Onis, offered her mediation. However the fact may be, it is evident that Spain and Great Britain have some serious misunderstandings with each other, and it can scarcely be expected that the policy, which England is adopting in relation to South America, will tend to conciliate them.

From the complexion of the debates in the House of Representatives, during the session of Congress which terminates this day, you will infer the great and increasing interest felt in this country with regard to the events occur-

---

¹ "3. That by requiring of Spain satisfaction upon their own complaints, as the price of a tender of mediation for the differences of Spain with us, the British government connected an interest of their own with the issue, which obviously tended to influence their conduct as mediators."—*Original draft.*

² Adams, *Memoirs*, April 14, 1818.

ring in that part of the American hemisphere. The part pursued by the government of the United States in this contest, has been unequivocal neutrality. None of the revolutionary governments has yet been formally acknowledged; but if that of Buenos Ayres should maintain the stability which it appears to have acquired since the declaration of independence of 9 July, 1816, it cannot be long before they will demand that acknowledgment of right.[1] And however questionable that right may be now considered, it will deserve very seriously the consideration of the European powers, as well as of the United States, how long that acknowledgment can rightfully be refused. Since beginning this letter I have received your despatch No. 60 of 26 February, enclosing the memoir of Russia on these South American affairs. We have been promised a communication of the proposals of Great Britain; but the receipt of them has been delayed longer than we had reason to expect.

The proceedings of Congress will also show the sensibility excited in this country by the unjust and long continued imprisonment of R. W. Meade. Nothing but the expecta-

---

[1] "J'avoue que ma dernière conversation avec M. Adams [May 5] m'a paru être une sorte de disparate du caractère propre de ce ministre. Il m'a parlé de l'Espagne avec une aigreur sans égale, du peu de l'intérêt qu'avait, après tout, la République à traiter aux conditions proposées par le gouvernement fédéral. Il m'a répété plusieurs fois que, si ces propositions n'avaient point été faites, on se garderait bien de les faire aujourd'hui, et que, si elles n'étaient point acceptées d'ici au prochain congrès, il devenait plus que probable qu'alors il ne serait plus au pouvoir de l'administration de traiter sur de pareilles bases. Mr. Adams a peut-être eu pour but de faire arriver par nous un tel avis à la cour d'Espagne, afin d'accélérer un arrangement quelconque. Les Florides, a-t-il dit, doivent être à nous et ne peuvent être qu'à nous. Que l'Espagne consente ou non à les céder, elles seront à nous. . . . Je ne dois pas taire qu'il m'a été aisé de voir que les dernières nouvelles reçues d'Europe paraissaient donner à M. Adams une assurance qu'il n'avait pas il y a quelques mois." *Hyde de Neuville to the Duc de Richelieu*, June 4, 1818. Hyde de Neuville, *Mémoires et Souvenirs*, II. 367.

tion that he will very speedily be released has induced the forbearance of Congress from resorting to measures of reprisal.

The information given you that W. D. Robinson had been released from his imprisonment, by virtue of the *indulto* was incorrect. He was sent on board the frigate *Iphegenia* from Vera Cruz to be conveyed to Spain. But that ship proving to be unfit for sea, was obliged to put into the port of Campeachy, where she was condemned as not seaworthy. Mr. Robinson was kept in close confinement on shore, where he remained on the 4th of March last, to be transported by some other vessel to Spain. Eight other Americans are said by the public journals to be confined there with him. That he claimed the benefit of the *indulto* is certain. His detention, therefore, is in violation of the royal word. You will not fail, in the case of his arrival in Spain, earnestly to demand his release. I am with great respect, etc.

TO PETER PAUL FRANCIS DE GRAND

WASHINGTON, 20 April, 1818.

DEAR SIR:

I have received your letters of 21 and 22 March and 14 April; by the last I perceive with much pleasure that you are recovering the use of your right hand. I hope it will very shortly be restored to you entirely.

The German project yet remains a mystery to be unravelled. The accounts that we have from New Orleans are that 900 men, or 1,500, or 2,000, or 3,000—for all these numbers are mentioned in different accounts—have effected a landing at Galveston. But what are they to do there? They are upon the territories of the United States, and cannot remain there for any purpose friendly to them. It is also observed that the greater part of the funds with which the party sailed from Philadelphia were raised by the proceeds of the sales of the Tombigbee lands which Congress had generously granted to distressed French emigrants for the cultivation of the vine.[1]

I am, etc.

TO J. E. HALL

WASHINGTON, 27 April, 1818.

SIR:

My sincere acknowledgments are due to you for your obliging communication of my being elected a member of the American Philosophical Society, and they are in an especial manner to be given to you as the person at whose proposal this honor was conferred upon me. If I can in any respect consider myself competent to be associated with persons thus distinguished in literature and science, it is only from the ardent attachment to those pursuits which I have always felt, though I have during the greater part of my life been deprived both of the time and the means for indulging it.

With regard to the biographical sketch mentioned in a note received from you some time since, I have heard that it has already been published in a newspaper, though I have never seen it in print. It was written, not for publication, but merely as a memorandum, at the request of a gentleman who contemplated publishing a history of the United States, and who in the collection of his materials adopted the singular expedient of writing a circular letter to many individuals asking them to give an account of themselves.

[1] See Adams, *Memoirs*, April 30, 1818.

There were obvious objections to such interrogatories, and few of the persons questioned returned, I believe, any answer. I did not think myself bound to be so fastidious, and answered without hesitation. The intended historian, however, as I have understood, died without accomplishing his purpose. My answer to his inquiries fell into other hands and was published with the consent, and perhaps revisal of my father.[1] To its publication I can have no other objection than the unwillingness to occupy with a subject of so little interest the pages of your miscellany which may be devoted to a more useful purpose. At the same time, I cannot but be highly gratified at the kindness with which you recollect me as one of the earliest and most copious contributors to the *Port Folio*, of whose original editor the remembrance is the "memory of joys that are past."

I am very respectfully, etc.

TO ALBERT GALLATIN

DEPARTMENT OF STATE,
WASHINGTON, 19 May, 1818.

SIR:

Your dispatches to number 65, inclusive, have been received, with the packets of newspapers and books, occasionally transmitted with them. During the session of Congress, which closed on the 20th ulto. it was found impossible to pay that immediate attention to your communications as from time to time they were received, which their importance demanded. In reviewing them at this time that which appears to require the most immediate and particular notice is your letter of 17 January, No. 59.

[1] See Vol. III. 292, *supra*.

By the newspapers and public documents transmitted to you, the extraordinary interest which has been felt in the contest between Spain and the South American provinces will be disclosed, in the various forms under which it has occupied the deliberations of Congress. You will see how it has been complicated with our own Spanish relations, by the transactions relating to Amelia Island, by the negotiation which Spain has thought fit to have the appearance of keeping alive, and by the question incidental to our neutrality in that warfare, which the course of events has frequently produced.

The correspondence between Mr. Onis and this government has been little more than a repetition on both sides, of that which had taken place at Aranjuez, at the period of the extraordinary mission to Spain in 1805, and it has terminated in a note from Mr. Onis stating that he is under the necessity of sending again a messenger to Spain for new instructions, and a further enlargement of his powers; on the strange allegation that his government had always supposed that the United States, in proposing to agree to the river Colorado, as the western boundary of Louisiana, had reference to the Red River of Natchitoches and not to the Colorado which falls into the Gulph of Mexico. Mr. Onis's messenger is gone, and Mr. Onis expects his return in August next, till when nothing further will be done in the negotiation, nor does the nature of this proceeding afford any encouragement to suppose that after his return its progress will be more satisfactory.

Mr. Onis thought proper to address several notes of protestation against the occupation of the United States of Amelia Island. At the time when that measure was taken, instructions were forwarded to Mr. Erving, to give such explanations to the Spanish government relating to it, as it was concluded could not but be satisfactory. The documents on that subject communicated to Congress at two different periods of the session have shown the necessity and the urgency by which the step was dictated and justified. Mr. Onis's remonstrances have excited very little attention; but some dissatisfaction at the measure has been manifested by the more ardent friends of the South American revolutionists.[1] The disclosure of the transactions, in which McGregor's expedition originated, of the manner and materials of its execution, and of the pernicious influence which it had and portended to important interests of our own country, have conciliated to the proceedings of this government the general acquiescence and assent of the public opinion of the country.

A motion was made in the House of Representatives, while the general appropriation bill was under consideration, to introduce the appropriation of an outfit and a year's salary for a minister to be sent to the provinces of La Plata, if the President should think proper to make such an appointment. The object of this motion was to obtain the sanction of a legislative opinion, in favor of the immediate acknowledgment of the government of Buenos Ayres; but it was rejected by a majority of 115 to 45. Independently of the objection to it that it had the appearance of dictating to the executive with regard to the execution of its own duties, and of manifesting a distrust of its favorable disposition to the independence of the colonies for which there was no cause, it was thought not advisable to adopt any measure of importance upon the imperfect information then possessed, and the motive for declining to act was the stronger, from the circumstance that three commissioners

---

[1] "By whom it was considered, as in its operation favoring so much the cause of Spain as to be scarcely reconcilable with our neutrality."—*Original draft.*

had been sent to visit several parts of the South American continent, chiefly for the purpose of obtaining more precise and accurate information.

Dispatches have been received from them, dated 4 March, immediately after their arrival at Buenos Ayres. They had touched on their way, for a few days, at Rio de Janeiro; where the Spanish Minister, Count Casa Flores, appears to have been so much alarmed by the suspicion that the object of this mission was the formal acknowledgment of the government of La Plata, that he thought it his duty to make to Mr. Sumter an official communication that he had received an official despatch from the Duke of San Carlos, the Spanish Ambassador at London, dated the 7th of November last, informing him *that the British government had acceded to the proposition made by the Spanish government of a general mediation of the powers to obtain the pacification of Spanish America, the negotiation of which it was upon the point of being decided whether it should be at London or at Madrid.*

This agitation of a Spanish Minister, at the bare surmize, of what might be the object of the visit of our commissioners to Buenos Ayres, affords some comment upon the reserve which *all* the European powers have hitherto observed in relation to this affair, towards the United States. No official communication of this projected general mediation has been made to the government of the United States, by any one of the powers, who are to participate in it; and although the Duke de Richelieu and the Russian Ambassador both, in conversation with you, admit the importance of the United States to the subject, and of the subject to the United States, yet the former abstains from all official communication to you of what the allies are doing in it, and the latter apologizes for the silence of his government to us, concerning it, on the plea that, being upon punctilious terms with England, they can show no mark of confidence to us but by concert with her.

On the 27th of January last, Mr. Bagot, at the same time when he informed us of the proposal of Spain to Great Britain to mediate between the United States and Spain, did also by instruction from Lord Castlereagh state that the European allies were about to interpose in the quarrel between Spain and her revolted colonies; and that very shortly a further and full communication should be made to us of what was proposed to be done—with the assurance that Great Britain would not propose or agree to any arrangement in which the interests of all parties concerned, including those of the United States, should not be placed on the same foundation. Nearly four months have since elapsed; and the promised communication has not been made;[1] but we have a copy of the Russian *answer*, dated in November at Moscow, to the first proposals made by Great Britain to the European allies, and we know the course which will be pursued by Portugal in regard to this mediation. If the object of this mediation be any other than to promote the total independence, political and commercial, of South America, we are neither desirous of being invited to take a part in it, nor disposed to accept the invitation if given. Our policy in the contest between Spain and her colonies has been impartial neutrality. The policy of all the European states has been hitherto the same. Is the proposed general mediation to be a departure from that line of neutrality? If it is, which side of the contest are the allies to take? The side of Spain? On what principle, and by what right? As contending parties in a civil war, the South

[1] It was not made until October 19, 1818. See Adams, *Memoirs*, under that date, and Castlereagh, *Memoirs*, XII. 66.

Americans have rights, which other powers are bound to respect as much as the rights of Spain; and after having by an avowed neutrality admitted the existence of those rights, upon what principle of justice can the allies consider them as forfeited, or themselves as justifiable in taking side with Spain against them?

There is no discernible motive of justice or of interest, which can induce the allied sovereigns to interpose for the restoration of the Spanish colonial dominion in South America. There is none even of policy; for if all the organized power of Europe is combined to maintain the authority of each sovereign over his own people, it is hardly supposable that the sober senses of the allied cabinets will permit them to extend the application of this principle of union to the maintenance of colonial dominion beyond the Atlantic and the Equator.

By the usual principles of international law, the state of *neutrality* recognizes the cause of both parties to the contest *as just*—that is, it avoids all consideration of the merits of the contest. But when abandoning that neutrality, a nation takes one side in a war of other parties, the first question to be settled is the *justice* of the cause to be assumed. If the European allies are to take side with Spain, to reduce her South American colonies to submission, we trust they will make some previous inquiry into the justice of the cause they are to undertake. As neutrals we are not required to decide the question of justice. We are sure we should not find it on the side of Spain.

We incline to the belief that on a full examination of the subject, the allies will not deem it advisable to interpose in this contest, by any application of force. If they advise the South Americans to place themselves again under the Spanish government, it is not probable their advice will be followed. What motives can be adduced to make the Spanish government acceptable to them? Wherever Spain can maintain her own authority she will not need the co-operation of the allies. Where she cannot exact obedience, what value can be set upon her protection?

The situation of these countries has thrown them open to commercial intercourse with other nations, and among the rest with these United States. This state of things has existed several years, and cannot now be changed without materially affecting our interests. You will take occasion not by formal official communication, but verbally as the opportunity may present itself, to let the Duke de Richelieu understand that we think the European allies would act but a just and friendly part towards the United States by a free and unreserved communication to us of what they do, or intend to do in the affair of Spain and South America. That it is our earnest desire to pursue a line of policy at once just to both parties in that contest, and harmonious with that of the European allies. That we must know their system, in order to shape our own measures accordingly; but that we do not wish to join them in any plan of interference between the parties, and above all that we can neither accede to nor approve of any interference to restore any part of the Spanish supremacy in any of the South American provinces.

I have the honor to be, etc.

TO RICHARD RUSH [1]

DEPARTMENT OF STATE,
WASHINGTON, 20 May, 1818.

SIR:

Your dispatches to number eleven, inclusive, with their respective enclosures, have been duly received. . . .

From the tenor of your conference with Lord Castlereagh, reported in your dispatch number seven, as well as from the communications made here on the same subject by Mr. Bagot, it appears that the British government have acceded to the proposal heretofore made on our part, to refer the question which has arisen upon the construction of the first article of the treaty of Ghent, in relation to the restitution of slaves carried away from the United States after the ratification of the treaty of peace, to the arbitration of a friendly sovereign. This accession is understood to be absolute and unconditional; but accompanied with the suggestion of a wish on the part of the British cabinet, to try as a previous measure the expedient adopted for the adjustment of other questions between the two countries of submitting the case to the decision of commissioners mutually chosen by the two parties. Submitting at the same time to the same or other commissioners appointed in like manner, the ascertainment and demarcation of a boundary line from the northwest corner of the Lake of the Woods, westward, and the right and title of the United States to a settlement at the mouth of Columbia River, on the Pacific Ocean.

If the proposal to refer to commissioners the decision of the question relating to the slaves, before having recourse

[1] Printed in part in *American State Papers*, Foreign Relations, IV. 853.

to the arbitration had been confined to that object, it would have been accepted without hesitation or delay. But it has been so connected with the others that Lord Castlereagh at last avoided committing his government to the engagement of disposing in that manner of this particular point of difference by itself. Mr. Bagot's statement of the proposal is of the same character. Without explicitly declaring that the British government would decline submitting the slave question alone to commissioners, he did not profess to be authorized to agree to it separately, and urged on various grounds the expediency of arranging as soon as possible, and by the same means, all the subjects which might even be hereafter occasions of misunderstanding between the two countries.

Taken altogether as a complicated proposal it involves a multitude of considerations, which require some deliberation before a definitive answer can be given. As soon as the President shall have come to a determination concerning it the result will be immediately communicated to you. In the meantime it may be proper that you should assure Lord Castlereagh that it was entirely owing to accident, and to the communications which had previously passed between the late Secretary of State and Mr. Baker concerning the restitution of the post at the mouth of Columbia River, that the *Ontario* was dispatched for the purpose of resuming our possession there, without giving notice of the expedition to Mr. Bagot, and to his government. Copies of these communications are herewith enclosed, from which it was concluded that no authorized English establishment existed at the place; and as they intimated no question whatever of the title of the United States to the settlement which existed there before the late war, it did not occur that any such question had since arisen, which could make it an object of interest to Great Britain. You are authorized to add, that notice of the departure of the *Ontario* and of the object of her voyage would nevertheless have been given, but that the expedition was determined and the vessel dispatched during the President's absence from the seat of government, the last season.[1]

These explanations have already been given to Mr. Bagot, who has expressed himself entirely satisfied with them, and his conviction that they will be equally satisfactory to his government. As it was not anticipated that any disposition existed in the British government to start questions of title with us on the borders of the South Sea, we could have no possible motive for reserve or concealment with regard to the expedition of the *Ontario*. In suggesting these ideas to Lord Castlereagh rather in conversation than in any more formal manner, it may be proper to remark the minuteness of the present interest, either to Great Britain or the United States, involved in this concern; and the unwillingness for that reason of this government, to include it among the objects of serious discussion with them. At the same time you might give him to understand, though not unless in a manner to avoid everything offensive in the suggestion, that from the nature of things, if in the course of future events, it should ever *become* an object of serious importance to the United States it can scarcely be supposed that Great Britain would find it useful or advisable to resist their claim to possession by systematic opposition. If the United States leave her in undisturbed enjoyment of all her holds upon Europe, Asia, and Africa, with all her actual possessions in this hemisphere, we may very fairly expect that she will not think it consistent either with a wise or a friendly policy

---

[1] See Schafer, "British Attitude toward the Oregon Question," in *American Historical Review*, XVI. 282.

to watch with eyes of jealousy and alarm every possibility of extension to our natural dominion of North America, which she can have no solid interest to prevent, until all possibility of her preventing it shall have vanished.

 This circumstance will afford also a very suitable occasion for opening to the British government the wish of the President, for a frank, candid, and unreserved mutual communication of the views of policy entertained by each party upon objects of serious interest to both; among which the affairs of South America, are preëminently deserving of attention. The reserve with which it appears from your No. 11 that everything done by the European allies on this subject has been withheld from you, is the more remarkable by the consideration, that the Russian Ambassador at Paris, has alleged to Mr. Gallatin the necessity under which his government felt itself of not being more communicative without the concurrence of England, as an apology for a like reserve on their part. To England, therefore, it is attributed by her allies. On the 27th of January last, Mr. Bagot, in communicating the request of Spain that Great Britain would undertake the mediation between her and us, at the same time gave us an assurance from Lord Castlereagh that a full communication should *very shortly* be made to us of the whole proceedings of the European allies in this affair of South America. Not a line upon the subject has since then been received by Mr. Bagot, and a mere accident has put us in possession of an official communication from the Duke of San Carlos to the Spanish Minister at Rio Janeiro, written in *November* last, and announcing that Great Britain had acceded to the proposal of Spain, that there should be a general mediation of the European alliance, for the pacification of the Spanish Colonies, and that it was then to be immediately determined whether the negotiation should be held at London or at Madrid. This communication was made with great earnestness by Count Casa Flores to Mr. Sumter, on the mere entrance of the *Congress* frigate, with our commissioners to South America at Rio de Janeiro. That Spanish Minister, apprehensive that the object of our mission was to acknowledge the independence of the government of Buenos Ayres appears to have supposed that this critical disclosure of the intention of the allies, would have been a sufficient inducement for our commissioners to retrace their steps, and instead of proceeding to Buenos Ayres to return immediately home. His alarm was premature. But among the reflections suggested by this incident is, the importance to the European alliance, as well as to the United States, that this government should be frankly and candidly and fully informed of what the allies do, and of what they intend to do with regard to South America. Hitherto the policy of Europe, and that of the United States in this matter, has been the same—*neutrality*. It cannot have escaped the recollection of Lord Castlereagh how often he has been assured of the wish of this government to proceed in relation to South American affairs, in good understanding and harmony with Great Britain; most especially so long as their mutual policy should be neutrality. He will probably recollect his having observed that in *their* idea of neutrality the non-acknowledgment of the independence of the colonies was an essential point, which so long as their independence is the precise question of the war is undoubtedly true. But it is also true that the non-acknowledgment of the colonial supremacy of Spain, during the contest, is equally essential to *neutrality*. The proclamation of the Prince Regent, prohibiting British subjects from serving on either side in this war, is a signal acknowledgment of the principle, and a plain admission of the obligation of neutral duties, as well towards the South Americans as towards Spain. Now the first point upon which we desire and think ourselves entitled to explicit information from the alliance is, whether their plan of mediation and of pacification proceeds upon the basis of *neutrality*. If so, the allies are pledged to take no part against the South Americans. If not, upon what principle of right will the allies, upon what principle will especially Great Britain, depart from the neutrality which she has observed and proclaimed? If the plan of pacification is to be founded upon the basis of neutrality, it must be offered to the free acceptance of the South Americans, without any pretence or intention of compulsion. We think there is no prospect that any such proposal to them will be successful, even if it should be backed by the new armament and the Russian fleet lately purchased by Spain. From this transaction as well as from some other indications, among which is the purport of the memorial from Moscow, dated the 17th of November, 1817, to serve for instructions to the Russian ministers at the several allied courts, the disposition of Russia, to say the least, appears to incline strongly against the South Americans. The substance of that memorial is an exhortation to Spain by certain territorial concessions to Portugal on the Rio de la Plata, to secure the coöperation of the government of Brazil against the South American insurgents, and then with the support of the whole European alliance, to offer certain privileges to the South Americans, as the condition of their return to subjection. It does not, however, contemplate the exercise of force on the part of the allies, but intimates that the fate of South America may be settled by general treaties, like those of Vienna for the abolition of the slave trade. This memorial refers to one previously received from the British cabinet;

and adheres to certain conditions upon which they proposed that the interposition of the allies should be granted, and to other particulars in the British memorial, involving the questions of armistice, coöperation, guarantee and neutrality which naturally arose from the subject. All these the Russian memorial sets aside as objects of a subordinate nature, approving, however, a remark of the Spanish government that the term *armistice* might have a dangerous impression upon the insurgent South Americans.

It is hoped that the free communication promised by Lord Castlereagh, through Mr. Bagot, will have been forwarded from England before you receive this letter. But should the reserve towards you noticed in your No. 11 on South American concerns be still continued, you will take occasion to remind Lord Castlereagh of this promise, remarking the satisfaction which it gave to the President, and the entire confidence with which he is expecting its fulfilment. You will observe that if the European alliance are undertaking jointly to arrange the affairs of Spain and South America, the United States have so deep an interest in the result, that it will be no more than justice to them on the part of the alliance to give them clear, explicit and immediate notice, not only of their acts but of their intentions; not only of their final decisions, but of the propositions of each of their members. If they do not think proper to *consult* the United States before coming to their conclusions, they will of course expect that the United States will come to their conclusions without consulting them. What we ask, and what we promise, is immediate notice of what is done or intended to be done. You will at the same time bear in mind, and if the occasion should be given by any intimation of a disposition to invite the United States to to take a part in the negotiation, you will let it be known that we have no desire to participate in it; and above all that we will join in no plan of pacification founded on any other basis than that of the entire independence of the South Americans.

It is presumed that this will very soon be, if it is not already, the real policy of Great Britain; however, in deference to the powerful members of the European alliance, she may acquiesce in the project of a compromise under the sanction of the alliance between political resubjugation, and commercial liberty or privileges. We believe this compromise will be found utterly impracticable, at least as a permanent establishment; and we conjecture that the British cabinet have already made up their minds to the total independence of South America, placing little reliance on the issue of this joint negotiation. When they have satisfied their sense of duty to their ties of amity with Spain, it is supposed they will soon discover the great interest of Great Britain in the total independence of Spanish America, and will promote that event just so far as their obligations towards Spain will permit. The time is probably not remote, when the acknowledgment of the South American independence will be an act of friendship towards Spain herself. When it will be kindness to her to put an end to that self-delusion under which she is wasting all the remnant of her resources in a war, infamous by the atrocities with which it is carried on, and utterly hopeless of success. It may be an interesting object of your attention to watch the moment when this idea will become prevalent in the British councils, and to encourage any disposition which may consequently be manifested to a more perfect concert of measures between the United States and Great Britain towards that end—the total independence of the Spanish South American provinces.

Among the symptoms of the approach of that period, we cannot overlook the sentiments avowed by Lord Castlereagh in Parliament, in his answer to some observations of Mr. Lyttleton in the debate upon the late slave-trade abolition treaty with Spain. The policy which he in that speech recommends, of throwing open all the gates of commerce, and the universal approbation with which it was received, show the direction in which the current of opinion is running, and we may fairly hope will find its application not only in all the questions relating to South America, but also in the commercial arrangements which must soon be resumed between us and Great Britain. I shall in another letter make known to you the President's views on this subject, and in the meantime remain with much respect, etc.

TO RICHARD RUSH [1]

DEPARTMENT OF STATE,
WASHINGTON, 21 May, 1818.

SIR:

Among the laws enacted at the last session of Congress, which will be found in the file of the *National Intelligencer* regularly forwarded to you, there are two materially affecting our relations with Great Britain, and which will require your particular attention. The first directs the return of all extra duties, whether of tonnage or upon merchandise, levied upon British subjects after the 3d of July, 1815, the date of the commercial convention, upon condition that the same principle shall be sanctioned and ob-

---

[1] It was in preparing this dispatch that Adams devised a system of a diplomatic index to papers received in the Department of State, a system in use at the present time (1915). *Memoirs*, May 20, 1818.

served by the British government with regard to the extra duties levied upon American citizens and property in the British dominions in Europe. As this provision was necessary on both sides to carry the convention into effect, and as the principle was fully sanctioned with regard to a part of the duties by the act of Parliament of 30 June last, it cannot be doubted that complete effect will now be given to it by the additional act necessary for that purpose. In your conversation with Lord Castlereagh on this matter reported in your letter No. 2, he closed the topic by promising to consult upon it, Mr. Robinson, now President of the Board of Trade. This gentleman was one of the negotiators of the convention of 3 July, 1815, and knows that the intention of the parties was, conformably to the letter of the convention, that its operation should commence from its date. He is a man of perfectly fair and candid mind; and of a conciliatory and obliging disposition. If on receiving this despatch, the act of Parliament corresponding to that of Congress to which I know refer, shall not have passed, it may facilitate despatch, if, with the assent of Lord Castlereagh, which he will readily give, you should call upon Mr. Robinson himself at the office of the Board of Trade, and obtain the aid of his influence to carry the act through. The law of Congress is in the *National Intelligencer* of 4 May.[1]

The other law to which I have called your attention is an act concerning navigation passed on the 18th and published in the *National Intelligencer* of the 21st of April. It meets the British prohibitive colonial system by direct and countervailing prohibition, to commence from and after the 30th of September next. The vote upon its passage in the Senate where it originated was all but unanimous; and in the

---

[1] A part of this dispatch was printed in *American State Papers*, Foreign Relations, IV. 371, beginning at this point.

House of Representatives the opposition to it amounted only to 15 or 16 votes.

Although no formal communication of this law to the British government will be necessary, it may naturally be expected that it will be noticed in your occasional conversations with Lord Castlereagh. He will doubtless remember, and may be reminded of, the repeated efforts made by this government to render it unnecessary by an amicable arrangement, which should place on an equitable footing of reciprocity the intercourse between the United States and the British colonies. He will remember the repeated warnings given that to this result it must come, unless some relaxation of the British prohibitions should take place; and his own equally repeated admissions that the exercise of the prohibitive right on the part of the United States would be altogether just, and would give no dissatisfaction whatever to Great Britain. You are nevertheless authorized to assure him that the President assented to this measure with great reluctance, because, however just in itself it may be, its tendencies cannot but be of an irritating character to the interests which it will immediately affect, and because his earnest desire is to remove causes of irritation and to multiply those of a conciliatory nature between the two countries. Such has manifestly been on both sides the effect of the equalizing and reciprocal provisions of the convention of July, 1815, and such he has no doubt would be the effect of the extension of its principles to the commercial intercourse between the United States and the British colonies in the West Indies and on this Continent. And you are authorized again to repeat the offer of treating for a fair and equitable arrangement of this interest. A further inducement for making this offer may be stated in the expediency of looking forward without further delay to the expiration of the convention of 1815, which has now little more than one year to remain in force. It is important that the commercial part of the community, both here and in Great Britain, should have timely notice of the state in which the relations between the countries are to stand after the termination of that convention; and as there are other objects of moment to be adjusted, the President desires you to propose an immediate general negotiation of a commercial treaty, to embrace the continuance for a further term of [ ] years of the convention, and also the other subjects in discussion between the two governments, namely, the question concerning the slaves, that relating to the Fisheries, the boundary line from the Lake of the Woods, and the Columbia River settlement. The President prefers taking this course to that of submitting to commissioners, at least immediately, questions upon which he thinks it probable the two governments may thus by a shorter process come to a mutual understanding between themselves.

If upon making this proposal, the British government agree to this negotiation, the President proposes that Mr. Gallatin and you should be authorised jointly as plenipotentiaries to conclude the treaty, which it is very desirable may be concluded in season to arrive here by the commencement of the next session of Congress, which is to be on the third Monday in November.[1] Instructions will be transmitted immediately to Mr. Gallatin to hold himself in readiness to repair to London upon receiving notice from you, should plenipotentiaries be appointed to treat with you; and besides the instructions which formed the basis of the existing convention, and others already in your possession, further documents will be forwarded to you as

[1] Adams, *Memoirs*, May 19, 1818.

soon as possible which may assist you in the management of the negotiation.

We entertain hopes that this measure may result in a new treaty which will remove most, if not all, of the causes of dissension between us and Great Britain. The satisfaction with which we have observed the avowal of the most *liberal* commercial principles by Lord Castlereagh in Parliament has already been noticed in my last letter. The opening, if not at all, at least of a great portion, of the ports of South America to the commerce of the world, which under every possible course of events must be now considered as irrevocable, and the bill which we perceive was before Parliament for establishing free ports in the British-American colonies, all tend to convince us that Great Britain must see that a relaxation from her colonial restrictions has become the unequivocal dictate of her own interest.[1]

The *National Intelligencer* of 25 April contains the proclamation of the President issued in consequence of the official communication by Mr. Bagot of the law of the province of Nova Scotia, repealing that upon which the counteracting law of Congress had been adopted. The retaliatory prohibitions of our law have accordingly ceased in respect to the province of Nova Scotia.[2] But no such communication has been made to us from the province of New Brunswick; and from the public prints it appears that, although their legislature were equally convinced of the expediency of repealing their plaister law, the measure was not consummated, from a difference of opinion between the legislative

---

[1] "That she will make upon an enlarged scale the same discovery, which has already been made by the legislature of the province of Nova Scotia, in regard to the trade in plaister of Paris."—*Original draft.*

[2] Dated St. George's Day, April 23, 1818. See Adams, *Memoirs,* under that, date.

Assembly and the Council, whether the repeal could take effect without the previous sanction of the king in Council. Our counter restrictions of course remain in operation with respect to the province of New Brunswick.

Mr. Bagot has personally delivered to me the warrant to the Governor General of Canada and to the officer commanding in Nova Scotia for the delivery of the islands in the Bay of Passamaquoddy conformably to the decision of the commissioners under the fourth article of the treaty of Ghent.

I am, etc.

TO ALBERT GALLATIN [1]

DEPARTMENT OF STATE,
WASHINGTON, 22d May, 1818.

SIR:

. . . .

The President is willing that the convention of 3 July, 1815, should be continued for eight or even ten years as it stands. Its operation has indeed been in some respects disadvantageous to the United States and favorable to Great Britain, owing to the revival of the interdiction of access to our vessels to the British West India and North American colonies, while our intercourse with them has been exclusively confined to British vessels. Yet that the injury to our navigation and shipping interest has not been very essential we have many indications, among which one is the return of trade just received from Liverpool for the last half year of 1817, a return exhibiting the entry of

[1] This dispatch is printed in part in *American State Papers*, Foreign Relations IV. 371.

235 American vessels, and a burthen of 73,000 tons, at that port during that time; to which the consul adds that a constant preference has hitherto been shown to our vessels for freight from thence. Another is the notice even now from our Southern ports, that the shipping there is not sufficient to take the produce ready for exportation. A third is the fact that in our trade with the British dominions in Europe the majority of vessels and of tonnage has hitherto been American. The moral effect of the equalization of duties on both sides in softening national asperities has been unequivocal, and is an object of much importance, deserving to be cherished and improved by both governments. The encouragement which the convention has given to our trade with the British possessions in the East Indies is more questionable, as that trade operates upon us as a continual and embarrassing drain of specie. But as it has been a trade of profitable returns, and as it would still to a great extent be carried on with the native states of India if we should be excluded, or our intercourse should be burthened and restricted with the British territories, the President will be satisfied to leave it as it is, and subject to the increasing competition of the British private traders with India, which will be likely to affect the interests of the British company more than ours.

The other interests which the President hopes may be adjusted by this negotiation are:

1. The intercourse with the British colonies in the West Indies and North America. You are well acquainted with the failure of the attempt to extend the convention of 1815 to this intercourse at the negotiation of the convention, and at a subsequent period, when four additional articles were proposed on the part of Great Britain—a copy of which you have. There was reason to believe that Lord Castle-

reagh was personally well disposed to a more liberal expansion of the colonial intercourse, although the Cabinet was not entirely prepared for it. The manner in which he has recently avowed a liberal commercial principle in Parliament, and the approbation with which that avowal was received; the obvious though not declared bearing which those sentiments had, both upon the South American contest, and upon those relations between the United States and the British colonies; the free-port acts, which we understand have been introduced into Parliament, and are even said to have passed, strongly and concurrently indicate that a change is taking place in the policy of the Cabinet on this subject, and we hope that now is precisely the favorable time for taking advantage of it. Our own navigation act may perhaps contribute to the same effect, and even should it operate otherwise, and confirm them in their obstinate exclusion of our vessels from those ports, as it will make their exclusion from ours to the same extent reciprocal, it leaves us the more free to agree to the renewal of the convention of July, 1815, if nothing more can be obtained.

2. Indemnity to the owners of the slaves carried away from the United States by British officers after the ratification of the peace of Ghent, and contrary to a stipulation in the first article of that treaty.

Copies of the correspondence between the two governments on this subject are in the possession of Mr. Rush. They disagreed in their construction of the stipulation alluded to, and each party adhering to its own view of it, a proposal was made nearly two years since on our part to refer it to the arbitration of some friendly sovereign. This proposal which Mr. Rush upon his arrival in England renewed has now been accepted by the British government, but with a further proposal to refer it and two other subjects for arrangement in the first instance to commissioners, like those under the 4th, 5th, 6th and 7th articles of the treaty of Ghent. 3, 4. These other subjects are the boundary line from the north-west corner of the Lake of the Woods westward; which you remember was all but agreed upon, and went off upon a collateral incident at Ghent; and our *title* to the settlement at the mouth of Columbia River.

The expediency of referring any of these questions to two commissioners, one belonging to each of the two countries, is very doubtful. With regard to the slaves and to Columbia River, it was scarcely to be expected that the commissioners of either party would ultimately entertain an opinion different from that already pronounced by his own government, and if concession upon one point is to be made the condition of corresponding concession upon the other, it may with more propriety be effected by compromise between the two governments than by judiciary powers given by them to individuals under allegiance to the two countries themselves. As to the line from the Lake of the Woods, as some dissatisfaction has already been excited here by the expense occasioned by the two commissions already employed in settling the boundary, another commission to draw a line through the depth of the deserts, and to an indefinite extent, would be still more liable to censure; besides the apprehension which it might raise that the issue of the commission would be to bring the British territory again in contact with the Mississippi.

5. The fisheries. The correspondence between the two governments on this subject leaves it still in the unsettled state in which it was left at the peace. Two proposals have been made on the part of the British government neither of which proving acceptable, a counter proposal from us has been promised, and will be contained in the further de-

tailed instructions which will be prepared and forwarded to Mr. Rush to assist you in the conduct of the negotiation.

I am, etc.

TO JONATHAN RUSSELL

DEPARTMENT OF STATE,
WASHINGTON, 24 May, 1818.

SIR:

I have had the honor of receiving your Letter of 11 March enclosing a letter from the King of Sweden, Charles John addressed to the President and Senate of the United States announcing the decease of the late King.[1] The President's answer is herewith enclosed which you will deliver in person to the King together with your new letter of credence. A copy of it is also transmitted, which according to the usage you will communicate to the Minister of Foreign Affairs before you deliver the original.

By the third section of the second article of the constitution of the United States it is provided that the President "shall receive ambassadors and other public ministers." It is therefore to him that their credential letters and consequently all public letters of foreign sovereigns to the government of the United States should be addressed. Neither the House of Representatives, nor the Senate, nor the two Houses in Congress assembled hold correspondence with foreign princes or states. The European sovereigns, none of whom appears to understand or to have attended to this part of our constitution, have addressed their letters sometimes to the Congress of the United States, sometimes

[1] Charles XIII died February 5, 1818, and was succeeded by Bernadotte, who took the title of Charles XIV. He had been adopted by Charles XIII under the name of Charles John.

to the President and Congress, and sometimes to "the United States." This is the first letter which has been received addressed to the President and Senate, a formulary probably suggested to the Swedish government by the occasion which they have had to observe the agency attributed to the Senate by our constitution with regard to the ratification of treaties and to the appointment of our own public ministers abroad. This conclusion is, however, incorrect, because I have noticed the authority to *receive* foreign ministers is vested exclusively in the President, and in practice all the letters from foreign sovereigns, however addressed, are opened and answered only by him. You may take occasion to state this to the Swedish Minister of Foreign Affairs as a reason why the King's letter, though addressed to the President and Senate, is answered only by the President. At the same time you may intimate that although its address should have been to the President alone, he was disinclined to be punctilious on a mere point of form, and received it without hesitation, not doubting that the style of address conformable to our constitution, when known to the Swedish government, will in the case of any future correspondence be observed.

I am with great respect, etc.

TO ABIGAIL ADAMS

WASHINGTON, 25 May, 1818.

MY DEAR MOTHER:

I am ashamed to find upon my file of letters *to be answered* one from you of 29 January, besides two or three from my father of as old standing. You know, however, the only cause which has occasioned so long a postponement of my reply. There has been I believe no change in the office of collector at Plymouth, and it was with much pain I learnt it was probable there would be.[1] Should it happen I will present your recommendations in the proper quarter.

Although I have the pleasure of a personal acquaintance with Mr. Wirt, I have not been able to read his life of Patrick Henry; for as my office gives me from four to six hours of indispensable reading every day, and other employment for an equal or greater proportion of the time, I can scarcely indulge myself for half an hour with anything else, without finding that some duty has been neglected. To travel through such a volume as that of Mr. Wirt has therefore been impracticable, but I have read large extracts from it in the newspapers and reviews. My father's letters in *Niles' Register*, and those to Judge Tudor, have given me greater pleasure;[2] but General Dearborn's account of the battle of Bunker's Hill and the controversy which has arisen from it have affected me quite otherwise.[3] I can excuse that sort of partiality which manifests itself in aggrandizing the patriots and warriors of our Revolution; but it grieves me to see the reputation of any of them assailed thirty years after death, and to find co-temporaries and eye-witnesses disputing with each other whether Putnam was a hero or a coward.

The late session of Congress has exhibited the parties of this country in a new and extraordinary point of view. The divisions heretofore so keen and bitter, between federalists and republicans, were scarce perceptible. Party spirit,

---

[1] Henry Warren was then the collector, and Major William Hamet was suggested as a successor.

[2] *Niles' Weekly Register*, XIV. 17, 33, 137, 177.

[3] *Account of the Battle of Bunker's Hill*, Boston, 1818. It called out a reply from Daniel Putnam.

inextinguishable in a country like ours, was in search of a leader, and the leader in search of party spirit, and both in search of pretexts. They all were found, and found out each other; but the political atmosphere was calm and the attempts to blow up a gale were not successful. Neither South America, nor internal improvement, could be made to produce much agitation among the people. The foundations, however, were laid for the future fabric of opposition. The ground for conflict was surveyed, and musters of force more than once took place. Since the close of the session there is nothing stirring to produce excitement in the country, and although federalism still retains its stronghold in Massachusetts, it will even there continue to lose its virulence, and will preserve its supremacy only by annulling the influence of the state.

. . . .

I am, etc.

TO RICHARD RUSH

WASHINGTON, 29 May, 1818.

DEAR SIR:

. . . . . .

The *inexorable economy* of the legislature in regard to the expenses of foreign intercourse has been manifested in various ways during the late session. The expenditures of the existing commissions under the Ghent treaty occasioned so much dissatisfaction, that after a thorough investigation by the Committee of Ways and Means, and a still more minute investigation by two special committees of enquiry, a resolution actually passed the House of Representatives the last evening of the session, to request the President to propose to the British government some mode of accomplishing the business in a less expensive manner. Want of time alone prevented the Senate from acting upon this resolution and probably from concurring in it.

The appropriations proposed in the estimates for agents for seamen and claims at Amsterdam and Madrid, at salaries of $2,000 each, were struck out. That for the agent at Copenhagen was equally omitted in the appropriation bill reported by the Committee of Ways and Means, and it was only upon a representation that the agent actually there could not receive notice of the discontinuance of his salary till a considerable part of the year will have elapsed, that an appropriation was finally agreed to of $1,500 for three-quarters of the present year, after which it will cease.

Unequivocal evidence was manifested of an *expectation* by Congress that the missions to Sweden and the Netherlands should in the course of the present year be reduced, and chargés d'affaires take the place of the ministers plenipotentiary residing at those courts. The arrangements of the executive had already been made conformably to this provision. Mr. Eustis is expected home within one or two months, and Mr. A. H. Everett will be appointed as chargé d'affaires to the Netherlands. New credentials are transmitted to Mr. Russell at Stockholm; but it is not supposed he will protract his residence there beyond the present year, and on taking leave he is to commit the charge of the affairs of the legation to Mr. Hughes.

You see Congress are determined we shall have a great revenue—*magnum vectigal parsimonia*. Yet they have been bountiful to the remaining warriors of our revolution; and for my own part, when I consider the principles by which they were actuated, both in their economy and their liberality, I think them honorable to the legislature and to the country.

On a still broader scale, you will remark in reference to the policy pursued towards foreign nations a well tempered combination of liberality and of national spirit. The negotiation for a commercial treaty with the Netherlands, which had been attempted last summer at The Hague, was unsuccessful; but the act of that government exempting the vessels of the United States from extra tonnage duty as foreigners has been met by a regulation more than reciprocal on our part—the act of Congress removing not only all extra tonnage duties from the vessels of the Netherlands, but also all extra duties upon the merchandise imported in them, and looking back in bestowing this benefit to the time when the regulations of the Netherlands in favor of our navigation themselves commenced. At the same time the British system of excluding our vessels from their colonial ports has been equally met by a counteracting system of total exclusion. This measure being merely experimental, it would be presumptuous to reckon with much confidence upon its effects; but the point of view in which you will take pleasure in considering it is the prevalence of a national feeling over those partial and sectional interests and prejudices which heretofore prevented the experiment from being made. How the British free-port act, which is said to have passed in Parliament, will operate upon this measure, and whether it was adopted in anticipation of the act of Congress, you can perhaps assist us in forming a correct opinion.

In the public despatches you will be informed of the President's view with regard to South American affairs. Mr. Sumter writes that he sent you a copy of his correspondence with Casa Flores concerning our three commissioners to Buenos Ayres. That Spanish Minister's panic at the appearance of our commissioners disclosed to us a secret worth knowing. The European alliance appear to have been disposed to settle affairs between Spain and South America without asking our opinion, and without even letting us know what they were about. It may also disclose a secret quite as valuable to them—that we have some concern with that question, and that they ought not to settle it without consulting us. We say they ought not to interfere at all; and most especially not to restore any part of the dominions of Spain. We think it impossible that they should interfere with any effect to that end, and we believe that the British government neither expects nor intends it. If Count Palmella, the Portuguese minister, should be still in London when you receive this, let me recommend it to you to cultivate his acquaintance and friendship, to converse with him on these affairs as freely as you may find will be agreeable to him. You may probably derive much useful information from him. Have the goodness to bring me to his recollection, with the assurance of the great respect and esteem for his personal character that I entertain, and the pleasure with which I remember the acquaintance that I enjoyed with him in London.

The President's health during the last winter has been infirm, and he had one severe attack of illness which confined him three weeks to his chamber. He has however entirely recovered, and yesterday left the city with the Secretaries of War and the Navy upon a tour down the Chesapeake to Norfolk, upon which he expects to be absent about three weeks. He will not extend his journey further south this winter.

Mr. Pinkney arrived a few days since at Annapolis. Mr. G. W. Campbell, is appointed Minister to Russia, and is to sail in the course of the next month from Boston in the *Guerriere* for Cronstadt.

A copy of Mr. Wirt's *Life of Patrick Henry*, and two or three copies of Mr. Pitkin's statistical work will be sent you.

I am, etc.

TO RICHARD RUSH [1]

Department of State,
Washington, 30 May, 1818.

Sir:

I had the honor of receiving yesterday your dispatch dated 15 April, No. 14. The President had left this city the day before on a short tour from Annapolis down Chesapeake Bay to Norfolk. It is expected his absence will be of about three weeks, and upon his return the particular instructions relative to the negotiation of the commercial treaty to take place in the event of the acceptance by the British government of the proposal contained in my last dispatch will be forwarded to you. The sentiments of the President with regard to the proposed coöperation of the United States for the suppression of the slave trade by a *naval police*, and a restricted mutual right of search, will be transmitted at the same time. It would have been agreeable, and might have enabled us to judge more immediately of the propriety of our acceding to any contemplated arrangements of this kind, if the articles themselves as proposed had been communicated to you, instead of a bare verbal description of their purport by Lord Castlereagh. On this subject, as well as upon the mediation between Spain and South America, it may be proper to suggest in the most friendly manner, that whenever the coöperation of the United States to any measure *concerted* by

---

[1] An extract from this dispatch is in *American State Papers*, Foreign Relations, IV. 372.

the European alliance is thought useful or desirable, it may with more propriety and facility be obtained by communicating unreservedly with them while the arrangements are forming, than by a mere notification of what *has been* done.

From the substance of Lord Castlereagh's remarks with regard to our intercourse with the British colonies in the West Indies and North America, the prospect is less favorable than had been anticipated of a further relaxation of their exclusive colonial system, and Lord Castlereagh's commercial liberality in his answer to Mr. Lyttleton must, it seems, be received with exceptions reserved. The free-port act, however, of which nothing appears to have been said in your conference with him, is itself an important modification of that system. Our navigation act of the last session you will see has gone further than the proposed bill reported by the Committee of Foreign Relations. It is entire prohibition. And although the President takes the first moment after its enactment, and even before it goes into operation, to hold out again to Great Britain the hand of liberal reciprocity, yet in the event of a negotiation, he will not wish that the British cabinet should be pressed upon this point. It will be sufficient to make the offer. If not accepted, we must be content to abide by the issue of our own prohibitions.

It is not our desire to embarrass the proposed commercial negotiation with any of the questions of maritime regulations adapted to a state of warfare. We do not wish that blockades, contraband trade with enemies or their colonies, or even impressment, should be drawn into the discussion, unless such a wish should be manifested on the British side.

Mr. Bagot has been informed that this negotiation will be proposed, and that in the event of its being agreed to, another plenipotentiary will be joined with you to confer and conclude with those who may be appointed on the part of Great Britain. He is not aware that there will be any objection to it; but if there should be any, and the British government should determine to keep the renewal of the commercial convention distinct from every other subject to be arranged between the two countries, you will of course not give the notice to Mr. Gallatin to repair to London mentioned in my last despatch. If the British cabinet agree to negotiate, it is hoped that the special instructions to be prepared and forwarded to you will reach you as soon as Mr. Gallatin will find it convenient to meet you in London. If the British cabinet prefer by a single article to renew the convention of July, 1815, for a term of eight, ten, or even twelve years, or any shorter period, your full power heretofore given will be still in force, and will enable you to conclude such an article, subject to the ratification here, by and with the advice and consent of the Senate.

I am, etc.

TO JOSEPH HOPKINSON

WASHINGTON, 1st June, 1818.

DEAR SIR:

Your favor of the 25th ultimo has been duly received, and I tender you my best thanks for the information of Moll's *Atlas* of 1720 containing the map of Louisiana as then claimed by France.[1] The map to which you refer was not known to me, though from your description of it there is a great probability of its having been that from which De Lille's map was afterwards copied.[2] The French map of

---

[1] "A new map of the North Parts of America claimed by France," dated 1720.

[2] Guillaume Del' Isle, 1703. See Phillips, *List of Maps of America*, 366.

1717 having been published so immediately after St. Denis's second journey, and having his route marked upon it, indicates that it was occasioned by that event. The map which you have seen is, therefore, a valuable document, and if you can obtain it we shall be thankful for it. Since my letter to Mr. Onis several documents confirmative of our claim to the river Bravo have been transmitted to the Department, and I have so thoroughly convinced myself that it is just, that by my good will the offer shall never again be made to Spain which she had slighted, of taking the Colorado for the western boundary at the Gulf. I would henceforth never recede an inch from the Bravo. It will afford me peculiar satisfaction also to receive evidence in support of our title from *you*.

I am, etc.

TO JOHN D. LEWIS

WASHINGTON, 18 June, 1818.

DEAR SIR:

. . . .

The affidavit of Mr. Kücel of Archangel concerning the conduct of Mr. L. Harris as consul in 1808 and 1809, copy of which was enclosed in your letter of 13 August, I felt it to be my duty to lay before the President, to whom Mr. Harris had expressed a desire to be again employed in the public service. The President directed that a copy of it should be transmitted to Mr. Harris himself, for such explanation as he might think proper to give concerning the transactions to which it referred. Mr. Harris gave explanations accordingly, and during the late session of Congress was several weeks himself in this city. After a conversation with me, in which I stated to him without disguise my own impression on the subject, he intimated to the President that he was apprehensive I entertained prepossessions unfriendly to him, and expressed the wish that the examination of the charges against him and of his vindication of himself might be referred to other persons, members of the administration. To this the President with my entire acquiescence and approbation assented. The reference was accordingly made to the Secretary of the Treasury and the Secretary of War, Messrs. Crawford and Calhoun. Mr. Harris's defence consisted chiefly in the proofs of approbation of his conduct by all the administrations of the United States under which he had served; by the favor of the Emperor Alexander which he had constantly enjoyed; and by Count Romanzoff and the American ministers who have successively resided at St. Petersburg, and in impeaching the character of his accusers. He represented Kücel and Rodde of Riga as worthless men, by whom he had been deceived, and altogether undeserving of credit. He attributed to your enmity and *ingratitude* all these accusations against him, and attempted also to destroy your credit by allegations against you, and by a certificate from Mr. Coxe, formerly Consul at Tunis.

As these papers seem to require some explanation from you, I told Mr. Harris that I thought it a justice due to you that they should be made known to you, and that copies of them would be furnished you. They are accordingly herewith enclosed, and I entreat you to give me a fair and candid exposition of the facts, that I may have the opportunity of proving to those who are not personally acquainted with you, the uprightness of your conduct, of which those who do know you need no proof. Mr. Harris had also a letter to himself from Mr. Rodde of Reval, expressing his strong displeasure at the proceedings of his brother of Riga, and having the appearance of contradicting his statements to Harris's disadvantage. I was much surprised I own at the sight of this letter from Rodde of Reval, because he had told me with his own lips at Reval, the whole story of his brother's and his own transactions with Harris, and had shown me the letters that had passed between them at the time of their differences.

Mr. Crawford and Mr. Calhoun, after the examination of all the papers, gave it as their opinion that some further explanation was necessary with regard to Kücel's affidavit, and Harris has sent to Russia for further testimonials in his favor. My knowledge was of course all hearsay, and from parties concerned only in the cases of Donovan and Rodde of Reval. I advised Mr. Harris, if he had received no part of the money which he admitted had been occasionally paid for the admission of vessels with *irregular* papers, to procure from the brothers Cramer a copy of his accounts of partnership as settled with them, and their declaration upon oath, together with that of James Alexander Smith, that in this settlement Harris had received nothing as a proportion of such gratuities paid for the consular certificate in favor of vessels for which it could not have been obtained gratis. Whether he will attempt to obtain such a declaration from the Cramers and Smith I do not know. But he will undoubtedly continue to make every possible effort to justify himself and to cast discredit upon his adversaries. In communicating to you what he has done with this view against you, I make it an express condition that you will not at any future period make it a subject of personal violence between him and you. I know your feelings and do full justice to them; but you must give me your word of honor that you will never call him to what you call the account of a gentleman, and I tell you candidly that if I were not persuaded that you will give me this promise without hesitation, I should not feel myself bound to give you this opportunity of justifying your own character.

This leads me to assure you of the great regret and concern which the affair between your brother[1] and J. L. Harris has given me. Of this transaction I have a very clear and doubtless correct idea, having received full statements of it from you, from Harris himself, and from Mr. Pinkney, whose conduct relating to it has been marked with the impartiality which his station required, and at the same time with a sincere friendship and esteem both for your brother and yourself. I have not the pleasure of a personal acquaintance with your brother; but from what I have heard of him from all who do know him, I entertain a high respect for his character, and esteem him as your next of kin in disposition as well as in blood. Now you cannot have forgotten that while I had the pleasure of enjoying your acquaintance at St. Petersburg, I more than once took the liberty of advising you most earnestly to coolness and forbearance towards persons who had injured you; and I cannot but wish I had been in a situation to give the same advice to your brother, and that he had shown as much attention to it. I expect that Mr. Harris will resign his office and leave Russia. Of his conduct from the time when your brother assaulted him upon the exchange, it is not necessary for me to give an opinion; but neither is it possible so entirely to take side with your brother in the affair, as to approve the time, place and manner, in which he gave this affront to a public officer of his country. I say this in entire confidence to you, and to explain the motive for with-

[1] W. D. Lewis.

holding the consular appointment from your brother. I mentioned his name to the President, and showed him your letter declining the appointment for yourself and asking it for your brother. He thought it would have the appearance not only of taking side with your brother in the quarrel, but of rewarding him for an act certainly not conformable to the Russian laws, and not calculated to do honor to our own national character. I very sincerely lament the inconveniences that your brother has suffered in consequence of it, and wish it had been in my power to prevent them; nor should I now express my opinion upon the transaction, but that I feel it a duty to open to you my impressions upon it entirely without reserve. When I say that it was not calculated to do honor to our national character, I refer only to the impression which under any circumstances it must have produced upon the by-standers. If Harris had resented the attack with ordinary spirit, the scene upon the exchange must have been very painful and entirely adverse to the American character. If by his forbearance he degraded himself, still the American character suffered by his degradation. If in a course of time hereafter these considerations should lose their weight as the whole transaction falls into oblivion, they must have their effect at the present moment, and I have thought it best in regard both to you and to your brother to make them known to you. I hope that both he and you will consider them as perfectly compatible with the most earnest disposition on my part to befriend him, if any occasion should ever present itself in which I can indulge myself in that desire.[1]

Mr. Campbell will deliver you this letter. I beg leave to recommend him and his family to every attention and service that you can render them. Mrs. Adams is well

[1] Adams, *Memoirs*, March 5, 1819.

and wishes to be kindly remembered to you. Charles has grown a great boy and is at school at Boston.

I am, etc.

TO JONATHAN RUSSELL

DEPARTMENT OF STATE,
WASHINGTON, 22 June, 1818.

SIR:

. . . . . .

From your letter of 4 February it appears that there exists a disposition on the part of the Swedish government to proceed further than the treaty as now ratified stipulates, in opening and placing upon a liberal footing the commercial intercourse between the two countries. The policy of this government in relation to this subject generally has been disclosed in its utmost extent by two acts of Congress passed at their last session, one of which is a navigation act, meeting by direct and total prohibition the British system of exclusion of our vessels from their colonies in the West Indies and on this continent, and the other is an act by which the foreign tonnage duties are repealed in favor of the vessels of the Netherlands. The latter of these acts was a measure of reciprocity, corresponding with a regulation of the same kind which had been adopted in the kingdom of the Netherlands in favor of the vessels of the United States. An attempt was made last summer to negotiate a new treaty of commerce with the Netherlands, which was unsuccessful. These mutual regulations, however, may accomplish the liberal views of both parties as effectually as if they were effected by treaty. You are authorized to assure the Swedish government that there is no doubt the same principles will be adopted with Sweden upon the same condition of reciprocity, and that we are willing to admit Swedish vessels and the merchandise imported in them into our ports upon an equal footing with our own, if we can obtain admission upon the same terms for our vessels and their cargoes in Sweden. But we cannot accede to an exception of the article of salt or any other, the objection to which is the same as to the ten per cent additional duties in the expunged articles of the treaty—namely, that they belong properly to neither of the systems, but form a halfway term between the two. We prefer that of opening our commerce to fair and equal competition, and we adopt that of countervailing and restrictive measures only in self-defence. . . .

TO ALEXANDER HILL EVERETT

WASHINGTON, 22 June, 1818.

DEAR SIR:

When I advised you never to solicit an office for yourself, I did not mean to preclude you from the exercise of your influence in favor of your friends. It would have given me pleasure if your brother [1] could have received one of the two new appointments of appraisers of goods at Boston, and your letter was laid before the President. But the appointments were regularly made through the channel of the Treasury Department, and the choice had been fixed upon before your letter was received.

My advice was founded upon the opinion that your talents and services would of themselves operate as a sufficient recommendation of you for any office which may be a worthy object of your ambition. When you reënter the

[1] Probably Oliver Everett.

diplomatic career, the opportunity of rendering useful services will be in your hands. Its judicious improvement will be the best of recommendations.

Mr. Eustis was expected at The Hague on the 15th of April, and was to embark shortly afterwards for the United States. His arrival may now be daily expected. I have received a letter from him giving the explanations which I had requested of the passages in former letters of his relating to you, of which you have had notice. They are entirely satisfactory and honorable to you. It is, of course, very desirable that if you should meet him on his return home, you should not in any manner give him to understand that you have had notice of his remarks concerning you which have given you uneasiness. They were on his part quite confidential, and as now appears written without any unfriendly disposition towards you.[1] It was proper on the prospect of your re-appointment to an important public trust that their full import should be unequivocally ascertained as they have been to the complete justification of your character.

Mr. Campbell is to proceed in the course of a few days to Boston to embark in the frigate *Guerriere* for Russia. But the President does not think proper to make the appointment of a chargé d'affaires to the Netherlands until after the arrival of Mr. Eustis in this country, and it is probable that the frigate will go not through the channel but north about.

[1] "His love of retirement which appeared to me to have acquired the strength of habit and prevented him from frequenting society sufficiently to become acquainted with passing events, formed the only objection to his usefulness at a foreign court. To his integrity, perfect honor and capacity to discharge faithfully any trust committed to him; to his learning, information and talents, I can most cheerfully add my testimony to that bestowed by all who know him. With all this it did appear to me that talents inferior with habits more social might be more useful." *William Eustis to John Quincy Adams,* February 7, 1818. Ms.

Since beginning this letter I have received one from Mr. Eustis dated at The Hague, 21 April. He was making preparations for his departure and still expected to embark about the beginning of May.

I remain, etc.

TO CHRISTOPHER HUGHES

WASHINGTON, 22 June, 1818.

DEAR SIR:

I have had the pleasure of receiving from you private letters of 30 July, 25 August, 8 October, 17 January, and 6 February last. In a public dispatch I acknowledged the receipt of the first and second, without being able to answer them in particular detail. And although there are parts of your private correspondence which I value very highly, you will I am sure make allowance for the impossibility of answering your private letters with punctuality when I assure you that I have upon my unanswered file letters that have lain there for months from my own father. To the example which you allege of my predecessors, I have no other reply than "non omnia possumus omnes." They must have had a greater degree of *facilite de travail* than I have. It certainly was considered by Mr. Madison that the public duties of the Department of State were more than sufficient for one man, as you know one of the last acts of his administration was the proposal to take part of them off, by the establishment of a home department. Congress, however, thought otherwise. For myself I can only assure you that I have found the duties of the Department to be more than I can perform. Some of them are therefore not performed, among which, as it becomes necessary to give the preference of neglect to those which bear least upon the public interest, is that of answering letters relating to the private interests of the writers, or to the disposition, temper, and affections of the head of the department. You will immediately perceive, my dear Mr. Hughes, the decisive reason which has deprived me of the pleasure which I should have taken in answering every one of your every kind and friendly letters. It is one of the sarcastic remarks of Rochefoucauld, that the reason why the conversation of lovers is so delightful to them is that it turns exclusively upon themselves. But these repasts of sweetmeats require the stomachs of lovers to digest them, and the parts of your correspondence which I have assured you I highly value are not precisely those which relate to your affairs or to my virtues, but precisely those which relate to anything else.

However deeply, for instance, I sympathized in your disappointment at the return of Mr. Russell to Stockholm, it was not in my power to prevent it; and if it had been, there was a consideration due also to him, and his feelings, and his interests, so far as they were not incompatible with those of the public. His treaty had been advised for ratification by the Senate with exceptions. It was not unnatural or unreasonable that he should wish to complete the negotiation which had been thus far managed by himself. You had chosen to go to Stockholm with a full knowledge that he might return there, and I had explicitly given you my opinion when I had the pleasure of seeing you in England, that he would return. The recital of your distresses upon his return is very pathetic; but *que puis-j'y faire, mon cher ami?* I could not answer you anything that would be agreeable to you, and when you receive this letter, I am not without my suspicion that you will think it would have been quite as well if I had now persevered in not answering you at all.

As to your regard, and kindness, and esteem for me, I receive the assurances of them with a full conviction of their sincerity, and I trust with a suitable sentiment of gratitude. And now, that matter being settled between us, let me entreat you never to write me another word upon the subject. Let me henceforth take it for granted that you have a good opinion both of my character and capacity, and that there are no doubts in that respect, which it requires the confirmation of fresh assurances to remove.

Your letter of 6 February, enclosing one for General Smith, was received by me after the close of the session of Congress, and I accordingly forwarded that for the General immediately to him at Baltimore. I received from him a few days afterwards a letter inquiring how long Mr. Russell would probably remain in Sweden, which I answered by stating that from his late letters, he might be detained a few months longer than he would have been, if the accession of a new king had not made it necessary for him to deliver a new credential letter; but that it was still expected his mission would terminate before the close of the present year. The time is, of course, left to his own choice and convenience.

I suppose you will by the commencement of the next year find yourself again the chargé d'affaires at Stockholm; but as a friend I advise you neither to calculate with much confidence upon remaining there many years, nor to expect any appointment elsewhere in Europe. Sweden has now no diplomatic character of any rank in the United States, nor do her interests appear to require that she should have any. We have lately heard rumors as if Mr. De Kantzow expected to come here again. If he comes, he will certainly be received with all due complacency and respect; but neither the President, nor Congress, nor the spirit of our country, are at all inclined to countenance any useless exchange of diplomatic missions. If Sweden should see no necessity for keeping a chargé d'affaires here, we shall not only concur in that opinion, but shall very soon recollect how very easy it is for us to live in perfect good understanding with Sweden, without any diplomatic personage at Stockholm. Your career in that case will be short. It was a maxim of Mr. Jefferson's, which I find is also approved by Mr. Monroe, that Americans, and especially young Americans, should for their own sake, as well as for that of their country, make no long residences in a public capacity at the courts of Europe. He thought the air of those regions so unfriendly to American constitutions that they always required after a few years to be renovated by the wholesome republican atmosphere of their own country. The practice of the present administration will be altogether conformable to these principles.

From what I have here said, you will infer my wish that in future your letters may relate to anything else but ourselves. And, for example, write me everything that you can learn about the affairs and interests of Sweden, not only in their direct relations with the United States, but with every part of Europe and with all the rest of the world. Write me whether any peculiar characteristic marks the administration of the present king, how he stands with the several orders of the states of the kingdom. Who are his most confidential ministers and advisers? What sort of character and reputation is formed or forming by his son, the Duke of Sudermania?[1] The names and characters of the principal noblemen in office about the court. Whether any persons of distinction in the country are considered as unfriendly to the present establishment, and how their standing in

[1] He ascended the throne in 1844 as Oscar I.

society is affected by it. What part the king takes in the general affairs of Europe, if any, and the state of his relations with Russia, France, England, Austria, Denmark, the Porte, and the *European* and the *Holy* Alliance. How he stands with Spain, and whether he or his Cabinet have any opinions about the affairs of South America. Keep a constant eye upon all your diplomatic colleagues, obtain their friendship and confidence by those winning ways of yours, find out all their secrets and those of their masters, and without ever betraying the confidence of any one (of which I know you are incapable and which we never would ask), let us have the full benefit of all your discourses. Turn in a word all your sagacity, all your activity, and all your ingenuity, to the account of your country, and whether you write me public dispatches or private letters, *they shall be answered*.

I beg to be most respectfully remembered to Mrs. Hughes, and congratulate you upon the increase and prosperity of your family. Mrs. Adams also begs to be affectionately remembered to her. George is at the University at Cambridge and will be much gratified by your kind remembrances. Believe me, etc.

CASE OF OBED WRIGHT [1]

The Opinion of the Secretaries of State, and of the Treasury, and of the Attorney General, in the case of Captain Obed Wright, is that a prosecution should be directed before the circuit court of the United States in the first instance; and that if that court should disclaim jurisdiction of the

[1] Obed Wright, by whose orders the friendly Indians of the Chehaw village were killed.

crime, that he should be referred for trial by a court-martial under the direction of the executive of the state of Georgia.

Respectfully submitted to the President.

26 June, 1818.

WASHINGTON, June 28, 1818.

Let the prosecution be instituted in the manner proposed, and a commission be issued for the trial of Captain Wright. It is presumed that a commission ought to issue, provided the trial is to take place before the usual term, which is not till November or December next, to which period it would be improper to postpone it, if to be avoided. Of this mode of proceeding General Jackson ought to be advised, and of the time when the trial will be commenced, that witnesses may be ordered to attend. Governor Rabun should likewise be apprised of it for the same reason.

An officer of rank should be ordered to visit the Chehaw town in the name of the executive of the United States, to examine into the loss and damage that indemnity may be made and to console the survivors. I wish Mr. Adams to have these purposes carried into effect, giving the necessary advice to the Department of War when its agency is necessary.

JAMES MONROE.

TO GEORGE WASHINGTON CAMPBELL

DEPARTMENT OF STATE,
WASHINGTON, 28 June, 1818.

SIR:

The Swedish government have agreed to ratify the treaty negotiated by Mr. Russell, with the exception of the 3d, 4th, and 6th articles, conformably to the advice and consent given by the Senate of the United States. The ratifications are to be exchanged at Stockholm.

The ratified treaty is herewith committed to your charge.

On your passage of the Sound to enter the Baltic you will have occasion to come to anchor at least for a few hours in the road of Elseneur. You will then give the treaty to Mr. Burrows,[1] whom the President has directed shall have the accommodation of a passage in the frigate, with directions to proceed immediately with it and deliver it to Mr. Russell at Stockholm. His expenses on the journey may be paid by you and charged separately in your accounts. Should any unforeseen circumstance render it inconvenient for Mr. Burrows to undertake this journey, an officer belonging to the ship, upon the selection of whom you will consult Captain McDonough, may be substituted in his stead. . . .

As in your passage into the Baltic you must necessarily pass immediately before the city of Copenhagen, you will perhaps find it convenient to anchor there, and to go yourself on shore for two or three days. As there are two objects upon which it will be desirable to have some explanation with the Danish government, an informal letter of introduction is furnished you to the Minister of Foreign Affairs, Rosencrantz, for the purpose of enabling you to communicate with him upon objects of public concernment.

An intimation was given a few months since through the Danish Minister in London to Mr. Rush, that they wished to see from the United States at the court of Denmark a minister of equal rank with the Danish minister residing here.

If you see Mr. Rosenkrantz, you will inform him that entertaining the most friendly dispositions towards the government of Denmark, if the President has forborne to accede immediately to his suggestion, it has by no means proceeded from any intentional disrespect, but from the nature of our constitutions, and the established policy of

[1] S. E. Burrows.

the country of keeping no government diplomatic missions at foreign courts except where the continuance of occasions for discussion of important topics of public interest render it indispensably necessary. You will observe that although Mr. Pedersen [1] unites with the character of Consul General that of Minister Resident, and although the President with views of accommodation and deference to the appointment by his Danish Majesty very readily acquiesced in this combination, yet as Mr. Pedersen has never resided at the seat of government, as the other foreign ministers are expected to do and are indeed officially required, we have considered his official rank rather as a personal favor or privilege conferred upon him than as of a character requiring a corresponding diplomatic officer from the United States in Denmark. That the combination itself of the *legational* and *consular* character is not without inconveniences, so well understood by the European governments that it is very rarely if ever practised by them in their intercourse with one another. That we are not insensible to them, and although the President is entirely satisfied with the conduct of Mr. Pedersen, and in no wise desirous that his diplomatic rank and privileges should be withdrawn from him, yet whenever the king of Denmark shall think proper to terminate his public mission, it will be quite satisfactory to us, if in future the offices of consul and of public minister should be kept entirely distinct, and the appointment of the one, or the other, or of both, will be received by this government with equal satisfaction, as it may suit the views of the government of Denmark to make them.

Denmark possesses in the West Indies the two islands of Saint Croix and St. Thomas. The Governor General resides at Saint Croix; but St. Thomas has the privileges of a free

[1] P. Pedersen, stationed at Philadelphia.

port. We have lately had as Consuls, Robert Jaques at the former, and Robert Monroe Harrison at the latter. Mr. Harrison at a very early period fell into misunderstandings with the local authorities of the island of St. Thomas, and afterwards with the Governor General, against whom he reported a complaint for severe and illegal treatment of an American seaman. The documents furnished on that occasion were such as required the animadversion of the Danish government, and complaint was made by Mr. Forbes, upon which it is hoped that a suitable investigation will have been made, and the conduct of the Governor General, if culpable as alleged, duly reprehended. As upon the complaints of the Governor General against Mr. Harrison, Mr. Pedersen, the Danish Minister, made a formal demand for the revocation of that officer's commission, the President thought proper to comply with the request and Mr. Harrison was dismissed. This measure was not known to the Danish government when they came to the determination that Mr. Jaques should be recognized as consul of the United States at St. Croix, but that *no* Consul should be admitted at the island of St. Thomas. The resolution to recognize Mr. Jaques was communicated by Mr. Rosenkrantz in a written note to Mr. Forbes; that rejecting *any* Consul at St. Thomas was only mentioned verbally; and with the addition that Mr. Jaques would be permitted to appoint an agent under him for the island of St. Thomas.

It is hoped that when you arrive at Copenhagen the Danish government will have been informed of the removal of Mr. Harrison, and that they will reconsider the decision to allow no consul at St. Thomas. You will state that St. Croix is a place not much frequented by American vessels, while St. Thomas is constantly crowded with them. That it will probably be much more so when our navigation act of the last session of Congress goes into operation. The number of American vessels that entered at St. Thomas the last half of the year 1801 was near 130, from which it is evident how often the services of a consul must have been needed. If a *deputy* from the consul at St. Croix is freely admitted, we cannot discern a solid motive for denying to the government of the United States the right of appointing its own agents, or reducing them to the necessity of prescribing to one of their officers the appointment of another as his deputy. This, however, at the present moment must be done. Mr. Jaques will, therefore, be directed to appoint Mr. Nathan Levy as his agent, and he will be furnished with a commission as consul, to be presented if the Danish government should finally conclude to receive him.

Dispatches have already been forwarded to Mr. Forbes instructing him to present these views of both the subjects here noticed to Mr. Rosenkrantz. But he may possibly leave the country before he receives them and they may have more weight if presented again to his consideration, though informally, by you.

With respect to the claims of indemnity of our citizens upon the government of Denmark, which have long been due, and the recovery of which was the principal object of the mission of Mr. Erving and of the late agency of Mr. Forbes, you will in stating to Mr. Rosenkrantz that you have no instruction to enter upon the discussion of them with him, give him distinctly to understand that they have not been, and will not be abandoned by this government.

The consulate at St. Petersburg is in a situation somewhat peculiar. Mr. John Levett Harris still holds the appointment; but having got into a personal altercation with an American citizen residing there, named W. D. Lewis, his conduct in the transactions to which that incident gave occasion has been such that the President is of opinion that he ought not consistently with a due regard to the public service longer to hold the office. Unwilling, however, to resort to the harsh measure of immediately removing him, the President assented to the wish expressed by his uncle, Mr. Levett Harris, at whose solicitation he had been appointed, that the Consul might be invited by *him* to return to the United States and resign. Some months having already elapsed since this arrangement was settled, it is expected that on your arrival at St. Petersburg Mr. Harris will be no longer there. Should it, however, prove otherwise the President wishes you to signify to Mr. Harris his expectation that he would resign; and should that intimation not prove sufficient, a letter to him is herewith furnished you to be delivered to him only in case of such resistance on his part to the milder course adopted at the request of his uncle. Should there be no necessity for delivering this letter, you will please to send it back to this Department.

If the consular office should thus upon your arrival, or shortly afterwards, be vacant, it may be necessary that you should make some temporary provision for the performance of its duties. The same William D. Lewis above mentioned and his brother, John D. Lewis, a very respectable American merchant, who has been several years residing at St. Petersburg, have both been strongly recommended to the President; but a decisive objection against the appointment of either of them is, that it would in effect be taking part with them in their quarrel with Harris, a course, in the President's opinion, which would be improper in itself; and especially so, as the conduct of W. D. Lewis, on the occasion referred to appears to have been itself not altogether unexceptionable. If Mr. Harris returns, as is expected in the course of the summer, an appointment to the consulate will be immediately made, so that the interval of vacancy in the office may be as short as possible.

Among the complaints against J. L. Harris has been that of making excessive and illegal charges for the performance of consular functions. Complaint of this nature gave rise indeed to his quarrel with Lewis. It was upon the 81st section of the collection law of 2d March, 1799, and the certificate therein required to be authenticated by the consul upon the landing of goods in foreign port, and upon which he is allowed to charge a fee of one dollar for *each* certificate. Harris, it seems, alleging the invariable practice for his warrant, insists that there should be a separate certificate for each shipper of goods; which, however, is manifestly not required by the law; the very form of the certificate prescribed in it including several shipments by different persons and of different articles in one certificate. When appealed to by the parties, Mr. Pinkney gave the same opinion that such was the necessary construction of the law. As the consuls of the United States in Europe have no other allowance than a few of these official fees, there is a propensity among some of them to increase them as much as possible. Without supposing a necessity for the minister to interfere with the consul's discharge of his functions, so long as there is no complaint against him, you will in any case when appealed to take care to keep the consul strictly within the terms of the law.

It may in conclusion be observed that in the present circumstances and condition of Europe among the most important of your duties will be that of observing with the most attentive assiduity the movements of negotiation between the principal European powers, and in an especial manner those of Russia. A friendly intercourse with the other ministers residing at the Russian court, and a frequent and confidential correspondence with the other ministers of the United States in Europe, will contribute to extend the sphere and to multiply the sources of information. The European alliance appear to be still closely united in reference to French affairs. They have not yet agreed upon any concert of operations with regard to Spain and South America. It will be acceptable to learn as early as possible whatever determination, and even whatever deliberations, occur between them on that subject, as well as on any others to which the course of events may give rise. The President relies with confidence, on your vigilance, your penetration, and your discretion. I have, etc.

TO GEORGE WASHINGTON CAMPBELL

DEPARTMENT OF STATE,
WASHINGTON, 28 June, 1818.

SIR:

The relations, whether commercial or political, between the United States and the Empire of Russia have undergone so little variation since the instructions were prepared for your immediate predecessor, that it might be sufficient to furnish you with the copy of them, which you will receive herewith for the general government of your official conduct on the important mission to which you have been appointed. It may be proper to add, however, a few observations suggested chiefly by the communications received from him during his residence at St. Petersburg.

The government of the United States, from the period of their declaration of independence, have been generally desirous, and always willing to settle and establish their commercial intercourse with the several powers of Europe by treaties of commerce. Very soon after the peace of 1783 a special commission was appointed, with authority to negotiate such treaties with all or any of the European states who might be disposed to treat with them. Since then, whenever a disposition has been manifested for such a negotiation by any European power, it has been readily met by a corresponding disposition on the part of the United States; and they have frequently been proposed by themselves to those powers with whose dominions any considerable direct intercourse has existed; and among the rest to Russia. But all their commercial negotiations, actual or proposed, have been invariably animated by the principles of liberality and reciprocity. For the intercourse of peace their object has been to remove restrictions and to generalize privileges, to obtain and to grant every advantage enjoyed by the subjects or citizens of other nations, but not to claim or to bestow any other. The commercial treaties negotiated by other nations were almost always combinations for exclusive privileges or concessions of monopoly. But the spirit of the American revolution was emphatically the spirit of liberty and of equal rights. It was manifested not only in their internal institutions, but in the influence which they exercised from the first moment of their admission into the community of nations. It was proclaimed to the world, in a manner appropriate to its own excellence and to their dignity, in the first treaty that they concluded with a European power—that of 6th February, 1778, with France. The preamble to that memorable instrument declares that the King of France and the United States,

willing to fix in an equitable and permanent manner the rules which ought to be followed relative to the correspondence and commerce which the two parties desire to establish, between their respective countries, States, and subjects, *have judged that the said end could not be better obtained than by taking for the basis of their agreement the most perfect equality and reciprocity, and by carefully avoiding all those burthensome preferences which are usually sources of debate, embarrassment and discontent; by leaving, also, each party at liberty to make, respecting commerce and navigation, those interior regulations which it shall find most convenient to itself; and by founding the advantage of commerce solely upon reciprocal utility and the just rules of free intercourse; reserving withal to each party the liberty of admitting at its pleasure other nations to a participation of the same advantages.*

It may be a subject at once of honest exultation and of serious admonition to Americans of this day, that while their declaration of independence contained the first solemn recognition by a nation at the moment of its bursting into birth of the great and sacred principles of civil society, upon which alone rightful government can be founded, their first national compact, though concluded with an absolute monarchy, proclaimed in like manner the only just and magnanimous principles which ought to govern the intercourse of nations with each other. It was "in the spirit of that intention, and to fulfill those views," that the first treaty with France was concluded; and the same spirit and intention have pervaded all the commercial negotiations of the United States, from that day to the present. One of their principal motives for renewing more than once the offer of a commercial negotiation with Russia has been the impression that Russia has herself been among the foremost assertors of liberal principles, especially in their application to the commercial intercourse of nations, in times of maritime war. It appears, however, from the coolness with which the overtures of the United States to negotiate a commercial treaty with Russia have at three different periods been received, that there is a reluctance on the part of the Emperor to enter upon any such negotiation. The first of these proposals was made soon after the first interchange of diplomatic missions between the two countries; the second at the appointment of the extraordinary mission upon the Emperor's offer of mediation between the United States and Great Britain; and the third by your immediate predecessor. They have all been declined, and there is no adequate inducement for us to repeat them again. From a paper drawn up by Mr. Pinkney, and of which a copy has been furnished you, it appears that there are no preferences granted in the Russian ports to other foreigners, from which American citizens are excluded; no extraordinary duties, from which they could be relieved; no prohibitions, but such as bear on the subject of other nations as much as on them; no advantages, which could be obtained for them without equivalents more than equal to their values. It may be added that religious toleration being established in all the Russian dominions, no treaty stipulation is necessary to secure to our citizens resorting thither the rights of conscience; that consuls are mutually received and acknowledged on the reciprocal footing of the most favored nation; and that all the benefits which could be obtained on either side by the most amicable treaty of commerce, are in fact enjoyed by their citizens and subjects respectively under the municipal regulations of the two countries. We have therefore no reason to regret the aversion of the Emperor to the shackles of a commercial treaty, as the same disposition which deters him from entering into such engagements with the United States, will guard him from yielding any concession to other nations prejudicial to them.

It will, however, be worthy of your attention to be informed of the charges to which the citizens of the United

States frequenting the Russian ports for commercial purposes may be subjected; and perhaps your official interposition may be occasionally required to secure them from imposition. The merchants of St. Petersburg, and of the other Russian ports generally, are mere consigners. They are little else than brokers between the foreigners who arrive with cargoes from abroad, and the people in the interior who bring their produce to markets in the sea ports. All business is done by a few houses, mostly foreigners—English and Germans. Much of the American business has been done by these English houses; and there is even now only one American merchant settled there. From this mode of transacting business the Americans who arrive there with cargoes are very much at the mercy for their purchases, sales and port-charges, of the merchant to whom they commit themselves, and consign their property. The consignee often sells the cargo to a secret partner or agent of his own. He has often a stock on hand of the articles wanted for the return cargo, which he makes a show of purchasing for his employer; and in both cases having an interest directly opposite to his, and a thorough acquaintance with the market and the means of operating upon it, sacrificing the interests of the employer to the profit of his own, charging heavy commissions both for purchases and sales really made on his own account; gratuities to custom house officers, perhaps never paid, and many other charges equally unprincipled and burdensome. You may be surprised to learn that practices of this nature are not uncommon among the commercial houses of the first consideration in Russia. Among the papers transmitted to the Department by Mr. Pinkney, and of which you will have a copy, is a list of the usual port-charges paid by foreigners in the Russian ports. One of them under the name of *church-money*, he observes, is paid by other foreigners, but not by Americans. Yet it is often charged in their portage bills; and indeed is founded in better reasons than some of the charges which are still constantly paid. It is a small contribution exacted from all the British vessels and cargoes arriving there, for the support of two English churches, one at St. Petersburg and one at Cronstadt; and the clergymen officiating at them. As these churches afford the means of religious worship in their own language, and according to their own forms, to the merchants and mariners of the British nation, while they are abiding there, it may be very proper that they should contribute towards the expense of supporting them. The objection to a general participation by Americans in the burden and the benefit of their establishments is that they are exclusively English, encumbered with all the *political* parts of the English ritual, in which no American may be a willing associate; and with the sectarianism of the Church of England, in which a great majority of the American seamen who visit Russia, would not more readily join.

It is the peculiar duty of the American consul to watch over these mercantile charges to which our countrymen trading in that country are liable, and to guard their interests against the impositions, which under the form of *usage* are sometimes attempted to be practiced upon them. It seldom but sometimes happened that the interference of the minister in such cases is required, and hence it is important that he should be well acquainted with the practical details of the foreign commerce of Russia, and it is the more essential when, as will generally happen, the consul himself is a partner of some commercial house at St. Petersburg.

With regard to the views of Russia upon the north-west

coast of this continent it is necessary to add only a few words to the instructions given to your predecessor. The Emperor Alexander, has never shown any symptoms of the passion which so vehemently prompted his ancestor Peter to make Russia a naval power; and in which the late Empress Catherine participated in so considerable a degree. The sale of line of battleships and frigates to Spain, is one proof among many, of his indifference to that instrument of power. The circumstances of the European world may have contributed to confirm him in this departure from the most remarkable and profoundest part of Peter's policy. The irresistible control over the north of Europe which he had acquired by the conquest of Finland and of Poland; the approximation in which they have brought him to the heart of Europe; and the ascendancy which, together with the late events, they have given him in all the European counsels, have probably taken such exclusive possession of his mind, that it has neither leisure nor inclination to occupy itself with the remote and contingent importance which can possibly be attached to the possession of a navy, in the future history of Russia. With the neglect of the navy, that of navigation and commercial shipping naturally follows; and without these, however the establishment of distant colonies may be attempted they can never flourish. It may be proper to observe attentively the movements of Russia with regard to their settlements on the north western coast; but they can never form a subject of serious difference, or jarring interest between that Empire and the United States.

Recent incidents have made it probable that those regions will be more liable to raise new controversies between the United States and Great Britain. Before the commencement of the late war a settlement by American citizens was formed at the mouth of Columbia River. During the war it was broken up by a British armed force, and purchased by certain agents of the North-West Company. After the conclusion of the peace, the restoration of the post was demanded, conformably to the stipulation in the first article of the treaty of Ghent, by a note from the Secretary of State to Mr. Baker, the British chargé d'affaires. The answer of Mr. Baker intimated that no British post had been retained there. The *Ontario* Sloop of War, was despatched in October last to resume possession of that post, and in some appropriate manner to reassert the title of the United States. Very soon afterwards a remonstrance against this measure was addressed to the Department of State by the British Minister residing here, which has since been renewed by Lord Castlereagh in verbal conference with our Minister at London. A proposal has been made on the part of the British Cabinet that the question, together with that of the boundary line to run from the north-west corner of the Lake of the Woods westward, as the boundary between the United States and the British possessions on the continent, and that concerning the slaves carried away from the United States by British officers, after the restoration of the peace, should be referred to the decision of commissioners like those appointed under the 4th, 5th, 6th, and 7th articles of the treaty of Ghent; and in case of disagreement between the commissioners, in like manner, to the decision of some friendly sovereign. Instead of adopting this proposal, the President has determined to propose to the British government a general negotiation of a commercial treaty, including the continuance for another term of years of the convention of 3 July, 1815, as well as the adjustment of these and other objects of difference between us and Great Britain. Whether this proposition will be accepted by the British cabinet or not we can not now ascertain; but it has already been agreed between the two governments that the question with regard to the slaves shall be referred to a third party—"some friendly sovereign or state." In the expectation that one or more of the three commissions appointed under the treaty of Ghent might eventuate in the disagreement of the commissioners, and that the recourse provided by the treaty on that contingency would become necessary, the minister of the United States in England has already been instructed to propose or to agree to the Emperor of Russia, as the sovereign to whom these appeals in the last resort should be submitted. Under these circumstances not only the views of the Russian government, with reference to their own settlements and pretensions on the north-west coast, acquire additional interest; but the whole system of Russian policy, as it bears on her relations with Great Britain, with the European alliance, with Spain and the South American affairs, may require the most steady and attentive observation, as it may link itself with objects of importance to the interests and welfare of the United States.

Of the European alliance, the Emperor of Russia may now be considered as the head; of the so-called Holy Alliance he is undoubtedly the founder. The latter is a compact of a character entirely new and unexampled in the history of the world—a personal compact between several sovereigns, by which as individuals, and not through the medium of their ministers, they bind themselves as sovereigns to observe towards one another and towards their subjects the precepts of the Christian religion; "precepts of Justice, of Charity, and of Peace," which they declare "far from being applicable only to private life, ought, on the contrary, to have a direct influence on the resolutions of Princes and govern all their measures, as being the only means of consolidating human institutions and of remedying their imperfections."

To this compact the British government is not a party, because the sovereign of Great Britain can make no autographic contracts binding upon his nation; but it was declared by Lord Castlereagh in Parliament, that they had full communication of the treaty at its formation and that its principles have the entire approbation of his Royal Highness the Prince Regent, a circumstance the more remarkable, as the fundamental principle of the compact is in direct opposition to the doctrines of the most celebrated late British writers on natural law—Bishop Horsley and Dr. Paley. The Prince Regent's approbation of the principles of the Holy Alliance must, therefore, be understood as extending no farther than his constitutional authority—that is, as approving that other sovereigns and nations should be bound by the compact, while the sovereign and nation of Great Britain should be restricted by no such obligations.

But although no party to the *Holy Alliance*, Great Britain is a member, and perhaps the most powerful and effective member of the *European alliance;* an association of the principal governments of Europe, the present object of which is to consolidate the settlement of European affairs, which they have established upon the ruins of the revolutionary system of France. The settlement having left a leaven of internal discontent fermenting among the people of almost every part of Europe, the sovereigns have felt the necessity of peace, and close alliance among themselves. The influence of these principles may account for the part which the Emperor of Russia has hitherto taken in the quarrel which has arisen between Spain and Portugal from the occupation by the latter of Montevideo, and for the sentiments which he has manifested with regard to the contest between Spain and her American colonies.

The Portuguese government of Brazil took Montevideo and the eastern banks of the River La Plata from the possession, not of Spain, but of the revolutionary South Americans, who had cast off the authority of the Spanish monarchy. Spain unable to defend herself either against her revolted subjects, or against the Brazilian invasion, immediately appealed for support to the European alliance, against the attack of Portugal. The European alliance, apparently not reflecting that they could not interfere in this affair without making themselves parties both to the controversy between Spain and Portugal, and to that between Spain and her colonies, took up the cause of Spain with a decision equally precipitate and peremptory; offered their mediation to Portugal, with high encomiums upon the moderation and magnanimity of Spain in asking for it, and with unqualified menaces that if Portugal should decline their mediation, and withhold the explanations which they demanded, they would throw the whole weight of their power on the side of Spain. Portugal accepted the mediation and gave the explanations. And although she had old pretensions to the territory which she had occupied, and an unsettled claim for the restoration of Olivenza in Europe, she offered to waive all these demands, and to restore Montevideo to Spain, whenever Spain should be in a condition to receive it; that is, when she should have subdued the revolution in the provinces of La Plata. Spain utterly unable to comply with this condition, without which she saw that her demand upon Portugal for the restoration of Montevideo was not only nugatory but ridiculous, was now reduced to the humiliation of imploring the mediation of the European alliance between her and her revolted colonies; or in other words of asking the aid of the allied force to recover her authority over her American dominions.

The Emperor of Russia, who as the conservator of the peace of Europe had already sided with Spain against the aggression of Portugal, seems now to have taken the same bias against the colonies, as the restorer of what he considered legitimate authority. Having no immediate interests of his own involved in the question, he appears to have viewed it only as a question of supremacy and obedience between the sovereign and his subjects, and to have taken it for granted that the sovereign must have the right, and the subjects the wrong of the cause. But Great Britain, the other efficient member of the alliance, had a great and powerful interest of her own to operate upon her consideration of the case. The revolution in South America had opened a new world to her commerce which the restoration of the Spanish colonial dominion would close against her. Her Cabinet therefore devised a middle term, a compromise between legitimacy and traffic; a project by which the political supremacy of Spain should be restored, but under which the Spanish colonies should enjoy commercial freedom, and intercourse with the rest of the world. She admits all the pretensions of legitimacy until they come in contact with her own interest; and then she becomes the patroness of liberal principles and colonial emancipation.

In the correspondence between the European allies which has hitherto taken place on this subject we have seen only the memoir of the Russian Cabinet, dated at Moscow on November, 1817, from which it would seem that the Russian project is a compromise between Spain and Portugal, and then a coöperation between them to reduce the South Americans to submission. The memoir speaks in vague and general terms of certain favors or privileges to be promised and secured to the colonies; but its general import shows the design of restoring the entire authority of Spain.

It is remarkable that the European allies have hitherto withheld from the government of the United States all their proceedings on this intended mediation between Spain and her colonies. That they had acceded to the request of Spain to that effect, we should know only by unauthenticated rumor, but for the accident of our commissioners to South America having touched at Rio de Janeiro. The Spanish Minister there, in a moment of alarm lest the object of their mission should be to recognize the government of Buenos Ayres, and seemingly with the hope of intimidating them from proceeding, made a formal disclosure to Mr. Sumter of this proposed interference of the European alliance. In January last, Mr. Bagot by instructions from Lord Castlereagh, informed me that he expected *very shortly* to make to us a full communication of their proceedings in this concern, but we have to this day heard no further from him of it. There is some reason to believe that nothing decisive will be agreed upon until the meeting of sovereigns, expected to be held in the course of the present summer, and then ulterior measures may probably depend on the expedition to be fitted out from Cadiz of the ships of war lately sold by the Emperor of Russia to Spain.

At the time of your arrival at St. Petersburg, it is probable that the Emperor will have returned from his excursion; and it will be among the most interesting objects of your enquiry, to ascertain the results of that meeting. Perhaps it will no longer be deemed necessary by the allies to withhold from the government what they have done and what they intend, in relation to the affairs of Spain and South America. Instructions have been forwarded to Mr. Gallatin and to Mr. Rush, to give the French and English Cabinets informally to understand that the interests of this nation are so deeply concerned, and the feelings of the country are so much excited on this subject that we have a just claim to be informed of the intentions as well as the acts of the European alliance concerning it. That our policy hitherto has, like that of the European powers, been neutrality between Spain and the colonies. That we earnestly wish to pursue a course for the future in harmony with that of the allies; but that we will not participate in and cannot approve any interposition of other powers, unless it be to promote the total independence, political and commercial, of the colonies. That we believe it must eventually come to this result, and that it is rendering no service to either of the parties to endeavor to prevent or to retard it. In your interview with the Russian ministry it may be proper that you should express similar sentiments to them; avoiding, however, all animadversion which might be understood as censuring the part taken by the Emperor in favor of Spain.

It is not unlikely that Spain in her general recurrence to the allies to support her against all her adversaries and to extricate her from all her difficulties, may have resorted to them, and particularly to the Emperor of Russia, for countenance in her differences with the United States. Some features of resemblance have been remarked between the capture of Amelia Island by our forces and that of Montevideo by the Portuguese; and the Emperor of Russia having in that case manifested at the outset a disapprobation of the proceeding of Portugal, may, perhaps, have been more readily accessible to a prejudice against a step in some respects similar taken by the United States. The motives for the occupation of Amelia Island, have been so fully disclosed and so thoroughly discussed, that if any occupation should arise in which an explanation and justification of them may be advisable, your information is already so complete for that purpose that it is presumed no further elucidation of it is necessary. The entrance of our troops into East Florida in pursuit of the savages, who after desolating our frontiers attempted to take refuge there, and their occupation of posts essential for holding them in check, will as easily admit of justification. The positive stipulation of Spain by treaty to restrain the Indians within her territories from all hostilities against the United States, and her notorious failure to fulfill that engagement rendered those measures on our part indispensable for the protection of our own people against the most barbarous and unrelenting of enemies. You may add that notwithstanding the manifest wrongs which for a series of years we have suffered from Spain, we are and shall continue to be always ready to adjust upon the most equitable terms all our differences with her, whenever she shall adopt the same disposition.

I have, etc.

TO WILLIAM PLUMER

WASHINGTON, 6 July, 1818.

DEAR SIR:

. . . . . .

Very shortly after I received your letter and that of your son respecting the publication of the Journal of the Convention which formed the present Constitution of the United States, in the Senate there was a resolution offered to the same effect, which in the course of the session was adopted by both Houses, with the addition of a direction for the publication also of part of the correspondence of the old Congress during the Revolution. Presuming that this legislative provision would supersede the intention of your son's, I have forborne to take any further steps in relation to it.

You have been kind enough upon several occasions, and upon various topics of public interest, to give me your opinions in the candor and sincerity of friendship. Those opinions have always been much respected by me; when the measures of the President have met your approbation, it has given me as much pleasure as if they had been my own. When you have censured, I have always perceived with new regret that it was not without reason. There have been, however, motives for the steps which you think objectionable of which you have not perhaps been aware. The opinion given by the President in the message at the commencement of the late session against the constitutional power of Congress in regard to internal improvement,[1] was thus declared to avoid the complaint which had been made against his predecessor of having *withheld* his opinion upon the same question until Congress had matured an act for making such improvements, and then defeating the measure by his *veto*. Many of the members of the former Congress had showed dissatisfaction at this course, and had urged that it would be fairer and save the time of Congress and the nation if the chief magistrate should explicitly make known his opinion beforehand, so as to spare the majority of the legislature the necessity of coming in direct collision with his negative. These reasons certainly have their weight, but in fact the exercise of actual control by the President over the opinions and wishes of a majority of the legislature will never be very palatable in what form soever it may be administered.

I hope the appointment to Russia will prove more satisfactory than your anticipations. The difficulty of filling

[1] *Messages and Papers of the Presidents*, II. 17.

the foreign missions well is great and increasing. You are aware that the compensation allowed to our ministers at the principal European courts is not only inadequate, but to such a degree that no man can accept and hold one of them more than one or two years, without the sacrifices of private property which few of us are able to bear. Mr. Pinkney with the advantage of a double outfit has been driven home at the end of two years, by the excess of his expenses as much as by the rigor of the Russian climate. Our countrymen and Congress are not yet convinced of the necessity of making further provision for the support of the missions abroad; but men of the first rate talents have discovered that they can do better for themselves and their families at home. The missions to England and to Russia were both *declined* by men of whose abilities you would have been fully satisfied. This state of things will be felt in consequences which may cost the nation millions for every thousand saved by their parsimony in this instance. I am no friend to profusion for the payment of public service. I am convinced that it is just and politic in the people to make all their offices of high trust and honors rather burthensome than lucrative. Real patriotism will cheerfully bear some pecuniary sacrifices, and the appetite of ambition for place is sufficiently sharp set without needing the stimulant dram of avarice to make it recur. But in the missions abroad there are expenses and a general style of living which your ministers cannot avoid without personal and national degradation. Men of affluent fortunes may be willing to accept as a salary for a year that which will little more than defray their necessary expenses for a quarter; but throughout the United States how many men are there able by their private resources to be laid under this contribution? And of that number, small as it is, how many possess talents suited to represent the nation with honor and to execute the trust of its most important interests which must be confided to them?

The state of our relations with Spain continues to be critical, and has been rendered more so by the recent events in Florida. The dispatches from General Jackson which will explain his motives for the capture of Pensacola have not yet been received.

We are in daily expectation of the arrival of two commissioners from South America. You will see in the newspapers some interesting details of affairs in Chili, with an address to Captain Riddle of the *Ontario*.

I am, etc.

TO THE PRESIDENT

[JAMES MONROE]

WASHINGTON, 8 July, 1818.

SIR:

I had the honor of receiving this morning your letter of the 6th instant. The only letters received from the Commissioners to South America are of 23 April, the day before they sailed from Buenos Ayres on their homeward voyage, and advising drafts upon the Department. No dispatches from them have come to hand, a circumstance which excites no small surprise. Until I received your letter, I had supposed they might have been addressed directly to you and received since you left the city.

Yesterday the dispatches from General Jackson to the War Department, containing the documents relating to the capture of Pensacola, were received by Mr. Hambly and forwarded to you.

Last evening I received a note from the Spanish Minister informing me that he had just arrived here, and requesting an interview as soon as possible on affairs of the last importance to Spain and the United States. He has been with me this day and delivered to me a new note on the affair of Pensacola, the translation of which is in hand. Mr. de Neuville sent this morning to ask an interview upon an affair of importance, and has also been with me. Pensacola was also the burden of his song.[1] As there was something tragical in the manner of both these gentlemen, I told them that they must take for nothing whatever I said to them, until I should have the honor of receiving your instructions; but that in my private opinion you would approve General Jackson's proceedings. That we could not suffer our women and children on the frontiers to be butchered by savages, out of complaisance to the jurisdiction which the King of Spain's officers avowed themselves unable to maintain against those same savages, and that when the governor of Pensacola threatened General Jackson, to drive him out of the province *by force*, he left him no alternative but to take from him the means of executing his threat. Onis for the first time since I have held communication with him manifested symptoms of perturbation.[2]

I am, etc.

---

[1] Onis had not only entered his protest against the act of hostility and claimed restitution and indemnification, but had also asked the other foreign ministers resident in the United States severally to protest in a similar manner against the proceedings of the American army. Bagot was out of the city, but assured Onis that in his opinion such action on his part would be premature.

[2] See Adams, *Memoirs*, July 8, 1818.

"M. Adams, qui me témoigne toujours beaucoup d'égards et me parle avec une extrême confiance, me dit que je pouvais mauder à mon cour que j'avais le certitude que le général Jackson avait agi de son propre mouvement, et que, jusqu'à présent, l'administration n'avait reçu de lui aucun rapport officiel. . . . Cette confidence fut suivie de beaucoup d'observations, dont il m'est impossible

TO THE PRESIDENT

[JAMES MONROE]

SIR:

I shall with your permission notify Mr. Bagot that you will receive him at one o'clock to-morrow. The other suggestions in your note shall be attended to. I will bring with me to you this day General Jackson's correspondence, and wish once more to submit certain particulars to your consideration with a view to the question whether he was not fully justified under his orders, and whether it should not be so stated in the answer to Mr. Onis? Accept assurances, etc.[1]

Monday Morning, 20 July, 1818.

de ne pas reconnaître la justesse; je me suis déjà plusieurs fois trop étendu sur ce sujet. Je me bornerai donc à répéter qu'il faut, si on veut traiter avec le gouvernement fédéral et arriver promptement à un résultat, non seulement s'occuper de ses propres difficultés, mais faire la part de celles du cabinet de Washington. Vouloir négocier avec lui comme on le ferait avec les cabinets de Paris ou de Londres même, c'est ne point connaitre la nature de ses institutions." *Hyde de Neuville to the Duc de Richelieu*, July 15, 1818. Hyde de Neuville, *Mémoires et Souvenirs*, II. 374.

[1] Monroe was away from Washington when Jackson's report on the taking of Pensacola reached the War Department, and returned on the 12th. In a meeting of the cabinet on July 15, the President and all the members present except Adams were of the opinion that Jackson had acted "not only without, but against, his instructions; that he had committed war upon Spain, which cannot be justified, and which, if not disavowed by the Administration, they will be abandoned by the country." Adams believed Jackson justified by the necessity of the case and by the misconduct of the Spanish officers. For a full week, in six meetings of the cabinet the matter received consideration, and resulted in a reply to Onis "on the grounds of the President's original sketch," sent to the Spanish Minister on the 23d. See Adams, *Memoirs*, July 15–23, 1818.

TO DON LUIS DE ONIS [1]

Department of State,
Washington, July 23, 1818.

Sir:

I have had the honor of receiving your letters of the 24th June and 8th instant, complaining of the conduct of Major General Jackson in entering West Florida with the forces under his command, taking the Spanish ports of St. Mark and Pensacola, etc.

Without recurring to the long standing and heavy causes of complaint which the United States have had against Spain; to the forbearance with which they have been borne, without despairing of obtaining justice from her by amicable means; to the efforts equally unceasing and unavailing which they have made to obtain that justice; or to the extraordinary delays by which it has been protracted and is still withheld, it is thought proper on this occasion to call your attention to a series of events which necessitated and justified the entrance of the troops of the United States upon the Spanish boundary of Florida, and gave occasion to those transactions of the commander of the American forces against which you complain.

It cannot be unknown to you that, for a considerable time before the government of the United States issued the orders for military operations in that quarter, the inhabitants of their frontier had been exposed to the depredations, murders, and massacres of a tribe of savages, a small part of which lived within the limits of the United States, far the greater number of them dwelling within the borders of Florida. The barbarous, unrelenting, and exterminating

[1] Printed in *American State Papers*, Foreign Relations, IV. 497.

character of Indian hostilities is also well known to you; and, from the peculiar local position of these tribes, it was obvious that there could be no possible security for the lives of the white inhabitants of those borders unless the United States and Spain should be reciprocally bound to restrain the portion of the Indians respectively within their territories from committing robbery and butchery upon the citizens and subjects of the other party. So forcibly was this necessity felt by both, that in the fifth article of the treaty of 27th October, 1795, the following remarkable stipulation is contained:

The two high contracting parties shall, by all the means in their power, maintain peace and harmony among the several Indian nations who inhabit the country adjacent to the lines and rivers which, by the preceding articles, form the boundaries of the two Floridas; and, the better to obtain this effect, both parties oblige themselves expressly to restrain by force all hostilities on the part of the Indian nations living within their boundaries, so that Spain will not suffer her Indians to attack the citizens of the United States, nor the Indians inhabiting their territory; nor will the United States permit these last mentioned Indians to commence hostilities against the subjects of his Catholic Majesty, or his Indians, in any manner whatever.

Notwithstanding this precise, express, and solemn compact of Spain, numbers, painful to recollect, of the citizens of the United States inhabiting the frontier—numbers, not merely of persons in active manhood, but of the tender sex, of defenceless age, and helpless infancy, had at various times been butchered, with all the aggravations and horrors of savage cruelty, by Seminole Indians, and by a banditti of negroes sallying from within the Spanish border, and retreating to it again with the horrid fruits of their crimes.

At a former period the governor of Pensacola had been called upon, by a letter from Major General Jackson, conformably to the stipulated engagement of Spain and to the duties of good neighborhood, to interpose by force and break up a stronghold of which this horde of savages and fugitive slaves had possessed themselves on the territory of Florida. The answer acknowledged the obligation, but pleaded an incompetency of force for its fulfilment. Copies of these important documents are herewith transmitted to you;[1] and it may be within your knowledge and recollection that the orders and the competent force which General Zuniga stated in his letter that he had solicited from his governor general, and without which he declared himself unable to destroy this fort, created upon Spanish territory for purposes of united civilized, savage, and servile war against the United States, were never furnished; and that the United States were finally compelled to accomplish its destruction by their own force.

The permanent and unvarying policy of the United States, with regard to all the Indian tribes within their borders, is that of peace, friendship, and liberality; and so successful has this policy been, that, for many years, no instance has occurred of their being in hostility with any Indian tribe, unless stimulated by the influence of foreign incendiaries. Even after the repeated commission of these depredations and massacres by the Seminole Indians, at the very moment when the government of the United States was reluctantly compelled to employ their own military force for the protection of their people, offers of peace were tendered to them, and rejected.

Nor has the respect manifested by this government for the territorial rights of Spain been less signal and conspic-

---

[1] Printed in *American State Papers*, Foreign Relations, IV. 499.

uous, even after the full and formal notice, by the governor of Pensacola, of the incompetency of his force either to perform the duties of neutrality, or to fulfil the obligations of the treaty. When it became necessary to employ the military force of the United States for the protection of their frontier, on the 30th October last, the commanding officer in that quarter, while directed to take other measures for suppressing the hostilities of the Indians, was expressly instructed not on that account to pass the line, and make an attack upon them within the limits of Florida, without further orders. On the 2d of December instructions to the same effect were repeated. On the 9th of December they were again renewed, with the modification suggested by the continuation of Indian outrages, that, should the Indians assemble and force in the Spanish side of the line, and persevere in committing hostilities within the limits of the United States, the American officer was authorized in that event to exercise a sound discretion as to the propriety of crossing the line, for the purpose of attacking them, and breaking up their towns. On the 16th of December, upon information that an officer of the United States, with a detachment of forty men, had been attacked, and all destroyed, with the exception of six who made their escape, four of whom were wounded, the instruction, of which the following is a copy, was issued from the Department of War to the American general then in command:

On receipt of this letter, should the Seminole Indians still refuse to make reparation for their outrages and depredations on the citizens of the United States, it is the wish of the President that you consider yourself at liberty to march across the Florida line, and to attack them within its limits, should it be found necessary, unless they should shelter themselves under a Spanish fort. In the last event, you will immediately notify this Department.

These, with a subsequent instruction of the 26th of December to the commander in chief, referring to them, and directing him, with a view to them, to adopt the necessary measures to terminate a conflict which it had ever been the desire of the President, from considerations of humanity, to avoid, but which was made necessary by the settled hostilities of the Indians, are all the instructions given in relation to Florida.

By the ordinary laws and usages of nations, the right of pursuing an enemy, who seeks refuge from actual conflict within a neutral territory, is incontestable. But, in this case, the territory of Florida was not even neutral. It was itself, as far as Indian savages possess territorial right, the territory of Indians, with whom the United States were at war. It was their place of abode, and Spain was bound by treaty to restrain them by force from committing hostilities against the United States— an engagement which the commanding officer of Spain in Florida had acknowledged himself unable to fill. Of the necessity there was for crossing the line, what stronger proofs could be adduced than that it was within that line that the American general met the principal resistance from the Indians which he encountered in the whole campaign; that within that line, at their towns which he destroyed, he found displayed, as barbarous trophies, the mutilated remnants of our wretched fellow-citizens, the murdered women and children, the accumulated barbarities of many years?

You have seen that no instruction or authority, inconsistent with the declaration in the message of the President of the United States of the 25th of March last to Congress, was ever issued to the commander of the American forces. The possession which he took of the fort of St. Mark, and consequently of Pensacola, was upon motives which he himself has explained, and upon his own responsibility. For his justification in the adoption of both those measures, he states them to have been necessary upon the immutable principles of self-defence.

That, at an early period of his operations, he had given full notice of their object to the governor of Pensacola, by a communication, dated the 25th of March last, warning him that every attempt on his part to succor the Indians, or prevent the passage of provisions for the American troops in the Escambia, would be viewed as acts of hostility:

That, in defiance of this admonition, the governor of Pensacola did both give succor to the Indians, and delay the passage of the provisions to the American army, and thereby subjected them to the severest privations:

That the governor of Pensacola had caused it to be directly reported to the American general that Fort St. Mark had been threatened by the Indians and negroes; and expressed serious apprehensions, from the weakness of the garrison and defenceless state of the work, for its safety:

That this information was confirmed to the American general from other sources, upon which he could rely, and completely warranted the amicable occupation by him of that fort:

That, upon his entering the fort, evidence, clear, unequivocal, and manifold, was evinced of the duplicity and unfriendly feeling of the commandant—evidence demonstrating, beyond the power of denial, that, far from acting in the spirit of that sacred engagement of his sovereign, to restrain by force his Indians from hostilities against the United States, he had made himself, by every act in his power, a partner and accomplice of the hostile Indians, and of their foreign instigators:

That the same spirit of hostility to the United States was

discovered by the governor of Pensacola himself, by his refusal to permit, unless by the payment of exorbitant duties, the passage of provisions to the American army; by the reception and succors given to the Indians at various times; and, finally, by a letter which he sent to the American general, denouncing his entry into Florida as an aggression against Spain, and threatening, unless he should immediately withdraw from it, and should he continue what he thus styled aggression, that he would repel force by force. This was so open an indication of hostile feeling on the part of Governor Mazot, after he had been early and well advised of the object of General Jackson's operations, that this officer no longer hesitated on the measures to be adopted—the occupation of Pensacola and of the fort of Barrancas.

The charges alleged by General Jackson against the commandant of St. Mark's are not known even to have been denied. The governor of Pensacola has *partly*, and but partly, contradicted those which applied to himself. He assured General Jackson that the information received by him of the numbers of Indians who had been received and harbored at Pensacola was erroneous. It is possible that the numbers may have been somewhat exaggerated in the reports which General Jackson had received. But within ten days after the time stated in his letter to the governor of Pensacola of this assemblage of Indians at that place, a large body of them were overtaken, surprised, and defeated by the forces of the United States, within one mile of Pensacola. Nor was it until after that event that the governor issued his proclamation for refusing them supplies, and gave them the advice under which eighty-seven of them surrendered themselves to the American officer. But the measures of General Jackson were not founded upon one solitary fact. A combination of circumstances, all tending to convince him of the hostile spirit of the governor, remains yet uncontradicted; and the general has furnished proofs that Governor Mazot's assertion, that there had been, since the surrender of those eighty-seven Indians to Captain Young, only two in Pensacola, and those in jail, was itself very incorrect. Besides the Alabama chief, included in the capitulation, one wounded Indian was found in the fort of Barrancas. Holmes, a noted Red Stick chief, left Pensacola but the day before the American troops took possession, and a number of other Indians were seen about the same time within a few miles of Pensacola, and succeeded, with the aid of Spanish officers, in eluding the pursuit of the American troops.

A conduct not only so contrary to the express engagements of Spain, but so unequivocally hostile to the United States, justly authorizes them to call upon his Catholic Majesty for the punishment of those officers, who, the President is persuaded, have therein acted contrary to the express orders of their sovereign. In the full confidence that your government will render to the United States ample justice in this regard, the President has directed all the proofs relating thereto to be embodied, as the ground of an application to that effect to your government.

In the meantime, I am instructed by the President to inform you that Pensacola will be restored to the possession of any person duly authorized on the part of Spain to receive it; that the fort of St. Mark, being in the heart of the Indian country, and remote from any Spanish settlement, can be surrendered only to a force sufficiently strong to hold it against the attack of the hostile Indians; upon the appearance of which force it will also be restored.

In communicating to you this decision, I am also directed to assure you that it has been made under the fullest conviction, which he trusts will be felt by your government, that the preservation of peace between the two nations indispensably requires that henceforth the stipulations by Spain to restrain by force her Indians from all hostilities against the United States should be faithfully and effectually fulfilled.

I pray you to accept, etc.

TO ALBERT GALLATIN AND RICHARD RUSH [1]

DEPARTMENT OF STATE,
WASHINGTON, 28 July, 1818.

GENTLEMEN:

In the expectation that the government of Great Britain have accepted the proposal which Mr. Rush was instructed to make for negotiating a treaty of commerce, embracing the continuance of the convention of 3 July, 1815, for an additional term of years, and including other objects of interest to the two nations, I have now the honor of transmitting to you the President's instructions to you for the conduct of the negotiation.

1. With regard to the commercial convention of 3 July, 1815, you have already been informed that the President is willing that it should be continued without alteration for a further term of eight or ten years. We had flattered ourselves from the liberal sentiments expressed by Lord Castlereagh in Parliament, and from various other indications, that the British Cabinet would have been now prepared to extend the principles of the convention to our commercial intercourse with their colonies in the West Indies and North

[1] An extract from this dispatch is printed in *American State Papers*, Foreign Relations, IV. 375.

America; but from the report of two conferences between Mr. Rush and Lord Castlereagh since received, it appears that our anticipations had been too sanguine, and that with regard to our admission into their colonies they still cling to the system of exclusive colonial monopoly.

Our navigation act passed at the last session of Congress, was well calculated to bring this system to a test by which it has not hitherto been tried, and if experiment must be made complete so that the event shall prove to demonstration which of the two countries can best stand this opposition of counter-exclusions, the United States are prepared to abide by the result. Still we would prefer to remove them at once; if for no other reason that it would have a tendency to promote good humor between the two countries. We wish you to urge this argument upon the British Cabinet, to remind them of the principles avowed by Lord Castlereagh in Parliament, to which I have before referred, and of their precise bearing upon this question. It may also be proper to suggest that while Great Britain is pressing upon Spain the abandonment of her commercial monopoly throughout the continent of South America, her recommendation must necessarily gain great additional weight by setting the example with her own colonies; while at the same time her own interest in her monopoly must be reduced to an object too trifling for national consideration, when the Spanish Colonies shall be open to the commerce of the world. Finally, it may be observed that the free-port act, passed at the late session of Parliament, goes already so far towards the abandonment of their system that it can scarcely be perceived why they should adhere to the remnant of it any longer. Other arguments may occur to your own reflections and result from your thorough knowledge of the subject. You will urge them with earnestness, though giving it always to be understood that we shall acquiesce in their ultimate determination.

Whenever this subject has been presented to the British Cabinet since the peace, their only objection to the proposals and arguments of the United States has been that their system has been long established. Lord Castlereagh has invariably acknowledged his own doubts whether it was wise or really advantageous to Great Britain; but placed the determination to preserve it upon the single ground of its having long existed. Whatever weight there is in the reasoning, it would bear in favor of all those other exclusions which he congratulated Parliament and the country at having been abolished as much as in support of this. It is the argument of all existing abuse against reformation, of mere fact against reason and justice. The commercial intercourse between the United States and the West Indies is founded upon mutual wants and mutual convenience; upon their relative geographical position; upon the nature of their respective productions; upon the necessities of the climate, and upon the convulsions of nature. When the British ministry say against all this, our ancestors established a system and therefore we must maintain it, we may reply, if your ancestors established a system in defiance of the laws of nature, it is your interest and your duty to abolish it. But who can overlook or be blind to the changes of circumstances of the establishment and growth of the United States as an independent power; to the expulsion of the French from St. Domingo; to the revolution in progress in South American provinces? Every system established upon a condition of things essentially transient and temporary must be accommodated to the changes produced by time.

Besides the free-port act, a printed copy of which has now

been received from Mr. Rush, and which we find is limited to ports specially appointed by the Crown in the provinces of Nova Scotia and New Brunswick, we have seen in the public journals a bill, for permitting a certain trade between the British West Indies and *any colony or possession in the West Indies, or on the Continent of America, under the dominions of any foreign European sovereign or state.* This measure appears intended to counteract the effects of our late navigation act, and gives further manifestation of the adherence of the British government to their colonial exclusions. It is the President's desire that nothing should be omitted which can have the tendency to convince them that a change would promote the best interests of both countries, as well as the harmony between them. Should your efforts prove ineffectual, we can only wait the result of the counteracting measures to which we have resorted, or which may be found necessary hereafter.

In carrying the convention of 3 July, 1815, into execution, the British government have sanctioned the practice with regard to some of the foreign tonnage duties, first to levy them, as if the convention were not in force; and then upon petition of the persons interested to have them returned. If this practice cannot be given up altogether, it will be necessary that some regulation should be adopted by which the extra duties shall be returned of course, and without putting the parties to the trouble and expense and delay of obtaining it by petition. At present, unless the petition is presented the duties are not returned. It happens sometimes that masters of vessels pay the duties without knowing that they are entitled to have them returned, in which case they are lost to them or their owners. It will be proper, therefore, to require the adoption of some general regulation, in virtue of which it shall be made the duty of the officers of the customs to repay the extra duties in all cases in which they shall have been levied, without exposing the individual to lose his right by his own ignorance, or by the negligence or infidelity of his consignee.

2. *Slaves*. The British government have accepted the proposal of referring to the decision of some friendly sovereign or state, the question concerning the slaves carried away from the United States by British officers after the ratification of the peace. They propose, however, a previous reference of it to two commissioners, appointed like those under the 4th, 5th, 6th, and 7th articles of the treaty of Ghent, and to proceed with similar powers and committing to the same commissioners the power of fixing definitively the boundary between the United States and the possessions of Great Britain westward from the northwest corner of the Lake of the Woods, and of pronouncing upon the right of the United States to the settlement on the shores of the Pacific Ocean, at the mouth of Columbia River. Those objects are so entirely different from one another, the principles, the character of the evidence, and the reasoning which must lead to the result, are so disconnected and incongruous, that if submitted at all to commissioners, it is obviously proper to refer them to different commissions. The question concerning the slaves is a question of construction upon the terms of the first article of the treaty; and the two governments having already discussed it, each after discussion adhering to its own opinion, there is little prospect that either of the commissioners will come to a conclusion different from that of his own government. The present offer of the British government, connecting it with another question of boundary, bears the appearance of a disposition to make it an affair of compromise, and that they are willing to concede something to us on one of the points, upon condi-

tion of a concession from us upon the other. If this be their object these mutual concessions may be made with more convenience by direct and immediate agreement between the two governments, and by an article of the treaty, than by the means of commissioners, whose functions are rather of the judicial than the ministerial character, and whose duties are to decide and not to compromise.

3. *Boundary from the Lake of the Woods westward.* By the second article of the treaty of peace of 1783 the boundaries of the United States, after having been traced from the northwest angle of Nova Scotia, to the most northwestern point of the Lake of the Woods, and pursued "from thence on a *due west* course to the river Mississippi; thence by a line to be drawn along the middle of the said river Mississippi until it shall intersect the northernmost part of the thirty-first degree of North Latitude."

By the fourth article of the treaty of 1794 it was declared to be uncertain whether the river Mississippi extended so far to the northward, as to be intersected by a line due west from the Lake of the Woods; and a joint survey of the river from one degree below the falls of St. Anthony to the principal sources of the said river and of the parts adjacent thereto, was stipulated; and if on the result of the survey it appeared that the river could not be intersected by the line, the parties were to regulate the boundary line by amicable negotiation, according to justice and mutual convenience, and in conformity to the intent of the treaty. This joint survey never took effect.

By a convention signed on the 12th of May, 1803, by Mr. King and Lord Hawkesbury, but which was not ratified, it was agreed that the boundary should be by a line from the northwest corner of the Lake of the Woods, by the shortest line until it touched the river Mississippi. Until then the Mississippi River had been the western boundary of the United States. The cession of Louisiana gave them a new and extensive territory westward of that river.

In the negotiation of 1807 between Messrs. Monroe and W. Pinkney, and the Lords Holland and Auckland, there were three successive drafts of articles for the settlement of this boundary. The first, proposed on the British side (Art. 5, p. 198, Docts.), was a line due west from the Lake of the Woods along the 49th parallel of north latitude, as far as the territory of the United States extends in that quarter, and the line *to that extent* was to form the boundary; with a proviso that the article should not be construed to extend to the northwest coast of America; or to the territories westward of the Stony Mountains.

The second, proposed on the part of the United States (p. 202), took a line due north or south as the case might be, from the most northwestern point of the Lake of the Woods, until it shall intersect the 49th parallel of north latitude, and then due west along the parallel for the boundary between the territories of the parties, with the proviso excluding the northwest coast and all territories westward of the Stony Mountains.

The third, was agreed to by both parties; and varied from the second only by an additional clause purporting that this should be the boundary *as far as the respective territories of the parties extend in that quarter.*

That convention was not ultimately concluded.

At the negotiation of the peace of Ghent, the 8th article of the first project presented by the American plenipotentiaries, was a transcript from this article last above mentioned; and the article proposed by the British plenipotentiaries on returning the project was the same as that which had been first proposed by Lords Holland and Auckland;

with an additional paragraph stipulating free access to the British subjects through the territories of the United States to the Mississippi, and the free navigation of that river. In the conferences that ensued the substance of the article so far as it regarded the boundary was agreed to on both sides; but as the American plenipotentiaries could not accede to the additional paragraph, the article was finally altogether omitted.

From the earnestness with which the British government now return to the object of fixing the boundary, there is reason to believe that they have some other purpose connected with it which they do not avow, but which in their estimation gives it an importance not belonging to it, considered in itself. An attempt was at first made by them at the negotiation of Ghent, to draw the boundary line by a line from Lake Superior to the Mississippi. But as they afterwards not only abandoned that pretension, but gave up even the pretension to an article renewing their right to the navigation of the Mississippi, it was to have been expected they would thenceforth have considered this western boundary of no importance to them. The new pretension, however, of disputing our title to the settlement at the mouth of Columbia River, either indicates a design on their part to encroach by new establishments of their own upon the forty-ninth parallel of latitude, south of which they can have no valid claim upon this continent, or it manifests a jealousy of the United States, a desire to check the progress of our settlements, of which it might have been supposed that experience would before this day have relieved them. Their projects for the line, both in the negotiation of Messrs. Monroe and Pinkney in 1806, and at Ghent in 1814, were to take the 49th parallel of latitude from the Lake of the Woods west, as far as the territories *of the United States* extend in that direction, with a caveat against its extension to the South Sea or beyond the Stony Mountains. Upon which two observations are to be made: first, that it is uncertain whether any part of the Lake of the Woods is in latitude 49; and secondly, that they always affected to apply the indefinite limit of extension "*as far as the territories extend*" to the territories of the United States, and not to those of Great Britain, leaving a nest-egg for future pretensions on their part south of latitude 49. The counter projects for the lines on our part, therefore, at both those negotiations were from the northwest corner of the Lake of the Woods, the point already fixed and undisputed, a line due north or south as the case may be to the 49th parallel of latitude, and thence along that parallel due west as far as the territories *of both parties* extend in that direction, and adopting the caveat against extension to the Pacific or beyond the Stony Mountains.

4. *Settlement at the mouth of Columbia River.* From the late correspondence with the Spanish Minister Onis, it appears that the claim of Spain upon the shores of the South Sea extends to the 56th degree of north latitude. But there is a Russian settlement in 55, besides a temporary lodgment connected with it as far south as 42. The pretensions of the British government may on this occasion be disclosed. We know not precisely what they are, nor have they explained the grounds or the motives upon which they contest our right to the settlement called Astoria, formed before the late war and broken up by the British sloop of war *Raccoon* in the course of it. The papers enclosed marked from A to I contain all the information material to the subject possessed by this Department. It appears that at the time when the American settlement was broken up during the war, the property was purchased by certain

agents of the British North West Company. This, however, could in no manner divest the United States of their jurisdiction. As the British government admit explicitly their obligation under the first article of the treaty of Ghent to restore the post, there can be no question with regard to the right of the United States to resume it.[1] We do not perceive how or why this question should be referred to two commissioners of the respective nations; and as Russia herself has pretensions on that coast, it deserves the consideration of both parties whether the ultimate determination in the almost unavoidable case of a difference between the commissioners could with propriety be referred to her sovereign. Mr. Rush has been instructed in the event of a final difference between the commissioners under the existing commissions, to propose the Emperor of Russia as the sovereign to whose decision the reference stipulated on that contingency in the treaty should be made. It cannot be doubted that he was the sovereign contemplated by both parties, at the time when the treaty was concluded, and it might be difficult to designate any other in whom the confidence of both parties would be so strong and clear, as to secure their cordial acquiescence in his decision.

The expedient itself of submitting questions of territorial rights and boundaries in discussion between two nations to the decision of a third, was unusual, if not entirely new, and should the contingency occur, will probably encounter difficulties of execution not foreseen at the time when the stipulation was made of resorting to it. The subjects in controversy are of a nature too intricate and complicated, requiring on the part of the arbitrator a patience of investigation and research, historical, political, legal, geographical and astronomical, for which it is impossible to conceive that

[1] Schafer, in *American Historical Review*, XVI. 286.

the sovereign of a great Empire could *personally* bestow the time. It follows of consequence, that if he should accept the trust which would thus be offered him, the investigation upon which his decision would be founded must be referred to one of his imperial Councils, or to a special commission of individuals selected by him for the purpose. Whoever is acquainted with the influence exercised by the British government over the general dispositions and opinions of the individuals at the head of all the branches of administration in Russia, as well as in other countries of Europe, must be aware to what extent the decisions in such a case would be dependent upon the individuals selected for the arbitration, and how much the door would be opened for the operation of diplomatic management and court intrigues to obtain a decision unfavorable to the United States. These ideas are suggested with a view to recommend the attempt rather to come to an agreement between the parties themselves upon all objects which have not been thoroughly discussed between them, than to cast their difficulties upon commissioners who can scarcely be expected to agree concerning them, and then upon a foreign sovereign, of whose personal integrity no doubt can be entertained, but who cannot have leisure to sift the subjects in dispute to the bottom, and whose own interests may be found to interfere with his entire impartiality.

On the whole the President will be well satisfied if these three objects, of indemnity for the slaves carried away, of the western boundary from the Lake of the Woods, and of the settlement at the mouth of Columbia River, can be adjusted by this negotiation, rather than referred to commissions which must be expensive, and so constituted as to make it at least probable that they will decide nothing; and then to a friendly sovereign, still at great expense and other inconveniences to both parties. With regard to the slaves, it is highly probable that if the British government would agree to pay for them at once, it would cost them little more than it will to go through the process of a commission and of a reference to a friendly sovereign, even if the final decision should be in their favor. On the other hand, should the decision be that the slaves shall be paid for, it would after this cumbrous and complicated process cost the United States as much to obtain this justice to their citizens, as the amount of the payment itself. The question which it was proposed by them should be submitted to the decision of an impartial arbitrator was merely on the construction of one paragraph in an article of the treaty of Ghent. This was so simple, and requiring so little research or investigation of any kind, that it might have been decided immediately by the sovereign himself, upon an inspection of the article, and a short statement of the facts to which both parties would have agreed. But the delineation of an unsettled boundary across the western deserts of this continent; the title to establishments on the Pacific Ocean, where the arbitrator himself is not without his pretensions, and where save pretensions there is no object to any party worth contending for, to create burdensome commissions, and make solemn references to a foreign sovereign—for these appear scarcely to be necessary if altogether justifiable. The whole amount of the sum with which Great Britain could make indemnity for the captured slaves would be inconsiderable.[1] As to the line from the Lake of the Woods; you are authorized to agree to that which was agreed upon by the plenipotentiaries on both sides in 1807, but not to any line which would bring the British in contact with the Mississippi; nor to anything which would authorize the British to trade with

---

[1] "Probably not exceeding one hundred thousand pounds."—*Original draft.*

Indians within the boundaries of the United States. Of the inconveniences of allowing such trade, even by licenses, a recent instance has occurred, copies of the papers relating to which are transmitted to you.

5. *Fisheries.* The proceedings, deliberations and communications upon this subject, which took place at the negotiation of Ghent, will be fresh in the remembrance of Mr. Gallatin. Mr. Rush possesses copies of the correspondence with the British government relating to it after the conclusion of the peace, and of that which has passed here between Mr. Bagot and this government. Copies of several letters received by members of Congress during the late session from the parts of the country most deeply interested in the fisheries are now transmitted.

The President authorizes you to agree to an article whereby the United States will desist from the liberty of fishing, and curing and drying fish within the British jurisdiction *generally,* upon condition that it shall be secured as a permanent right, *not liable to be* impaired by any future war, from Cape Ray to the Ramean Islands, and from Mount Joli on the Labrador coast through the strait of Belle Isle, indefinitely north along the coast. The right to extend as well to curing and drying the fish, as to fishing.

By the decree of the judge of the Vice Admiralty Court at Halifax on the 29th of August last, in the case of several American fishing vessels which had been captured and sent into that port, a copy of which is also now transmitted to you, it appears that all those captures have been *illegal.* An appeal from this decree was entered by the captors to the Appellate Court in England, and the owners of the captured vessels were obliged to give bonds to stand the issue of the appeal. Mr. Rush was instructed to employ suitable counsel for these cases if the appeals should be entered, and as we have been informed by him has accordingly done so. If you do not succeed in agreeing upon an article on this subject, it will be desirable that the question *upon the right* should be solemnly argued before the Lords of Appeal; and that counsel of the first eminence should be employed in it. Judge Wallace agreed with the Advocate General, that the late war completely dissolved every right of the people of the United States acquired by the treaty of 1783; but it does not appear that this question had been argued before him, and the contrary opinion is not to be surrendered on the part of the United States upon the *dictum* of a Vice Admiralty Court. Besides this we claim the rights in question not as acquired by the treaty of 1783, but as having always before enjoyed them, and as only recognized as belonging to us by that treaty, and therefore never to be divested from us but by our own consent. Judge Wallace, however, explicitly says that he does not see how he can condemn these vessels without an *act of Parliament*, and whoever knows anything of the English constitution must see that on this point he is unquestionable right. He says indeed something about an Order in Council, but it is very clear that would not answer. It is a question of forfeiture for a violated *territorial* jurisdiction, which forfeiture can be incurred, not by the law of nations, but only by the *law of the land*. There is obviously no such law.

The argument which has been so long and so ably maintained by Mr. Reeves, that the rights of *ante-nati* American as British subjects, even within the kingdom of Great Britain, have never been divested from them, because there has been no act of Parliament to declare it, applies in its fullest force to this case, and connected with the article in the treaty of 1783 by which this particular right was recognized, confirmed, and placed out of the reach of an act of

Parliament, corroborates the argument in our favor. How far it may be proper and advisable to use these suggestions in your negotiation must be left to your sound discretion; but they are thrown out with the hope that you will pursue the investigation of the important questions of British law involved in this interest, and that every possible advantage may be taken of them, preparatory for the trial before the Lords of Appeal, if the case should ultimately come to their decision. The British government may be well assured that not a particle of these rights will be finally yielded by the United States without a struggle which will cost Great Britain more than the worth of the prize.

These are the subjects to which the President is willing that your negotiation should be confined. With regard to the others of a general nature, and relating to the respective rights of the two nations in times of maritime war, you are authorized to treat of them and to conclude concerning them conformably to the instructions already in possession of Mr. Rush; or if the difficulty of agreeing upon the principles should continue as great as it has been hitherto, you may omit them altogether.

You will not fail to transmit by duplicates the result of your conferences at as early a period as may be found practicable.[1]

I am, etc.

---

[1] On July 29 Adams wrote to Gallatin requesting him to go to London to negotiate, if the British government had accepted the proposition made to it. *American State Papers*, Foreign Relations, IV. 378.

TO RICHARD RUSH

Department of State,
Washington, 30 July, 1818.

Sir:

Your dispatches to No. 20, inclusive, dated 4 June, 1818, have been received, with their respective enclosures and the regular packages of newspapers and other documents.

With this letter you will receive the instructions for the contemplated negotiation of a commercial convention, to take effect at the expiration of that of 3 July, 1815. A duplicate of the full power to Mr. Gallatin and yourself is likewise enclosed. It is supposed Mr. Gallatin will be in England before you receive this letter, if the British government shall have agreed to the negotiation.

A letter from the Prince Regent announcing the marriage of his sister, the Princess Elizabeth,[1] has been delivered to the President by Mr. Bagot. The President's answer and a copy of it are herewith enclosed. You will ask an audience to deliver the answer, or send it to Lord Castlereagh, as circumstances may render proper, and in the manner which will be most agreeable to his Royal Highness.

You will have seen that the free-port act, upon which the Order in Council received with your despatch No. 20 was founded, had excited the attention of this government even before the bill had gone through Parliament. We are disposed still to consider it as a partial departure from the rigor of the British colonial monopoly, and we hope it will lead to more general measures of a similar character. We are not anxious to enquire whether it was the result of the liberal principles avowed by Lord Castlereagh on the Spanish slave

[1] She married, April 7, 1818, Frederick, Prince of Hesse Homburg.

treaty debate, or whether it has been extorted by the navigation act to which we have found it necessary to resort. So far as it goes, it admits us explicitly to our portion of the trade which we have been so long and so fruitlessly endeavoring to obtain by amicable and voluntary compact. In speculating upon the probable operation of these acts, it would seem that their effect will be to favor the interest of the ports designed as free, at the expense partly of the two nations, but principally of the other British settlements and colonies. How far they will be satisfied with this policy is for the enquiry of Great Britain, and not ours; but it is very clear that both governments will be carefully watching its effect, and that each will adopt future measures, to the good or ill effect to its own interests which experience will disclose as resulting from these. We most sincerely wish that the British government would once fairly try the effect of a *conciliating* instead of a *counteracting* policy.

Among the acts of the last session of Congress you will find one (Ch. 109, p. 102) authorizing the Secretary of the Treasury to repay all the alien extra duties levied upon British subjects after the 3d of July, 1815, provided, the corresponding and reciprocal provision shall be made by the British government. You mentioned in one of your early dispatches having spoken of this matter to Lord Castlereagh, but have not since informed us what was the result. As this measure on both sides is indispensable for carrying the convention into effect with good faith, if an act of Parliament is necessary for that purpose, it is hoped it has not been overlooked.

During the last session of Congress no small dissatisfaction was manifested at the extraordinary expense and the very slow progress made by the commissions under the 5th, and under the 6th and 7th articles of the treaty of Ghent. At the close of the session a resolution passed the House of Representatives, a copy of which is herewith enclosed. It was not acted upon by the Senate, and therefore not formally communicated to the President. As an expression of the opinion and wishes of the House of Representatives it is, however, deserving of attention. The President wishes you to have some communication with the British government on the subject. An intimation to the commissioners of the propriety of expediting as much as possible their labors, and with a particular attention to economy, is the only measure supposed at present to be advisable. The American commissioners, both of whom were here part of last winter, have already had such intimations of the sense of the public and of Congress on this point, as was suited to impress upon them the importance of proceeding with all possible frugality and dispatch.

As the British free-port acts open to American shipping the ports of Halifax and St. John, as that of Bermuda was already opened, an obvious necessity arises of admitting a consul or commercial agent of the United States at those ports, upon which you will consult with Lord Castlereagh, and give notice as early as possible whether such officers will be received and permitted to exercise their functions. The same question may be extended to the ports of Calcutta, Madras and Bombay, in the East Indies.

The public papers now forwarded will give you the current events of the day. The transactions of General Jackson in his campaign against the Indians have excited great interest here, and will probably occasion some excitement in Europe. The execution of two British subjects by sentences of a court-martial has already been noticed by Mr. Bagot, and may perhaps give rise to animadversions in England. By some accident for which we are unable to account, the proceedings of the court-martial with the documents upon which the convictions were founded have not yet been received. When they come it is presumed we shall be enabled to give explanations of those proceedings which will be satisfactory to the British government. Pensacola is to be restored to Spain.

The *Congress* frigate has returned with two of the commissioners who went to Buenos Ayres. Judge Bland proceeded to Chili. Their unanimous opinion is that the resubjugation of the provinces of La Plata to Spain is impossible. Of their internal condition the aspect is more equivocal.

Mr. Campbell sailed last week for St. Petersburg in the *Guerriere* frigate from Boston. As he will probably land at Copenhagen, he is authorized to give proper explanations to the Danish government for declining to make the appointment of a permanent minister of the United States at that court, according to the suggestion of the Danish minister in London to you, which you will accordingly communicate to him.

I am, etc.

TO FRANCIS CALLEY GRAY

WASHINGTON, 3 August, 1818.

DEAR SIR:

I have received your letter of the 16th ultimo, with a copy of your oration delivered on the anniversary of Independence, which I have read with great pleasure.

Mr. Campbell, on finding that you declined the appointment of Secretary of Legation, sent me back the letter which I had written to you by him. I now enclose it to you wishing you to consider it as a testimonial of my regard.

I cannot disapprove the principle upon which you have preferred adhering for the present to your professional career at home, to entering upon that of American diplomacy abroad. My advice to every young American in reference to the public service would be, to maintain a high sense of personal independence, and nothing can more effectually serve this than an established reputation at the bar. But this requires indefatigable industry and arduous persevering application. Now the same qualities, in the same degree, applied to the duties of a Secretary of Legation and to the studies congenial to that character, would, I think, qualify you for serving your country with as much and perhaps more usefulness than applied in a like portion of time to increasing practice at the bar.

My theory of accordance between the duties of self respect, and devotion to the public according to the genius of our institutions, is this. The individual owes the exercise of all his faculties to the service of his country. Whether he shall serve his country in a public capacity, should in the first instance be determined by the country (through its constitutional organs) and not by the individual. He ought not to obtrude, nor even to offer himself directly or indirectly, nor to use by himself or his friends any means whatever to obtain an appointment. But when invited to the public service by the regular authority, the rule of duty changes, and in general cases the obligation of the citizen is to accept the call and to assume the station assigned to him. To this rule, as to all others, there are exceptions, of which the individual must be the judge, but upon which he is bound to determine, not upon light or capricious or selfish motives, but with a due regard to the claims of his country upon him, as well as to his own interests and feelings. I am far from thinking that you have in this instance judged and acted otherwise than with perfect propriety. By persevering in your professional practice you will secure a more entire personal independence than you can enjoy in *any* public station. There are other forms of public service in which you may be engaged without being necessarily withdrawn from your employments at the bar. An introduction to the public service by means of popular suffrage is more creditable, and brings one in upon a more solid foundation than that by executive appointment. Service at home requires few or none of those sacrifices of domestic affections which must be made by long and distant absence from one's family, friends and country. For these most precious human enjoyments, next to those of the *mens conscia recti*, there is no substitute for an American holding a public station in Europe. He can form no friendships there, can contract no attachments there. If he does, it will be his misfortune, for every such new and uncongenial tie must proportionably loosen his hold upon his country. Public service at home is not liable to the same temptations nor exposed to the same dangers as that in foreign lands. An American, especially a young American in Europe, breathes an atmosphere full of the most deadly infection to his morals. He has incessant incitements to dissipated habits, idleness, intemperance and sensuality, to resist which calls for a perpetual exercise of self-control and self-denial. The very gratification of his curiosity by visiting the marvellous objects accumulated in the European capitals for the gaze of strangers is generally but a variety of wasted time. One of my motives for recommending you to the President and to Mr. Campbell as Secretary of Legation in Russia was that, having once passed through that ordeal and returned home a sound American still, you would have been better prepared for passing safely through it again. That you would have revisited Europe, not to gaze, and wonder, and glut upon delicious novelties; but as a place, where you had business to transact and studies to pursue for the service of your country. I regret on the public account that the proposal did not meet your views; but on your own I am willing to believe and hope that you have chosen the better part.

Whatever your future course may be, I pray you to be assured that I shall always take a warm interest in your welfare, and that I remain, etc.

TO ALEXANDER HILL EVERETT [1]

DEPARTMENT OF STATE,
WASHINGTON, 10 August, 1818.

SIR:

The Minister Plenipotentiary [Eustis] who for some years past has represented this government at the court of the Netherlands having returned to the United States, the President has thought proper to appoint a chargé d'affaires to reside there in future, and has conferred the temporary appointment upon you; with the intention of presenting your name to the Senate for their advice and consent to the same nomination at their next session.

The relations between the United States and the new kingdom of the Netherlands are altogether commercial. A treaty of amity and commerce, concluded in the year 1782 with the United Provinces of the Netherlands, is acknowledged by both governments to be still in force, so far as it is adapted to the present circumstances of the two nations; both of which have since its conclusion undergone revolutions of government, and obtained acquisitions of

[1] These instructions were finished and laid before the President July 24.

territory to which the engagements of the treaty are understood to extend.

Immediately after the termination of the late war between the United States and Great Britain, and when the turn of events in Europe presented the first prospects of a period of general peace and tranquillity, during which it was to be expected that all the maritime nations would foster their respective commercial interests, Congress by an act of 3 March, 1815, manifested to the world the liberal spirit with regard to commercial intercourse which it has always been the policy and the desire of the United States to promote. This act contained an offer to repeal all the discriminating duties of tonnage, and upon merchandise imported in foreign vessels into the United States, in favor of any nation which would accede to the same measure in favor of the United States, limited, however, in respect to the merchandise, to the produce or manufacture of the nation to which the vessel should belong.

This proposal was shortly afterwards partially carried into effect by the commercial convention of 3 July, 1815, with Great Britain. Adhering, however, to the exclusive monopolizing and colonial system with regard to her possessions in the West Indies and on this continent, she accepted the principle of equalizing the duties only for the intercourse between the United States and her European possessions. She still persists in the same system, and the navigation act passed at the last session of Congress meets her regulations by a corresponding exclusion of British vessels coming from ports into which the vessels of the United States are permanently denied access.

The government of the Netherlands, very soon after the conclusion of the convention of 3 July, 1815, between the United States and Great Britain, declared their readiness to enter into arrangements of the same kind. They offered an immediate equalization of *tonnage* duties, and by an erroneous construction of the act of Congress of 3 March, 1815, they appear to have considered it as having taken effect in favor of the vessels of the Netherlands from the time when they made this offer. By the express terms of the act, however, it related to the duties on merchandise as well as on tonnage; nor could the President give effect to the acts in favor of any foreign nation, until he was satisfied that *all* discriminating or countervailing duties of such nation, so far as they operated to the disadvantage of the United States, had been abolished.

By a law of 3 October, 1816, the government of the Netherlands declared that from and after the first of January, 1817, the tonnage duties on vessels of the United States in the ports of the Netherlands should be the same as on the vessels of the nation. This law, with an instruction to the officers of the customs conformable to it, was transmitted by Mr. Eustis in January, 1817, in a despatch to the Department of State, which appears by some accident not to have been received. Nor was the chargé d'affaires from the Netherlands residing here furnished with a copy of it to be communicated to the government of the United States. The regulation is stated in late letters from Mr. Eustis to have been adopted in the confidence that the same advantage would immediately be secured to the vessels of the Netherlands in the ports of the United States, by virtue of the act of Congress of 3 March, 1815. And Mr. Eustis in several late letters repeats this intimation, that the government of the Netherlands had taken much dissatisfaction, at his not being enabled to inform them that this measure of reciprocity had been adopted in favor of the Dutch vessels. He seems, indeed, impressed with the idea that the failure of the negotiation of a new commercial treaty by Mr. Gallatin and himself last summer, was in a great measure attributed to this untoward incident. It appears also by late communications from him and Mr. Appleton, whom during his late absence in France he left as chargé d'affaires at The Hague, that the Dutch government did actually reëstablish the discriminating duties against vessels of the United States from the 1st of March last; but with a promise, which was all that he was able to obtain, that they should cease whenever the United States should repeal the discriminating *tonnage* duties upon the vessels of the Netherlands.

It has already been remarked that the letter of Mr. Eustis, dated January, 1817, containing the first information that the vessels of the United States were exempted from extra-tonnage duties in the Netherlands, appears never to have been received at the Department, and that no official communication was made of that law by the chargé d'affaires from that country, until after the commencement of the last session of Congress. The measure of the Dutch government, therefore, not being known, could not be reciprocated. But had it been known, as it related exclusively to tonnage duties, it could not have been reciprocated by an order of the President under the act of 3 March, 1815, which authorized him not to declare the tonnage duties alone repealed, but those also upon merchandise, the produce or manufacture of the country to which the vessel should belong. The law and regulation of the Netherlands were not co-extensive with the offer in the act of 3 March, 1815, and if there were in the Netherlands no extra duties upon merchandise imported in American vessels, nor any other discriminating or countervailing duties to their disadvantage, the fact had not been officially communicated, and could not be known to the President. Early in the course of the last summer a full-power was transmitted to Messrs. Gallatin and Eustis authorizing them to conclude a new treaty of commerce, embracing all the objects interesting to the two countries, and founded upon principles of perfect reciprocity. The causes of the failure of that negotiation are set forth in documents, a copy of which will be furnished you. The report of its issue was received here during the last session of Congress, and the difficulties upon which the conferences had been suspended, appearing to be of a nature not removable by a renewal of the negotiation, immediate measures were taken to secure by act of Congress to the vessels of the Netherlands in the ports of the United States, all the advantages which had been granted to American vessels in the Dutch ports by the law of 3 October, 1816. The act of Congress is retrospective, operating from the time when the reciprocal law of the Netherlands took effect in favor of the American vessels, that is, from the 1st of January, 1817. It repeals the discriminating duties, not only of tonnage, but upon merchandise imported in vessels of the Netherlands; whether such merchandise be of the produce or manufactures of the territories in Europe of the king of the Netherlands, or "such produce and manufactures as can only be, or most usually are first shipped from a port or place in that Kingdom." This last provision goes further than the act of Congress of 3 March, 1815, and removes the principal difficulty on our part upon which the conferences of the last summer were suspended. It places the vessels of the Netherlands in our ports, so far as respects the Dutch territories in Europe, entirely upon the same footing as our own, and upon a footing better than that of our vessels in the Netherlands, inasmuch as our tonnage duty upon our own vessels is lower than theirs. So that while American vessels in the ports of the Netherlands are paying a tonnage duty of [ ] the Dutch vessels in ours pay only six cents a ton.

From the manner in which the conferences at The Hague terminated, and from the tenor and complexion of a note transmitted *after they had terminated* by the Dutch plenipotentiaries to Mr. Eustis, it would seem as if there had been on their part some excitement of temper. Mr. Eustis is persuaded that a change of policy in the Dutch government itself was effected during the progress of the negotiation. He thinks it had excited the commercial jealousy of the merchants of Amsterdam, who roused an influence to prevent any liberal concession of the government in regard to our intercourse with their colonies, and he conjectures that an external and political interposition was likewise used to defeat the negotiation. The above detail of the transactions between the two governments since our peace with Great Britain has been given, that you may be enabled on a suitable occasion to satisfy the Dutch Minister of Foreign Affairs, and through him the government of the Netherlands, of the perfect fairness and candor of our proceedings towards them, and of the earnest desire which we have invariably entertained of establishing the commercial intercourse between the two countries on the most liberal and conciliatory principles. The chargé d'affaires of the Netherlands residing here has intimated a wish that the negotiation for a new commercial treaty might be resumed; but it is not certain whether he has in that respect expressed the wishes of his government, or merely a sentiment of his own. As it is highly probable that a renewal of the negotiation would revive those counteracting influences which are supposed to have affected the suspension of the conferences, and as experience has shown that their result is not only to prevent the mutual agreement of the parties, but to alienate them from each other, and to raise asperities between them which would not otherwise exist, the President has thought it most advisable to leave the negotiation of the treaty incomplete, and to endeavor to accomplish its objects by the regulations of the respective governments independent of formal compact. If anything should be said to you by the Minister of Foreign Affairs, importing a wish for a renewal of the negotiation, you will inform him that the President will accede with the utmost readiness and satisfaction to that wish; but without alluding to the *sources* of the obstacles to the success of the late conferences, or discovering any suspicion of the adverse interests, commercial or political, homebred or foreign, you will notice the natural tendency of *discussion*, unless it terminates in agreement, to generate mutual coolness and opposition. You will observe not by way of complaint, but as matter of fact, that this general effect was exemplified in the progress and event of the late conferences. That a second abortive attempt would probably be more strongly marked with the same result; and that the very earnestness of our desire to be on terms of cordial good-understanding with the Netherlands has led the President to the conclusion, that if the formal negotiation of a new treaty should be resumed, it would be more certain of terminating to the satisfaction of both parties, by ascertaining as a preliminary the principles upon which the two governments can agree.

In the negotiation of last summer it appeared that the Dutch plenipotentiaries were desirous of obtaining modifications of the treaty of 1782, to which the United States cannot accede. They expressed the disposition to set aside the 8th article, which pledges each of the parties to protect the property of the other within its jurisdiction; and the part of the eleventh article, which stipulates that free ships shall make free goods and *persons*. As the first of these is an obligation binding upon every *independent* nation, without needing an engagement by treaty, the very attempt to be released from it is an acknowledgment of dependence upon another power, which takes away the reliance upon any compact to be agreed upon with a nation thus trammelled; and although the principle of free ships free goods may probably hereafter be far less useful to the United States than to the Netherlands in a treaty between them, we cannot consent to expunge an article, the omission of which would have the appearance of giving countenance to the practice of impressment.

The repeal of the discriminating duties has been on our part as complete as the government of the Netherlands could wish. The vessels of that nation and the merchandise imported in them are placed upon the footing of importations in our own. Our plenipotentiaries endeavored to obtain in return for this advantage an article securing to our vessels admission into the Dutch ports of the East and West Indies, upon the footing of the most favored nation, but without success. We have nothing more to grant by treaty than we have already conceded by the law. The admission of our vessels into the Dutch colonies may remain upon its present footing, so long as the government of the Netherlands find their interest in giving it no further extension. They are now in fact admitted upon the footing of the most favored nation; but the Dutch government declined stipulating for the continuance of this advantage, without the promise of an equivalent on our part—adhering to the decayed and rotten principles of the exclusive European colonial system, as if they had forgotten or wilfully overlooked the forty last years of the history of the world.

The whole of this colonial system, as first established by

Spain and Portugal, and since adopted by other nations from whose institutions more liberal results were to have been expected, is an outrage upon the first principles of civil society. The revolution of North America, and that which is now in progress on the southern continent of this hemisphere, the removal of the Portuguese government to Brazil, and the expulsion of the French from the island of St. Domingo, together with the progress of the human mind towards emancipation, which no efforts of existing power can suppress, must within a period not very remote demolish all the remnants of that absurd and iniquitous system. The United States may without material inconvenience wait for the consummation of this event, and leave the government of the Netherlands to discover the necessity of accommodating themselves to it.

The principles assumed by the Dutch plenipotentiaries in their note of 10 September, 1817, to Messrs. Gallatin and Eustis, afford the strongest illustration to these remarks. They recur to the general *monopolizing* features of the colonial system, not as just and proper in themselves, but as founded upon and justified by established European usage. They affirm that while the Netherlands in Europe enjoy the privileges of a free constitutional government, their *colonies* in the East and West Indies are under the servitude of absolute subjection to the will of the king. Locked up as an exclusive possession to be administered, not for their own benefit but for the benefit of the inhabitants of the Netherlands, that access to them by foreigners is to be obtained, not upon the broad and equitable principle of mutual wants and mutual convenience, but as a participation of one monopoly in return for participation of another monopoly. So that the United States, to obtain such access must begin by establishing some such arbitrary monopoly of their own, and then by relaxing from it in favor of the Netherlands, yield an equivalent for a like admission to the Dutch colonies. When it was observed to them by Messrs. Gallatin and Eustis that the important commerce of Louisiana, though always closed against them as colonial, had been opened to them since its annexation to the United States, and thus by a fair application even of their own principle gave us a claim of admission to their colonies, they contended that our admission to the Belgian provinces was to be considered as an equivalent for theirs to Louisiana; as if the Belgian provinces had not been open to us as much before their annexation to the kingdom of the Netherlands as they have been since.

The establishment of this principle by the powers of Europe possessing colonies, of granting access to the colonies of each other as a mutual barter of monopoly, is nothing less than a commercial conspiracy against the United States, the only nation whom it materially injures, and the only nation extensively commercial and maritime which possesses no colonies. In the present state of the world it is obvious that it cannot be carried into effect, but this government cannot too cautiously avoid acquiescing in it. The prospect being thus unfavorable of an agreement between the two governments upon the principles of any further stipulation important to their common intercourse, it is hoped no further wish will be intimated to you for a renewal of the negotiation; in which case it will not be necessary for you to introduce the subject, or to present the ideas here unfolded. You will neither seek nor avoid the discussion. But if commenced, you will be especially careful to avoid everything offensive in the manner, and to conduct it with the moderation and urbanity compatible with the firm adherence to our rights and consistent with the friendly disposition possessed and entertained by this government towards that of the Netherlands.

The claims of citizens of the United States upon the government of the Netherlands, to be indemnified for the depredations upon their property committed under color of ordinances and decrees of the French government, or that of Holland under Louis Buonaparte, having formed the subject of instructions to the late minister plenipotentiary, are well known to you. A copy of those instructions is herewith enclosed. The documents in support of the claims it is presumed have been left in the hands of Mr. Appleton, who will deliver them over to you. A copy of the printed opinion of John Woodward, an eminent lawyer of New York, on the case of the Brig *St. Michaels* and her cargo, is also now transmitted, and contains a discussion of principles and a collection of authorities from the writers on the laws of nations generally applicable to all the claims. The printed documents relating to the late negotiation with Naples, for claims founded partly on the same principles, may also be usefully consulted in maintaining the argument of *right* in support of those which it will be your duty to recommend to the justice of the government of the Netherlands.

No principle of international law can be more clearly established than this: that the *rights* and the *obligations* of a nation in regard to other states are independent of its internal revolutions of government. It extends even to the case of conquest. The conqueror who reduces a nation to his subjection, receives it subject to all its engagements and duties towards others, the fulfillment of which then becomes his own duty. However frequent the instances of departure from this principle may be in point of fact, it cannot with any color of reason be contested on the ground of right. On what other ground is it indeed that both the governments of the Netherlands and of the United States now admit that they are still reciprocally bound by the engagements, and entitled to claim from each other the benefits, of the treaty between the United States and the United Provinces of 1782? If the nations are respectively bound to the stipulations of that treaty now, they were equally bound to them in 1810, when the depredations for which indemnity is now claimed were committed; and when the present king of the Netherlands came to the sovereignty of the country, he assumed with it the obligation of repairing the injustices against other nations which had been committed by his predecessors, however free from all participation in them he had been himself. It is fully understood that the European allied powers have acted upon this principle in their support of the claims of indemnities of their subjects upon the present government of France, and France on her part claims from the United States, not only the advantage of every stipulation contracted by the United States with the government of Napoleon, but by a latitude of construction of her own, privileges which were not intended to be conceded by them.

With regard to the facts upon which the claims of indemnity of our citizens upon the government of the Netherlands are founded, it is supposed they are of a nature not to be contested. They are generally cases of seizure and confiscation by decrees and orders of the government, of the most arbitrary and unjustifiable character. Some of them were doubtless attended with circumstances of more aggravation than others. That of the *St. Michaels*, as represented in the pamphlet herewith forwarded, is particularly recommended to your attention. In using every proper exertion in your power to obtain from the Dutch government a recognition of the justice of these claims and provision for them, you will carefully avoid both in the manner and substance of your applications, every appearance of useless importunity, and every expression of an irritating or offensive character. They must understand that although pursued with moderation and forbearance, the claims will not be abandoned or renounced.

Your principal remaining duty will be to obtain and report to this Department, from time to time, all the interesting information that you can collect with reference to the country where you are to reside, and to the general affairs of Europe. The local situation of that country being nearly central to the whole range of European concern, is favorable to this development; and as the United States have no diplomatic agent in any part of Germany, your assiduous attention may with usefulness and propriety be turned to the course of events in that portion of Europe. A friendly intercourse with the other diplomatic characters at the court of the Netherlands, and a correspondence with the ministers of the United States at the principal European courts, will give you great facilities for obtaining early and correct information, and your judgment will be well exercised in distinguishing between that, and the groundless rumors which are in constant circulation, and sometimes from sources where nothing but authenticity might be expected. It is understood that about the time when you will reach the place of your destination, a meeting is to be held in its immediate vicinity between several of the most powerful sovereigns of Europe, the principal members of the European alliance. At that meeting objects of the first importance to the civilized world will doubtless be agitated, and perhaps arrangements formed for settling interests of the highest moment to Germany, France, Italy, Spain, Portugal, and perhaps South America. In the latter only the interests of the United States will be to any considerable extent involved. The best and most particular information that you can obtain from that quarter will be very acceptable. You understand that the policy of the government of the United States is to favor by all suitable means compatible with a fair neutrality the total independence of the South American provinces. It is presumed that the ultimate policy of the European powers in general will be the same. But hitherto it has been fluctuating, and unsystematic, and somewhat discordant. . . .

The consuls of the United States within the kingdom of the Netherlands are Alexander McRae, at Amsterdam; George Joy, at Rotterdam; David Parish, at Antwerp, and Emmanuel Wambersie, at Ostend, the last of whom is believed to be the only one now at his post. Mr. McRae was appointed during the last session of the Senate and has not yet embarked for Europe. The vacancy at Antwerp, having been made known since the adjournment of the Senate, has been filled by the appointment of Mr. Parish, who will also be nominated at their next meeting. His commission is now forwarded to you, with the request that after obtaining the necessary exequatur you will forward it to his house at Antwerp. The consuls will, of course, correspond with you, and will receive from you every official aid in the performance of their duties which may be necessary, and which you can give them.

I am, etc.

TO THE PRESIDENT

[James Monroe]

Washington, 12 August, 1818.

Sir:

I have the honor of enclosing the following letters and documents which have just been received, and of requesting concerning them the favor of your instructions.

1. A letter from the Spanish Minister Onis, in reply to that by which he was informed of your determination that Pensacola should be restored, with three enclosures.
2. Translation of a letter from Don M. H. de Aguirre, the agent from Buenos Ayres.
3. A letter from the Governor of Georgia, giving the information that Captain Obed Wright had made his escape.
4. A letter from Mr. King of the Senate.
5. A letter from Mr. Eustis, late Minister to the Netherlands.
6. A letter from George Sullivan, requesting authority to commence a certain suit in the name of the United States.

Mr. Onis has given out that he waits for instructions from his court to make new propositions for a definite arrangement of differences. A false report from Cadiz through the Havana, that the Floridas have been ceded by Spain to the United States by a treaty signed at Madrid, has been published and repeated in most of the newspapers with a confidence indicating private speculation behind the scenes. It is stated to have come directly from the American consul at Cadiz. It seems desirable that this person should be speedily replaced by another.

Mr. Aguirre is now here and will wait till I can communicate to him the answer which I may be enabled by your direction to give to his proposals. He came with bitter complaints that he had been several times personally arrested in New York, notwithstanding his public character.[1] I told him that I was sure you would regret this circumstance, but that it was not in the power of the executive to exempt him from arrest, not only for the reason given by Judge Livingston, that his government was not recognized, but because his commission was not that of a public minister. He then gave me a history of his mission to this country and its special object, which was to build and dispatch six sloops of war for the governments of La Plata and Chile. But his actual funds being adequate to pay only for two, he had built no more. That they are now ready for sea; but to give them the appearance of a mercantile speculation and to clear them out, he was obliged to have them registered in the names of his two captains, in consequence of which they have both been attached for personal debts of those captains. That the Spanish consuls and agents have seduced some of his officers and individuals of the crews. That his funds are exhausted, and the vessels are now lying at New York at an expense of a thousand dollars a day. That finding the execution of the object of his government impracticable, he has concluded to give it up, and if possible to sell his two ships in their present condition. That being built for vessels of war, they are not saleable among the merchants, and he therefore offers them to the government of the United States. I inquired what price he proposed to ask for them. He said he could not now exactly tell; but if the proposal should be deemed by you admissible, he would immediately ascertain.[2]

[1] Adams, *Memoirs*, August 8, 1818.
[2] "Your answer to Mr. Aguirre, informing him that he could not be protected

If you think Mr. King's construction of the Navigation Act of the last session of Congress correct, I submit to your consideration whether it will not be proper that instructions should be immediately issued from the Treasury Department to the collectors of the customs and published, giving notice that British vessels will not be admitted to entry from the ports of Halifax and St. John's after the 30th of September, and that notice of the same should be given by me to Mr. Bagot. Mr. Calhoun, the comptroller of the Treasury [Anderson], and myself, consider the act in the same point of view as Mr. King. The Attorney General being at Baltimore I have not had the opportunity of consulting him.

. . . .

I propose to leave the city about the 20th instant and to be absent about two weeks, unless sooner recalled by the state of business of the Department, or by your direction.

I am, etc.

TO THE PRESIDENT

[James Monroe]

WASHINGTON, 13 August, 1818.

SIR:

I have the honor of receiving your letter of the 10th instant with the enclosures this morning. The zeal of the

against arrest for the reasons stated, was very correct. He ought to have known the fact, and not mentioned it; but, in truth, his whole proceeding here has manifested his utter incompetency for his trust; or that, misguided by others, he has believed that he could, by taking advantage of the public feeling in favor of the colonies, force the government into measures forbidden by our laws, disgraceful to the character and repugnant to the national interest." *Monroe to Adams*, August 17, 1818. Ms.

Spanish official agents in New York and the present arrangements and dispositions of the military agent of Buenos Ayres and Chile appear to have rendered it unnecessary to give any immediate answer to Mr. Onis's load of affidavits. Mr. Stoughton did, it seems, cause Mr. Aguirre and the captains of his two ships to be arrested for a violation of the neutrality law of the last session of Congress. Judge Livingston discharged them, on the ground that the case of violation of the law had not been made out. The judge also explicitly declared that the prosecution for breach of the law might be carried on without any interference of the executive, a fact which may serve for answer to many of Mr. Onis's notes. Mr. Aguirre, however, seems determined that his real object should not be misunderstood, and that if the executive is not implicated in it, the fault shall not be in him. He makes no secret that his intention was to arm, and equip, and fit out, and man from our ports ships of war, to be dispatched as mercantile speculations and under the flag of the United States, but to be metamorphosed into armed ships with Buenos Ayrean officers and crews the moment they should be beyond the territorial jurisdiction of the United States. I now enclose the translation of his letter of proposals, upon which I am to request your instructions. He waits for the answer here, though his letter announces him to be under an indispensable necessity of returning immediately to New York.

. . . . . .

I am, etc.

TO RICHARD RUSH

DEPARTMENT OF STATE,
WASHINGTON, 15 August, 1818.

SIR:

The act of Parliament passed at the last session of that body, and the Order of the British Council of 27 May last consequent upon it, copies of which have been received at this Department from you, are understood to have made no alteration in the British *ordinary laws of navigation and trade*. They merely open to the admission for certain specified purposes of vessels of the United States the ports of Halifax in Nova Scotia and of St. John's in New Brunswick, for a limited time, and by a regulation revocable at the pleasure of the council. They cannot therefore in any manner affect the operation of the act of Congress concerning navigation of 18 April last, and the ports of the United States will be after the 30th of next month closed against British vessels from Halifax and St. John's, in like manner as if no such act of Parliament and order in council had issued.

[Referring to my late letters on the subject of South American affairs, I am now directed to inquire what part you think the British government will take in regard to the dispute between Spain and her colonies, and in what light they will view an acknowledgment of the independence of the colonies by the United States? Whether they will view it as an act of hostility to Spain, and in case Spain should declare war against us in consequence, whether Great Britain will take part with her in it?] [1]

I am, etc.

[1] This last paragraph was sent in cypher. The same questions were asked of

TO RICHARD RUSH

Private.   WASHINGTON, 20 August, 1818.
DEAR SIR:

Since I had the pleasure of writing you last (except from the Department) I have received your letters of 25 April, 3d and 25 May. The letter relating to Parry [1] was delivered, as you desired, to Commodore Rodgers. Parry himself has lately arrived at Norfolk, and has been here to offer his services to the Commissioners of the Navy. I have not heard with what success. You know that here, as well as elsewhere, there are so many native candidates for every kind of public employment that it is difficult for foreigners in competition with them to obtain it. Mr. Parry's manuscripts about which he was solicitous were all safely lodged by Commodore Barney in the public offices, but in all the departments of naval architecture and even of ordnance we are, or fancy ourselves, a little more than upon a par with the invention and ingenuity of the old countries.

I did also receive, and I am very sorry to say, several months ago, a letter from Mr. Tigere and a box containing prussiate of potash. He had explained to me while I was in England his ingenious invention for preparing paper from which the oxymuriatic acid should not extract ink without leaving traces, and his wish to obtain a patent for it in the United States. At that time there were paper mills at this place which I supposed were at work, and to the owners of which I thought I could offer Mr. Tigere's proposals. But

---

Gallatin in France, and Campbell in Russia, and were suggested by the President in a letter to Adams, dated August 10.

[1] William Parry, described by Rush as an "ingenious and respectable mechanic in the shipbuilding line."

they are at a stand, or abandoned, and I know not where to present Mr. Tigere's invention with a prospect of obtaining for him an associate who will agree to his terms. By our patent laws the patent could not be taken out in another name, nor in that of Tigere himself without a residence of two years or a special act of Congress. Finally, trifling as the cost of a patent right is here, there is much reason to believe that the benefit to be derived from it in this case would not defray the expense of taking it out. If Mr. Tigere should call upon you again for an answer to his letter to me, have the goodness to convey these ideas to him in such manner as may best suit the patience of his temper, and, if possible, without suggesting to him any doubts either of the ingenuity, originality, or virtue of his invention.

I am very sorry to find that Lord Castlereagh appears to have felt hurt at a remark in a report of a committee of the House of Representatives in Congress upon the fourth of the articles proposed by him to be added to the commercial convention of 3 July, 1815.[1] He has sent to Mr. Bagot a copy of a note which he addressed to you on the subject about the first of June, though no mention is made of it in your dispatches down to the 9th of that month. He is very unwilling to be suspected of a disposition to tamper with our Indians in time of peace. The execution of two Englishmen by a sentence of a court-martial in the late campaign against the Seminoles will startle him still more. Mr. Bagot has already applied to me several times for some explanation of this transaction, but by some accident for which we are yet unable to account the proceedings of the court-martial, which were forwarded by General Jackson to the War Department the first week in May, have never been

[1] Adams, *Memoirs*, August 1, 1818. The article interfered with the settled policy of the United States in regard to trade with the Indians.

received and we are yet without them. Copies are expected in the course of a few days.[1]

Notwithstanding the decision of the judge of Vice Admiralty at Halifax last year, that American fishing vessels could not be condemned as forfeited *without an act* of Parliament, the British cruisers on that coast have captured several of them again this season, some of which have been released, and others detained for trial, and it is said will be condemned. Mr. Bagot has informed me that orders were again issued from the British government in May to Admiral Milne, to suspend captures again for the present year. As I think you will not come to an agreement for an article upon this subject, we must defend our whole right to the last extremity. Judge Wallace's decision that they cannot condemn without an act of Parliament is so obviously just that I can hardly believe another judge would decide otherwise. But if he should, we shall take care to have the cause carried by appeal to the Supreme Court of Admiralty in England and shall then rely upon your exertions to have all possible justice done to it. That counsel shall be employed, not only who are of the first ability, but who shall take *our* view of the treaty of peace of 1782 and '83, as a treaty in its nature not to be affected by a subsequent war;

[1] "Mr. Bagot has called upon me a third time to inquire for information of the proceedings of the court-martial in the cases of Arbuthnot and Ambrister; and as the editors of newspapers in Georgia and New York have apparently information not yet received by the government, he manifested a little impatience, and said he had reason to believe that the information was in everybody's hands but his. The Secretary of War has this week received a letter from Captain Gadsden written by direction of General Jackson, stating that on the 5th of May a detailed report of his proceedings till that time was forwarded to the War Department, together with the original proceedings of the court-martial, and the original letters upon which those two men were condemned. The miscarriage of that dispatch affords materials for much conjecture. General Jackson promises copies of the documents, the arrival of which is daily expected." *To the President*, August 20, 1818. Ms.

as a treaty of *partition* and recognition as well as of peace, and who shall exhibit and illustrate this position in all its strength. To this must be added the argument of *Mr. Reeves*, which has never been answered by any English lawyer, and which applies to this case in its utmost force. Then the principle of Judge Wallace that the forfeiture cannot accrue, nor the seizure be legal, without an act of Parliament. Every one of these points should be argued with all the talent and eloquence that Doctors Commons can supply, with a shorthand reporter to take down every word of the trial for publication. If the Lords of the Council are prepared to set at naught the character of the treaty of independence, the whole body of their own law of alienage and allegiance, and parliamentary authority by arbitrary prerogative in time of peace, let us have their determination at full length and in a tangible shape. From their decision there will still be an appeal to the sense and spirit even of their own nation, and still more of ours.

I will thank you to procure and send by as early an opportunity as possible to New York or Philadelphia, with suitable directions for their transmission here by any good coasting vessel, a *table* copying press of the best kind, with two reams of folio copying paper, two of quarto paper, two dozen papers of the proper ink powder, wetting and drying books of the largest dimensions in use, and all the ordinary apparatus of such a press. It is for the use of the Department, and you will charge for the expense of it in your accounts.

I remain.

TO THE PRESIDENT

[JAMES MONROE]

WASHINGTON, 23 August, 1818.

SIR:

Your letter of the 20th instant was received yesterday. Having found nothing on the files of the Department which can ascertain the fact that Mr. Barlow's [1] detention here, from the time of his appointment until his departure upon his mission to France in 1811, was at the suggestion of the government, further explanation from Mr. Lee [2] (who is yet absent) becomes necessary before a definitive answer to Mr. Barlow's present representatives in relation to the time from which his salary is to be allowed. I omitted to mention in my former letter the other question respecting the allowance to Mr. Thomas Barlow as the secretary of legation. My own opinion is that he is in justice entitled to it until he delivered up his trust to Mr. Crawford, but I do not feel authorized to approve of any allowance questioned by the accounting officers of the Treasury in cases which occurred before my appointment to the Department without your express sanction.

Mr. Calhoun concurs in the opinion that the additional allowance of 3,000 dollars each should be made to Messrs. Rodney and Graham on account of their late mission. I shall consult the Attorney General upon it to-morrow, and if he assents, shall leave directions for the payment to be made them.

Mr. Calhoun doubts the expediency of issuing a proclama-

[1] Joel Barlow.
[2] William Lee.

tion offering a reward for the apprehension of Captain Wright. I shall write further on this subject after consulting with Mr. Wirt.

You will I presume this day receive the warrant of execution of the mail robbers to be signed, if approved by you. I have no doubt of the authority to issue it, but with the Attorney General I think it would be proper that a uniformity of practice throughout the United States should be established by an act of Congress, for all such cases tried by courts of the United States. I incline farther to the opinion that no execution ought ever to take place without such a warrant from the President. For as the power of pardon is given to him by the constitution, and as it is a power beneficent in its nature, it is the dispensation of the national mercy, the last and most precious right reserved to the culprit convicted of capital transgression. If the execution of the sentence follows of course upon conviction and by the appointment of the court, it may take place without the President's knowing even that there has been a trial. It is altogether in the spirit of our institutions, as well as conformable to those of humanity, that in *every* case of capital conviction the President should decide upon a full and solemn consideration, whether he ought to grant or to withhold the exercise of this awful power of human life or death. If no execution could take place without his warrant, he must necessarily have the question brought before him. By the other mode of practice, it may always and doubtless often will happen that the question will not be brought before him at all.

I now enclose a draft of a letter to Mr. Aguirre, in which I have endeavored to accomplish the object of your instructions in your letter of the 17th instant. I have to ask of you the favor after making such alterations and such marginal additions as you may think proper, to send it back to the Department to be finally copied and transmitted to me to New York for my signature. Mr. Aguirre being himself at New York, it will there reach him without loss of time. I propose to leave the city next Wednesday the 26th,[1] and calculate upon being at New York on Tuesday the first of next month, and to proceed the next morning in the steamboat. If your answer to this can be here next Saturday morning, the letter prepared may be dispatched to me the next day and will reach me at New York on Tuesday.

The copy of Mr. Rush's statement of the conversation between him and Mr. Aguirre is also enclosed herewith, chiefly for the purpose of asking you whether it would not be expedient to omit in the copy to be sent to Mr. Aguirre the last paragraph, relating to sentiments expressed by him concerning the probable future constitution of Buenos Ayres. This paragraph having no connection with the reception or treatment that he has experienced here, nor with the object or execution of his mission to this country, may it not have the appearance of a disposition to take advantage of words which may have been unguardedly spoken by him, and which may operate to his disadvantage in his own country? On the other hand, as his conduct has been marked with no respect or delicacy to this government, if, as is highly probable, all these documents will be published at the next session of Congress, it may perhaps be more candid to give Mr. Aguirre the whole of Mr. Rush's statement, and thereby afford him an opportunity of giving such explanations of the sentiments attributed to him in the last paragraph as he may think proper. I leave the whole to your determination.

The other present enclosures are applications for office,

[1] Adams, *Memoirs*, August 27, 1818.

and from Mr. Lewis[1] at Port at Prince concerning his salary. I would request the return to the Department of these and all other papers enclosed to you, except such as you have occasion for retaining.

The dispatches last received from Mr. Rush will be transmitted to you to-morrow and will require your attention.

I am, etc.

TO THE PRESIDENT

[JAMES MONROE]

WASHINGTON, 24 August, 1818.

SIR:

Since I had the honor of writing you yesterday, I have received several dispatches from Mr. Gallatin, none of them relating to objects of general importance, except that which with its enclosure is now transmitted to you, together with the dispatches from Mr. Rush yesterday noticed. Mr. del Real, the deputy from New Granada, the author of the protest, was well known to me during my residence in England, and was a very respectable and rational man. His paper, as well as that of Mr. Rivadavia,[2] prove at how much greater distance the British government have even to this time kept the South American agents than we have.

In the draft of a letter to Mr. Aguirre which was to have been forwarded to you yesterday, but which by the course of the mail I find cannot go till this day, I have stated to him the grounds upon which the government of the United

---

[1] Jacob Lewis, commissioner of claims.

[2] Deputy in London from the United Provinces of La Plata.

States have been deterred from acknowledgment of that of Buenos Ayres, as including the dominion of the whole vice royalty of La Plata. The result of the late campaign in Venezuela, by comparing the royal and the republican bulletins, has been so far disadvantageous to the latter that they have totally failed in obtaining possession of any part of the coast. They have therefore at least one more campaign of contest to go through, for which they will need several months of preparation. Bolivar appears to have resigned the chief military command to Paez, and the army is to be reorganized. But the royalists do not appear to have gained any ground, and are evidently too much weakened by their losses to act upon the offensive. In this state the independence of Venezuela can scarcely be considered in a condition to claim the recognition of neutral powers. But there is a stage in such contests when the party struggling for independence have, as I conceive, a right to demand its acknowledgment by neutral parties, and when the acknowledgment may be granted without departure from the obligations of neutrality. It is the stage when the independence is established as a matter of fact, so as to leave the chance of the opposite party to recover their dominion utterly desperate. The neutral nation must, of course, judge for itself when this period has arrived, and as the belligerent nation has the same right to judge for itself, it is very likely to judge differently from the neutral and to make it a cause or a pretext for war, as Great Britain did expressly against France in our Revolution, and substantially against Holland. If war thus results in point of fact from the measure of recognizing a contested independence, the moral right or wrong of the war depends upon the justice, and sincerity, and prudence with which the recognizing nation took the step. I am satisfied that the cause of the South Americans, so far as it consists in the assertion of independence against Spain is *just*. But the justice of a cause, however it may enlist individual feelings in its favor, is not sufficient to justify third parties in siding with it. The fact and the right combined can alone authorize a neutral to acknowledge a new and disputed sovereignty. The neutral may indeed infer the right from the fact, but not the fact from the right. If Buenos Ayres confined its demand of recognition to the provinces of which it is in actual possession, and if it would assert its entire independence by agreeing to place the United States upon the footing of the most favored nation (which you recollect Pueyrredon declined in his pseudo treaty with Worthington, upon the avowed intention of reserving some special favors to Spain as compensation for his abandonment of her claims of sovereignty), I should think the time now arrived when its government might be recognized without a breach of neutrality. I did not think it necessary or proper to say this in the letter to Mr. Aguirre, but I submit the observations to your consideration.

From the proposals [1] made to Mr. Rush by Lord Castlereagh in relation to the measures to be agreed upon for the abolition of the slave trade, I presume they will be repeated in case of the negotiation of a new commercial convention or treaty. I therefore send you all the treaties communicated by Lord Castlereagh, and request your directions whether any, and if any, what instructions shall be given to Mr. Gallatin and Mr. Rush on the subject.

You will see that the British government have shown some dissatisfaction at an observation made in a printed report of the Committee of Foreign Relations on the projected four articles to be added to the commercial conven-

[1] June 20, 1818. Printed in Rush, *Memoranda of a Residence at the Court of London* (2nd Ser.), 33.

tion of 1815. Mr. Bagot has also been instructed on this affair, and a copy of Lord Castlereagh's note to Mr. Rush was some time since received by him.

I am, etc.

TO DON LUIS DE ONIS [1]

DEPARTMENT OF STATE,
WASHINGTON, 24 August, 1818.

SIR:

I have received your letters of the 27th ulto. and of the 5th inst.[2] with their respective enclosures, all of which have been laid before the President. With regard to the two vessels alleged to have been equipped at New York for the purpose of cruising under the flag of Buenos Ayres, against Spanish subjects, the result of the examination which has taken place before a judge of the Supreme Court of the United States has doubtless convinced you that no prosecution, commenced by the government of the United States against the persons charged with a violation of their laws and their neutrality, could have been necessary or useful to you, no transgression of the laws having been proved against them.

It would be equally superfluous and unseasonable to pursue the discussion with you, relative to the proceedings of the American commander in chief in entering Florida and his conduct there; and to the misconduct of the governor of Pensacola and of the commandant of St. Marks, in aiding and abetting the savage enemies of the United States, whom Spain by solemn treaty bound herself to restrain by

[1] Printed in *American State Papers*, Foreign Relations, IV. 508.
[2] *Ib.*, 500, 504.

force from committing hostilities against them. But you will permit me to observe that the obligation of Spain was positive and unqualified; and that an attempt to evade its force by the allegation that Spain could not carry it into effect until she knew what hostilities they *had* committed, and the possible causes of, or provocations to them, would be equally unwarranted by the express terms of the article, and by the intentions of the contracting parties to the treaty. The stipulation of Spain was not to punish her Indians for murders committed upon the aged and the infirm, the woman and children of the United States; but to restrain them by force from committing them, and the insinuation that the Indians themselves had been provoked to such atrocious acts would be as disingenuous on the part of Spain to escape from the sacred duties of her compact, as it would be unfounded in point of fact.

The letter from General Jackson to the governor of Pensacola, a copy of which was transmitted to you in mine of the 23d ulto. and with its answer, was written, not as you allege at the turbulent period of the late war between the United States and Great Britain, but, as their dates will show, more than a year after the conclusion of the peace. The fort had been built upon Spanish territory, under the sufferance of the Spanish authorities, by British officers, during the war, for annoyance against the United States. After the peace it remained the stronghold of fugitive negro and Indian robbers and murderers, which the governor of Pensacola, when summoned by General Jackson to destroy, alleged his inability to do it without reinforcement and further orders, which as the event proved were never received.

I have the honor to inform you that orders have already been forwarded to the commanding officers at Pensacola and

St. Marks to deliver up those places, conformably to the notice in my letter to you of 23d ulto., to the former governor of Pensacola and commandant of St. Marks respectively, or to any person duly authorized from you or from the governor general of the Havannah to receive them.

I am further instructed by the President to assure you of the satisfaction with which he has seen in the last paragraph of your letter, your expectation of being speedily enabled to make proposals containing the bases of a treaty which may adjust to mutual satisfaction all the existing differences between our two nations, and his earnest hope that this expectation, in the fulfilment of which this government have confided and adopted measures corresponding with it, may be realized at an early day.

I have the honor, etc.

TO DON MANUEL H. DE AGUIRRE

DEPARTMENT OF STATE,
WASHINGTON, 27 August, 1818.

SIR:

Your letter of the 10th instant has been laid before the President, who has directed me to inform you that the executive administration is not authorized to make the purchase of the two ships which have been built under your direction at New York, and which you now propose for sale.

From the time when the civil war between Spain and her South American colonies commenced, it has been the declared policy of the United States, in strict conformity to their existing laws, to observe between the parties an impartial neutrality. They have considered it as a civil war, in which as a foreign nation they were [by the ordinary duties of nations towards each other, under no obligation to interpose. It had been their steady and invariable policy during the long and numerous wars which from the establishment of the constitution of the United States had agitated Europe, and was laid in the deepest foundations of their own freedom and independence, the permanent establishment of which essentially depended upon the principle of pacific dispositions towards all nations, and the firm determination to resort to war for no interests other than their own.] [1]

In the month of July, 1816, the congress assembled at Tucuman issued a declaration of independence for the province of La Plata, including, as you have heretofore stated, all the provinces previously comprehended within the vice-royalty of that name. From that period the United States have considered the question of that independence as the precise question and object of the war. [As a question of right between Spain and Buenos Ayres, the United States could not decide it without taking a part inconsistent with neutrality, with the party in whose favor they should decide. They could not recognize the sovereignty of Spain over the colony as still existing, nor the independence of the colony as established, without becoming a party to the very question of the war. As a question of *fact*, as little could they recognize the government of Buenos Ayres as supreme over the provinces of La Plata, while Montevideo, the Banda Oriental, and Paraguay, were not only possessed in fact by others, but under governments disclaiming all dependence upon Buenos Ayres, no less than upon Spain.] [2]

[1] The sentences within the brackets were struck out by the President, who suggested as a substitute: "they authorized to allow to the parties engaged in it equal rights, which equality the colonies have invariably enjoyed in the United States."
[2] For the sentences in brackets the President substituted the following: "The

The government of the United States have nevertheless extended to the people of Buenos Ayres, all the advantages of a friendly intercourse which are enjoyed by other nations, and every mark of friendship and good will which were compatible with a fair neutrality. Besides all the benefits of a free commerce and of national hospitality, and the admission of their vessels into our ports, the agents from Buenos Ayres have, though not recognized in form, had the freest communication with the administration, and have received every attention to their representations which could have been given to the accredited officers of any independent power. No person has ever presented himself from your government with the credentials or commission of a public minister. Those which you have exhibited give you the express character of *agent* only; which neither by the laws of nations, nor by those of the United States, confer the privilege of exemption from personal arrest. That you have been, as mentioned in your letters, subjected to the inconvenience of such an arrest, is sincerely regretted by the President, but is a circumstance which he had no power to prevent—by the nature of our constitution the supreme executive, possessing no authority to dispense with the oper-

President is of opinion, that Buenos Ayres has afforded strong proof of its ability to maintain its independence; a sentiment, which he is persuaded, will daily gain strength with the powers of Europe, especially should the same career of good fortune continue in its favor. In deciding the question respecting the independence of Buenos Ayres, many circumstances claim attention in regard to the colonies, as well as to the United States, which make it necessary that we should move in it with caution. Without mentioning those relating to the United States which he is bound to weigh, it is proper to notice one in regard to the colonies, which presents a serious difficulty. You have requested the recognition of the independence of the government of Buenos Ayres, as supreme over the provinces of La Plata, while Montevideo, the Banda Oriental, and Paraguay, are not only possessed in fact by others, but under governments disclaiming all dependence upon Buenos Ayres, no less than upon Spain."

ation of the laws, except in cases prescribed by the laws themselves.

This observation appears to be the more deserving of your consideration as you mention as your motive for communicating to the acting Secretary of State [Rush] at the time of your arrival in this country, in July, 1817, the object of your agency—the building of a number of vessels of war for the government of Buenos Ayres and Chile—namely, that you believed the President had a discretionary power to suspend the laws against fitting out, equipping and arming in our ports vessels of war for the belligerent purposes of other powers. Of the conversation which passed between you and the then acting Secretary of State, a statement has been drawn up by him, a copy of which is herewith enclosed. He informed you, that to maintain the neutral obligations of the United States, the laws prohibited the arming of vessels in our ports for the purpose of committing hostilities against any nation with which they were at peace; and also prohibited our citizens from enlisting or being enlisted within the territory or jurisdiction of the United States in the service of any foreign state, as a soldier or as a marine or seaman on board of any vessel of war, from accepting and exercising any commission; but that vessels, even suited for warlike purposes, and arms and ammunition of every kind might be purchased within our country, as articles of merchandise, by either of the belligerent parties, without infringement of our laws or neutrality. How far this condition of our laws was compatible with the practical execution of the commission with which you were charged, you were to judge, and in the case of doubts entertained by yourself were advised to consult the opinion of counsel learned in the law, from any of whom you might obtain information under which your course of proceeding would be correct and safe; but that the executive possessed no power to dispense with the execution of the laws; and was, on the contrary, bound by his official duty and his oath to take care that they should be faithfully executed.

On the 14th of November last I had the honor of receiving a note from you, in which, after referring to this previous conversation with my predecessor, you stated that you had proceeded to carry into immediate execution the orders of your government upon the terms of that conversation, but that finding it impossible to conduct the business as had been your desire with secrecy, which you were engaged in the execution of formal contracts, an act of Congress was presented to you, prohibiting, under heavy penalties, all persons from fitting out vessels of the description of those you had ordered to be built at New York, and which must consequently be unable to proceed to their destination, and you requested of me information on these points.

Through the medium of two of the commissioners then about to proceed to South America, you were again reminded that the Secretary of State could not with propriety draw the line or define the boundary which you should not pass; that the interpretation and exposition of the laws, under our free institutions, belonged peculiarly to the judiciary; and that if, as a stranger, unacquainted with our legal provisions, you wanted any advice on this subject, there were professional men of eminence in every state, to whom, in common with others, you might recur for their opinions. It was understood that you were fully satisfied with this explanation.

You have, therefore, constantly been aware of the necessity of proceeding in such a manner, in executing the orders of your government, as to avoid violating the laws of the United States, and although it has not been possible to extend to you the privilege of exemption from arrest (an exemption not enjoyed by the President of the United States himself, in his individual capacity) yet you have had all the benefit of those laws which are the protection of the rights and personal liberties of our own citizens. Although you had built, and equipped, and fitted for sea, and manned, two vessels suitable for purposes of war, yet as no proof was adduced that you had armed them, you were immediately liberated and discharged by the decision of the judge of the Supreme Court, before whom the case was brought. It is yet impossible for me to say that the execution of the orders of your government is impracticable; but the government of the United States can no more countenance or participate in any expedient to evade the intention of the laws than it can dispense with their operation.

Of the friendly disposition of the President towards your government and country many proofs have been given. I am directed by him to renew the assurance of that disposition, and to assure you that it will continue to be manifested in every manner compatible with the laws of this Union, and with the observance of its duties towards others. I am, etc.

TO THOMAS SUMTER, JR.

Department of State,
Washington, 27 August, 1818.

Sir:

. . . . . .

Your correspondence with the Spanish Minister, Count Casa Flores, had the effect of first disclosing to us with official authenticity the mediation which the five great European allied powers have *projected* between Spain and her South American colonies. The allies have not been very communicative with the United States with regard to their measures and intentions in this respect; but we know that they have not, and we have strong reason to believe that they will not, agree upon any coercive measures in the case. There is little doubt that the real policy of Great Britain is to promote the cause of the independents, and although they will not aid them by a public acknowledgment, and will take no step of which Spain can complain, they will take special care that the European alliance shall take no active measures against the independents. The agents of Buenos Ayres and of New Granada in England have sent in to the British government *protests* against the interposition of the allies, unless upon the basis of the total independence of the colonies, unanswerable upon the argument both of right and fact; and the views of Great Britain and Russia, as to what *is to be done*, are so widely apart, with so little desire on either side to come upon this point to an agreement, that there can be no doubt but this appeal of Spain to the thunderbolts of the allies will terminate in utter disappointment.

Two of the late commissioners to South America, Messrs.

Rodney and Graham, have returned to this country. Mr. Bland, as you doubtless know, proceeded to Chile.

The President, having determined that the *Macedonian*, Captain [John] Downes, should be sent to the Pacific Ocean, has directed him to touch on the passage at Pernambuco, at Rio de Janeiro, and at the river of La Plata. I avail myself of that opportunity to forward this dispatch.

The consul at Pernambuco, Joseph Ray, has become involved in several very unpleasant altercations with the local government of that place. Several persons, among whom his secretary, have been arrested in his house, and are in confinement as prisoners. He has been charged with improper conduct in relation to the insurrection of the last year, and has thought himself under the necessity of making a formal protest against the proceedings of the governor concerning him. In a letter to this Department of 11 April last he mentions having written to you on the subject of his grievances, but that he had no acknowledgment of the receipt of his letters. Having only his representations of the facts, we are unable to form upon them the deliberate judgment which they might require, and even upon his statements there is reason to conjecture that his conduct has been, to say the least, indiscreet. We should be glad to hear from you upon the subject.

A letter from seven American seamen, landed on the coast of Brazil in consequence of their mutiny against the captain of the schooner *Penguin*, to which they belonged, has been received by the collector at New York. They state that since the month of February, when they landed, they have been kept in prison by the government at Pernambuco, they know not for what cause; that they have ineffectually claimed the protection of the consul, and that they are suffering harsh treatment. Captain Downes will be instructed on touching at Pernambuco to ascertain the circumstances relating to their imprisonment, to endeavor to obtain their liberation, if upon examination he shall think it proper to demand it, and whatever may be the success of his application, to call and make report of it to you at Rio de Janeiro. If any coöperation of yours should be necessary you will take such steps as you shall think proper and expedient.

Mr. Henry Hill has been appointed consul at Rio de Janeiro and Mr. Samuel Hodges, Junr., at the Cape de Verde Islands. Some difficulty has heretofore occurred, respecting the acknowledgment of a consul appointed from hence at the Cape de Verde. Perhaps an order from the government of Brazil to the authorities in the islands may be necessary to secure the recognition of Mr. Hodges; in which case you are requested to take the proper measures for having it expedited. The complaints against Mr. Halsey,[1] of having improperly taken part in privateering under the South American authorities, were too well founded, and he was for that reason some months since dismissed from his office as consul at Buenos Ayres.

Your renewed request for permission to return to the United States has been submitted to the consideration of the President, who not without reluctance has eventually concluded to comply with it. At the ensuing session of Congress a person will be nominated to the Senate as your successor at Rio de Janeiro, and it is hoped that the delay until then will be compatible without material inconvenience with your arrangements.

I am, etc.

[1] Thomas L. Halsey.

TO DON LUIS DE ONIS [1]

DEPARTMENT OF STATE,
WASHINGTON, October 31, 1818.

SIR:

Your letter of the 24th instant, with the proposals contained in it,[2] offered as a basis of a treaty for the adjustment of all the subjects in discussion between the United States and Spain, has been received, and laid before the President of the United States.

I am directed by him to forbear entering into any examination of the historical disquisition concerning the original pretensions of Spain to all the territories bordering on the Gulf of Mexico, and the whole country included in the French colony of Louisiana, which you have thought proper to introduce into your note. The right of the United States to the river Mississippi, and all the waters flowing into it, and to all the territories watered by them, remains as entire and unshaken by anything now adduced by you as by anything which had ever preceded it in the discussions between the two governments. It is established beyond the power of further controversy; nor could it answer any useful purpose to reproduce proofs which have already more than once been shown, and which, remaining unim-

---

[1] Printed in *American State Papers*, Foreign Relations, IV. 530.

[2] *Ib.*, 526. Monroe was much dissatisfied with the proposals made by Onis, "considering them not only as altogether inadmissible, but as merely another experiment upon the patience and long-suffering of this Government. He said it was time to bring Onis to a point, and, if he would not agree to reasonable terms, to break off the negotiations." Adams, *Memoirs*, October 26, 1818. The draft of the reply to Onis was with the President on the 28th and after three days' consideration in cabinet received its final form.

paired, must henceforth be considered by the United States as not susceptible of refutation.

In confining my attention to the propositions which you offer as the basis of a treaty, I have to observe that any further proceedings upon the first of them have been rendered unnecessary by the determination promptly taken by this government, and communicated to you, to restore the forts of Barrancas and St. Marks, together with Pensacola, to any person duly authorized by your government to receive them. You have been informed of the evidence inculpating the governors of those places, not only as having utterly neglected to carry into effect the stipulation in the treaty of 1795, by which Spain was bound to restrain, *by force*, the Indians within her territories from committing hostilities against the United States or their citizens, but as having deeply participated in the hostilities of those same Indians. You have been informed that these were the real and only causes of the occupation of these places by the commander of the American forces. Under these circumstances, however the United States may regret the necessity of that occupation, it is for the Spanish officers themselves to answer to their own sovereign for the consequences of their own conduct; and the forbearance of the United States, as well as their respect for the rights and the honor of Spain, are sufficiently manifested by their readiness to restore the possession and to consign to oblivion the hostile conduct of those officers of his Catholic Majesty.

The uselessness of any stipulation on the subject of this first proposition is further demonstrated by the nature of the second, in which you announce your authority to cede all the property and sovereignty possessed by Spain in and over the Floridas. The effect of this measure being necessarily to remove all cause of contention between the contracting parties with regard to the possession of these territories, and to everything incidental to them, it would be worse than superfluous to stipulate for restoring them to Spain in the very treaty by which they are to be ceded in full sovereignty and possession to the United States. Neither can the United States recognize as valid all the grants of land until this time, and at the same time renounce all their claims, and those of their citizens, for damages and injuries sustained by them, and for the reparation of which Spain is answerable to them. It is well known to you, sir, that notice has been given by the minister of the United States in Spain to your government that all the grants of land lately alleged to have been made by your government within those territories must be cancelled, unless your government should provide some other adequate fund, from which the claims above referred to of the United States and their citizens may be satisfied.

From the answers of Don José Pizarro to this notice, we have reason to expect that you will be sensible of that necessity, and that some time must be agreed upon subsequent to which no grant of the lands within the territories in question shall be considered as valid.

The boundary line proposed by you, west of the Mississippi, can as little be assented to by the United States. Instead of it, I am authorized to propose to you the following, and to assure you that it is to be considered as the final offer on the part of the United States.

Beginning at the mouth of the river Sabine, on the Gulf of Mexico, following the course of said river to the thirty-second degree of latitude; the eastern bank and all the islands in said river to belong to the United States, and the western bank to Spain; thence, due north, to the northernmost part of the thirty-third degree of north latitude, and until it strikes the Rio Roxo, or Red River, thence, following the course of the said river, to its source, touching the chain of the Snow mountains, in latitude thirty-seven degrees twenty-five minutes north, longitude one hundred and six degrees fifteen minutes west, or thereabouts, as marked on Melish's map, thence to the summit of the said mountains, and following the chain of the same to the forty-first parallel of latitude; thence, following the said parallel of latitude forty-one degrees, to the South Sea. The northern bank of the said Red River, and all islands therein, to belong to the United States, and the southern bank of the same to Spain.

It is believed that this line will render the appointment of commissioners for fixing it more precisely unnecessary, unless it be for the purpose of ascertaining the spot where the river Sabine falls upon latitude thirty-two degrees north, and the line thence due north to the Red River, and the point of latitude forty-one degrees north on the ridge of the Snow mountains: to which appointment of commissioners this government will readily agree.

The United States will agree to the proposal that the contracting parties shall mutually renounce all claims for damages or injuries which they, their citizens or subjects, have received from each other, until the date of the treaty; it being always understood that all grants of lands in any parts of the territories to be ceded by Spain to the United States subsequent to the year 1802 are to be held null and void.

This renunciation on the part of the United States will be understood to extend

1st. To all the cases of claims provided for by the convention of 1802.

2d. To all cases of claims on account of captures by

French privateers, and condemnations by French consuls, within the territorial jurisdiction of Spain.

3d. To all claims of indemnities, on account of the suspension of the right of deposit at New Orleans, in 1802.

4th. And to all claims of citizens of the United States upon the government of Spain, statements of which, soliciting the interposition of the government of the United States, shall have been, before the date of this treaty, and since the date of the convention of 1802, presented either to the Department of State, or to the minister of the United States in Spain; but not to claims which the individuals of the United States may have against those of Spain, or against the Spanish government, on any other account.

The United States will exonerate Spain from all demands in future on account of the above-mentioned claims, and undertake to make satisfaction for the same to an amount not exceeding five millions of dollars.

To ascertain the full amount and validity of those claims, a commission, to consist of three commissioners, shall be appointed by the President of the United States, by and with the advice and consent of the Senate; which commission shall meet at Washington, and within the space of three years shall receive, examine, and decide upon the amount and validity of all claims coming within the descriptions above mentioned. And the Spanish government shall furnish all such documents and elucidations as may be in their possession, for the adjustment of the said claims, according to the principles of justice; the said documents to be specified when demanded at the instance of the said commissioners.

Your fifth proposition is, that the treaty of limits and navigation of 1795 shall remain in force in all and each of its articles, with the exception of that part of the fifteenth article which stipulates *that the flag shall cover the property.*

The 2d, 3d, 4th, 21st, and the second clause of the 22d articles of the treaty of 1795 have either received their entire execution, and can no longer be considered as remaining in force, or have been rendered inoperative by subsequent events. Whatever relates in them to limits or to the navigation of the Mississippi, has been extinguished by the cession of Louisiana to France, and by her to the United States; with the exception of the line between the United States and Florida, which will also be annulled by the cession of Florida, which you now propose. I am authorized to agree to the confirmation and recognition of all the remaining articles of that treaty as still in force; and to assent to the exception proposed by you of part of the fifteenth article, to this extent: that if, hereafter, either of the contracting parties shall be at war with a third party, and the other neutral, the flag of the neutral shall cover the property of enemies whose governments recognize the same principle, and not of others.

Your sixth proposition is inadmissible. The United States do not know that any additional laws or declarations are necessary to secure the fulfilment, on the part of Spain, of her engagements in the treaty of 1795. Numerous and just as their complaints have been of the violations of that treaty, under the authority of Spain, they consider the Spanish government fully competent to make reparation for them, and to secure the faithful observance of their engagements, in future, without new laws or declarations. Nor are they aware of any vague or arbitrary interpretation in any of the ports of this Union, by which, contrary to the laws of nations, or to the stipulations of the treaty of 1795, the law is eluded. The interpretation or construction given to the stipulations of the treaty of 1795 within the United States is subject to the decisions of the judicial tribunals of the United States, who are bound to consider all treaties as the supreme law of the land. Their proceedings are all public, and their decisions upon all questions of interpretation are recorded and published. In this there is surely nothing vague or arbitrary; nothing requiring new laws or declarations. Of the many complaints which you have addressed to this government in relation to alleged transactions in our ports, the deficiency has been, not in the meaning or interpretation of the treaty, but in the proofs of the facts which you have stated, or which have been reported to you, to bring the cases of complaint within the scope of the stipulations of the treaty.

In consideration of the cession of the Floridas by Spain, to redress and cancel the claims of the United States and their citizens upon Spain, and always understood that the late grants of the lands for which the indemnity for these claims is to be sought, shall be held null and void, the government of the United States will certify that they have not received any compensation from France for the injuries suffered from French privateers, consuls, and tribunals on the coasts and in the ports of Spain, and will present an authentic statement of the prizes made, and of their value, that Spain may avail herself of it in such a manner as she may deem just and proper. Upon the basis offered by your propositions, modified conformably to the observations now submitted to you, I am authorized to conclude a treaty with you; but, as the session of Congress is at hand, I am directed to request your immediate and frank reply to this communication. The President is deeply penetrated with the conviction that further protracted discussion of the points at issue between our governments cannot terminate in a manner satisfactory to them. From your answer to this letter,[1] he must conclude whether a final adjustment of all our differences is now to be accomplished, or whether all hope of such a desirable result is, on the part of the United States, to be abandoned.

I pray you, etc.

TO JOHN ADAMS [2]

WASHINGTON, 2 November, 1818.

MY EVER DEAR AND REVERED FATHER:

By a letter from my son John, I have this day been apprised of that afflictive dispensation of Providence which has bereft you of the partner of your life; me of the tenderest and most affectionate of Mothers, and our species of one whose existence was virtue, and whose life was a perpetual demonstration of the moral excellence of which human nature is susceptible. How shall I offer you consolation for your loss when I feel that my own is irreparable? Where shall I entreat you to look for comfort in that distress which earth has nothing to assuage? Ten days have elapsed since we received in a letter from Harriet Welsh, the first intimation of my mother's illness; and in every anxious hour, from mail to mail, I have felt that I ought to write to you, and endeavor to soothe by the communion of sorrows, of hopes and fears, that anguish which I knew was preying upon your heart. Do not impute, my dear and only Parent, the silence that I have kept to neglect of that sacred duty which I owe to you. If I have refrained even from good

---

[1] Dated November 16. It is in *American State Papers*, Foreign Relations, IV. 531.

[2] Adams, *Memoirs*, November 2, 1818.

words, it was because in the agitation of my own heart I knew not how to order my speech, nor whether on receiving my letter, it would come to you seasonably to sympathize with your tears of gratitude or of resignation.

The pangs of dissolution are past, and my Mother, I humbly hope, is a spirit, purified even from that little less than heavenly purity which in her existence here was united with the lot of mortality. I am advised that you have endured the agony of her illness with the fortitude that belongs to your character; that after the fatal event that fortitude rose, as from you I should have expected, with renewed elasticity from the pressure under which it had been bowed down. Will the deep affliction of your son now meet in congenial feeling with your own, without probing the wound which it is the dearest of his wishes to alleviate? Let me hear from you, my dearest father, let me hear from you soon. And may the blessings of that God, whose tender mercies are over all his works, still shed rays of heavenly hope and comfort over the remainder of your days.

Your distressed but ever affectionate and dutiful son.[1]

---

[1] "You have lost, my dear son, one of the kindest and most precious of parents, for such she truly was to you and to all my children. If you live as I hope and pray you may to an age as advanced as hers, you will never meet on earth one to whom you will owe deeper obligations, or who will be to you a more faithful and affectionate friend. May it be your lot in life to enjoy the society even of a few spirits so nearly approaching to perfection as hers; and above all, my son, may he who is the Supreme good inspire and guide your conduct through your worldly career, so that at the final scene you may surrender your spirit to its creator as unsullied as was hers. I have no greater blessing to bestow—be it yours, and be it that of your brothers." *To John Adams, Jr.*, November 2, 1818. Ms.

TO ALBERT GALLATIN AND RICHARD RUSH [1]

DEPARTMENT OF STATE,
WASHINGTON, 2 November, 1818.

GENTLEMEN:

From the dispatches, which since I last had the honor of writing to you, have been received at this Department from Mr. Rush, dated the 24th and 26th of June, and the 15th of August, it appears that there are two subjects likely to be brought under consideration in your conferences with the British plenipotentiaries, which were not contemplated by the President at the time when your former instructions were prepared. Impressment and the slave trade.

Impressment. In the notes Nos. 1 and 2, delivered by Mr. Rush to Lord Castlereagh, the first on the 18th of April, and the second on the 20th of June,[2] both the offers had been made to the British government warranted by his former instructions of legislative measures for excluding British seamen from the naval and merchant service of the United States, on condition of a formal stipulation on the part of Great Britain, that the impressment of men from the vessels of the United States shall henceforth cease. Both these proposals at the time when they were offered, or shortly afterwards, had been rejected with an intimation from Lord Castlereagh to Mr. Rush in the latter instance, that the objections of the British cabinet against them would be presented in writing.

Afterwards, however, on the 14th of August,[3] he expressed

---

[1] Printed in *American State Papers*, Foreign Relations, IV. 399.

[2] See Rush, *Memoranda of a Residence at the Court of London* (1st Ser.), 205 289.

[3] *Ib.*, 329.

his willingness that the subject should be taken up in the proposed negotiations of a commercial treaty, and avowed as an opinion of his own, upon which he had indeed not consulted with his colleagues in the cabinet, that these proposals might with certain modifications, which he thought very important to Great Britain and of little moment to the essential object of the United States, be rendered acceptable. These were: 1. That the treaty containing the stipulation should be limited to a duration of ten or twelve years, with liberty to each party to be absolved from its stipulations on a notice of three or six months. 2. That the British boarding officer entering American ships at sea for a purpose justified under the laws of nations, should have the liberty of calling for a list of the crew, and if he saw a man whom he knew or suspected of being an Englishman, he should without taking the man have the privilege of making a record or *procès-verbal* of the fact, to be presented to the consideration of the American government.

These suggestions have received the fullest and most deliberate consideration of the President, with the earnest disposition on his part to view them in the most favorable light.[1] He welcomes them especially as the first indications of a consciousness in the British Cabinet, that the permanency of peace between the two countries is utterly incompatible with the resumption of the practice of impressing men from our vessels on the high seas—a conviction so profoundly impressed upon his own mind, that he scarcely thinks any discouragement could justify a remission of our efforts to remove this inevitable cause of future collisions, so long as the practice hitherto persevered in shall continue to exist.

It is readily agreed that the treaty to contain the stipu-

[1] Adams, *Memoirs*, October 29 and 30, 1818.

lation shall be limited in duration to eight, ten, or twelve years, but that either party should have the liberty of putting an end to the whole treaty by a notice of three or six months, would seem to place the whole commercial relations between the two countries upon too precarious a foundation. Some of the stipulations proposed in your negotiation are in their nature intended to be permanent, even in the event of a war. Others would require legislative regulations to protect interests which would be deeply affected by the sudden termination of the treaty. The President nevertheless authorizes you to agree, that besides the general limitation of the temporary articles of the treaty to eight, ten or twelve years, either party shall be at liberty to dissolve them after a notice of two years given to and received by the other. Or if preferable, to the British government, the article relative to impressment may be made a separate article distinct from the rest of the treaty, and limited to a term of four years. This course would indeed be most convenient, as it would give us the opportunity of taking the sense of the Senate upon it without implicating it with the other parts of the treaty. Our intention and expectation is that the practice of taking men from our ships being once formally renounced by Great Britain, she will in point of fact never recur to it again.

If the intention of Lord Castlereagh was that this right of dissolving the compact by a notice of three or six months should apply only to the article against impressment, its acceptance is objectionable on other grounds. The engagement to exclude all British seamen from our sea service will operate immediately from its commencement with some inconvenience to our merchants. Since the peace and the dispersion of the vast number of seamen disbanded from the British navy, there are, no doubt, considerable numbers of them who have found employment on board of our vessels, and their exclusion from them will not be accomplished without some inconvenience. The effect of the stipulation of Great Britain, to take no men from our vessels, is remote and contingent upon the event of her being engaged in a maritime war with other powers. The onerous part of the engagement is therefore to us immediate and certain; the benefit to be derived from it distant and eventual. If to this apparent inequality should be added a power reserved by Great Britain to cancel the bargain by a simple notice of three or six months, we could scarcely consider it as a contract. It would be a positive concession and sacrifice on our part, for the mere chance of a future equivalent for it, altogether dependent upon the will of the other party. The alternatives now proposed, it is hoped, will answer the purposes intended by this expedient suggested by Lord Castlereagh, without being equally liable to the difficulties which arrest our assent to it, otherwise than as thus modified. It would also be desirable that the commencement of the engagement to exclude British seamen should be postponed for some time, say to the first of October, 1820, that a sufficient notice may be given to the merchants and mariners whose interests will be affected by it.

The second proposal, that British officers entering our merchant vessels for purposes warranted by the law of nations shall be authorized to call for the list of the crew, and if they should find or suspect an Englishman to be on board, make a record of the fact for the purpose of remonstrance to the government of the United States, is in the view of the President still more objectionable. In the first place, the distrust which it implies, that the laws for excluding British seamen will, though stipulated, not be faithfully executed, is not warranted by any experience, nor can this government give countenance to it by assenting to any stipulation which would be considered as resulting from it. If the United States bind themselves to this exclusion, they will sincerely and faithfully carry it into execution. It was not expressly asked by Lord Castlereagh in his proposal as reported by Mr. Rush, that the officer in calling for the shipping paper, should also have the power of mustering the crew to examine them by comparison with the list; but as the mere view of the list would be useless unless coupled with that power, we consider it as having been intended to be included in the proposal, and this very inspection of the crews of our vessels by a foreign officer has been found among the most insulting and grievous aggravations of the practice of impressment. Besides this, the tendency of such an examination in every single instance would be to produce altercation between the British officer and the commander of the American vessel. If the officer should be authorized to make a record of his suspicions, the master on his side, and the suspected seamen, must of course have the privilege of making their counter record, and as there would be no tribunal to judge between them, the probable ultimate result would be no other than that of exciting irritation between the two nations and fractious discussions between the governments. If the engagement to exclude British seamen from our service should fail of being executed to an extent worthy of the slightest attention of the British government, they could not avoid having notice of it, by proofs more effectual and more abundant than could be furnished by this sort of scrutiny. A failure of execution on our part to any such extent, would give them not only the right of remonstrating to ours, but even of cancelling their obligation within a lapse of time, which must guard them against the danger of any material national injury.

We have the fullest confidence that if the engagement on both sides be once contracted, Great Britain will thenceforward have no lawful or even plausible motive, either for wishing it cancelled, or for inspecting the crews of our vessels in search of men.

Slave trade.[1] The President desires that you would make known to the British government his sensibility to the friendly spirit of confidence with which the treaties lately contracted by Great Britain with Spain, Portugal, and the Netherlands, and the legislative measures of Parliament founded upon them, have been communicated to this government, and the invitation to the United States to join in the same or similar arrangements has been given. He wishes you also to give the strongest assurances that the solicitude of the United States for the accomplishment of the common object, the total and final abolition of that odious traffic, continues with all the earnestness which has so long and so steadily distinguished the course of their policy in relation to it. As an evidence of this earnestness he requests you to communicate to them a copy of the act of Congress of the last session, in addition to the act of 1807 to prohibit the importation of slaves into the United States (Acts of the last session, chap. 86, p. 81); and to declare the readiness of this government within their constitutional powers, to adopt any further measures which experience may prove to be necessary for the purpose of attaining so desirable an end.

But you will observe that in examining the provisions of the treaties communicated by Lord Castlereagh, all their essential articles appear to be of a character not adaptable to the institutions or to the circumstances of the United States.

The power agreed to be reciprocally given to the officers

[1] Adams, *Memoirs*, October 30, 1818.

of the ships of war of either party, to enter, search, capture, and carry into port for adjudication, the merchant vessels of the other, however qualified and restricted, is most essentially connected with the institution by each treaty of two mixed courts, one of which to reside in the external or colonial possessions of each of the two parties respectively. This part of the system is indispensable to give it that character of reciprocity, without which the right granted to the armed ships of one nation to search the merchant vessel of another would be rather a mark of vassalage than of independence. But to this part of the system the United States, having no colonies either on the coast of Africa or in the West Indies, cannot give effect.

You will add, that by the constitution of the United States it is provided that the judicial power of the United States shall be vested in a Supreme Court, and in such inferior courts as the Congress may, from time to time, ordain and establish. It provides that the judges of these courts shall hold their offices during good behavior, and that they shall be removable by impeachment and conviction of crimes and misdemeanors. There may be some doubt whether the *power* of the government of the United States is competent to institute a court for carrying into execution their penal statutes beyond the territories of the United States—a court consisting partly of foreign judges, not amenable to impeachment for corruption, and deciding upon the statutes of the United States without appeal.

That the disposal of the negroes found on board the slave trading vessels which might be condemned by the sentence of these mixed courts cannot be carried into effect by the United States. For if the slaves of a vessel, condemned by the mixed court, should be delivered over to the government of the United States as freemen, they could not but by their own consent be employed as servants or free laborers. The condition of the blacks being in this Union regulated by the municipal laws of the separate states, the government of the United States can neither guarantee their liberty in the states where they could only be received as slaves, nor control them in the states where they would be recognized as free.

That the admission of a right in the officers of foreign ships of war to enter and search the vessels of the United States in time of peace, under any circumstances whatever, would meet with universal repugnance in the public opinion of this country. That there would be no prospect of a ratification by advice and consent of the Senate to any stipulation of that nature. That the search by foreign officers, even in time of war, is so obnoxious to the feelings and recollections of this country, that nothing could reconcile them to the extension of it, however qualified or restricted to a time of peace. And that it would be viewed in a still more aggravated light, if, as in the treaty with the Netherlands, connected with a formal admission that even vessels under convoy of ships of war of their own nation should be liable to search by the ships of war of another.

You will therefore express the regret of the President that the stipulations in the treaties communicated by Lord Castlereagh are of a character to which the peculiar situation and institutions of the United States do not permit them to accede. The constitutional objection may be the more readily understood by the British Cabinet, if they are reminded that it was an obstacle proceeding from the same principle which prevented Great Britain from becoming formally a party to the Holy Alliance. Neither can they be at a loss to perceive the embarrassment under which we should be placed by receiving cargoes of African negroes, and be bound at once to guarantee their liberty, and to employ them as servants. Whether they will be as ready to enter into our feelings, with regard to the search by foreign navy lieutenants of vessels under convoy of our own naval commanders, is perhaps of no material importance. The other reasons are presumed to be amply sufficient to convince them, that the motives for declining this overture are compatible with an earnest wish that the measures concerted by these treaties may prove successful in extirpating that root of numberless evils, the traffic in human blood, and with the determination to coöperate to the utmost extent of our powers in this great vindication of the sacred rights of humanity.[1]

TO PETER PAUL FRANCIS DE GRAND

WASHINGTON, 16 November, 1818.

DEAR SIR:

. . . . . .

I shall commit to the Secretary of the Treasury your plan for creating a circulating medium of government paper. Men more conversant with the practical details of commerce than I am, and equally upright and intelligent with the author of the plan, but taking other views, may perhaps perceive objections to it which have not presented themselves to me. I have an indistinct idea, however, that this circulating medium once issued, would take almost entirely

[1] In his *Memoranda of a Residence at the Court of London* (1st Ser.), 354, Rush gives a summary of the negotiations of the joint mission of Gallatin and himself to November 1. See also Adams, *Writings of Gallatin*, II. 82-85. The convention resulting from the negotiations, signed October 20, 1818, covered the subjects of fisheries, boundary, and restoration of slaves; and extended the convention of July 3, 1815, for a period of ten years.

the place at least of U. S. Bank notes and thereby reduce the profits, if not substantially infringe upon the charter of the Bank. There is also some question upon my mind with regard to the *right* of the government to issue paper which costs them nothing (but the value of paper and cost of printing), and charging the Bank an interest of three per cent upon it. The Bank of course would not pay this interest. The purchasers or borrowers of the paper would pay in part a tax of six per cent upon it, which would be shared between the government and the Bank and for which neither of them would give anything. I have so obstinate an opinion that governments have no right to take anything from the people without giving them a *quid pro quo*, and so ineradicable a prejudice that paper as a representative *cannot* usurp with impunity the prerogative of its constituents, that my first impression is averse to anything which has the appearance of it. In this point of view [stands] a government paper creating a fictitious capital and charging six per cent a year. It is true that most of the commercial business of Amsterdam is transacted by the transfers of credits in the bank; but observe that the credit there is always a representative and nothing more. It always has its constituent, that is, the merchant who holds the credit in bank has always given something for it—a full equivalent —and when he transfers the credit he receives an equivalent for it. The credit, therefore, however frequently transferred, always represents something. It is the shadow of a substance. It strikes me that your government paper would be the shadow of a shade.

. . . .

TO GEORGE WILLIAM ERVING [1]

Department of State,
Washington, 28 November, 1818.

Sir:

Your dispatches to No. 92, inclusive, with their enclosures, have been received at this Department. Among these enclosures are the several notes addressed to you by Mr. Pizarro in relation to the transactions during the campaign of General Jackson against the Seminole Indians, and the banditti of negroes combined with them, and particularly to his procedings in Florida without the boundaries of the United States.

In the fourth and last of those notes of Mr. Pizarro, he has given formal notice that the king, his master, has issued orders for the suspension of the negotiation between the United States and Spain until satisfaction shall have been made by the American government to him for these proceedings of General Jackson, which he considers as acts of unequivocal hostility against him, and as outrages upon his honor and dignity; the only acceptable atonement for which is stated to consist in a disavowal of the acts of the American general thus complained of, the infliction upon him of a suitable punishment for his supposed misconduct, and the restitution of the posts and territories taken by him from the Spanish authorities, with indemnity for all the property taken, and all damages and injuries, public or private, sustained in consequence of it.

Within a very few days after this notification, Mr. Pizarro must have received, with copies of the correspondence be-

[1] Printed in *American State Papers*, Foreign Relations, IV. 539. The first draft was begun on November 8.

tween Mr. Onis and this Department, the determination which had been taken by the President to restore the places of Pensacola, with the fort of Barrancas, to any person properly authorized on the part of Spain to receive them, and the fort of St. Marks, to any Spanish force adequate to its protection against the Indians, by whom its forcible occupation had been threatened for purposes of hostility against the United States. The officer commanding at the post has been directed to consider two hundred and fifty men as such adequate force, and in case of their appearance with proper authority, to deliver it to their commander accordingly.

From the last-mentioned correspondence, the Spanish government must likewise have been satisfied that the occupation of these places in Spanish Florida by the commander of the American forces was not by virtue of any orders received by him from this government to that effect, nor with any view of wresting the province from the possession of Spain, nor in any spirit of hostility to the Spanish government; that it arose from incidents which occurred in the prosecution of the war against the Indians, from the imminent danger in which the fort of St. Marks was of being seized by the Indians themselves, and from the manifestations of hostility to the United States by the commandant of St. Marks and the governor of Pensacola, the proofs of which were made known to General Jackson, and impelled him, from the necessities of self-defence, to the steps of which the Spanish government complains.

It might be sufficient to leave the vindication of these measures upon those grounds, and to furnish, in the enclosed copies of General Jackson's letters, and the vouchers by which they are supported, the evidence of that hostile spirit on the part of the Spanish commanders, but for the terms in which Mr. Pizarro speaks of the execution of two British subjects taken, one at the fort of St. Marks, and the other at Suwanee, and the intimation that these transactions may lead to a change in the relations between the two nations, which is doubtless intended to be understood as a menace of war.

It may be, therefore, proper to remind the government of his Catholic Majesty of the incidents in which this Seminole war originated, as well as of the circumstances connected with it in the relations between Spain and her ally, whom she supposes to have been injured by the proceedings of General Jackson; and to give to the Spanish Cabinet some precise information of the nature of the business, peculiarly interesting to Spain, in which these subjects of her allies, in whose favor she takes this interest, were engaged, when their projects of every kind were terminated in consequence of their falling into the hands of General Jackson.

In the month of August, 1814, while a war existed between the United States and Great Britain, to which Spain had formally declared herself neutral, a British force, not in the fresh pursuit of a defeated and flying enemy, not overstepping an imaginary and equivocal boundary between their own territories and those belonging, in some sort, as much to their enemy as to Spain, but approaching by sea, and by a broad and open *invasion* of the Spanish province, at a thousand miles or an ocean's distance from *any* British territory, landed in Florida, took possession of Pensacola and the Fort of Barrancas, and invited by public proclamations, all the runaway negroes, all the savage Indians, all the pirates and all the traitors to their country, whom they knew or imagined to exist within reach of their summons, to join their standard, and wage an exterminating war against the portion of the United States immediately bordering upon this neutral and thus violated territory of Spain. The land commander of this British force was a certain Colonel Nicholls, who, driven from Pensacola by the approach of General Jackson, actually left to be blown up the Spanish fort of Barrancas when he found it could not afford him protection; and, evacuating that part of the province, landed at another, established himself on the Appalachicola river, and there erected a fort from which to sally forth with his motley tribe of black, white, and red combatants against the defenceless borders of the United States in that vicinity. A part of this force consisted of a corps of colonial marines, levied in the British colonies, in which George Woodbine was a captain, and Robert Christie Ambrister was a lieutenant.[1]

As between the United States and Great Britain, we should be willing to bury this transaction in the same grave of oblivion with other transactions of that war, had the hostilities of Colonel Nicholls terminated with the war; but he did not consider the peace which ensued between the United States and Great Britain as having put an end, either to his military occupations, or to his negotiations with the Indians against the United States. Several months after the ratification of the treaty of Ghent, he retained his post, and his parti-colored forces in military array. By the ninth article of that treaty the United States had stipulated to put an end, immediately after its ratification, to hostilities with all the tribes or nations of Indians with whom they might be at war at the time of the ratification, and to restore to them all the possessions which they had enjoyed in the year 1811. This article had no application to the Creek nation, with whom the United States had already made

[1] *American State Papers,* Foreign Relations, IV. 548, 604.

peace, by a treaty concluded on the ninth day of August, 1814, more than four months before the treaty of Ghent was signed. Yet Colonel Nicholls not only affected to consider it as applying to the Seminoles of Florida, and the outlawed Red Sticks, whom he had induced to join him there, but actually persuaded them that *they* were entitled, by virtue of the treaty of Ghent, to all the lands which had belonged to the *Creek* nation within the United States in the year 1811, and that the government of Great Britain would support them in that pretension. He asserted also [1] this doctrine in a correspondence with Colonel Hawkins, then the agent of the United States with the Creeks, and gave him notice in their name, with a mockery of solemnity,[2] that they had concluded a treaty of alliance, offensive and defensive, and a treaty of navigation and commerce, with Great Britain, of which more was to be heard after it should be ratified in England. Colonel Nicholls then evacuated his fort, which, in some of the enclosed papers, is called the fort at Prospect Bluff, but which he had denominated the *British* post on the Appalachicola; took with him the white portion of his force, and embarked for England with several of the wretched savages whom he was thus deluding to their fate, among whom was the prophet Francis or Hillis Hadjo, and left the fort, amply supplied with military stores and ammunitions, to the negro department of his allies. It afterwards was known by the name of the Negro fort.

Colonel Hawkins immediately communicated to this government the correspondence between him and Nicholls, here referred to, (copies of which marked Nos. 1 to 5 are herewith enclosed,) [3] upon which, Mr. Munroe, then Secre-

---

[1] *American State Papers*, Foreign Relations, IV. 548.
[2] *Ib.*, 552.
[3] *Ib.*, 547–550.

tary of State, addressed a letter [1] to Mr. Baker, the British chargé d'affaires at Washington, complaining of Nicholls' conduct, and showing that his pretence that the ninth article of the treaty of Ghent could have any application to his Indians was utterly destitute of foundation. Copies of the same correspondence were transmitted to the minister of the United States, then in England, with instructions [2] to remonstrate with the British government against these proceedings of Nicholls, and to show how incompatible they were with the peace which had been concluded between the two nations. These remonstrances were accordingly made, first in personal interview with Earl Bathurst and Lord Castlereagh, and afterwards in written notes addressed successively to them, (copies of which, together with extracts from the dispatches of the American minister to the Secretary of State, reporting what passed at those interviews, are enclosed).[3] Lord Bathurst, in the most unequivocal manner, confirmed the facts, and disavowed the misconduct of Nicholls; declared his disapprobation of the pretended treaty of alliance, offensive and defensive, which he had made; assured the American minister that the British government had refused to ratify that treaty, and would send back the Indians whom Nicholls had brought with him, with advice to make their peace on such terms as they could obtain. Lord Castlereagh confirmed the assurance that the treaty would not be ratified; and if, at the same time that these assurances were given, certain distinctions of public notoriety were shown to the prophet Hillis Hadjo, and he was actually honored with a commission as a British officer, it is to be presumed that these favors were granted

---

[1] *American State Papers*, Foreign Relations, IV. 553.
[2] *Ib.*, 554.
[3] *Ib.*, 554, 555.

him as rewards of past services, and not as encouragement to expect support from Great Britain in a continuance of savage hostilities against the United States; all intention of giving any such support having been repeatedly and earnestly disavowed.

The Negro fort, however, abandoned by Colonel Nicholls, remained on the Spanish territory, occupied by the banditti to whom he had left it, and held by them as a post from whence to commit depredations, outrages, and murders, and as a receptacle for fugitive slaves and malefactors,[1] to the great annoyance both of the United States and of Spanish Florida. In April, 1816, General Jackson wrote a letter to the Governor of Pensacola, calling upon him to put down this common nuisance to the peaceable inhabitants of both countries. That letter, together with the answer of the Governor of Pensacola,[2] has already been communicated to the Spanish Minister here, and by him doubtless to his government. Copies of them are, nevertheless, now again enclosed; particularly as the letter from the Governor explicitly admits that this fort, constructed by Nicholls in violation both of the territory and neutrality of Spain, was still no less obnoxious to his government than to the United States; but that he had neither sufficient force nor authority, without orders from the Governor General of the Havana, to destroy it. It was afterwards,[3] on the 27th of July, 1816, destroyed by a cannon shot from a gun vessel of the United States, which, in its passage up the river was fired upon from it. It was blown up with an English flag still flying as its standard, and immediately after the barbarous murder of a boat's crew belonging to the navy

---

[1] *American State Papers*, Foreign Relations, IV. 555.
[2] *Ib.*, 556.
[3] *Ib.*, 559.

of the United States, by the banditti left in it by Nicholls.

In the year 1817, Alexander Arbuthnot, of the island of New Providence, a British subject, first appeared as an Indian trader in Spanish Florida, and as the successor of Colonel Nicholls in the employment of instigating the Seminole and outlawed Red Stick Indians to hostilities against the United States, by reviving the pretence that they were entitled to all the lands which had been ceded by the Creek nation to the United States in August, 1814. As a mere Indian trader, the intrusion of this man into a Spanish province was contrary to the policy observed by all the European powers in this hemisphere, and by none more rigorously than by Spain, of excluding all foreigners from intercourse with the Indians within their territories. It must be known to the Spanish government whether Arbuthnot had a Spanish license for trading with the Indians in Spanish Florida, or not; but they also know that Spain was bound by treaty to restrain by force all hostilities on the part of those Indians against the citizens of the United States; and it is for them to explain how, consistently with those engagements, Spain could, contrary to all the maxims of her ordinary policy, grant such a license to a foreign incendiary, whose principal if not his only object appears to have been to stimulate those hostilities which Spain had expressly stipulated by force to restrain. In his infernal instigations he was but too successful.[1] No sooner did he make his appearance among the Indians, accompanied by the prophet Hillis Hadjo, returned from his expedition to England,[2] than the peaceful inhabitants on the borders of the United States were visited with all the horrors of savage

---

[1] *American State Papers*, Foreign Relations, IV. 580.
[2] *Ib.*, 596.

war—the robbery of their property, and the barbarous and indiscriminate murder of women, infancy, and age.

After the repeated expostulations, warnings, and offers of peace, through the summer and autumn of 1817, on the part of the United States, had been answered only by renewed outrages, and after a detachment of forty men, under Lieutenant Scott,[1] accompanied by seven women, had been waylaid and murdered by the Indians,[2] orders were given to General Jackson, and an adequate force was placed at his disposal to terminate the war. It was ascertained that the Spanish force in Florida was inadequate for the protection even of the Spanish territory itself against this mingled horde of lawless Indians and negroes; and, although their devastations were committed within the limits of the United States, they immediately sought refuge within the Florida line, and there only were to be overtaken. The necessity of crossing the line was indispensable; for it was from beyond the line that the Indians made their murderous incursions within that of the United States. It was there that they had their abode; and the territory belonged, in fact, to them, although within the borders of the Spanish jurisdiction. There it was that the American commander met the principal resistance from them; there it was that were found [3] the still bleeding scalps of our citizens, freshly butchered by them; there it was that he released the only *woman* who had been suffered to survive the massacre of the party under Lieutenant Scott. But it was not anticipated by this government that the commanding officers of Spain in Florida, whose especial duty it was in

---

[1] *American State Papers*, Foreign Relations, IV. 598.
[2] *Ib.*, 605.
[3] *Jackson to the Secretary of War*, March 25, 1818, printed in *American State Papers*, Foreign Relations, IV. 572.

conformity to the solemn engagements contracted by their nation, to restrain by force those Indians from hostilities against the United States, would be found encouraging, aiding, and abetting them, and furnishing them supplies for carrying on such hostilities. The officer in command immediately before General Jackson was, therefore, specially instructed to respect, as far as possible, the Spanish authority, wherever it was maintained; and copies of those orders were also furnished to General Jackson, upon his taking the command.

In the course of his pursuit, as he approached St. Marks, he was informed direct from the governor of Pensacola that a party of the hostile Indians had threatened to seize that fort, and that he apprehended the Spanish garrison there was not in strength sufficient to defend it against them. This information was confirmed from other sources, and by the evidence produced upon the trial of Ambrister, is proved to have been exactly true. By all the laws of neutrality and of war, as well as of prudence and of humanity, he was warranted in anticipating his enemy by the amicable, and, that being refused, by the forcible occupation of the fort. There will need no citations from printed treatises on international law to prove the correctness of this principle. It is engraved in adamant on the common sense of mankind. No writer upon the laws of nations ever pretended to contradict it. None, of any reputation or authority, ever omitted to assert it.

At the Fort St. Marks, Alexander Arbuthnot, the British Indian trader from beyond the seas, the firebrand by whose touch this negro-Indian war against our borders had been re-kindled, was found [1] an inmate of the commandant's

---

[1] *Jackson to José Mazot*, May 23, 1818, printed in *American State Papers*, Foreign Relations, IV. 567.

family; and it was also found that, by the commandant himself, councils of war had been permitted to be held within it by the savage chiefs and warriors; that the Spanish storehouses had been appropriated to their use; that it was an open market for cattle known to have been robbed by them from citizens of the United States, and which had been contracted for and purchased by the officers of the garrison; that information had been afforded from this fort by Arbuthnot to the enemy of the strength and movements of the American army; that the date of departure of express had been noted by the Spanish commissary; and ammunition, munitions of war, and all necessary supplies furnished to the Indians.

The conduct of the Governor of Pensacola was not less marked by a disposition of enmity to the United States, and by an utter disregard to the obligations of the treaty, by which he was bound to restrain, by force, the Indians from hostilities against them. When called upon to vindicate the territorial rights and authority of Spain, by the destruction of the Negro fort, his predecessor had declared it to be not less annoying and pernicious to the Spanish subjects in Florida than to the United States, but had pleaded his inability to subdue it. He himself had expressed his apprehensions that Fort St. Marks would be forcibly taken by the savages from its Spanish garrison; yet, at the same time, he had refused the passage up the Escambia River, unless upon the payment of excessive duties, to provisions destined as supplies for the American army, which, by the detention of them, was subjected to the most distressing privations. He had permitted free ingress and egress at Pensacola to the avowed savage enemies of the United States. Supplies of ammunition, munitions of war, and provisions had been received by them from thence. They had been received and sheltered there from the pursuit of the American forces, and suffered again to sally thence, to enter upon the American territory, and commit new murders. Finally, on the approach of General Jackson to Pensacola, the Governor sent him a letter [1] denouncing his entry upon the territory of Florida as a violent outrage upon the rights of Spain, commanding him to depart and withdraw from the same, and threatening, in case of his non-compliance, to employ force to expel him.

It became, therefore, in the opinion of General Jackson [2] indispensably necessary to take from the Governor of Pensacola the means of carrying his threat into execution. Before the forces under his command, the savage enemies of his country had disappeared. But he knew that the moment those forces should be disbanded, if sheltered by Spanish fortresses, if furnished with ammunition and supplies by Spanish officers, and if aided and supported by the instigation of Spanish encouragement, as he had every reason to expect they would be, they would reappear, and, fired, in addition to their ordinary ferociousness, with revenge for the chastisement they had so recently received, would again rush with the war-hatchet and the scalping-knife into the borders of the United States, and mark every footstep with the blood of their defenseless citizens. So far as all the native resources of the savage extended, the war was at an end; and General Jackson was about to restore to their families and their homes the brave volunteers who had followed his standard, and who had constituted the principal part of his force. This could be done with safety, leaving

---

[1] *José Mazot to Jackson*, May 23, 1818, printed in *American State Papers*, Foreign Relations, IV. 567.

[2] *Jackson to the Secretary of War*, May 5, 1818, printed in *American State Papers*, Foreign Relations, IV. 601.

the regular portion of his troops to garrison his line of forts, and two small detachments of volunteer cavalry to scour the country round Pensacola, and sweep off the lurking remnant of savages who had been scattered and dispersed before him. This was sufficient to keep in check the remnant of the banditti against whom he had marched, so long as they should be destitute of other aid and support. It was, in his judgment, not sufficient, if they should be suffered to rally their numbers under the protection of Spanish forts, and to derive new strength from the impotence or the ill-will against the United States of the Spanish authorities.

He took possession, therefore, of Pensacola and of the fort of Barrancas, as he had done of St. Marks, not in a spirit of hostility to Spain, but as a necessary measure of self-defense; giving notice that they should be restored whenever Spain should place commanders and a force there able and willing to fulfil the engagements of Spain towards the United States, or of restraining by force the Florida Indians from hostilities against their citizens. The President of the United States, to give a signal manifestation of his confidence in the disposition of the king of Spain to perform with good faith this indispensable engagement, and to demonstrate to the world that neither the desire of conquest, nor hostility to Spain, had any influence in the councils of the United States, has directed the unconditional restoration, to any Spanish officer duly authorized to receive them, of Pensacola and the Barrancas, and that of St. Marks, to any Spanish force adequate to its defense against the attack of the savages. But the President will neither inflict punishment, nor pass a censure upon General Jackson, for that conduct, the motives for which were founded in the purest patriotism; of the necessity for which he had the most immediate and effectual means of forming a judgment; and the vindication of which is written in every page of the law of nations, as well as in the first law of nature—self-defense. He thinks it, on the contrary, due to the justice which the United States have a right to claim from Spain, and you are accordingly instructed to demand of the Spanish government that inquiry shall be instituted into the conduct of Don José Mazot, Governor of Pensacola, and of Don Francisco C. Luengo, Commandant of St. Marks, and a suitable punishment inflicted upon them, for having, in defiance and violation of the engagements of Spain with the United States, aided and assisted these hordes of savages in those very hostilities against the United States which it was their official duty to restrain. This inquiry is due to the character of those officers themselves, and to the honor of the Spanish government. The obligation of Spain to restrain, *by force*, the Indians of Florida from hostilities against the United States and their citizens, is explicit, is positive, is unqualified. The fact that, for a series of years, they have received shelter, assistance, supplies, and protection, in the practice of such hostilities, from the Spanish commanders in Florida, is clear and unequivocal. If, as the commanders both at Pensacola and St. Marks have alleged,[1] this has been the result of their weakness rather than of their will; if they have assisted the Indians against the United States to avert their hostilities from the province which they had not sufficient force to defend against them, it may serve in some measure to exculpate, individually, those officers; but it must carry demonstration irresistible to the Spanish government, that the right of the United States can as little compound with impotence as with perfidy, and that Spain must immediately make her election, either to place a force

---

[1] *José Mazot to Jackson*, April 30, and *Francisco Caso y Luengo to Jackson*, April 7, 1818, printed in *American State Papers*, Foreign Relations, IV. 563, 575.

in Florida adequate at once to the protection of her territory, and to the fulfilment of her engagements, or cede to the United States a province, of which she retains nothing but the nominal possession, but which is, in fact, a derelict, open to the occupancy of every enemy, civilized or savage, of the United States, and serving no other earthly purpose than as a post of annoyance to them.

That the purposes, as well of the negro-Indian banditti, with whom we have been contending, as of the British invaders of Florida, who first assembled and employed them, and of the British intruding and pretended traders, since the peace, who have instigated and betrayed them to destruction, have been not less hostile to Spain than to the United States, the proofs contained in the documents herewith enclosed are conclusive. Mr. Pizarro's note of 29th August speaks of his Catholic Majesty's profound indignation at the "sanguinary executions on the Spanish soil of the subjects of powers in amity with the king"—meaning Arbuthnot and Ambrister. Let Mr. Pizarro's successor take the trouble of reading the enclosed documents,[1] and he will discover who Arbuthnot and Ambrister were, and what were their purposes; that Arbuthnot was only the successor of Nicholls, and Ambrister the agent of Woodbine, and the subaltern of McGregor. Mr. Pizarro qualifies General Jackson's necessary pursuit of a defeated savage enemy beyond the Spanish Florida line as a *shameful invasion of his Majesty's territory*. Yet that territory was the territory also of the savage enemy, and Spain was bound to restrain them by force from hostilities against the United States; and it was the failure of Spain to fulfil this engage-

---

[1] *Proceedings of a special court at Fort St. Mark's*, April 26, and Ambrister's *Memorial to the Duke of York*, printed in *American State Papers*, Foreign Relations, IV. 580, 604.

ment which had made it necessary for General Jackson to pursue the savage across the line. What, then, was the character of Nicholls's invasion of his Majesty's territory? and where was his Majesty's profound indignation at that? Mr. Pizarro says, his Majesty's forts and places have been violently seized on by General Jackson. Had they not been seized on, nay, had not the principal of his forts been blown up by Nicholls, and a British fort on the same Spanish territory been erected during the war, and left standing as a negro fort, in defiance of Spanish authority, after the peace? Where was his Majesty's profound indignation at that? Has his Majesty suspended formally all negotiation with the sovereign of Colonel Nicholls for this shameful invasion of his territory, without color of provocation, without pretence of necessity, without shadow or even avowal of a pretext? Has his Majesty given solemn warning to the British government that those were incidents "of transcendent moment, capable of producing an essential and thorough change in the political relations of the two countries?" Nicholls and Woodbine, in their invitations and promises to the slaves to run away from their masters and join them, did not confine themselves to the slaves of the United States. They received with as hearty a welcome, and employed with equal readiness, the fugitives from their masters in Florida as those from Georgia. Against this special injury the governor of Pensacola did earnestly remonstrate with the British admiral, Cockburn.[1] But against the *shameful invasion* of the territory; against the violent seizure of the forts and places; against the blowing up of the Barrancas, and the erection and maintenance, under British banners, of the negro fort on Spanish soil; against the nego-

---

[1] Sob. Kindelan to Cockburn, February 18, 1835, printed in *American State Papers*, Foreign Relations, IV. 561.

tiation by a British officer, in the midst of peace, of pretended treaties, offensive and defensive, and of navigation and commerce upon Spanish territory, between Great Britain and Spanish Indians, whom Spain was bound to control and restrain—if a whisper of expostulation was ever wafted from Madrid to London, it was not loud enough to be heard across the Atlantic, nor energetic enough to transpire beyond the walls of the palaces from which it issued, and to which it was borne.

The connection between Arbuthnot and Nicholls, and between Ambrister, Woodbine, and McGregor, is established beyond all question, by the evidence produced at the trials before the court-martial. I have already remarked to you on the very extraordinary circumstance that a British trader from beyond the sea should be permitted by the Spanish authorities to trade with the Indians of Florida. From his letter to Hambly, dated 3d May, 1817,[1] it appears that his trading was but a pretence, and that his principal purpose was to act as the agent of the Indians of Florida, and outlaws from the Creeks, to obtain the aid of the British government in their hostilities against the United States. He expressly tells Hambly there that the chief of these outlaws was the principal cause of his (Arbuthnot's) being in the country, and that he had come with an answer from Earl Bathurst, delivered to him by Governor Cameron, of New Providence, to certain Indian talks, in which this aid of the British government had been solicited.

Hambly himself had been left by Nicholls as the agent between the Indians and the British government; but having found that Nicholls had failed in his attempt to prevail upon the British government to pursue this clandestine war in the midst of peace, and that they were not prepared to

[1] Printed in *American State Papers*, Foreign Relations, IV. 588.

support his pretence that half a dozen outlawed fugitives from the Creeks were the Creek nation, when Arbuthnot, the incendiary, came, and was instigating them, by promises of support from Great Britain, to commence their murderous incursions into the United States, Hambly, at the request of the chiefs of the Creeks themselves, wrote to him,[1] warning him to withdraw from among that band of outlaws, and giving him a solemn foreboding of the doom that awaited him from the hand of justice if he persevered in the course that he pursued. Arbuthnot nevertheless persisted, and while he was deluding the wretched Indians with the promise of support from England, he was writing letters for them [2] to the British minister in the United States, to Governor Cameron, of New Providence, to Colonel Nicholls, to be laid before the British government, and even to the Spanish governor of St. Augustine, and the Governor General of the Havana,[3] soliciting, in all quarters, aid and support, arms and ammunition, for the Indians against the United States, bewailing the destruction of the negro fort, and charging the British government with having drawn the Indians into war with the United States, and deserting them after the peace.

You will remark among the papers produced on his trial, a power of attorney,[3] dated June 17, 1817, given him by twelve Indians, partly of Florida, and partly of the fugitive outlaws from the United States. He states that this power and his instructions were to memorialize the British government and the Governor General of the Havana. These papers are not only substantially proved as of his handwriting on the trial, but, in the daily newspapers of London

---

[1] Printed in *American State Papers*, Foreign Relations, IV. 578.
[2] *Ib.*, 585.
[3] *Ib.*, 589.

of 24th and 25th of August last, his letter to Nicholls [1] is published, (somewhat curiously garbled,) with a copy [2] of Hambly's above-mentioned letter to him, and a reference to this power of attorney to him,[3] *approved by the commandant of St. Marks, F. C. Luengo.* Another of the papers is a letter written in the name of the same chiefs, by Arbuthnot, to the Governor General of the Havana,[4] asking of him permission by Arbuthnot to establish a warehouse on the Apalachicola, bitterly and falsely complaining that the Americans had made settlements on their lands within the Spanish lines, and calling upon the Governor General to give orders to displace them, and send them back to their own country. In this letter they assign as a reason for asking the license for Arbuthnot, their want of a person to put in writing for them their talks of grievances against the Americans, and they add: "The commander of the fort of St. Marks has heard all of our talks and complaints. He approves of what we have done and what we are doing, and it is by his recommendation we have thus presumed to address your excellency." You will find those papers in the printed newspapers enclosed, and in the proceedings of the court-martial, and will point them out to the Spanish government, not only as decisive proofs of the unexampled compliances of the Spanish officers in Florida to foreign intrusive agents and instigators of Indian hostilities against the United States, but as placing beyond a doubt that participation of this hostile spirit in the commandant of St. Marks which General Jackson so justly complains of, and of which we have so well-founded a right to demand the

---

[1] Printed in *American State Papers*, Foreign Relations, IV. 578, 587.
[2] *Ib.*, 579.
[3] *Ib.*, 580, 589.
[4] *Ib.*, 588.

punishment. Here is the commandant of a Spanish fort, bound by the sacred engagement of a treaty to restrain by force the Indians within his command from committing hostilities against the United States, conspiring with those same Indians, and deliberately giving his written approbation to their appointment of a foreigner, a British subject, as their agent to solicit assistance and supplies from the Governor General of the Havana, and from the British government, for carrying on these same hostilities.

Let us come to the case of Ambrister. He was taken in arms, leading and commanding the Indians in the war against the American troops; and to that charge, upon his trial, pleaded guilty. But the primary object of his coming there was still more hostile to Spain than to the United States. You find [1] that he told three of the witnesses who testified at his trial that he had come to this country *upon Mr. Woodbine's business at Tampa Bay*, to see the negroes righted; and one of them, that *he had a commission in the patriot army under McGregor*, and that he expected a captaincy. And what was the intended business of McGregor and Woodbine at Tampa Bay? It was the conquest of Florida from Spain, by the use of those very Indians and negroes whom the commandant of St. Marks was so ready to aid and support in war against the United States. The chain of proof that establishes this fact is contained in the documents communicated by the President to Congress at their last session, relating to the occupation of Amelia Island by McGregor. From these documents you will find [2] that while McGregor was there, Woodbine went from New Providence in a schooner of his own to join him, that he arrived at Amelia Island just as McGregor, abandoning

---

[1] *American State Papers*, Foreign Relations, IV. 604.
[2] *Ib.*, 603.

the companions of his achievement there, was leaving it; that McGregor, quitting the vessel in which he had embarked at Amelia, went on board that of Woodbine, and returned with him to New Providence; that Woodbine had persuaded him they could yet accomplish the conquest of Florida with soldiers to be recruited at Nassau from the corps of colonial marines which had served under Nicholls during the late war with the United States, which corps had been lately disbanded, and with negroes to be found at Tampa Bay, and 1,500 Indians already then engaged to Woodbine, who pretended that they had made a grant of all their lands there to him. Among the papers, the originals of which are in our possession, are in McGregor's own handwriting instructions [1] for sailing into Tampa Bay, with the assertion that he calculated to be there by the last of April or first of May of the present year; a letter [1] dated 27th December last, to one of his acquaintances in this country, disclosing the same intention; and the extract of a proclamation [1] which was to have been issued at Tampa Bay, to the inhabitants of Florida, by the person charged with making the settlement there before his arrival, announcing his approach for the purpose of liberating them from the despotism of Spain, and of enabling them to form a government for themselves. He had persuaded those who would listen to him here that his ultimate object was to sell the Floridas to the United States. There is some reason to suppose that he had made indirect overtures of a similar nature to the British government. This was Ambrister's business in Florida. He arrived there in March, the precursor of McGregor and Woodbine; and immediately upon his arrival he is found [2] seizing upon Arbuthnot's

---

[1] *American State Papers*, Foreign Relations, IV. 604.
[2] *Ib.*, 580.

goods, and distributing them among the negroes and Indians; seizing upon his vessel, and compelling its master to pilot him, with a body of armed negroes, towards the fort of St. Marks, with the declared purpose of taking it by surprise in the night; writing letters to Governor Cameron, of New Providence, urgently calling for supplies of war and of cannon for the war against the Americans, and letters to Colonel Nicholls, renewing the same demands of supplies, informing him that he is with 300 negroes, "a few of our Bluff people," who had *stuck to the cause*, and were relying on the faith of Nicholls's promises. "Our Bluff people" were the people of the negro fort, collected by Nicholls and Woodbine's proclamations during the American and English war; and "*the cause*" to which they stuck was the savage, servile, exterminating war against the United States.

Among the agents and actors of such virtuous enterprises as we have unveiled, it was hardly to be expected that there would be found remarkable evidences of their respect, confidence, and good faith towards one another. Accordingly, besides the violent seizure and distribution by Ambrister of Arbuthnot's property, his letters to Cameron and to Nicholls are filled with the distrust and suspicions of the Indians that they were deceived and betrayed by Arbuthnot; while, in Arbuthnot's letters to the same Nicholls [1] he accuses Woodbine of having taken charge of poor Francis the prophet, or Hillis Hadjo, upon his return from England to New Providence, and, under pretence of taking care of him and his affairs, of having defrauded him of a large portion of the presents which had been delivered out from the King's stores to him for Francis's use. This is one of the passages of Arbuthnot's letter [2] to Nicholls, *omitted* in the publication of it last August in the London newspapers.

[1] *American State Papers*, Foreign Relations, IV. 587.   [2] *Ib.*, 578.

Is this narrative of dark and complicated depravity; this creeping and insidious war, both against Spain and the United States; this mockery of patriotism; these political filters to fugitive slaves and Indian outlaws; these perfidies and treacheries of villains incapable of keeping their faith even to each other; all in the name of South American liberty, of the rights of runaway negroes, and the wrongs of savage murderers—all combined and projected to plunder Spain of her province, and to spread massacre and devastation along the borders of the United States—is all this sufficient to cool the sympathies of his Catholic Majesty's government, excited by the execution of these two "subjects of a Power in amity with the King?" The Spanish government is not at this day to be informed that, cruel as war in its mildest forms must be, it is, and necessarily must be, doubly cruel when waged with savages; that savages make no prisoners, but to torture them; that they give no quarter; that they put to death, without discrimination of age or sex. That these ordinary characteristics of Indian warfare have been applicable, in their most heart-sickening horrors, to that war left us by Nicholls as his legacy, reinstigated by Woodbine, Arbuthnot, and Ambrister, and stimulated by the approbation, encouragement, and aid of the Spanish commandant at St. Marks, is proof required? Entreat the Spanish minister of state for a moment to overcome the feelings which details like these must excite; and to reflect, if possible, with composure, upon the facts stated in the following extracts from the documents enclosed:

Letter from sailing master Jairus Loomis to Commodore Daniel T. Patterson, 13th August, 1816, reporting the destruction of the negro fort:[1]

[1] *American State Papers,* Foreign Relations, IV. 559.

On examining the prisoners, they stated that Edward Daniels, ordinary seaman, who was made prisoner in the boat on the 17th July, *was tarred and burnt alive.*

Letter from Archibald Clarke to General Gaines, 26th February, 1817:[1]

On the 24th instant the house of Mr. Garret, residing in the upper part of this county, near the boundary of Wayne County (Georgia), was attacked, during his absence, near the middle of the day, by this party (of Indians), consisting of about fifteen, who shot Mrs. Garret in two places, and then dispatched her by stabbing and scalping. Her two children, one about three years, the other two months, were also murdered, and the eldest scalped; the house was then plundered of every article of value, and set on fire.

Letter from Peter B. Cook (Arbuthnot's clerk) to Eliz. A. Carney, at Nassau, dated Sewanee, 19th January, 1818, giving an account of their operations with the Indians against the Americans, and their massacre of Lieutenant Scott and his party: [2]

There was a boat that was taken by the Indians, that had in it thirty men, seven women, and four small children. There were six of the men got clear, and one woman saved, and all the rest of them got killed. The children were taken by the leg, and their brains dashed out against the boat.

If the bare recital of scenes like these cannot be perused without shuddering, what must be the agonized feelings of those whose wives and children are from day to day, and

---
[1] *Message from the President of the United States to Congress,* March 25, 1818.
[2] *American State Papers,* Foreign Relations, IV. 605.

from night to night, exposed to be the victims of the same barbarity? Has mercy a voice to plead for the perpetrators and instigators of deeds like these? Should inquiry hereafter be made why, within three months after this event, the savage Hamathli-Meico, upon being taken by the American troops, was by order of their commander immediately hung, let it be told that that savage was the commander of the party by whom those women were butchered, and those helpless infants were thus dashed against the boat. Contending with such enemies, although humanity revolts at entire retaliation upon them, and spares the lives of their feeble and defenseless women and children, yet mercy herself surrenders to retributive justice the lives of their leading warriors taken in arms, and, still more, the lives of the foreign white incendiaries, who, disowned by their own governments, and disowning their own natures, degrade themselves beneath the savage character by voluntarily descending to its level, is not this the dictate of common sense? Is it not the usage of legitimate warfare? Is it not consonant to the soundest authorities of national law? "When at war (says Vattel) with a ferocious nation which observes no rules, and grants no quarter, they may be chastised in the persons of those of them who may be taken; they are of the number of the guilty; and by this rigor the attempt may be made of bringing them to a sense of the laws of humanity." And again: "As a general has the right of sacrificing the lives of his enemies to his own safety, or that of his people, if he has to contend with an inhuman enemy, often guilty of such excesses, he may take the lives of some of his prisoners, and treat them as his own people have been treated." The justification of these principles is found in their salutary efficacy for terror and for example.

It is thus only that the barbarities of the Indians can be

successfully encountered. It is thus only that the worse than Indian barbarities of European impostors, pretending authority from their governments, but always disavowed, can be punished and arrested. Great Britain yet engages the alliance and coöperation of savages in war; but her government has invariably disclaimed all countenance or authorization to her subjects to instigate them against us in time of peace. Yet, it so happened, that, from the period of our established independence to this day, *all* the Indian wars with which we have been afflicted have been distinctly traceable to the instigation of English traders or agents. Always disavowed, yet always felt; more than once detected, but never before punished; two of them, offenders of the deepest dye, after solemn warning to their government, and individually to one of them, have fallen, *flagrante delicto*, into the hands of an American general; and the punishment inflicted upon them has fixed them on high, as an example awful in its exhibition, but, we trust, auspicious in its results, of that which awaits unauthorized pretenders of European agency to stimulate and interpose in wars between the United States and the Indians within their control.

This exposition of the origin, the causes, and the character of the war with the Seminole Indians and part of the Creeks, combined with McGregor's mock patriots and Nicholls's negroes, which necessarily led our troops into Florida, and gave rise to all those incidents of which Mr. Pizarro so vehemently complains, will, it is hoped, enable you to present other and sounder views of the subject to his Catholic Majesty's government.

It will enable you to show that the occupation of Pensacola and St. Marks was occasioned neither by a spirit of hostility to Spain, nor with a view to extort prematurely the province from her possession; that it was rendered necessary by the neglect of Spain to perform her engagements of restraining the Indians from hostilities against the United States, and by the culpable countenance, encouragement and assistance given to those Indians, in their hostilities, by the Spanish governor and commandant at those places, that the United States have a right to demand, as the President does demand, of Spain the punishment of those officers for this misconduct; and he further demands of Spain a just and reasonable indemnity to the United States for the heavy and necessary expenses which they have been compelled to incur by the failure of Spain to perform her engagements to restrain the Indians, aggravated by this demonstrated complicity of her commanding officers with them in their hostilities against the United States; that the two Englishmen executed by order of General Jackson were not only identified with the savages, with whom they were carrying on the war against the United States, but that one of them was the mover and fomenter of the war, which, without his interference, and false promises to the Indians of support from the British government, never would have happened; that the other was the instrument of war against Spain as well as the United States, commissioned by McGregor, and expedited by Woodbine, upon their project of conquering Florida with these Indians and negroes; that as accomplices of the savages, and, sinning against their better knowledge, worse than savages, General Jackson, possessed of their persons and of the proofs of their guilt, might, by the lawful and ordinary usages of war, have hung them both without the formality of a trial; that, to allow them every possible opportunity of refuting the proofs, or of showing any circumstance in extenuation of their crimes, he gave them the benefit of trial by a court-martial of highly respectable officers; that the defense of one consisted solely and exclusively of technical cavils at the nature of part of the evidence against him, and the other confessed his guilt; finally, that, in restoring Pensacola and St. Marks to Spain, the President gives the most signal proof of his confidence that, hereafter, her engagement to restrain by force the Indians of Florida from all hostilities against the United States will be effectually fulfilled; that there will be no more murders, no more robberies, within our borders, by savages prowling along the Spanish line, and seeking shelter within it, to display in their villages the scalps of our women and children, their victims, and to sell, with shameless effrontery, the plunder from our citizens in Spanish forts and cities; that we shall hear no more apologies from Spanish governors and commandants of their inability to perform the duties of their office and the solemn contracts of their country—no more excuses for compliances to the savage enemies of the United States, from the dread of their attacks upon themselves—no more harboring of foreign impostors upon compulsion; that a strength sufficient will be kept in the province to restrain the Indians by force, and officers empowered and instructed to employ it effectually to maintain the good faith of the nation by the effective fulfilment of the treaty. The duty of this government to protect the persons and property of our fellow-citizens on the borders of the United States is imperative—it must be discharged. And if, after all the warnings that Spain has had; if, after the prostration of all her territorial rights and neutral obligations by Nicholls and his banditti during war, and of all her treaty stipulations by Arbuthnot and Ambrister, abetted by her own commanding officers, during peace, to the cruel annoyance of the United States; if the necessities of self-defense should again compel the United States to take possession of the Spanish forts and places in Florida, declare, with the frankness and candor that become us, that another unconditional restoration of them must not be expected; that even the President's confidence in the good faith and ultimate justice of the Spanish government will yield to the painful experience of continual disappointment; and, that, after unwearied and almost unnumbered appeals to them for the performance of their stipulated duties in vain, the United States will be reluctantly compelled to rely for the protection of their borders upon themselves alone.

You are authorized to communicate the whole of this letter, and the accompanying documents, to the Spanish government. I have the honor, etc.[1]

[1] "I propose then that you select Mr. Adams's four principal letters on the Spanish subject, to wit, that which establishes our right to the Rio Bravo which was laid before the Congress of 1817-18; his letters to Onis of July 23 and November 30, and to Erving of November 28; perhaps also that of December 2. Have them well translated into French, and send English and French copies to all our ministers at foreign courts, and to our consuls. The paper on our right to the Rio Bravo, and the letter to Erving of November 28 are the most important and are among the ablest compositions I have ever seen, both as to logic and style. . . . It is of great consequence to us, and merits every possible endeavor, to maintain in Europe a correct opinion of our political morality. These papers will place the event with the world in the important cases of our western boundary, of our military entrance into Florida, and of the execution of Arbuthnot and Ambrister." *Jefferson to Monroe,* January 18, 1819. *Writings of Jefferson* (Ford), X. 122.

"Mr. Adams seems to have taken the course in his essay on the Seminole war and the murder of Ambrister and Arbuthnot—for I feel it to be this crime—which his enemies would have pointed out to him as most calculated to promote their views.

"If Mercer does justice to the subject—and I am much inclined to hope and believe he will—I think the noble Secretary will writhe under the lashes which he has most indiscreetly and unnecessarily courted." *Christopher Gore to Jeremiah Mason,* January 20, 1819. *Memoir of Mason,* 210.

"I agree with you in opinion of the character of General Jackson's conduct, and am glad to see the subject taken up with so much spirit in the House of Representatives of the United States. I hope the debate will terminate in a censure of Jackson. I really think it a national concern. The barbarous conduct of Jackson and his court-martial, and not less barbarous doctrine by which it is attempted

TO DON LUIS DE ONIS [1]

Department of State,
Washington, 30 November, 1818.

Sir:

I have had the honor of receiving your letter of the 16th instant, and am directed by the President to inform you that, in making to you the proposal contained in my letter of the 31st of last month, with regard to the western boundary between the United States and the bordering territory of Spain, it was with the view, by the magnitude of the sacrifice which it involved on the part of the United States, to manifest the deep solicitude which he felt in terminating, by a general adjustment of all the differences which have been so long in discussion between the two nations, a state of things so unpropitious to the good understanding between them, and so much to be regretted by both.

As it was believed this article could alone present an ultimate obstacle to the agreement thus earnestly desired, I was directed frankly to present you at once the utmost extent to which the government of the United States felt itself warranted, consistently with its duties to the rights

---

to be justified, will, unless disclaimed, disgrace us in the opinion of the civilized world." *Jeremiah Mason to Christopher Gore*, January 31, 1819. *Ib.*, 211.

"I am of opinion that Mr. Adams has lost credit with his New England friends, by his bold attempt at a justification. I think it unfortunate for him that he did not confine himself to the repelling of the complaint of Spain, where there seems to be much ground for recrimination at least, without attempting so broad and entire justification of the whole transaction in all respects. I see no ground on which the execution of Arbuthnot and Ambrister can be justified, nor much in the circumstances of the case to excuse the act, which must, in the common opinion of mankind, be held to have been cruel and barbarous." *Jeremiah Mason to Rufus King*, January 31, 1819. *Ib.*, 212.

[1] Printed in *American State Papers*, Foreign Relations, IV. 545.

and interests of the nation, to concede, of those unquestionable rights, to accommodate the wishes and to quiet the pretensions of your sovereign; but, in yielding thus much, you were explicitly notified that the proposition was final, and that upon your acceptance of it depended the only remaining hope, in the mind of the President, of a termination to this negotiation satisfactory to both parties.

As you have now declared that you are not authorized to agree, either to the course of the Red River (Rio Roxo) for the boundary, or to the forty-first parallel of latitude, from the Snow mountains to the Pacific Ocean, the President deems it useless to pursue any further the attempt at an adjustment of this object by the present negotiation. I am, therefore, directed to state to you that the offer of a line for the western boundary, made to you in my last letter, is no longer obligatory upon this government.

Reserving, then, all the rights of the United States to the ancient western boundary of the colony of Louisiana by the course of the Rio Bravo del Norte, I am yet authorized to conclude a convention or treaty with you upon the other subjects of existing difference. But it is proper, in the first instance, and in reference to the first of the propositions made by you on the 24th of last month,[1] to correct an erroneous impression which you entertain, and which is certainly not warranted by any communication which you have received from this government. You have been informed that the contingencies upon which General Jackson adopted those measures, which you represent as hostilities and outrages, not having been anticipated, had not been provided for in his instructions; that they were unforeseen emergencies upon which, judging measures of energy necessary, he had recurred to them upon his own responsibility,

---

[1] *American State Papers*, Foreign Relations, IV. 526.

and upon motives which he had himself explained; that these measures were dictated by the hostile spirit, not of the American commander against Spain, but of the Spanish commanders against the United States. I informed you that the President of the United States had directed that the proofs of this hostility to the United States of those Spanish officers, furnished by General Jackson, should be embodied and presented to the government of his Catholic Majesty, with a demand that the misconduct of those officers should be suitably punished. I have now the honor of stating to you that it has accordingly been done; that the proofs collected by General Jackson, together with other accumulating demonstration of the justice of his charges against Don José Mazot, Governor of Pensacola, and Don Francisco C. Luengo, Commandant of St. Mark's, have been forwarded to the minister of the United States in Spain, with instructions to lay them before your government, and to call for their just animadversion upon the violation, by those officers, of the solemn engagements of their country to the United States.

After a full and deliberate examination of these proofs, the President deems them irresistibly conclusive that the horrible combination of robbery, murder, and war, with which the frontier of the United States bordering upon Florida has for several years past been visited, is ascribable altogether to the total and lamentable failure of Spain to fulfil the fifth article of the treaty of 1795, by which she stipulated to restrain, by force, her Indians from hostilities against the citizens of the United States. Without adverting to the transactions of the late war between the United States and Great Britain, who can mistake the character of the fact that a fort on Spanish soil was garrisoned by hundreds of negroes and Indians, with an English banner flying upon its wall, for the desolation of the American border; and that, sixteen months after the peace of America and of England, the governor of Pensacola, called upon by General Jackson to break up this lair of human tigers, pleaded his inability, and want of orders from his governor general, to comply with the request? Who can mistake the character of the fact, that, six months after the stronghold of these savage banditti had been blown up by a shot from an American gun-vessel, a pretended Indian trader, a foreigner both to Florida and to Spain, was permitted to come into a Spanish province, there to bribe the savages by presents, and to stimulate them by the grossest falsehoods and absurdest misrepresentations to war against the Americans? Do the governors of Florida, the instant they learn the appearance of this intending incendiary within their jurisdiction, seize and imprison him? Do they even command him to depart from the province? Nay, do they so much as require him to obey the laws and respect the engagements of their nation, and the duties of their stations? Far from it. Alexander Arbuthnot, a British subject from the island of New Providence, lands in the Spanish province of Florida, and there opens a warehouse for traffic with the Indians: by whose license or permission? It has not been the custom of Spain to allow the subjects of foreign powers to intrude upon her colonial possessions; and more than one American citizen is, at this moment, pining in the dungeons of Spain for having set his foot upon her soil. By whose permission, then, was Arbuthnot allowed to intermeddle in the province of Florida, even had it been only for the purpose of innocent trade with the Indians? Had he a license, or had he not? If he had, it is for the governors of Florida to explain by whom and upon what motive it was granted. If he had not, it is for them to show why he was suffered within their jurisdiction, to trample upon the laws of Spain with impunity. But innocent traffic was not the real purpose of Arbuthnot. He was there to stimulate as well the Indians of Florida as the fugitive outlaws from the Creek nation among them to war against the United States. He was goading them by the absurd pretence that the United States were bound by the treaty of Ghent to give up to them the lands within the borders of the United States which had been ceded by the Creek nation to the United States six months before the treaty of Ghent was signed. With the profoundest treachery to those Indians themselves, he was promising them that the British government would support them in this pretence, and was writing letters to the Governor of New Providence, to the British minister here, and through Colonel Nicholls, in England, to the British government, soliciting arms and ammunition for war against the United States. Nor was this all. He obtained from a number of Indian chiefs a power of attorney authorizing him to write letters and deliver talks in their name and behalf; and to the copy of that power, transmitted by him to England to be laid before the British government, were affixed the signature and *approbation* of F. C. Luengo, commandant of St. Marks. By virtue of the same power, he wrote, in the name of those Indians, a letter to the Governor General of the Havana, falsely pretending that the Americans were settling upon their lands, within the Spanish territory, and calling upon him for force to drive them out. This letter, too, asserts that its contents were sanctioned by the approbation of the commandant of St. Marks.

Arbuthnot was taken by General Jackson at St. Marks, and was then an inmate of the family of the commandant. Among his papers was found a letter from the commandant, written shortly before, styling him his *friend*, giving him notice of the approach of the American force, and advising him to come and provide for the safety of his *little affairs*, and hold consultation with him upon subjects which *could not with prudence be committed to writing.* What consciousness of participation in the abominable purposes of Arbuthnot is betrayed in those few words! What were those common concerns of an English Indian trader and of the Spanish commandant of a fort, which required so thick a veil of mystery to conceal them from detection that this officer should be afraid to expose them to the possibility of discovery by committing them to paper? They were, that St. Marks was the centre of Arbuthnot's intrigues with the Indians against the United States; that councils of the hostile Indians were held at the commandant's quarters, at which he personally attended; that white men, Spanish subjects, inhabitants of Florida, had been taken prisoners by the Indians, under the influence and by the direction of Arbuthnot; reserved by the Indians for torture; delivered as prisoners to the custody of the commandant of St. Marks; received by him as prisoners, and held as such until delivered by General Jackson's approach to that place. They were, in fine, that St. Marks had, in substance, become an Indian fort under a Spanish standard; and to such an extent did the commandant countenance the savages in their depredations upon the borders of the United States, that he actually contracted with some of them to purchase cattle to be robbed by them from the citizens of Georgia, actually purchased them after they had been robbed, and actually sold them as his private property to the purveying officers of General Jackson's army after he took possession of the fort.

It is to the artifices and instigations of Arbuthnot, thus, to say the least, tolerated by the Governor of Pensacola, and thus aided and abetted by the commandant of St. Marks, that this war with the Seminole Indians has been due. But for them it would undoubtedly never have happened. If no direct proof has appeared that the Governor of Pensacola was implicated in the criminal proceedings of Arbuthnot as deeply as the commandant of St. Marks, ample evidence has been produced of his having aided, assisted, and sheltered the Indians; of his having, as long as he dared, furnished them with supplies, including munitions of war. And his hostility to the United States has been sufficiently manifested by his exposing their army to the danger of famine, from the impediments opposed by his orders to the passage up the Escambia River of their supplies. That he harbored one Indian chief hostile to the United States, and not even belonging to Florida, is apparent by the article of capitulation which he obtained in his favor. That he suffered another, George Perryman, to escape from Pensacola upon General Jackson's approach, and go to England, there to renew, if possible, the negotiations of the prophet Francis, is announced as a late article of news in the English journals. That a number of other Indians were enabled, by the assistance of officers under his command, to escape from Pensacola on the very day that it was taken by General Jackson, is proved by the certificates of several witnesses. And, lastly, he did not hesitate to write a letter to that commander, before he took Pensacola, threatening, in the event of his not withdrawing immediately from Florida, to resist what he termed his aggressions by force.

It is therefore to the conduct of her own commanding officers that Spain must impute the necessity under which General Jackson found himself of occupying the places of their command. Had the engagements of Spain been fulfilled, the United States would have had no Seminole war. Far, then, from being under obligation to indemnify the crown of Spain for any losses which it may have sustained in consequence of this necessity, the United States are entitled to demand, and the minister of the United States at Madrid has been instructed accordingly, that the crown of Spain should indemnify them for the extraordinary and indispensable expenses which they have been compelled to incur by the prosecution of this war, which Spain was bound to prevent. The revenue collected in the places occupied is very far from being adequate to that object. As to the losses or injuries to the inhabitants, as private property, both at St. Marks and Pensacola, has been inviolably respected, no injury can have happened to them for which the United States should be responsible.

With respect to the other articles suggested in your propositions of 24th October, and your observations upon the modifications to them, proposed by me, as well as to other objects of minor concernment, to which your last note alludes, I am not aware of any insuperable obstacle to our coming to an agreement upon them. Should your instructions authorize you to waive the further consideration of the two articles upon which I have now communicated to you the final determination of the President, and to proceed in the discussion of the rest, I shall be happy to confer with you verbally concerning them as soon as may suit your convenience. After the explicit answer given you in my note of the 12th March last to your proposal of referring the differences between our governments to the mediation of Great Britain, and the reasons there assigned for declining that overture, the offer which you make of referring them to the allied monarchs, whom you state to be now assembled at Aix-la-Chapelle, was not to be expected. As you have, however, thought proper to make it, I refer you to my above-mentioned note for the grounds upon which it is declined. If you do not feel yourself at liberty to proceed in the negotiation on the terms proposed, postponing the articles relative to the western boundary and to the late transactions in Florida, I shall be ready, at your convenience, to exchange with you the ratifications of the convention of 1802.

I embrace with pleasure the occasion of renewing, etc.

TO ALBERT GALLATIN

DEPARTMENT OF STATE,
WASHINGTON, 30 November, 1818.

. . . .

As from the tenor of your dispatches it appears that the capture of Pensacola and those executions [of Arbuthnot and Ambrister], together with that of two of the hostile Indian chiefs had excited a sensation peculiarly unfavorable in France, and even in other parts of Europe; and as you know the solicitude of the President, that every act of his government in its relations with other powers and with the Indians should be not only conformable to the established laws and usages of nations, but peculiarly marked with a just deference to the well-considered opinions of the world, and to the principles of the most enlightened humanity, your attention is particularly invited to those parts of the statement and of the vouchers which have reference to those transactions. You will find that neither of them had been anticipated in the orders and instructions given to General Jackson. Their justification rests upon the reasons which he has himself assigned for resorting to those measures, and upon the facts disclosed in the vouchers furnished by him in vindication of them. Your observations to the Duke de Richelieu, and to the ministers of other powers having influence over Spain, as reported in your No. 84 were perfectly correct, excepting that without imputing to Spain the unjustifiable and hostile conduct of her commanding officers in Florida, General Jackson's proceedings were founded on the presumption that the fault was in those officers themselves. Had the situation and the duties of these officers been those of ordinary *neutrality*, their conduct would still have been altogether unwarrantable. But in the fifth article of our treaty of 1795 with Spain, which you transmitted to the Duke de Richelieu, he must have seen that this was a war to which she ought not to have been neutral. It was a war against hostilities, which she was in the most explicit and unqualified terms bound herself to prevent *by force*. General Jackson was performing that which Spain by solemn stipulation was bound to perform herself. The least that he could expect, therefore, was that every facility possible should be afforded by the Spanish commanders to his operations. That no assistance, supplies or shelter would be afforded by them to our savage enemies, who by the very tenor of the treaty were also theirs. Instead of which he found the commandant of St. Marks holding at his own quarters councils of war with the hostile Indians; contracting with them for the purchase of future plunder, to be robbed from the inhabitants on our borders; holding white men, Spanish subjects, settled in Florida, taken prisoners by the Indians, as prisoners for them; and confidentially corresponding with and harboring a pretended British agent (Arbuthnot), the mover, instigator and conductor of the Indians in their war against the United States. . . . The white men, as subjects of a European power with which we were at peace, could not be held as prisoners; a demand upon their own government to punish them would have been fruitless, their own government having no jurisdiction for the trial of their crime. To dismiss them with impunity would have been not only to let them loose to renew the same intrigues and machinations; but to leave their example a pernicious temptation to others to offend in like manner; an ignominious punishment, sparing life, would have little or no effect upon men to whom infamy was scarcely equivalent to any punishment at all. The Indian wars that we have suffered by the instigations of such characters, the hundreds and thousands of our citizens, of either sex and of every age, butchered with every horrible aggravation of savage cruelty, under the stimulus of these disavowed and unauthorized agents, are also to be considered. The necessity of a signal example was urgent and indispensable. It has been given; and if its operation should be, as we trust it will, to deter unauthorized foreign intruders from intermeddling between the United States and the Indians, it will be the greatest benefit ever conferred by a white man upon their tribes, since it will be the only possible means of redeeming them from the alternative otherwise unavoidable of their utter extermination.[1]

I am, etc.

[1] An extract from a dispatch to George W. Erving, dated December 2, 1818, is in the *American State Papers*, Foreign Relations, IV. 546.

To Rush he wrote, December 1: "In your communications with Lord Castlereagh upon this subject, the President desires that you will constantly observe a manner as mild and conciliatory as may be consistent with the explicitness indispensable for the vindication of our national character. . . . If the British government find in it [the dispatch to Erving] anything which calls for refutation or explanation from them, you will receive and report it, with the assurance that our proceedings have been exclusively dictated by the necessary justification of ourselves, and not with any view of crimination against them. . . . We hope the British government will definitively close all their concerns with the Indians and

TO DAVID C. DE FORREST [1]

Mr. Adams presents his compliments to Mr. De Forrest, and has the honor of assuring him by direction of the Presi-

negroes of Florida." The first part of this dispatch, relating to the rejection by the President of four articles proposed by the British government as additions to the commercial convention of July 3, 1815, is printed in *American State Papers*, Foreign Relations, IV. 401.

The British minister, Bagot, admitted that the case of Ambrister was clear, "both of his being taken in arms in the war of the negroes and Indians against us, and of his being there upon McGregor's project of conquering Florida;" but he raised doubts of Arbuthnot's connection with Woodbine. Adams sent to Rush, December 3, copies of the documents necessary to show this connection, and added:

"Mr. Bagot declared to me with the most positive and explicit asseveration that he never has received from his government one line of instructions respecting the Creek or Seminole Indians; nor one line directing him to attend to the interests of *any* Indians whatever. And he has shown me the copy of Colonel Nicholls' letter to Earl Bathurst of July, 1815, announcing his arrival in England with the treaty offensive and defensive and with the Prophet Francis; of Lord Bathurst's answer, disavowing the treaty, declaring to Nicholls that he had had no authority to make it, and that the British government would have nothing to do with it; of Lord Bathurst's letter to Francis himself, expressing regret that he and his tribe should still be at variance with the United States, informing him that a passage home would be provided for him, and recommending to him and them to come as soon as possible to a good understanding with the Americans, and sending him a present of a pair of silver mounted pistols, to which were added some implements of agriculture; and of a letter from Lord Bathurst to Mr. Baker, then chargé d'affaires here, dated 21 September, 1815 (the day after my note on the subject to Lord Bathurst), again disavowing Nicholls and his proceedings, and authorizing Baker to repeat the disavowal to this government. On these papers there is an endorsement by Mr. Baker, that he communicated their contents to Mr. Monroe, *at an interview* on the 6th of December, 1815.

"Here are written denials and disavowals enough, but a remark which cannot fail to occur is that here, as in England, none of them are communicated to us in writing. In the teeth of them all, Arbuthnot in his letters, not merely to Hambly and the commanding officer at Fort Gaines, but to Mr. Bagot himself and to

---

[1] Printed in *American State Papers*, Foreign Relations, IV. 416. See Adams, *Memoirs*, December 14, 1818.

dent of the United States, of the continued interest that he takes in the welfare and prosperity of the provinces of La Plata, and of his disposition to recognize the independent government of Buenos Ayres as soon as the time shall have arrived when that step may be taken with advantage to the interests of South America as well as of the United States.

In the meantime he regrets the exequatur to Mr. De Forrest, as Consul General of the United Provinces of South America, cannot be issued for reasons stated in part by the President in his message to Congress at the commencement of their present session, and further explained to Mr. De Forrest by Mr. Adams in the conversation which he has had the honor of holding with him. Mr. De Forrest must have seen that any privileges which may be attached to the con-

---

Nicholls for communication to Lord Bathurst himself declares, that on his leaving New Providence in the autumn of 1812, Governor Cameron gave him, to be communicated to the Indian chiefs a letter from Earl Bathurst, assuring them that the British minister at Washington was instructed to *attend to the rights and interests of the Indians.* In the teeth of them all, he and Ambrister both appeal to a promise stated by the Prophet Francis to have been made to him by the Prince Regent that they should be supplied with arms and ammunition by the governor of New Providence. . . .

"How far the British government may deem it necessary for the vindication of their own good faith and sincerity to deny or to explain the facts alleged by Arbuthnot and Ambrister and the Indian chief may be left to their own consideration. We do not wish to urge a discussion upon the subject, nor to anticipate in any respect the ultimate opinion of the world."

The reply of the British government is summarized in Adams, *Memoirs,* March 26, 1819, and Castlereagh's dispatch to Bagot, January 2, 1819, left no doubt of the opinion of the British government: "In whatever light the course of General Jackson's conduct in these and other proceedings connected with his late operations in the Floridas may be viewed, and to whatever comments certain parts of the evidence adduced upon the trials are open, yet it is impossible not to admit, that the unfortunate sufferers, whatever were their intentions, had been engaged in unauthorized practices of such a description as to have deprived them of any claim on their own government for interference on their behalf." See Rush, *Memoranda of a Residence at the Court of London* (1st Ser.), 450.

sular character cannot avail in the judicial tribunals of this country to influence in any manner the administration of justice, and with regard to the schooner brought into Scituate, such measures have been taken by the authorities of the United States as are warranted by the circumstances of the case and by the existing laws.[1]

With respect to the acknowledgment of the government of Buenos Ayres it has been suggested to Mr. De Forrest that, when adopted, it will be merely the recognition of a fact, without pronouncing or implying an opinion with regard to the *extent* of the territory or provinces under their authority, and particularly without being understood to decide upon their claim to control over the Banda Oriental, Santa Fé, Paraguay, or other provinces disclaiming their supremacy or dominion.

[1] "Of the persons composing the prize crew of the vessel at Scituate, and now in confinement upon charges of murder and piracy, it is understood that there are British subjects and one a citizen of the United States. It is known that commissions for private armed vessels, to be fitted out, armed and manned in this country, have been sent from Buenos Ayres to the United States, with the names of the vessels, commanders and officers in blank, to be filled up here, and have been offered to the avidity of speculators, stimulated more by the thirst for plunder, than by any regard for the South American cause. Of such vessels it is obvious that neither the captains, officers, nor crews, can have any permanent connection with Buenos Ayres, and from the character of those who alone could be induced to engage in such enterprises there is too much reason to expect acts of atrocity, such as those alleged against the persons implicated in the case of the vessel at Scituate. The President wishes to believe that this practice has been without the privity of the government of Buenos Ayres, and he wishes their attention may be drawn to the sentiment that it is incompatible both with the rights and the obligations of the United States: with their rights, as an offensive exercise of sovereign authority by foreigners within their jurisdiction, and without their consent; with their obligations, as involving a violation of the neutrality which they have invariably avowed, and which it is their determination to maintain. The President expects from the friendly disposition manifested by the Supreme Director towards the United States, that no instance of this cause for complaint will hereafter be given." *To David C. De Forrest*, January 1, 1819. Ms.

It was also observed that in acknowledging that government as independent it would be necessary for the United States to understand whether Buenos Ayres itself claims an entire or only an imperfect independence. From certain transactions between persons authorized by the supreme director and an agent of the United States (though unauthorized by their government), *after* the declaration of independence by the Congress at Tucuman and within the last year, it appears that the supreme director declined contracting the engagement that the United States should hereafter enjoy at Buenos Ayres the advantages and privileges of the most favored nation, although with the offer of a reciprocal stipulation on the part of the United States. The reason assigned by the supreme director was that Spain, having claims to the sovereignty of Buenos Ayres, special privileges and advantages might ultimately be granted to the Spanish nation as a consideration for the renunciation of those claims. It is desirable that it should be submitted to the consideration of the government of Buenos Ayres, whether while such a power is reserved their independence is complete, and how far other powers can rely that the authority of Spain might not be eventually restored. It has been stated by Mr. De Forrest that the Congress at Tucuman had passed a resolution to offer special advantages to the nation which should first acknowledge their independence: upon which the question was proposed whether such a resolution, if carried into effect, would not be rather a transfer of dependence from one nation to another than the establishment of independence—rather to purchase support than to obtain recognition. The United States have no intention of exacting favors of Buenos Ayres for the acknowledgment of its independence; but in acknowledging it, they will expect either to enjoy in their intercourse with it the same privileges and advantages as other foreign nations, or to know precisely the extent and character of the benefits which are to be allowed to others and denied to them. It should indeed be known to the supreme director, that while such an indefinite power is reserved of granting to any nation advantages to be withheld from the United States, an acknowledgment of independence must be considered premature.

In adverting to these principles it was observed to Mr. De Forrest that their importance could not be but peculiarly felt by the United States, as having been invariably and conspicuously exemplified in their own practice, both in relation to the country whose colonies they had been, and to that which was the first to acknowledge their independence. In the words of their declaration issued on the 4th of July, 1776, they resolved henceforth "to hold the British nation *as they hold the rest of mankind*, enemies in war, in peace friends:" and in the treaty of amity and commerce concluded on the 5th of February, 1778, between the United States and France, being the first acknowledgment by a foreign power of the independence of the United States, and the first treaty to which they were a party, the preamble declares that the king of France and the United States "willing to fix in an equitable and permanent manner the rules which ought to be followed relative to the correspondence and commerce which the two parties desire to establish between their respective countries, states, and subjects, have judged that the said end could not be better obtained than by taking for the basis of their agreement the most perfect equality and reciprocity, and by carefully avoiding all those burthensome preferences which are usually sources of debate, embarrassment, and discontent; by leaving also each party at liberty to make respecting commerce and navigation those interior regulations which it shall find most convenient to itself, and by founding the advantage of commerce solely upon reciprocal utility and the just rules of free intercourse reserving withal to each party the liberty of admitting at its pleasure other nations to a participation of the same advantage."

In the 2d article of the same treaty it was also stipulated that neither the United States nor France should henceforth grant any particular favor to other nations in respect of commerce and navigation, which should not immediately become common to the other nation freely, if the concession was free, or for the same compensation if conditional.

In answer to Mr. De Forrest's note of the 12th instant Mr. Adams has the honor of assuring him that the President has received with much satisfaction the information contained in it, and will have great pleasure from every event which shall contribute to the stability and honor of the government of Buenos Ayres.

Mr. Adams requests Mr. De Forrest to accept the assurance of his distinguished consideration.

Washington, December 31, 1818.[1]

---

[1] In a volume of *Letters from Washington,* published as "by a foreigner," but known to have been written by George Waterston, of the Library of Congress, during the winter of 1817-18, appeared a sketch of the Secretary of State. "Mr. Adams is in person short, thick, and fat, resembling a little in his face, the portrait of his father which you have seen; and neither very agreeable nor very repulsive. He is between forty-five and fifty years of age, and seems to be vigorous and healthy. He is regular in his habits, and moral and temperate in his life. To great talent, he unites unceasing industry and perseverance, and an uncommon facility in the execution of business. . . . Mr. Adams is extremely plain and simple, both in his manners and habiliments; and labors to avoid alike the foolery and splendor of 'fantastic fashion,' and the mean and inelegant costume of affected eccentricity. He is evidently well-skilled in the rhetorical art on which he has lectured, and in which he displays considerable research and ability; but whether he succeeded in reducing his principles to practice, while a member of the senate, I am not able to

TO RICHARD RUSH

Department of State,
Washington, 1 January,[1] 1819.

It is mentioned in one of your dispatches that Lord Castlereagh had made some enquiry of you, in what light the deputies from the South American revolutionary govern-

say. I should infer, however, that his speeches were more correct and polished, if they were not more eloquent, than those of his coadjutors in legislation. . . . From what I can learn, Mr. Adams, with all his knowledge and talent, did not attain the first rank among American orators. He wanted enthusiasm and fire; he wanted that nameless charm, which in oratory as well as poetry, delights and fascinates, and leads the soul captive, without the desire of resistance, or the consciousness of error. . . . In close argumentation, in logical analysis, in amplification and regular disposition, he is said to have been inferior to none. . . . Mr. Adams's prominent inclination, however, appears to be political. To be eminent as a statesman is his predominant ambition. . . . He is not one of those statesmen who theorize when experience can afford its aid, and avoids the application of abstract principles, when plainer and more obvious ones are calculated to subserve the object in view. He is sedate, circumspect, and cautious; reserved, but not distant; grave, but not repulsive. He receives, but seldom communicates, and discerns with great quickness, motives however latent, and intentions however concealed by the contorsions of cunning, or the drapery of hypocrisy. This penetration seems to be intuitive and natural. . . . It is the operation of native judgment and not the exercise of acquired cunning. . . . Mr. Adams has more capacity than genius; he can comprehend better than he can invent; and execute nearly as rapidly as he can design. Though as a public minister, he had no great opportunity to display his powers, yet, from the little he exhibited, a judgment may be formed of his ability in that character. He has all the penetration, shrewdness, and perseverance, necessary to constitute an able diplomatist, united with the capacity to perceive, and the eloquence to enforce, what would conduce to the welfare and interests of his country. . . . In short there is no public character in the United States, that has more intellectual power, the moral inclination to be more useful, or that will labor with greater assiduity to discharge the important duties he owes to himself and to his country." (Pp. 43–48.)

[1] This is the date on which the draft of the dispatch was begun. See Adams, *Memoirs*, January 2, 1819.

ments were considered by that of the United States? They have not been received or recognized in their official capacities, because that would have been equivalent to a formal recognition of the governments from which they come as independent; but informal communications have been held with them, both verbal and written, freely and without disguise. We have considered the struggle between Spain and those colonies as a *civil war*, the essential question of which was their independence of, or subjection to Spain. To this war the avowed and real policy of the United States has been to remain *neutral*, and the principles of neutrality which we consider as applicable to the case are these: First, that the parties have in respect to foreign nations *equal rights*, and are entitled, as far as is practicable, to equal and the same treatment. Secondly, that while the contest is maintained, on both sides, with any reasonable prospect of eventual success, it would be a departure from neutrality to recognize, either the supremacy contended for by Spain, or the independence contended for by the South Americans. For to acknowledge either would be to take the side of that party, upon the very question at issue between them.

But while this state of things continues, an entire equality of treatment of the parties is not possible. There are circumstances arising from the nature of the contest itself which produce unavoidable inequalities. Spain, for instance, is an acknowledged sovereign power, and as such has ministers and other accredited and privileged agents to maintain her interests and support her rights conformably to the usages of nations. The South Americans, not being acknowledged as sovereign and independent states, cannot have the benefit of such officers. We consider it, however, as among the obligations of neutrality to obviate this inequality as far as may be practicable without taking a side, as if the question of the war was decided. We listen, therefore, to the representations of their deputies or agents, and do them justice as much as if they were formally accredited. By acknowledging the existence of a *civil war*, the right of Spain, *as understood by herself*, is no doubt affected. She is no longer recognized as the sovereign of the provinces in revolution against her. Thus far neutrality itself operates against her and not against the other party. This also is an inequality arising from the nature of the struggle, unavoidable, and therefore not incompatible, with neutrality.

But this state of things is temporary; and neither do the obligations of neutrality require, nor do the rights, duties or interests of the neutral states permit that it shall be unreasonably protracted. It naturally terminates with the preponderating success of either of the parties to the war. If, therefore, we consider the civil war as no longer existing between Spain and Mexico, because there is no longer in that province an organized government, claiming to be sovereign and independent, and maintaining that claim by force of arms, upon the same principle though differently applied we think the period is fast approaching when it will be no longer a civil war between Spain and Buenos Ayres, because the independence of the latter will be so firmly established as to be beyond the reach of any reasonable pretension of supremacy on the part of Spain. The mediation of the allied European powers between Spain and her revolted colonies was solicited by Spain, with the professed object of obtaining from the allies a guarantee of the restoration of her sovereign authority in South America. But the very acceptance of the office of mediators, upon such a basis, would have been a departure from neutrality by the allies. This was clearly seen by Great Britain, who very explicitly and repeatedly declared that her intention was in no event whatever resulting from the mediation to employ force against the South Americans.[1]

The allies did, however, assent to become the mediators at the request of Spain alone, and upon the basis that the object of the mediation should be the restoration of the Spanish authority, though with certain modifications favorable to the colonies. As the United States were never invited to take a part in that mediation, so, as you have been instructed, they neither desired, nor would have consented to become parties to it upon that basis. It appears in one of your conversations with Lord Castlereagh, he expressed some regret that the views of this government in relation to that question were not precisely the same as those of the British cabinet, and that we disapprove of any interposition of third parties, upon any other basis than that of the total emancipation of the colonies.

[1] "The Russian government has indeed shown an interest in behalf of Spain which may perhaps not be reconcilable with a very rigid neutrality, by the sale of a whole squadron of ships of war, and by sending them during the war full-armed to the ports of Spain. Mr. Poletica, however, does not consider it in this light, but as a simple sale, without reference to the objects to which Spain might appropriate the ships, and without at all intending to take a decided part against the colonies. It is understood also that at the Congress of Aix-la-Chapelle the disposition of Russia against the colonies and in favor of Spain was more strongly marked than that of any other of the powers, and Mr. Poletica has made known to me that he was instructed, if the recognition of Buenos Ayres by the United States should not have taken place upon his arrival here, to use whatever influence he might possess, consistent with a due respect and deference for this government, to dissuade us from the adoption of this measure, as *an act of hostility* against Spain, the Emperor's ally. We have not recognized the independence of Buenos Ayres, nor is it the intention of the President to adopt that measure with precipitation. Should it take place after an adjustment of our own differences with Spain, it will certainly not be with any views of hostility to her." *To George Washington Campbell*, June 3, 1819. Ms.

Gallatin was in a good position to know the actual relations of Spain to the allied powers of Europe and the proposals of mediation made. Adams, *Writings of Gallatin*, I. 72-76.

The President wishes you to take an early and suitable occasion [1] to observe to Lord Castlereagh, that he hopes the difference between our views and those of Great Britain is more of form than substance—more founded in the degree of complacency respectively due by the parties to the views of Spain, than to any inherent difference of opinion upon the question to be solved. That as *neutrals* to the civil war, we think that no mediation between the parties ought even to be *undertaken*, without the assent of both parties to the war. That whether we consider the question of the conflict between Spanish colonial dominion and South American independence upon principles, moral or political, or upon those of the interest of either party to the war, or of all other nations as connected with them; whether upon grounds of right or of fact, they all bring us to the same conclusion that the contest cannot and ought not to terminate otherwise than by the total independence of South America. Anxious, however, to fulfil every obligation of good neighborhood to Spain, notwithstanding our numerous and aggravated causes of complaint against her, and especially desirous to preserve the friendship and good-will of all the allied European powers, we have forborne under circumstances of strong provocation to take any decisive step which might interfere with the course of their policy in relation to South America. We have waited patiently to see the effect of their mediation, without an attempt to disconcert or defeat any measures upon which they might agree for assuring its success. But convinced as we are that the Spanish authority never can be restored at Buenos Ayres, in Chile or Venezuela, we wish the British government and all the European allies to consider, how impor-

---

[1] Rush communicated the dispatch to Lord Castlereagh on February 12. *Memoranda of a Residence at the Court of London* (2nd Ser.), 15.

tant it is to them, as well as to us, that these newly formed states should be regularly recognized; not only because the right to such recognition cannot with justice be long denied to them, but that they may be held to observe on their part the ordinary rules of the laws of nations in their intercourse with the civilized world. We particularly believe that the only effectual means of repressing the excessive irregularities and piratical depredations of armed vessels under their flags, and bearing their commissions, will be to require of them the observance of the principles sanctioned by the practice of maritime nations. It is not to be expected that they will feel themselves bound by the ordinary duties of sovereign states while they are denied the enjoyment of all their rights.

The government at Buenos Ayres have appointed a consul general to reside in the United States. He applied as long since as last May, and again very recently, for an exequatur, which has not been issued, because that would be a formal recognition of his government. You will in the most friendly manner mention to Lord Castlereagh that the President has it in contemplation to grant this exequatur, or otherwise to recognize the government of Buenos Ayres at no remote period, should no event occur which will justify a further postponement of that intention. If it should suit the views of Great Britain to adopt similar measures at the same time and in concert with us, it will be highly satisfactory to the President. It will when adopted be a mere acknowledgment of the fact of independence, and without deciding upon the extent of their territory, or upon their claims to sovereignty in any part of the provinces of La Plata, where it is not established and uncontested.

I am, etc.

TO JOHN HOLMES [1]

DEPARTMENT OF STATE, January 20, 1819.

SIR:

In answer to the questions in your letter of the 16th instant I have the honor to state that Amelia Island is held under the authority of the act of Congress of January 15, 1811, and is intended to be held as long as the reasons upon which it was taken shall continue, subject, of course, to any other provision which Congress may deem necessary or expedient. It is under a military government. No customs are collected, no vessels being permitted to enter the port. Of its population the only evidence possessed is contained in the extract of a letter from Colonel Bankhead, a copy of which is herewith enclosed.

I am, etc.

TO DON LUIS DE ONIS [2]

DEPARTMENT OF STATE,
WASHINGTON, 29 January, 1819.

SIR:

Your letter of the 16th instant has been submitted to the consideration of the President of the United States, by

---

[1] Printed in *American State Papers*, Foreign Relations, V. 12. Bankhead's letter is also there printed.

[2] Printed in *American State Papers*, Foreign Relations, IV. 616.

Adams favored asking Congress to authorize the President to hold Pensacola and St. Marks and even the entire province of Florida, if Spain failed to fulfil her engagement to restrain the Indians within her territory from hostilities against the United States. Without such authority he believed nothing could be done in the negotiations on boundaries and claims so long pending between the United States whose direction I have the honor of informing you that the proposal to draw the western boundary line between the United States and the Spanish territories on this continent from the source of the Missouri to the Columbia River cannot be admitted. I have to add that for the purpose of an immediate arrangement of affairs with Spain, this government repeats the proposal contained in my letter to you of 31st October last; and if you are not authorized to agree to it, we are willing to adjust the other subjects of difference, leaving that to be settled hereafter. But if your powers are incompetent to accept either of these offers, the President thinks it useless to pursue the discussion any further of subjects upon which there can be no hope entertained of concluding an agreement between us.[1]

Be pleased to accept, etc.

---

and Spain. The discussion in the Cabinet on this question is given in Adams, *Memoirs*, January 2, 1819. Onis who had received new powers, expressed his earnest desire of concluding a treaty; but both the President and Adams were wearied by the fruitless discussion of matters on which an agreement was out of the question. As Onis insisted upon a reply to his note, the above was prepared. At the same time the President determined to make a concession on the western boundary, and with the French minister as intermediary, Adams prepared the way for a treaty. The *Memoirs* are full on the steps taken.

[1] On January 28 the Secretary of State sent to the President a report on the applications made by the independent governments of South America to have a minister or consul general accredited by the government of the United States. It was prepared in compliance with a resolution of the House of Representatives of January 14, and was laid before the House January 29. It is printed in *American State Papers*, Foreign Relations, IV. 412. See Adams, *Memoirs*, January 19, 20, 22.

TO JOHN ADAMS

WASHINGTON, 14 February, 1819.

MY DEAR SIR:

You have seen and heard something of the political agitation which has been excited at a late period of this session of Congress, and may perhaps have some perception of the unseen causes which produce the ostensible effects. You observe that I have become a favorite target for the sharpshooters, but there appears to me to be something very whimsical in the choice of their weapons. Of the transactions behind the scenes I know no more, perhaps not so much as you. That the South American horse should be ridden as long as he had legs to stand on, and that he should if possible be spurred rough-shod over me, was to be expected. But that the champions of Puyrredon and Bolivar should, at the next breath, become the champions of Pizarro and Onis; that the sympathies of Buenos Ayrean patriotism should melt into tender mercies for Arbuthnot and Ambrister; that General Jackson should be insinuated a murderer, for hanging murderers, and another officer extolled as a hero, for going out to be murdered to atone for a breach of discipline—all these, and numbers numberless more, are metamorphoses, logical and rhetorical, which put to shame all the metamorphoses poetical of Ovid. Pelion has been heaped upon Ossa to put down poor old Hickory—all with perfect respect for his character, with profound gratitude for his services, with entire conviction that those against whom he has perpetrated these enormous wrongs have a right to complain of them or demand satisfaction for them, with undoubting confidence in the purity and patriotism of his motives. Jackson was their friend—they admired him, they venerated him. But the Constitution! Oh! the Constitution and military usurpation, and cruel despotism! And so to guard the sacred Palladium of the Constitution, a bill of attainder upon Jackson's reputation was to be passed by one branch of the legislature, without hearing him in his own defense. As to the right of censuring without hearing him, who could doubt that? For it was not the man, it was only his conduct that was to be censured. And why should not a man be blamed as well as praised, without being heard for himself? Votes of thanks were always granted without calling upon the party to prove himself worthy of them, and why should not a vote of censure be passed, without calling upon the interested party to show that it was not deserved? From this style of argument may be inferred how much and how little of the real merits of the case operated on the *intended* vote of censure. But the event turned out different from what was contemplated. For a solemn vote of the House, passed by a considerable majority, has sanctioned every act that was to be blasted by a vote of disapprobation.

It has been asserted and maintained with some earnestness that this has not been treated as a party question; and to a certain extent it is undoubtedly true. All the known denominations of parties have been broken down by the debate and the vote. Neither the geographical, nor the political, nor the personal, standard has rallied all its votaries on either side. The inveterate avowed enemies of the Administration have, however, been the most decided in their virulence against Jackson. Many of those who at the last session voted against the Administration, have now been steadily in its power. Still more of those who were then its friends have now deserted its banners. Some are moved by state prejudices and resentments. Some by the doubts of really timorous consciences; some by considerations altogether personal. The art of a political partisan in Congress, at this time, is to unite as many various motives as possible under the banners of one pretext. In this instance the motives have been various and the pretext has been captivating. A strong minority therefore was formed, but a minority which will not be likely to adhere together upon any other important question; certainly not to form any permanent organized coalition. The views of those whose conduct has been governed principally by attachments to individuals have not been unanimous. And the individuals with whom the strongest combination of votes usually sympathizes, have considered the merits of the question in different lights, and come to opposite conclusions. New York and Georgia did not agree. Virginia was about equally divided against herself. So was Kentucky; and if the eloquence of the Speaker made some proselytes, he lost as many or more by the result of twenty days of discussion than he gained.

In one thing the enemies of General Jackson and mine heartily coalesced and completely succeeded. That is they involved me, and me alone, in the whole responsibility of all his acts. There was no other member of the Administration who had less or even so little concern with them, or agency over them, until long after they were past and irretrievable. The orders by which he was authorized to enter Spanish Florida had issued from the War Department, without my being consulted, and without my knowledge. His correspondence was entirely with that Department. But from the instant that the Spanish Minister, Onis, knew that Jackson had authority to enter Florida, he began to remonstrate against it, and every step that he advanced

Onis assailed me with a new and more vehement note of remonstrance. In proportion as the facts were made known to the Spanish government, the Minister of State there repeated his complaints with increasing heat of crimination and demand of satisfaction, until, on the 31st of August, he formally suspended all negotiation, and threatened war by a note which was communicated to all the courts and published in all the newspapers of Europe.

To all these complaints, and accusations and menaces, it was the duty of my office to answer, which I did by the letters to Mr. Erving of 23 November and 2 December. It was strictly and exclusively an answer to Spain and her complaints. But immediately after the meeting of Congress and of the Virginia legislature, an attempt was made to concert a joint attack by the latter, and by both houses of the former upon General Jackson and upon the President, but most especially upon the Secretary of State. At Richmond, after some preliminary skirmishing by the editor of the *Enquirer*,[1] forth came Jack the Giant Killer, Algernon Sydney,[2] and opened a battery upon the whole military career of General Jackson. A similar battery was immediately afterwards opened in the House of Representatives of Congress, by a member from Georgia; while in the Senate, another member from Georgia was working under him a mine to be blown up as soon as the favorable occasion should be presented. It was soon known that the complaints of the Spanish government had been answered by a dispatch from the Department of State to Mr. Erving, and immediately there came a call for it from the House. It was given, and no sooner printed in the *Richmond Enquirer*, than Alger-

[1] Thomas Ritchie.
[2] Benjamin Watkins Leigh. The letters were printed in a pamphlet, *Letters of Algernon Sydney in Defence of Civil Liberty*, Richmond, 1830.

non Sydney, transferring his attack from Jackson to me, filled in two numbers of falsehood and sophistry, eight or nine columns of that paper with invective against me for having defended Jackson against the complaints of Spain. Then came on the debates in Congress, Algernon Sydney having given the cue by pretending that I alone of the President's advisers had counselled the course pursued by him with regard to Jackson's proceedings, and that my letter to Erving was to be viewed, not as an answer to Pizarro and Spain, but as an elaborate effort to vindicate myself before the people of this country. The first of those assertions was false, and the second was a disingenuous misrepresentation, to which Clay, however, gave further countenance in his first speech on the subject. The object and result of it all was to identify the Secretary of State with all Jackson's sins and make him responsible for them all, and for those of the President, for not trying him by a court-martial, as well as for his own. Since this glorious conspiracy has failed, and neither the Virginia legislature, nor the House of Representatives, nor the Senate of the United States, has been bullied or inveigled into the plot, and as the whole proceeding is discountenanced by the popular opinion throughout the Union, I see the newspapers are contradicting Algernon Sydney's lie, that the Secretary of State *alone* counselled the course pursued by the President with regard to Jackson's proceedings, and stating, as was the fact, that it was with the unanimous concurrence of all the heads of Departments. The bunglers have found that what they meant for calumny was working as commendation.

I have barely room to assure you of my unalterable duty and affection.

TO DON LUIS DE ONIS

Mr. Adams presents his compliments to the Chevalier de Onis, and has the honor of sending him a copy of the treaty, as definitively drawn up and acceded to by the President of the United States, in our language, to which it will be necessary to have the Spanish copy made conformable. Mr. Onis will perceive that the President has consented to several of the modifications proposed on the part of Mr. de Onis and by him; the rest have on full deliberation been concluded to be inadmissible. Any variation from the draft now sent could have no effect other than of leading to new discussions which would defeat the common object of coming to an immediate conclusion. As soon as the Spanish copy shall have been prepared Mr. Adams will thank Mr. de Onis to have the originals in both languages made out so that they may be executed next Monday morning, and every assistance from this Department will be given to effect that object.[1]

Department of State, 19 February, 1819.

[1] The two projets of a treaty, the one submitted by Onis, on February 9, and the other by Adams, on February 13, are in *American State Papers*, Foreign Relations, IV. 617, 619. The illness of Onis led to an interview with the French minister, and the note embodying the objections and replies is in *Ib.*, 621. Adams, *Memoirs*, February 11-20, 1819, gives full details of the discussions between the negotiators of the treaty and in the President's Cabinet, and thus bears testimony to his own part, to which the successful issue was so largely due. The treaty was signed February 22, 1819, and on that day Adams summarized in his *Memoirs* the features of the treaty, the gains and possible dangers.

CERTIFICATE

WASHINGTON, 22d February, 1819.

I hereby certify that on the eleventh of June, 1815, I embarked in company with Mr. Jonathan Russell in the United States ship *John Adams*, Captain Samuel Angus, at Gothenburg, whence we proceeded to the Texel. There Mr. Russell and I went on by land to Ghent, and shortly afterwards the *John Adams* returned to the United States. That on the day when we embarked at Gothenburg Captain James Barron did apply to Captain Angus for a passage on board that vessel to the United States. That Captain Angus declared himself entirely disposed to give a passage to Captain Barron, referred him to Mr. Russell and myself for the opinion whether this could be done consistently with the cartel flag under which the ship was then sailing. That Captain Barron then stated to me that his motive for wishing to return to the United States at that time was his earnest desire to offer his professional services to his country in the war in which she was engaged, and to claim employment in the station to which he was entitled in the Navy. That Mr. Russell and myself highly approving the motive of Captain Barron, nevertheless felt ourselves compelled, though with reluctance, to give it as our opinion to Captain Angus that he could not consistently with his cartel give a passage to Captain Barron, which Captain Angus accordingly declined, to the great disappointment as I understood of Captain Barron. He then informed me that he had made the journey from Copenhagen to Gothenburg for no other purpose than that of obtaining his passage home in the above mentioned vessel.

TO HYDE DE NEUVILLE [1]

Private. WASHINGTON, [17] March, 1819.
SIR:
   I have the honor of requesting your answers to the following questions:
   1. Whether, during the negotiation of the late treaty between the United States and Spain, you were in constant confidential communication concerning it, and the subjects treated of in it, with the Spanish minister, Don Luis de Onis?
   2. Whether, in the week preceding the conclusion of the treaty, Mr. Onis was confined by indisposition to his house, and whether several communications, verbal and written, were made from him to me through your amicable intervention?
   3. Whether, through the whole course of the negotiation, it was explicitly understood by him, by yourself and by me, that the grants of lands in the Floridas, which had been rumored to have been made the preceding year by the King of Spain to the Duke of Alagon, Count Puñon Rostro and Mr. Vargas, were null and void, and to be so held under the treaty?
   4. Whether you expressly told me a few days before the signature of the treaty, that Mr. Onis felt a personal point

---

[1] Adams, *Memoirs*, March 17, 1819. Clay had told the President on March 8, the rumor that these grants of land in Florida bore date January 23, 1818, or one day earlier than that named in the treaty, subsequent to which all grants were declared null and void. In communicating this information to Adams, Monroe said, "If this is the case a most shameful fraud has been practiced." De Neuville gave assurance of his full understanding that these grants were null and void; but Onis, while admitting that he had the same understanding when he signed the treaty, said he should have insisted on their validity had he known of this prior date.

of honor, that those grants should be held null and void, inasmuch as rumors derogatory to his honor had been spread abroad, that he was personally interested in them?

5. Whether, since the conclusion of the treaty, a report having been circulated that those grants were made before the 24th of January, the date subsequent to which all grants are declared by the treaty to be null and void, you have mentioned this report to Mr. Onis, and whether he then assured you that it was his full and clear understanding that *all* the above mentioned grants were by the treaty null and void?

6. Whether you have told me that it was within your certain knowledge, that the Spanish government itself was fully aware that by the treaty all those grants would be null and void?

It is not to be expected that there will be any difference of understanding between the United States and Spain with regard to the operation of the article of the treaty relating to the grants of lands. The date of the 24th of January, 1818, was assented to at the proposition of Mr. de Onis, and with the understanding on both sides that the above mentioned grants were of a subsequent date. If Mr. Onis has committed an error in the date, it will only be necessary that it should be explained to the Spanish government at the exchange of the ratifications; to which effect Mr. Forsyth is instructed. No public use, therefore, is intended to be made of your answers now requested; but as everything on the part of the United States has been done in the most perfect *good faith*, and as you remember it was agreed that the articles concerning the cession should be drawn up in perfect good faith, and in such manner as to shield the honor of both countries, I am desirous of having your answers to the above questions, as a precaution, however unnecessary, to guard against the possibility of any future misunderstanding with regard to the interest and operation of that article of the treaty.

I pray you to accept, etc.[1]

TO DON LUIS DE ONIS

DEPARTMENT OF STATE,
WASHINGTON, 20 March, 1819.

SIR:

I have had the honor of receiving your letter of the 10th [2] instant, containing the candid declaration on your part that upon the signature of the treaty of 22 February last, it was your clear and explicit understanding that the grants of lands, said to have been made in the course of the preceding winter, to the Duke of Alagon, the Count of Puñon Rostro, and Mr. Vargas, were included among those declared by the 8th article of the treaty to be null and void, whatever their dates may have been. This frank explanation, with the declaration to the same effect which Mr. Forsyth is instructed to deliver on exchanging the ratifications of the treaty, will prevent the possibility of any misunderstanding between our two governments, and vindicate their unsullied good faith in this connection.[3] But to avoid alike the

---

[1] On March 17 an official inquiry was made of the French minister on these alleged grants, to which he replied on the following day. Both notes are printed in *American State Papers*, Foreign Relations, IV. 652, 653. Satisfactory as was the reply, the doubt remained, and on July 14, Adams submitted some "Observations" on the article of the treaty applying to land grants by the King of Spain. It is printed in *Ib.*, 653.

[2] Printed in *American State Papers*, Foreign Relations, IV. 651.

[3] The instructions to Forsyth, dated March 8, 1819, are in *American State Papers*, Foreign Relations, IV. 650.

chance of any transaction between individuals, which might arise from a premature and imperfect knowledge of the contents and intent of the treaty, and which might involve inconvenience or injury to them, I have to request that you would have the goodness to write immediately to the governor general of the island of Cuba, and to the governor of Florida at St. Augustine, and to the Spanish commanding officer at Pensacola informing him of the substance of that article, and of the intention and understanding between us, that under it, the above mentioned grants will be null and void. I would also further request you to give notice to those officers of the stipulation of the 2nd article, that all the documents and archives relating to the property and sovereignty of the two provinces are to be delivered up with them to the officers of the United States who may be duly authorized to receive them. And to recommend particularly to their attention that such care may in the interval be taken of the said documents and archives as may serve an effectual performance of this condition of the treaty. This suggestion has been rendered necessary by advices received at this Department of apprehensions entertained that in the event of the cession and evacuation of those provinces, there is an intention of carrying the documents and archives away.

I renew, etc.

TO HYDE DE NEUVILLE [1]

Department of State,
Washington, March 31, 1819

Sir:

The proposal contained in your letter of the 29th instant of concluding a consular convention between the United States and France, for the purpose of stipulating the mutual restoration of seamen deserting from the armed or merchant vessels of either nation in the ports of the other, has been submitted to the President of the United States, by whose direction I have the honor of informing you that he thinks a partial arrangement of one particular subject of interest in the commercial relations between the two countries would be liable to inconvenience, and less satisfactory, than a general review of those relations with the view of coming to arrangements concerning them, which may be calculated to promote the interests of both, and to strengthen and perpetuate the friendship and good understanding subsisting between them. . . .

I take this opportunity to acknowledge, also, the receipt of your note of the 20th instant, announcing your intention to avail yourself of a leave of absence from your sovereign to pay the visit to your country to which I have referred. I am directed by the President to assure you of the great satisfaction which he takes in bearing testimony to the propriety and friendliness of your conduct and deportment since you have resided here as the representative of France, and of his peculiar sensibility to the interest which, as the organ of your government, you have taken in promoting a conciliatory adjustment of the long standing and compli-

[1] Printed in *American State Papers*, Foreign Relations, V. 156.

cated differences between the United States and Spain. The minister of the United States in France has been instructed to make known to your government these sentiments of the President, to which I beg leave to add the assurance of my best wishes that your excursion may be prosperous and agreeable to you, and that at no distant day, if it suits your own views and those of your government, we may again welcome your return to your station at this place.

I pray you, etc.

TO THE PRESIDENT [1]

[JAMES MONROE]

WASHINGTON, 14 April, 1819.

DEAR SIR:

Mr. Hay called at the office of this Department yesterday with a copy of the correspondence between the Secretary of War and General Scott, immediately before the pamphlet [2] publication by that officer of his correspondence with General Jackson, with his comments upon it. Mr. Hay observed to me, that regretting on various accounts, but especially from motives of regard and friendship for General Scott, the publication, you had thought a question might arise from it, whether in the probable event of your meeting General Jackson in your present tour, anything which has yet occurred in this unfortunate difference between these two distinguished commanders would make it necessary or proper that your conduct towards General Jackson should be different from what it would have been, had the publi-

---

[1] Monroe left Washington March 30, for a southern and western tour.
[2] Adams, *Memoirs*, April 3 and 13, 1819.

cation not taken place, and considering it as a question involving public interests, it would be acceptable to you to have my opinion among those of persons in great confidence whom you would think proper to consult. If there is anything in the correspondence requiring public animadversion from the President of the United States in regard to the conduct of General Jackson, I believe it to be the invitation to a challenge at the close of his second letter to General Scott. Whether it is an express violation of the 25th Article of War or not, might be a question for legal subtlety and military candor to debate for the decision of a court-martial; but with a suitable portion of deference for the code of honor, I conceive that if the provocation to a duel had been regularly brought to the cognizance of the President of the United States, commander in chief of their armies, some token of discountenance to it would have been necessary from him, especially to counteract the pernicious effect of the example upon the whole army and the nation, thus given by one of the highest and most illustrious of its commanders. But, besides that this exceptionable part of General Jackson's conduct is made public without his consent and under circumstances which may not require the official notice of the President, I apprehend that this is not the point upon which you think deliberation to be requisite. It is but an incident, the tendency and character of which may be entirely overlooked at the present moment by the public and there are perhaps sound reasons for avoiding to make it a permanent feature of a contest which in the estimation of both parties and of the country presents points of public interest far otherwise important. I mention it now, because I do believe that if in consequence of what has happened or may happen, a meeting should take place between these two officers and either of them should fall, the country would look at the affair from a different point of view, and the Articles of War and the duty of the executive to take care that the laws shall be faithfully executed, and the odious side of duelling would be remembered. In that event, it might be inquired whether the President, with full knowledge of a challenge *standing* between two of the most eminent officers and valuable citizens of this nation, had thought proper in any manner to interpose with a view to prevent a catastrophe which in either case would be considered as a public calamity. But in submitting this reflection to your mind, I am far from thinking that a *public* manifestation of your displeasure at this part of the controversy could be either expedient on public considerations or tending to prevent the actual meeting. There is nothing else in the case which appears to me to call for any change in the forms of personal intercourse which may occur between the President and General Jackson. You may perhaps not think it necessary to decide whether the publication of General Scott is a violation of the order of 21 February, 1818, or not. If the decision can with propriety, I think it should be avoided. The public opinion to which he has appealed is, in the present stage of the controversy, not in his favor. He has not thought it necessary to observe much delicacy, either towards the President or the Secretary of War. But his charge against Governor Clinton upon surmises, very feebly supported upon his own statements, by the explicit denial of that gentleman, has recoiled upon Scott himself in a manner from which it is yet to be seen how he will extricate himself. Having a personal regard and friendship for him, as well as a very high sense of his public services, I should wish that no measure of severity should be taken by the executive against him in a case upon which it is probable the judgment of the tribunal to which he has had voluntary recourse, will bear more heavily upon him than he will find it easy to abide. I am, etc.

TO HYDE DE NEUVILLE

DEPARTMENT OF STATE,
WASHINGTON, 15 April, 1819.

SIR:

In reference to your official notes of 22 March and of the 8th of this month, I have the honor of informing you that instructions have been forwarded from this Department to the district attorney of the United States at Baltimore [1] directing him to examine the evidence in the cases of the privateers alleged to have been fitted out at that place, and to have committed piratical depredations upon French subjects and their property, as set forth in the documents enclosed with your notes, and to commence prosecutions in every case where the evidence is sufficient to support him.

You have justly observed, sir, in the acts of Congress and in the measures of the executive government of the United States to suppress these unlawful armaments in their ports, the earnest and constant solicitude with which that object has been, and will continue to be pursued.

With regard to the ideas suggested in your note of 22 March, of a common agreement to be adopted by all governments, or by several in amity with each other, to declare as pirate every privateer with a commission delivered with blanks left for the names, or unlimited in point of time, or whose captain and at least half the crew should not be natives of the country under whose flag the privateer shall be navigated, I would submit to your enlightened considera-

[1] Glenn.

tion, that independently of the question whether all or any of the nations of Europe are prepared to agree upon such a mutual stipulation, there might be great difficulty to the admission of the principle in the code of the United States. By the laws of nations the punishment denounced against the crime of piracy is capital, a severity which, by the institutions of the United States, is confined to very few crimes of the most atrocious character. It would scarcely be compatible with the sentiments prevailing in this nation to extend that heaviest of all penalties to offences the malignity of which might be so different in degree, according to the circumstances under which they might be perpetrated.

It is doubtless desirable to the whole community of civilized nations that the contest between Spain and the South Americans should be speedily terminated. But how far it may be the right of foreign nations to interpose for its termination, and upon what principles it should be promoted, are points upon which Europe is apparently not agreed, either with itself, or with the United States. It has hitherto been the policy of all, however, to take no part in the controversy affecting the rights or claims of either of the parties; and under the present circumstances would it be practicable to agree upon the rules in question, without formally admitting both parties to that controversy as parties to the compact which should adopt them, and without thereby recognizing both as sovereigns capable of contracting engagements binding upon the whole civilized world?

Notwithstanding these objections, the weight of which will be justly estimated by you, the regulations themselves, that commissions like those which you have designated, should be held irregular and unlawful, that captures made under them should be pronounced invalid, and even that penalties short of those inflicted for piracy should be prescribed to punish and deter the subjects of the several sovereigns who might mutually contract to prohibit them, appear to me to be fair subjects for discussion and agreement between friendly powers; and so far as concerns the United States and France, would very readily be on our part admitted among those upon which a new treaty of amity, commerce and navigation might be concluded. Such a treaty would, it is hoped, confirm and cement the harmony subsisting between our countries, and will be cheerfully entered upon by us, whenever it may suit the views and convenience of your government.

I repeat with pleasure, etc.

TO RICHARD RUSH

WASHINGTON, 2nd May, 1819.

DEAR SIR:

I am to acknowledge the receipt of your private letters of 9th September, and duplicate 28th October, and duplicate 28th November, and 12th January duplicate, with a sibylline leaf of 20th January, and if you could see my file of *unanswered letters* upon which they have been successively taking their places since I returned to this city on the 14th October last, I am afraid it would produce in you the determined resolution to break up our private correspondence altogether. This I should greatly regret; though without being *mendacior Parthis* I cannot promise more future punctuality of return than your past experience will warrant you to expect. You must put it upon the footing of charity and set down to the account of your good deeds every private letter that you write me. If indeed the measure of my occupations depended altogether upon the movements of the *corps diplomatique* accredited here, I should have reason to flatter myself with the hope of a long holiday, since the ministers of the three governments with which we have the greatest and most frequent *tracasseries* have all taken furloughs at the same time. Mr. Bagot will be the bearer of this letter, if it can reach him at Annapolis before he sails. Don Luis de Onis and his family are on their way to New York, where they are to embark in the *James Monroe* and sail for Liverpool on the 10th of this month. And Mr. Hyde de Neuville with his family are to follow in the course of another month. They all go upon leave of absence, but I believe all without any expectation of coming back. They are all regretted, for although Mr. Onis's mission began in a tempest and has been constantly *squally*, it has terminated with so much satisfaction to himself, and with the *prospect* of so much satisfaction to us, that we part very good friends. I say the *prospect* of satisfaction to us, because we have yet to wait for the ratification and execution of the treaty of 22nd February, and in the convulsive state of Spain we can reckon upon nothing as secure until it is in our actual possession. Mr. Bagot's career in this country has been much shorter and much easier than that of Don Luis; but the mission to the United States of a British minister (and as you well know *vice versa*) can never be a bed of roses. Mr. Bagot's conduct and deportment have been not merely and invariably unexceptionable, but have been truly those of a minister of peace, such as the diplomatic character ought to be, to answer the real, wise and benevolent purposes of its institution. His language has always been temperate and respectful, and his observance of the manners and feelings of the country always cautiously void of offense. The President wishes you to take some occasion to express in strong terms to Lord Castlereagh the satisfaction which Mr. Bagot has given in all his relations, official and individual, and the favorable impressions that it has produced on the government and on the public sentiment of the nation.[1] And as you are in a friendly personal intercourse with the family relations of Mrs. Bagot, it will be pleasing to them and very gratifying to me, if you will take care to let them know how justly and sincerely the virtues and accomplishments of that lady are estimated here, and how forcibly they have seconded and promoted the conciliatory disposition manifested through the whole period of his mission by her husband. In rendering this tribute of justice to her I take the greater satisfaction, as I have a grateful recollection of the many civilities for which I was indebted to her parents during my own residence in England, and also to her uncle, Mr. Villiers, to whose kind remembrance I am happy to have this opportunity of asking you to recall me.

Mr. de Neuville's return to his country I am apprehensive will not be a reception so satisfactory, or to friends in such high favor, as may be anticipated by Mr. Bagot. His diplomatic service here has had its difficulties and its asperities. But in all the intercourse that I have had with European statesmen, I have not met with a man of higher sentiments of honor, of kinder and more generous feelings, or of a fairer and more candid mind. I say this with the more pleasure because I came to be acquainted with him with an unfavorable previous prejudice against his character, and because I believe his opinions with regard to the internal policy of his own country as erroneous. But be they what they may, no foreign minister accredited to the United States since their existence as a nation has ever in serving his own government rendered at the same time a service so transcend-

---

[1] For a more full appreciation of Bagot's character, see Adams, *Memoirs*, April 14, 1819.

ently important to this country as Mr. Hyde de Neuville. The termination of the late negotiation with Spain (so far as it has been terminated) is, I am entirely convinced, in a great measure owing to his exertions. Immediately after my letter of 12th March, 1818, to Mr. Onis he began to take a part in the negotiation, and from that time pursued with great earnestness and zeal the object of having it brought to an amicable and mutually satisfactory close. So far as it could depend on him it has been effected, and Spain and the United States, as well as France, will have reason to thank him if the transaction shall be completed as the compact stands. You will consider the information as confidential. You remember the mediation of Great Britain and afterwards of the allied powers was proposed by Spain and declined by us. France without offering her mediation instructed her minister to use his good offices, and they were faithfully rendered. Their great efficacy was in the operation of their influence upon Spain. He operated upon Spain, first, by his counsels to Mr. de Onis, and secondly, by persuading his own government to act directly upon that of Spain. I believe this agency was not seen by any third party and was therefore not counteracted. I hope it will have produced its full effect before any available counteraction can be applied. But whether ultimately successful or not, Mr. de Neuville's efforts have been as active as his intentions have been sincere, and his conduct through the whole process has impressed me with a high sense of his integrity of heart and his friendliness of disposition.

The change of the Russian mission is not like the others, even nominally temporary. About six weeks since Mr. Daschkoff presented to the President his letters of recall; his successor, Mr. Poletica, has within these few days arrived at New York from Bordeaux, and has informed me that he may be shortly expected here. The President is not now here to receive him, having undertaken a southern and western tour of three months, upon which he left this city on the 30th of March. The last we have heard from him was from Georgetown, S. C. He was to enter Charleston last Monday morning. The Secretary of War, Mr. Calhoun, has accompanied him thus far.[1]

I have a dispatch to prepare for you to-morrow; but as it is very doubtful whether it be ready for you in time to reach Mr. Bagot, I now give you notice of it, and that your dispatches to No. 62, inclusive, have been received. I am glad to find that the pamphlet containing the documents which accompanied my letter of 28 November to Mr. Erving had been received by you, before the parliamentary discussion upon the execution of Arbuthnot and Ambrister was brought forward. As Mr. Bagot solemnly and repeatedly protested to me that he had never one line of instructions from his government about protecting or patronizing Indian rights or pretensions, and as Arbuthnot in his letters to Bagot himself refers to a very different statement of things from Lord Bathurst; as nothing can be more explicit on the one hand than the disavowals of Nicholls and his projects by Lord Bathurst to us, or than the assertions of the Prophet Francis to the contrary on the other, I have some curiosity to see how the most noble the Marquis of Lansdowne will have treated this part of the subject, as well as how my Lord Liverpool will work through with his positions that the execution of the incendiaries was wholly *unauthorized* by the American government. Unauthorized as a specific act it certainly was; but disavowed as the acts of Nicholls were by Lord Bathurst, it as certainly has not been and will not be. If the most noble Marquis, instead of concentrating

[1] He reached Washington May 24.

his indignations upon the punishment, will transfer a little of his meditation to the offenses of those two British worthies, he may come to a satisfactory result without charging either General Jackson or the American government with inhumanity. The most noble Marquis it seems, too, together with Mr. Wilberforce, is laying siege to us with that steam battery the slave trade. As the interferences of those gentlemen in this affair is altogether extra official and not remarkably delicate, I think you would do well to suggest to them that if the British government will begin by stipulating never from this day forth to the end of time to take by force a *white man* from an American merchant vessel on the high seas (unless as a prisoner of war), we will listen to proposals to let them search American vessels for *black men* in time of peace. And so long as their humanity for white freemen stops short of such an engagement for fear it should unman their navy, they may spare themselves the trouble of applying to us to unman our independence by trusting them to search our ships for black slaves to emancipate. I am not partial to the tribe of empirics whose infallible remedies are always worse than the disease.

I received the table copying press which is a very good one, and will thank you to send me two more reams of folio and two reams of quarto copying paper, and a *damping* box of the largest folio size. There was none with the press. Mr. Hamilton, Under Secretary of State, sent me through your kindness an eastern romance published by him—*Antar*. I pray you to offer him my thanks for his obliging present, and the assurance of the pleasure with which I always recollect my acquaintance with him, now of more than twenty years' standing.

I am, etc.[1]

[1] An official dispatch to Rush, dated May 7, 1819, on the commercial conven-

TO WARD NICHOLAS BOYLSTON

WASHINGTON, 24 May, 1819.

MY DEAR SIR:

I have observed with pleasure and gratitude your persevering efforts of beneficence to the University at Cambridge, and had heard of the institution of your prizes for elocution which cannot but be attended with good effects. Its operation by experience may perhaps suggest some rules for the distribution of the prizes which, if you should conclude to make the institution permanent, you may think it advisable to prescribe. Would it not for instance be useful to direct that if one of the *undergraduates* should obtain one of the first prizes he should not upon a second year be admitted as a competitor to speak *in the same language?* And would it not be proper to enlarge the circle of the languages in which the pieces may be spoken, at least by admitting the French? From the experience which I have had of the defects most common among young orators, I think it

---

tion of October 20, 1818, is in *American State Papers*, Foreign Relations, IV. 402.

"We are in expectation of seeing Mr. Baker here, and think he need not be alarmed by the prospect of Mr. Bagot's return to this country. Mr. Bagot himself has no such intention or inclination; for notwithstanding Mr. Erskine's remark to you, I doubt whether any British minister who ever was here felt any wish to return after getting home to come back *in the same capacity.* It is the real *purgatory*, and so is the condition of an American minister in England. Mr. Bagot and his family have been constantly very popular here, and at the same time very acceptable to this government. But they will be happier elsewhere, and we hope whoever comes to take their place will profit by their example. They sailed from Annapolis in the *Forth* frigate (a 74 in disguise) almost a fortnight since, and in another fortnight may be landed at Portsmouth." *To John Adams Smith*, May 17, 1819. Ms.

should be prescribed as an inflexible rule that no prompting should be allowed, and that whatever merit any speakers might display no prize should be given in any case where a failure of memory should be perceptible.

With regard to the professorship of rhetoric and oratory, I do most sincerely wish it would be given to a person capable of understanding its duties and of performing them. To Mr. McKean [1] it was a sinecure, given him for his wants and his vices, and not for any quality required by the place. I speak the whole truth to you, because nothing less can do any good. But the Corporation of Harvard University, though including some of the best men in the world, is and for many years has been more of a *Caucus Club* than a literary and scientific society—bigoted to religious liberality, and illiberal in political principle. When they have a place to fill, their question is not who is fit for the place, but who is to be provided for? And their whole range of candidates is a parson or a partisan, or both. From what I have seen of Mr. Norton and all that I have heard of him I have great respect for his character and abilities; but to make him professor of rhetoric and *oratory* could be equalled by nothing but by the appointment of a man born blind to lecture upon optics and make astronomical observations with the telescope.

I have been so long absent from this country that I have no knowledge of the young men whose talents would be their real recommendation to such an office, but I have no hesitation in saying that I think the clerical profession not well suited to it, and it would be as reasonable to take a professor of theology or of anatomy from the practising lawyers as a professor of eloquence from the pulpit. The

---

[1] Joseph McKean, who held the chair from 1809 to 1818. In 1819 Edward Tyrrel Channing was chosen Boylston Professor.

pulpit is indeed one of the scenes of practical oratory, but it is oratory of the lowest class. The pulpit orator has no antagonist. There may be triumph without a victory, but there can be no victory without a battle. Now as in the days of Cicero, the great struggle and the most splendid theatre of eloquence is at the bar.

It cannot be expected that any man very eminent as a public speaker will accept the appointment to this professorship. The talent commands a market of a higher order. Neither does the office require the exercise of the abilities necessary to a very distinguished orator, for a man may be excellent as a judge and instructor of eloquence without possessing its highest faculties himself. But an impediment of speech is a disqualification the exhibition of which in that professorship reflects disgrace upon those who made the appointment, and is an insult upon the founder of the institution. They would have done better to send to Hartford and to have offered the vacancy made by the death of Mr. McKean to *Mr. Laurent Clerk*.[1] He at least would have palsied no precept by his example.

Mrs. Adams joins me in requesting you to present our best respects to Mrs. Boylston and our joint thanks for her and your kind invitation, and believe me, etc.

[1] Laurent Clerk (1785–1869), who had lost the senses of smell and hearing, and was at the head of the asylum for deaf-mutes at Hartford, Conn.

TO HENRY CHANNING

WASHINGTON, 31 May, 1819.

SIR:

I duly received your letter of 19th November last, and also your private letter of 19 March, which according to your request I had considered as strictly confidential. Among the letters which the constant pressure of business renders it impossible to answer are those containing recommendations of persons to employment of any kind under the government. In such cases it has been the practice of the Department to consider the appointment of the person recommended or of another as the answer. The numbers of such recommendations which are received, and the uselessness and inconvenience of discussion upon their issue have contributed to establish this practice, from which it has been thought proper seldom to depart except in cases when the recommendation not being successful, an explanation of the reasons for which it was so is due to the persons who gave them.

The intimations of your letter of 19 March implicating the character of a person employed by the government of the United States have not been overlooked. I expect to go from New York to Norwich in the steam boats in the course of the month of July or the beginning of August. When I can fix upon the day I will give you notice of it, and shall be happy to meet you in the manner proposed by your letter.

I am, etc.

TO FREEMAN TYLER

WASHINGTON, 24 June, 1819.

SIR:

I beg you to present in my name to the stockholders of the Planters' Bank [1] the assurance of the very grateful sense which I entertain of the confidence with which they have honored me in electing me one of the directors of that institution for the ensuing year. And to add I should take great pleasure in accepting the trust and in serving them in that capacity, but for two considerations which I pray them to accept as my reasons for declining it:

The first, that having no command of my time I might not be able to attend a meeting of the directors even once in the year.

The second, that having doubts whether the office of a director in any bank would in strict propriety be compatible with that which I hold as a public servant, I had come to the conclusion of avoiding any such union of officers in my own person, before the stockholders of the Planters' Bank had done me this favor.

I regret very much that I shall be deprived of the pleasure of serving the stockholders to the best of my ability, and of being appointed in that service with the gentlemen whom they have chosen as the other directors.[2]

I avail myself of this occasion to acknowledge also the receipt of your letter informing me that the directors had rescinded the vote requiring absolutely the payment of the

---

[1] Of Prince George's County, Maryland.
[2] A similar incident in this year is given in Adams, *Memoirs*, March 25 and 26, 1819.

third instalment on the stock of the bank, leaving it optional with the stockholders individually.

Being of opinion that in the present circumstances of this country no bank capital can be employed *honestly, safely* and profitably, I should incline rather to reduce than to increase the stock that I hold in that species of property. Many banks have already suspended specie payments and many others will and must follow the example. If after such suspension they can retain any credit, large dividends may indeed for some time be made to the stockholders, but the end must be bankruptcy, as well of the bank as of their debtors. I wish to have no participation either in the process or in the result. I shall therefore not pay in the third instalment upon my shares at present and shall be happy to remain a stockholder in the Planters' Bank just as long as they continue to pay specie without hesitation, and preserve their capital safe and unimpaired.

I am, etc.[1]

---

[1] "The *Hornet* has arrived at New York, and Captain Read at this place, with dispatches from Mr. Forsyth to the 22d of June. There was no prospect of the ratification of the treaty.

"The Marquis of Casa Yrujo, who professed to be anxiously desirous of the ratification, was suddenly dismissed from office, and banished on the 14th of June. His successor *ad interim* was Mr. Salmon, brother-in-law of the Chevalier de Onis; and it is said to have been expected that Mr. Onis himself would be the minister of foreign affairs.

"On the 17th of June Mr. Salmon transmitted to Mr. Forsyth an answer to three notes addressed to his predecessor, urging the immediate ratification of the treaty. This answer was that his Majesty, considering the treaty of the highest importance, had determined to act upon it with the fullest deliberation." *To the President*, August 4, 1819. Ms.

A dispatch to John Forsyth, dated August 18, 1819, on the ratification by Spain of the treaty signed February 22, 1819, is in *American State Papers*, Foreign Relations, iv. 657.

TO HYDE DE NEUVILLE

Private and Confidential.

WASHINGTON, 23 October, 1819.

SIR:

I had the honor of receiving your letter by Mr. Picot, which I immediately transmitted to the President of the United States. I greatly regretted missing the pleasure of seeing you on my passage from Boston through New York.

The President duly appreciates the friendly disposition towards the United States which you have invariably manifested, and the conciliatory character of the interposition, as well of your sovereign as of yourself personally, in the transactions which we had flattered ourselves had satisfactorily terminated the long and painful misunderstanding between the United States and Spain.

In withholding the ratification of the treaty of 22 February last beyond the period limited for that object, the Spanish government has announced the intention of dispatching immediately a confidential person to ask certain *explanations*, the nature of which has not however been made known. The Duke of San Fernando has been inofficially mentioned as the person who would probably be employed for this purpose.

It has occurred to me, and upon suggesting the idea to the President it has met his approbation, that if you can without material inconvenience postpone your visit to France, it may serve at once the pacific and benevolent views of your government, and above all the honor and interest of Spain, if you conclude to return here and pass the ensuing winter at this place. It may be particularly useful that you should be here on the arrival of the confidential person above alluded to. By the earnest wishes of the American government I refer to that object so near to your heart and to that of his Majesty the King of France—the preservation of the peace of the world. By withholding the ratification of the treaty, Spain has given new and additional claims of satisfaction and indemnity to the United States, for which it will be indispensable that she should account to them. The preservation of peace continues to be an object of the most anxious desire to the President. Possibly your presence here under the critical circumstances which are to be anticipated, may contribute to maintain it; and should this most earnest hope be destined to fail, it may be satisfactory to your government, as it will be to us, that as you have witnessed the frankness and candor, and appealing to your own feelings, I will add the generosity with which the negotiation has been hitherto conducted on the part of the United States, so you may bear testimony to the patience and forbearance with which they will continue to act, till the last moment of possible endurance shall arrive.

In submitting this proposal to your consideration, it is not intended to urge your remaining here, should any imperious call require your adherence to the purpose of returning immediately to France. So far as considerations of a private and personal nature may contribute to your determination, you will not doubt the satisfaction with which in common with your many friends here we shall welcome your return to this city. . . .

Please to accept the renewed assurance of my very distinguished consideration.[1]

---

[1] "The President considers the King of Spain as bound in honor and justice to ratify the treaty, to which he pledged in unlimited terms his faith and royal word in the full power to Mr. Onis; and it being known that the terms of the treaty are

TO WILLIAM LOWNDES

DEPARTMENT OF STATE,
WASHINGTON, December 16, 1819.

SIR:
With reference to the question proposed by the committee, "whether the executive considers the Florida treaty as a subsisting one, valid according to national law, and within the limits of that minister's latest instructions, sanctioned by the Royal Council. If this obligation should be violated, it will remain for the United States to assert their rights in another form. Should the opinion of Congress concur with that of the President, possession will be taken of Florida, without any views of hostility to Spain, but holding her responsible for the expenses which may be occasioned by the measure. You will explicitly make known to the French government that it is not the intention of the United States to disturb the peace of Europe, and that if possession be quietly given of Pensacola and St. Augustine, when required, as it probably will be, the further claims of indemnities from Spain, arising from the refusal to ratify the treaty, will be reserved, subject to further amicable negotiation. Mr. Forsyth is instructed to remain at Madrid and await the result of the meeting of Congress." *To Albert Gallatin*, August 23, 1819. Ms.

"Je vis hier M. le secrétaire d'État et lui annonçai que, selon toute apparence, M. le général Vivès était en mer, que les intentions du cabinet de Madrid paraissaient de plus en plus très pacifiques et que tout ce que Sa Majesté Catholique semblait désirer, c'était qu'on en vînt à des explications franches sur certains points, particulièrement liés à la sûreté et à la dignité de la couronne d' Espagne.

"Il me fut aisé de voir, en abordant M. le secrétaire d'Etat, que l'horizon s'était un pur obscurci depuis notre dernier entretien. M. Adams se laisse facilement aller à ses impressions du moment, et sa physionomie décèle vite la pensée qui l'occupe.

"Ce que j'ai toujours prévu et redouté arrivera, en effet, si l'ambassadeur d'Espagne, au hier de venir pour s'assurer moralement du fait, demande officiellement qu'il demeure constaté par un acte quelconque. Plus cette demande sera péremptoire, plus on craindra qu'elle ne devienne publique, et plus alors on se croira dans la necessité de répondre avec énergie qu'on ne veut pas même discuter ce point, et qu'on reconnaitra l'indépendance des provinces espagnoles quand on le jugera convenable. Et cependant, non seulement l'intérêt des États-Unis n'est point de devancer à cet égard la politique des puissances d'Europe, mais le Président est bien éloigné d'y penser et surtout de le désirer." Hyde de Neuville, November 28, 1819 (?), in *Mémoires et Souvenirs*, II. 407.

giving the same perfect rights, and imposing the same perfect obligations, as if it had been ratified," I have the honor to state the President considers the treaty of 22d February last as obligatory upon the honor and good faith of Spain, not as a perfect treaty, (ratification being an essential formality to that,) but as a compact which Spain was bound to ratify; as an adjustment of the differences between the two nations, which the King of Spain, by his full power to his minister, had solemnly promised to *approve, ratify*, and fulfil. This adjustment is assumed as the measure of what the United States had a right to obtain from Spain from the signature of the treaty. The principle may be illustrated by reference to rules of municipal law relative to transactions between individuals. The difference between the treaty unratified and ratified may be likened to the difference between a covenant to convey lands and the deed of conveyance itself. Upon a breach of the covenant to convey, courts of equity decree that the party who has broken his covenant shall convey, and, further, shall make good to the other party all damages which he has sustained by the breach of contract.

As there is no court of chancery between nations, their differences can be settled only by agreement or by force. The resort to force is justifiable only when justice cannot be obtained by negotiation; and the resort to force is limited to the attainment of justice. The wrong received marks the boundaries of the right to be obtained.

The King of Spain was bound to ratify the treaty; bound by the principles of the law of nations applicable to the case; and further bound by the solemn promise in the full power. He refusing to perform his promise and obligation, the United States have a perfect right to do what a court of chancery would do in a transaction of a similar character between individuals, namely, to compel the performance of the engagement as far as compulsion can accomplish it, and to indemnify themselves for all the damages and charges incident to the necessity of using compulsion. They cannot compel the King of Spain to sign the act of ratification, and, therefore, cannot make the instrument a perfect treaty; but they can, and are justifiable in so doing, take that which the treaty, if perfect, would have bound Spain to deliver up to them; and they are further entitled to indemnity for all the expenses and damages which they may sustain by consequence of the refusal of Spain to ratify. The refusal to ratify gives them the same right to do justice to themselves as the refusal to fulfil would have given them if Spain had ratified, and then ordered the governor of Florida not to deliver over the province.

By considering the treaty as the term beyond which the United States will not look back in their controversial relations with Spain, they not only will manifest a continued respect for the sanctity of their own engagements, but they avoid the inconvenience of reëntering upon a field of mutual complaint and crimination so extensive that it would be scarcely possible to decide where or when negotiation should cease, or at what point force should be stayed for satisfied right; and by resorting to force only so far as the treaty had acknowledged their right, they offer an inducement to Spain to complete the transaction on her part, without proceeding to general hostility. But Spain must be responsible to the United States for every wrong done by her after the signature of the treaty by her minister; and the refusal to ratify his act is the first wrong for which they are entitled to redress.

I have the honor, etc.[1]

[1] See Hyde de Neuville, *Mémoires et Souvenirs*, II. 410.

TO WILLIAM LOWNDES

DEPARTMENT OF STATE,
WASHINGTON, December 21, 1819.

SIR:

In answer to the questions contained in your letter of the 10th instant, I have the honor to state for the information of the committee:

1st. That information has been received by the government of the United States, though not through a direct channel, nor in authentic form, that another motive besides those alleged in the letter of the Duke of San Fernando to Mr. Forsyth did operate upon the Spanish cabinet to induce the withholding of the ratification of the treaty, namely, the apprehension that the ratification would be immediately followed by the recognition by the United States of the independence of one or more of the South American provinces. It has been suggested that, probably, the most important of the explanations which the minister to be sent by Spain will be instructed to ask, will consist of an explicit declaration of the intentions of this government in that respect. There is reason, also, to believe that the impunity with which privateers fitted out, manned, and officered, in one or more of our ports, have committed hostilities upon the Spanish commerce, will be alleged among the reasons for delay, and perhaps some pledge may be required of the effectual execution against these practices of laws which appear to exist in the statute book.

It may be proper to remark that, during the negotiation of the Florida treaty, repeated and very earnest efforts were made, both by Mr. Pizarro at Madrid, and by Mr. Onis here, to obtain from the government of the United States, either a positive stipulation or a tacit promise that the United States would not recognize any of the South American revolutionary governments; and that the Spanish negotiators were distinctly and explicitly informed that this government would not assent to any such engagement, either express or implied.

2d. By all the information which has been obtained of the prospective views of the French and Russian governments in relation to the course which it was by them thought probable would be pursued by the United States, it is apparent that they strongly apprehended the immediate forcible occupation of Florida by the United States, on the non-ratification by Spain of the treaty within the stipulated time. France and Russia both have most earnestly dissuaded us from that course, not by any regular official communication, but by informal friendly advice, deprecating immediate hostility, on account of its tendency to kindle a general war, which they fear would be the consequence of a war between the United States and Spain. It was alleged that, in the present state of our controversy with Spain, the opinion of all Europe on the point at issue was in our favor, and against her; that, by exercising patience a little longer, by waiting, at least, to hear the minister who was announced as coming to give and receive explanations, we could not fail of obtaining, ultimately, without resort to force, the right to which it was admitted we were entitled; but that precipitate measures of violence might not only provoke Spain to war, but would change the state of the question between us, would exhibit us to the world as the aggressors, and would indispose against us those now the most decided in our favor.

It is not expected that, in the event of a war with Spain, any European power will openly take a part in it against the United States; but there is no doubt that the principal reliance of Spain will be upon the employment of privateers in France and England as well as in the East and West India seas and upon our own coast, under the Spanish flag, but manned from all nations, including citizens of our own, expatriated into Spanish subjects for the purpose.

3d. The enclosed copies of letters from Mr. Fromentin contain the most particular information possessed by the executive with regard to the subjects mentioned in your third enquiry. In the month of September, a corps of three thousand men arrived at the Havana from Spain, one-third of whom are said to have already fallen victims to the diseases of that climate. By advices from the Havana, as recent as the 4th of this month, we are assured that no part of this force is intended to be, in any event, employed in Florida.

4th. A communication from the Secretary of War, also herewith enclosed, contains the information requested by the committee upon this enquiry.

5th. At the time when Captain Read left Madrid (13 October), Mr. Forsyth had no positive information even of the appointment of the person who is to come out as the minister. Indirectly, we have been assured that he might be expected to arrive here in the course of the present month. I am, etc.

TO THE PRESIDENT [1]

[JAMES MONROE]

WASHINGTON, 25th December, 1819.

SIR:

The meeting held yesterday having terminated without any arrangement relative to the subject upon which it had upon desire been convened, and it being understood that it left the members of your administration free to pursue the course of conduct dictated by their sense of propriety respectively, to avoid being misunderstood in regard to that which I have hitherto pursued and to manifest my wish to pursue in future any other which you will please to direct or advise, I have thought necessary to submit the following observations to your candor and indulgence.

It has, I understood from you, been indirectly made a complaint to you [2] as a neglect of duty on the part of some of the members of your administration, or at least of the Secretary of State, that he omits paying at every session of Congress a first visit of form to every member of the Senate of the United States, and that his wife is equally negligent of her supposed duty, in omitting to pay similar visits to the ladies of every member of either House who visit the city during the session. The fact of omission, both as it regards my wife and myself, is acknowledged, and as you had the kindness to propose having any explanation of the motives of our conduct made known to those who to our

---

[1] These two letters, printed in Adams, *Memoirs*, concern a question of long standing at Washington, and one which confronted Adams soon after he became Secretary of State. See *Ib.*, January 5, 1818, December 16, 20, 22, 27.

[2] By Ninian Edwards (1775–1833), Senator from Illinois.

very great regret appear to be dissatisfied with it, the following statement is made to give that explanation.

I must premise that having been five years a member of the Senate, and having during four of the five sessions been accompanied at the seat of government by my wife, I never received a first visit from any of the heads of departments, nor did my wife ever receive a first visit from any of their ladies. We invariably paid the first visit and at that time always understood it to be the established usage. I do not mean to say that every Senator then paid the first visit to the heads of departments, but that the Senators neither exacted nor generally expected a first visit from them. Visiting of form was considered as not forming a part either of official right or official duty. I never then heard a suggestion that it was due in courtesy from a head of department to pay a first visit to all Senators, or from his wife to visit the wife of any member of Congress. When I came here two years ago I supposed the usual rules of visiting to remain as I had known them and practised them ten years before. Entertaining the profoundest respect for the Senate as a body, and a high regard for every individual member of it, I am yet not aware of any usage which required formal visits from me as a member of the administration to them as Senators.

The Senate of the United States, independent of its importance and dignity, is of all the associations of men upon earth that to which I am bound by every and the most sacred and indissoluble ties of personal gratitude. In a career of five and twenty years and through five successive administrations, scarcely a year has passed but has been marked in the annals of my life by manifestations of the signal confidence of that body. Unworthy indeed should I be of such confidence, if I had a heart insensible to those obligations. Base indeed should I feel myself if, inflated by the dignity of the stations to which their continued, uninterrupted and frequently repeated kindness has contributed to raise me, I were capable of withholding from them collectively or individually one particle of the reverence and honor due from me to them. But I was not conscious that this mode of showing my respect to them was either due or usual, and when the first intimation was given to me that there was such an *expectation* entertained by the Senators in general, I quickly learnt from other quarters that if complied with, it would give great offense to the members of the House of Representatives unless extended also to them. To pay visits of ceremony to every member of Congress at every session would not only be a very useless waste of time, but not very compatible with the discharge of the real and important duties of the departments, always peculiarly pressing during the session of Congress. Neither did the introduction of such a system of mere formality appear to me altogether congenial to the republican simplicity of our institutions. To avoid all invidious discrimination I have paid no first visit to any member of either house of Congress as such, but I have returned the visits of all who have pleased to visit me, considering it as perfectly optional between every member of either house and me whether any interchange of visits should take place between us or not. The rule which I have thought it best to adhere to for myself has also been pursued by my wife with my approbation. She has never considered as incumbent upon her to visit first ladies coming to this place *strangers* to her. She could draw no line of discrimination of strangers whom she should and strangers whom she should not visit. To visit all with the constantly increasing resort of strangers here, would have been impossible; to have visited only the ladies of members of Congress, would have been a distinction offensive to many other ladies of equal respectability; it would have applied even to the married daughter of the President. The only principle of Mrs. Adams has been to *avoid invidious distinctions*, and the only way of avoiding them is to visit no lady as a stranger. She first visits her acquaintance according to the usual rules of private life, and receives or returns visits of all ladies strangers who pay visits to her. We are aware that this practice has given offense to some members of Congress and their ladies, and we very sincerely regret the result. We think, however, that the principles properly understood cannot be offensive. To visit first *all* strangers or *none* appears to be the only alternative to do justice to all. Above all we wish it understood that while we are happy to receive any respectable stranger who pleases to call upon us, we have no claim or pretension to claim it of any one.

It only remains for me to add that after this frank exposition of what we have done and of our only motives for the course we have pursued, I am entirely disposed to conform to any other which you may have the goodness to advise.

With perfect respect I remain, etc.

TO THE VICE PRESIDENT [1]

[Daniel D. Tompkins]

WASHINGTON, 29th December, 1819.

DEAR SIR:

It has been suggested to me that some of the members of the Senate, entertaining the opinion that a formal visit in person or by card is due from each of the heads of the executive departments at the commencement of every session of Congress to every Senator upon his arrival at the seat of government, have considered this omission on my part to pay such visits as the withholding from them of a proper mark of respect, or even as implying a pretension to exact such a formality from them. Disclaiming every such pretension and every such claim on my part, I take the liberty of submitting to you the following explanation of the motives which have governed my conduct in relation to this subject.

I have invariably considered the government of the United States as a government for the transaction of business, and that no ceremonial for the mode or order of interchanging visits between the persons belonging to the respective departments in it had ever been established. I was myself five years a member of the Senate, and at four of the five sessions of Congress which I attended I was accompanied by my wife. During that time I never once received a first visit from any of the heads of departments, nor did my wife ever receive a first visit from any one of their ladies, except perhaps *once*, when she was sick, from Mrs. Madison. We always called upon them soon after our

[1] See Adams, *Memoirs*, January 22, 1820.

arrival at Washington, not from any opinion that it was an obligation of duty, but because we understood and believed it to be usual, and because we did not think it improper. We made an exception after the first session with regard to Mr. Gallatin, who never having returned my first visit was supposed not to incline to that sort of intercourse with us.

When I came to this place to reside two years since, I was under the impression that the usages with regard to visiting were as I had known and practised them ten years before, that as a member of the Administration I had no sort of claim to a first visit from any member of either house of Congress, but that neither had any member of Congress any claim to a first visit from me; that the interchange and order of visits was entirely optional on both sides; and that no rule of etiquette whatever existed which required that either party should pay the first visit, or indeed any visit to the other.

In the course of the winter of 1817–18 two members of the Senate, for both of whom I have the highest respect and with one of whom I had had the pleasure of sitting several years in the Senate, called on me at my office and informed me that there was a minute of a rule agreed upon, not officially but privately, by the members of the Senate of the first Congress, that the Senators of the United States paid the first visits to no person except the President of the United States. I observed to them that as during five years' service as a Senator I had never seen or heard of this rule I could hardly consider it as ever having been much observed, that I could, however, have no possible objection to the Senators prescribing any rule to *themselves* of visiting which they might think proper. But I asked them, if they understood the rule as implying an order that *other persons* should visit them? They answered, if I recollect right, by no means, and I supposed they viewed the whole affair as I did, as of little or no importance.

I have therefore paid no visits of form to members of the Senate, and though always [happy] to receive and return visits of those who pleased to call upon me, and happy to invite to my house every member of the Senate, whether he had or had not paid me a visit who would give me the honor of his company, I yet always respected the motives of those who declined paying me any visit, or even frequenting my house at all. I exacted nothing from them which they might think incompatible with their dignity. I presumed they would exact nothing from me not within the line of my official duty. I soon learnt that if I should make it a rule to pay the first visit to every Senator at each session, the same compliment would be claimed, if not by all, at least by a large proportion of the members of the House of Representatives, and I could find no republican principle which would to my own mind justify me in refusing to the members of one house that which I should yield as due to the members of another. At the commencement of each session of Congress I have visited the presiding member of each house, not from a sense of obligation but of propriety. I have not felt it my duty to pay first visits to any individual member of either house. Nor has it entered my imagination that a first visit was *due* from any member of either house to me.

If there is a body of men upon earth for whom more than for any other I ought to cherish any feelings of attachment superadded to every sentiment of reverence it is the Senate of the United States. Its importance and dignity as one of the branches of the legislature, as one of the component parts of the supreme executive, and as the tribunal of official honor and virtue cannot be more highly estimated by any man than by me. My father had the honor of being its first presiding officer. I had for five years that of being one of its members, and through every successive administration of this government, from the establishment of the national Constitution to this time, I have received frequent tokens of its confidence, which can never be obliterated from my memory and claiming all my gratitude. For every individual member of the body I feel all the respect due to his public character, and there is not one member towards whom I entertain a sentiment other than that of regard and esteem. If, therefore, the principle upon which I have omitted to pay them the first visits of form should ultimately fail of meeting their approbation, it will be serious cause of regret to me; but at all events I hope they will impute it to any other cause than intentional disrespect to them. I take this occasion of observing that with my approbation and advice, my wife has acted upon the same principle with regard to the ladies connected with members of the Senate or House of Representatives who have visited the place during the sessions of Congress, that I have pursued in relation to the members themselves. She has paid no first visits to ladies with whom she had not the advantage of being acquainted. She has received with pleasure and returned the visits of all ladies who have called upon her, whether connected with members of Congress or otherwise. She has visited her friends and acquaintances on the usual footing of private citizens, without pretension to claim and without being sensible of any obligation to pay any first visit. She would have paid with much pleasure the compliment to ladies of members of Congress had it been proper in her opinion to confine it to them. But she was aware that many other ladies, equally strangers to her and, though not immediately allied to members of Congress of character and standing in society equally respectable, occasionally came to spend some time in the city, and knowing it to be impossible that she should visit them all she declined the invidious task of discriminating whom she should and whom she should not visit first. If in observing this rule she has deviated from the practice of some other ladies in situations similar to her own, she has conformed to that which she constantly observed when she was herself the wife of a Senator at the seat of Government. She then always called upon the ladies of the heads of departments when she came to Washington, and always understood it to be the common practice. She lays no claim, however, to the same attention from any other lady, and having no pretension to visits of etiquette herself, thinks herself amenable to none from others. She has invited to her house without waiting for formal visits every lady of a member of Congress to whom she had not reason to believe such an invitation would be unwelcome, and while feeling it as a favor from those who have accepted her invitations, she has only regretted the more rigorous etiquette of those who have declined, inasmuch as it bereft her of the happiness which she would have derived from a more successful cultivation of their acquaintance. She would regret still more the error which should in any instance attribute her conduct to a pretension of any kind on her part, or to disregard of what is due to her from others.

I have thought this candid explanation of the motives of my conduct particularly due to those members of the Senate who, it has been intimated to me, have thought there was something exceptionable in it. I submit it to your indulgence and to their candor with the sincere and earnest assurance of my perfect respect for yourself and for them.

THE following pages contain advertisements of a few of the Macmillan books on kindred subjects.

The Writings of John Quincy Adams

EDITED BY WORTHINGTON C. FORD

To be complete in twelve volumes.   *Six volumes now ready*

Those writings which are of a permanent historical value and which are essential to a comprehension of the man in all his private and public relations only are chosen for this notable collection, the sixth volume of which is now ready. Nothing has been suppressed by the editor which can contribute to this main purpose. John Quincy Adams led a very eventful life, more than fifty years of it having been passed in public service. He was at all times a prolific writer and correspondent and has left behind him a great mass of material. A discriminating selection from this will be of the utmost value, not only because of the light which it throws upon one of the leaders of our early democracy, but also in that it will serve to vivify the social customs of an age that is past.

THE MACMILLAN COMPANY
Publishers   64-66 Fifth Avenue   New York

A NEW EDITION OF A STANDARD BIOGRAPHY

The Life of Andrew Jackson

BY JOHN SPENCER BASSETT, PH.D.

With illustrations. New edition. Two volumes in one

Cloth, 8vo.

This is a one-volume edition of a biography that has, since its first publication several years ago, come to be regarded as one of the most faithful stories of Jackson's life and of its effect on the nation that has ever been written. Professor Bassett has not slighted Jackson's failings or his virtues; he has tried to refrain from commenting upon his actions; he has sought to present a true picture of the political manipulations which surrounded Jackson and in which he was an important factor. The volume contributes largely to a clearer realization not only of the character of a great man but also of the complex period in which he lived.

THE MACMILLAN COMPANY
Publishers   64-66 Fifth Avenue   New York

Travels in the American Colonies, 1690–1783

By NEWTON D. MERENESS

Cloth, 8vo

This book consists of eighteen hitherto unpublished narratives, some written originally in English, others being translations from the French or German. They give accounts of travel on the Atlantic slope from Savannah to Albany; from Albany to Niagara Falls, Quebec, Hartford and Boston; through the Great Lakes from Detroit to Chicago; up the Mississippi from New Orleans to St. Louis; down the Ohio and the Mississippi from Pittsburg to New Orleans; up the Tennessee; through the country of the Choctaws, the Creeks and the Cherokees and through the backwoods from Pennsylvania to North Carolina. The traveler, usually an officer, is either on a tour of observation and inspection, or is attending to some other important business. In one instance a party of immigrants is removing to a new home in the wilderness.

THE MACMILLAN COMPANY
Publishers 64-66 Fifth Avenue New York

Japanese Expansion and American Policies

By J. F. ABBOTT
Of Washington University

Cloth, 12mo, $1.50

Here Professor Abbott sums up dispassionately and impartially the history of the diplomatic and social relations of Japan with the United States, and in particular gives the facts that will enable an American to form his own opinion as to the possibility of future conflicts between these two countries. The work is neither pro-Japan nor anti-Japan, but seeks, rather, to present the case justly. The author emphasizes the importance of an intelligent understanding of the subject, believing that in spite of the present lull owing to acute interest in European affairs, it is yet a problem that will periodically and persistently come to the fore until it is satisfactorily solved. Professor Abbott has given careful study to Far Eastern matters for the past fifteen years, has traveled at various times throughout the Orient and previous to the Russian War was an instructor in the Imperial Japanese Naval Academy.

THE MACMILLAN COMPANY
Publishers   64-66 Fifth Avenue   New York

/973.55A214W>C1>V6/